The Discontinuous Universe

THE DISCON

Edited by

Sallie Sears

Georgianna W. Lord

TINUOUS UNIVERSE

Selected Writings in Contemporary Consciousness

Basic Books, Inc., *Publishers*

New York *London*

Library of Congress Catalog Card Number: 74–169274
SBN 465–01667–7
Manufactured in the United States of America

Introduction

•(·)•

This book is a collection of documents in the contemporary arts and other disciplines including physics, anthropology, political philosophy and existential psychoanalysis. By and large, the writers assembled here have done most of their important work within the past two or three decades. In the absence of a god, "unsponsored" like the rest of their generation, they have spent their lives in the midst of the most terrible human possibilities without any real conviction that man can or even wishes to check himself before he destroys or maims the remaining life on his lone, already befouled, planetary home. In the face of such bleakness, their continuing will to create is itself an affirmation; indeed the capacity to make serious works of and about the imagination is not only very much alive on the contemporary scene, but is being realized frequently with an impressive brilliance and originality.

This art, however, is not easy. The writers here agree that man must impose some kind of order upon reality if he is to survive without being overwhelmed by confusion and inner disintegration. Yet the structures he has evolved in his efforts to render the world intelligible seem to them more a series of metaphors than anything else—interesting, effective, even magical perhaps, but arbitrary, interchangeable, with their ideal aim of corresponding to structures that "really" exist in the universe forever unverifiable.

The need for coherence, moreover, gains its urgency from the persistent, at times excruciating sense of chaos that has been central to modern experience and that carries to an extreme conclusion the fascination of the nineteenth century with nothingness, disintegration, and death. Flaubert was obsessed with the dream of writing a novel about nothing and Dostoyevski's narrator in *Notes from Underground* mercilessly analyzes the breakdown of his own personality. But both writers stopped short of yielding to madness and disbelief or of attempting the kind of radical experimentation with form that resulted in anti-mimetic art and undermined the conventions predicating a continuous, explicable, and ordered universe: the narrative past, ordinary chronology, the third person, the all-knowing "author," causality as a principle connecting episodes, the spatial-temporal coherence of events, and characterization that presumes to solve or at least contain the riddle of human irrationality. Indeed, for writers as diverse as Roland Barthes, Ionesco, R. D. Laing and Beckett, there is finally no such thing as an "irrational" response, in any ordinary sense, to an impenetrable universe shot through here and there with gleams of light, characterized otherwise by tedium and cruelty, bounded by death. Both celebrating and mocking the human imagination, shattering our familiar categories of thought, rejecting, in Harold Rosenberg's words, all imperatives to "conform to and uphold values of stability and permanence," while insisting upon its own capacity to enthrall, modern literature conjures a world of pure contingency. Reality is ambiguously, disturbingly, often self-destructively in flux; events "jeopardize" themselves and the same sentence, as Robbe-Grillet writes, "may contain an observation and its immediate negation." In the other arts, such hazard is reflected in works deliberately made not to last, in activities that blur distinctions among the different art forms, among genres within a given form, and between art and life: temporary sculpture, Happenings and other multi-media experiments, new integrations of art and technology.

At the moment, the work of artists like Cage and Beckett marks the outer limits of this revolt in art against its traditional role of reflecting a contained and intelligible reality. Beckett's "Three Dialogues" is the most revolutionary piece included here in its bald admission of a skepticism so total that all human activity—crucially that of the artist—has ceased to have any justification whatsoever. If he finds anything irrational, it is his own life force under the compulsion of which he continues to create. Prisoner of a world which confounds the mind and exhausts the feelings, he faces the problem not of how to comprehend its mystery but of how to endure its tedium and exercise a ferocious talent which he can neither justify nor repudiate. The assumption underlying all previous art, including virtually everything in the twentieth century, he insists, is that "the domain of the maker is the domain of the feasible." By contrast, the artist he speaks of is a maker without content, medium, or occasion for the artifacts he must make, yet has neither the desire nor the power to make. In an attempt to cope with these contradictions, Beckett remarked in 1961 that the task of the artist now must be to find forms which will for the first time incorporate rather than exclude chaos. The relation between the consciousness of chaos—which at its extreme finds something alien and terrible both within ourselves and in reality—and an indestructible if "occasionless" commitment to objects of beauty marks perhaps the broadest outlines of contemporary sensibility. To guide the reader along these outlines, we have placed the works under the following headings, with summaries of their major points suggestive of their central concerns:

PART I: THE DIVISION OF CONSCIOUSNESS AND THE DESTRUCTION OF CONVENTIONS

Around 1850, a division in human consciousness took place as the assumption that we lived in a coherent, ordered universe began to break down and, with it, the bourgeois values that had been dependent upon it. As man ceased to feel that his own and the natural world gave testimony to universal values, the artist began to reevaluate his relationship with the past. In particular, art began to destroy or undermine the conventions which had predicated a stable, continuous, "decipherable" universe: the narrative past, ordinary chronology, the fiction of the all-knowing "author" behind the work, for example. Language itself became problematic for the first time. "Meanings" of words were undermined or inverted; poets began deliberately destroying the relational elements in language.

PART II: MAN IN THE DISCONTINUOUS UNIVERSE

The New Art postulates a discontinuous, uncertain, fragmented universe which, excluding man from its attention, comes to seem inhuman and alien. In 1927, science articulates the principle of indeterminancy in physics. "Chance" or randomness of events becomes an underlying principle of our world view, and is reflected in the various arts. It is manifested in the reliance upon unconscious sources of imagery in surrealism; the chance-paintings of Jackson Pollock; the use of tables of random numbers to determine structures in dance, painting, or poetry; the deliberate employment of random sounds and rhythms in the music of John Cage; the improvisation and sudden use of the audience in Happenings; as well as their unpredictable duration.

PART III: TOWARD A NEW SET OF RELATIONS BETWEEN THE UNCONSCIOUS AND THE CONSCIOUS

Another aspect of the breakdown of the sense of a "rational" universe is that art predicates a new set of relations between the conscious and the unconscious. On the one hand, this involves revivifying and restoring the vitality of the unconscious. On the other hand, it involves disemburdening consciousness of its "neurotic" roles, such as the utilization of a "contaminated" language resulting from sexual repression and ideological distortions of various kinds. As the authority of the unconscious is acknowledged, it comes to play a contradictory role: restoring sensuality and a "magical" contact with the universe yet also creating the aesthetics of the nightmare, so that cruelty, terror and the grotesque become principles in certain arts and public acts (the agonized consciousness first celebrated by de Sade, Artaud's theatre of cruelty, and the theater of politics in America today). Madness itself becomes a decisive symbol for modern consciousness, either as it manifests itself in frenetic, self-devouring activity or else in emotional anesthesia and disrelation—a psychic closing off.

PART IV: PATTERNS AND CONSEQUENCES OF SELF-REFLECTIVE ART

The New Art reflects upon and undermines its own nature. Reexamining its relation both to the past and the present, it comes to conceive of its role as impermanent and no longer the bearer of "eternal" values. The artist acknowledges for the first time that "art" itself as a phenomenon may be displaced by some other form of expression emerging from technological advances. As this happens, the conventional boundaries between the arts break down, giving rise to experiments in various multi-media which merge techniques from film, dance, electronics, etc. Art as the "locus" of the values of stability and permanence is overthrown. Impermanence itself is erected into an aesthetic. In that sense, as Harold Rosenberg remarks, *all* works of art become Happenings. Traditional genres are undermined: the novel becomes the "anti-novel" and music "noise." The formal statement in political films becomes the impossibility of discourse. Like modern philosophy, modern film and novel tend to consciously meditate upon and question their own nature.

PART V: CONTEMPORARY VIOLENCE AND THE NEW SEARCH FOR COHERENCY

Contemporary art questions and reflects upon its own nature by means of structures which in one way or another are intelligible, even if their intelligibility lies solely in their formal aspects. The music of John Cage may consist of long silences or contain whatever chance sounds happen to be in the setting of the performance, but these are played off against created sounds (even if randomly selected) and both are played off against our experience of "traditional" compositions. Thus patterns consisting of various expectations and their violations are created, whether these be rhythmical, structural, based on the sound source, or whatever. Similarly, the novels of William Burroughs may ignore chronology, "story," the autonomy of both characters and settings yet, as in the case of *Naked Lunch,* create "mosaics" consisting of the repetition of key words and phrases or motifs which recur with slight variations throughout the novel. In physics, too, the emphasis has shifted from a material to a formal picture of the world, as it has been forced to abandon a strictly deterministic interpretation of natural events. Intelligibility still continues to be a basic assumption of the mind confronting the universe, and the capacity to predict future events still continues to be the primary criterion for the formulation of any natural law. But prediction is now limited to the probability, not the certainty, of future events. The whole definition of "intelligibility" has changed. It must provide for an area of uncertainty, hence of ambiguity, in our knowledge of the universe. At the same time, "structuring"—that is, providing abstract models which bear some coherent relation to the external world—continues to be the basic activity of the human mind whether in science, art, primitive thought, human play. No matter what its principles and methods, structuring has, Levi-Strauss claims, an intrinsic effectiveness in providing patterns of coherence. And though symbol-using animal as the first term in Burke's definition of man may be obvious, the implications of this formula are staggering: most of what we mean by "reality" has been put together by our "symbol systems." Survivors of extreme experiences—the atomic holocaust, the concentration camps—bear witness to the irreducible necessity of structuring in human life. Studies of the survivors of Hiroshima discovered that their capacity to live after physically enduring the explosion depended upon re-establishing forms within which the death immersion and the survivors' altered identity could be grasped and rendered significant. Similarly, what first moved Bruno Bettelheim to study himself and others in Nazi concentration camps as they were subjected to experiences designed to destroy all personal autonomy was the vital need to feel that he could not only physically survive deprivation and torture, but also continue to feel that his life had value. A standard technique in the camps, Hannah Arendt points out, was to create conditions in which prisoners were "utterly exposed to the arbitrary." In extreme situations, where survival is so precarious, what structures are adequate to subdue chaos?—what freedoms may man yet exercise to affirm his human identity?

Sallie Sears

Georgianna Lord

1972

Contents

• I THE DIVISION OF CONSCIOUSNESS AND THE DESTRUCTION OF CONVENTIONS

PART

I

1

Introduction from *Writing Degree Zero*

Roland Barthes

Hébert, the revolutionary, never began a number of his news-sheet *Le Père Duchêne* without introducing a sprinkling of obscenities. These improprieties had no real meaning, but they had significance. In what way? In that they expressed a whole revolutionary situation. Now here is an example of a mode of writing [1] whose function is no longer only communication or expression, but the imposition of something beyond language, which is both History and the stand we take in it.

It is impossible to write without labelling oneself: as with *Le Père Duchêne,* so equally with Literature. It too must signify something other than its content and its individual form, something which defines its limits and imposes it as Literature. Whence a set of signs unrelated to the ideas, the language or the style, and setting out to give definition, within the body of every possible mode of expression, to the utter separateness of a ritual language. This hieratic quality of written Signs establishes Literature as an institution and clearly tends to place it above History, for no limits can be set without some idea of permanence. Now it is when History is denied that it is most unmistakably at work; it is therefore possible to trace a history of literary expression which is neither that of a particular language, nor that of the various styles, but simply that of the Signs of Literature, and we can expect that this purely formal history may manifest, in its far from obscure way, a link with the deeper levels of History.

We are naturally concerned with a link the form of which may well vary with History itself; there is no need to invoke direct determinism in order to feel that History underlies the fortunes of modes of writing: this kind of functional front, which sweeps along events, situations and ideas in the current of historical time, does not so much produce effects as set limits to choice. History, then, confronts the writer with a necessary option between several moral attitudes connected with language; it forces him to signify Literature in terms of possibilities outside his control. We shall see, for example, that the ideological unity of the bourgeoisie gave rise to a single mode of writing, and that in the bourgeois periods (classical and romantic), literary form could not be divided because consciousness was not; whereas, as soon as the writer ceased to be a witness to the universal, to become the incarnation of a tragic awareness (around 1850), his first gesture was to choose the commitment of his form, either by adopting or rejecting the writing of his past. Classical writing therefore disintegrated, and the whole of Literature, from Flaubert to the present day, became the problematics of language.

This was precisely the time when Literature (the word having come into being shortly before) was finally established as an object. Classical art could have no sense of being a language, for it *was* language, in other words it was transparent, it flowed and left no deposit, it brought ideally together a universal Spirit and a decorative sign without substance or responsibility; it was a language "closed" by social and not natural bounds. It is a well-known fact that toward the end of the eighteenth century this transparency becomes clouded; literary form develops a second-order power independent of its economy and euphemistic charm; it fascinates the reader, it strikes him as exotic, it enthralls him, it acquires a weight. Literature is no longer felt as a socially privileged mode of transaction, but as a language having body and hidden depths, existing both as dream and menace.

This is important: literary form may henceforth elicit those existential feelings lying at the heart of any object: a sense of strangeness or familiarity, disgust or indulgence, utility or murder. For a century now, every mode of writing has thus been an exercise in reconciliation with, or aversion from, that objectified Form inevitably met by the writer on his way, and which he must scrutinize, challenge and accept with all its consequences, since he cannot ever destroy it without destroying himself as a writer. Form hovers before his gaze like an object; whatever he does, it is a scandal: if it stands resplendent, it appears outmoded; if it is a law unto itself, it is asocial; in so far as it is particular in relation to time or mankind, it cannot but mean solitude.

The whole nineteenth century witnessed the progress of this dramatic phenomenon of concretion. In Chateaubriand it is still only a trace, a light pressure of linguistic euphoria, a kind of narcissism in which the manner of writing is scarcely separable from its instrumental function and merely mirrors itself. Flaubert—to take only the typical stages of this process—finally established Literature as an object, through promoting literary labour to the status of a value; form became the end-product of craftsmanship, like a piece of pottery or a jewel (one must understand that craftsmanship was here made manifest, that is, it was for the first time imposed on the reader as a spectacle). Mallarmé's work, finally, was the crowning achievement of this creation of Literature as Object, and this by the ultimate of all objectifying acts: murder. For we know that the whole effort of Mallarmé was exerted towards the destruction of language, with Literature reduced, so to speak, to being its carcass.

From an initial non-existence in which thought, by a happy miracle, seemed to stand out against the backcloth of words, writing thus passed through all the stages of a progressive solidification; it was first the object of a gaze, then of creative action, finally of murder, and has reached in our time a last metamorphosis, absence: in those neutral modes of writing, called here "the zero degree of writing," we can easily discern a negative momentum, and an inability to maintain it within time's flow, as if Literature, having tended for a hundred years now to transmute its surface into a form with no antecedents, could no longer find purity anywhere but in the absence of all signs, finally proposing the realization of this Orphean dream: a writer without Literature. Colourless writing like Camus's, Blanchot's or Cayrol's, for example, or conversational writing like Queneau's, represents the last episode of a Passion of writing, which recounts stage by stage the disintegration of bourgeois consciousness.

What we hope to do here is to sketch this connection; to affirm the existence of a formal reality independent of language and style; to try to show that this third dimension of Form equally, and not without an additional tragic implication, binds the writer to his society; finally to convey the fact that there is no Literature without an Ethic of language.

The limited length of this essay (a few pages of which appeared in 1947 and 1950 in *Combat*) is sufficient indication that what is offered here is no more than an Introduction to what a History of Writing might be.

Translated by Annette Lavers and Colin Smith

NOTES

1 *Écriture,* which in French normally means only "handwriting" or "the art of writing," is now more and more frequently used as a substantive corresponding to all senses of the very *écrire,* generally to mean the style, the fact of composing a work, or the actions which properly belong to a writer. It is used here in a strictly technical sense to denote a new concept, and is translated as "writing," "mode of writing." This concept is discussed further in relation to that of "idiolect" in *Elements of Semiology* (I.I.6 and I.I.7), as is that of "zero degree."

2

The Death of the Author

Roland Barthes

In his story "Sarrasine," Balzac, speaking of a castrato disguised as a woman, writes this sentence: "It was Woman, with her sudden fears, her irrational whims, her instinctive fears, her unprovoked bravado, her daring and her delicious delicacy of feeling". Who is speaking in this way? Is it the story's hero, concerned to ignore the castrato concealed beneath the woman? Is it the man Balzac, endowed by his personal experience with a philosophy of Woman? Is it the author Balzac, professing certain "literary" ideas of femininity? Is it universal wisdom? or romantic psychology? It will always be impossible to know, for the good reason that all writing is itself this special voice, consisting of several indiscernible voices, and that literature is precisely the invention of this voice, to which we cannot assign a specific origin: literature is that neuter, that composite, that oblique into which every subject escapes, the trap where all identity is lost, beginning with the very identity of the body that writes.

Probably this has always been the case: once an action is *recounted,* for intransitive ends, and no longer in order to act directly upon reality—that is, finally external to any function but the very exercise of the symbol—this disjunction occurs, the voice loses its origin, the author enters his own death, writing begins. Nevertheless, the feeling about this phenomenon has been variable; in primitive societies, narrative is never undertaken by a person, but by a mediator, shaman or speaker, whose "performance" may be admired (that is, his mastery of the narrative code), but not his "genius". The *author* is a modern figure, produced no doubt by our society insofar as, at the end of the middle ages, with English empiricism, French rationalism and the personal faith of the Reformation, it discovered the prestige of the individual, or, to put it more nobly, of the "human person". Hence it is logical that with regard to literature it should be positivism, resume and the result of capitalist ideology, which has accorded the greatest importance to the author's "person". The *author* still rules in manuals of literary history, in biographies of writers, in magazine interviews, and even in the awareness of literary men, anxious to unite, by their private journals, their person and their work; the image of literature to be found in contemporary culture is tyrannically centered on the author, his person, his history, his tastes, his passions; criticism still consists, most of the time, in saying that Baudelaire's work is the failure of the man Baudelaire, Van Gogh's work his madness, Tchaikovsky's his vice: the *explanation* of the work is always sought in the man who has produced it, as if, through the more or less transparent allegory of fiction, it was always finally the voice of one and the same person, the *author,* which delivered his "confidence".

Though the Author's empire is still very powerful (recent criticism has often merely consolidated it), it is evident that for a long time now certain writers have attempted to topple it. In France, Mallarmé was doubtless the first to see and foresee in its full extent the necessity of substituting language itself for the man who hitherto was supposed to own it; for Mallarmé, as for us, it is language which speaks, not the author: to write is to reach, through a preexisting impersonality—never to be confused with the castrating objectivity of the realistic novelist—that point where language alone acts, "performs", and not "oneself": Mallarmé's entire poetics consists in suppressing the author for the sake of the writing (which is, as we shall see, to restore the status of the reader). Valery, encumbered with a psychology of the Self, greatly edulcorated Mallarmé's theory, but, turning in a preference for classicism to the lessons of rhetoric, he unceasingly questioned and mocked the Author, emphasized the linguistic and almost "chance" nature of his activity, and throughout his prose works championed the essentially verbal condition of literature, in the face of which any recourse to the writer's interiority seemed to him pure supersitition. It is clear that Proust himself, despite the apparent psychological character of what is called his *analyses,* undertook the responsibility of inexorably blurring, by an extreme subtilization, the relation of the writer and his characters: by making the narrator not the person who has seen or felt, nor even the person who writes, but the person who will write (the young man of the novel—but, in fact, how old is he, and *who* is he?—wants to write but cannot, and the novel ends when at last the writing becomes possible), Proust has given modern writing its epic: by a radical reversal, instead of putting his life into his novel, as we say so often, he makes his very life into a work for which his own book was in a sense the model, so that it is quite obvious to us that it is not Charlus who imitates Montesquiou, but that Montesquiou in his anecdotal, historical reality is merely a secondary fragment, derived from Charlus. Surrealism lastly—to remain on the level of this prehistory of modernity—surrealism doubtless could not accord language a sovereign place, since language is a system and since what the movement sought was, romantically, a direct subversion of all codes—an illusory subversion, moreover, for a code cannot be destroyed, it can only be "played with"; but by abruptly violating expected meanings (this was the famous surrealist "jolt"), by entrusting to the hand the responsibility of writing as fast as possible what the head itself ignores (this was automatic writing), by accepting the principle and the experience of a collective writing, surrealism helped secularize the image of the Author. Finally, outside of literature itself (actually, these distinctions are being superseded), linguistics has just furnished the destruction of the Author with a precious analytic instrument by showing that utterance in its entirety is a void process, which functions perfectly without requiring to be filled by the person of the interlocutors: linguistically, the author is never anything more than the man who writes, just as *I* is no more than the man who says *I:* language knows a "subject", not a "person", and this subject, void outside of the very utterance which defines it, suffices to make language "work", that is, to exhaust it.

The absence of the Author (with Brecht, we might speak here of a real "alienation", the Author diminishing like a tiny figure at the far end of the literary stage) is not only a historical fact or an act of writing: it utterly transforms the modern text (or—what is the same thing—the text is henceforth written and read so that in it, on every level, the Author absents himself). Time, first of all, is no longer the same. The Author, when we believe in him, is always conceived as the past of his own book: the book and the author take their places of their own accord on the same line, cast as a *before* and an *after:* the Author is supposed to *feed* the book—that is, he pre-exists it, thinks, suffers, lives for it; he maintains with his work the same relation of antecedence a father maintains with his child. Quite the contrary, the modern writer (*scriptor*) is born simultaneously with his text; he is in no way supplied with a being which precedes or transcends his writing, he is in no way the subject of which his book is the predicate; there is no other time than that of the utterance, and every text is eternally written *here* and *now*. This is because (or: it follows that) *to write* can no longer designate an operation of recording, of observing, of representing, of "painting" (as the Classic writers put it), but rather what the linguisticians, following the vocabulary of the Oxford school, call a performative, a rare verbal form (exclusively given to the first person and to the present), in which utterance has no other content than the act by which it is uttered: something like the *I Command* of kings or the *I Sing* of the early bards; the modern writer, having buried the Author, can therefore no longer believe, according to the "pathos" of his predecessors, that his hand is too slow for his thought or his passion, and that in consequence, making a law out of necessity, he must accentuate this gap and endlessly "elaborate" his form; for him, on the contrary, his hand, detached from any voice, borne by a pure gesture of inscription (and not of expression), traces a field without origin—or which, at least, has no other origin than language itself, that is, the very thing which ceaselessly questions any origin.

We know that a text does not consist of a line of words, releasing a single "theological" meaning (the "message" of the Author-God), but is a space of many dimensions, in which are wedded and contested various kinds of writing, no one of which is *original:* the text is a tissue of citations, resulting from the thousand sources of culture. Like Bouvard and Pecuchet, those eternal copyists, both sublime and comical and whose profound absurdity *precisely* designates the truth of writing, the writer can only imitate a gesture forever anterior, never original: his only power is to combine the different kinds of writing, to oppose some by others, so as never to sustain himself by just one of them; if he wants to express himself, at least he should know that the internal "thing" he claims to "translate" is itself only a ready-made dictionary whose words can be explained (defined) only by other words, and so on *ad infinitum:* an experience which occurred in an exemplary fashion to the young De Quincey, so gifted in Greek that in order to translate into that dead language certain absolutely modern ideas and images, Baudelaire tells us, "he created for it a standing dictionary much more complex and extensive than the one which results from the vulgar patience of purely literary themes" (*Paradis Artificiels*): succeeding the Author, the writer no longer contains within himself passions, humors, sentiments, impressions, but that enormous dictionary, from which he derives a writing which can know no end or halt: life can only imitate the book, and the book itself is only a tissue of signs, a lost, infinitely remote imitation.

Once the Author is gone, the claim to "decipher" a text becomes quite useless. To give an Author to a text is to impose upon the text a stop clause, to furnish it with a final signification, to *close* the writing. This conception perfectly suits criticism, which can then take as its major task the discovery of the Author (or his hypostases: society, history, the psyche, freedom) beneath the work: once the Author is discovered, the text is "explained", the critic has conquered; hence it is scarcely surprising not only that, historically, the reign of the Author should also have been that of the Critic, but that criticism (even "new criticism") should be overthrown along with the Author. In a multiple writing, indeed, everything is to be *distinguished,* but nothing *deciphered;* structure can be followed, "threaded" (like a stocking that has run) in all its recurrences and all its stages, but there is no underlying *ground;* the space of the writing is to be traversed, not penetrated: writing ceaselessly posits meaning but always in order to evaporate it: it proceeds to a systematic exemption of meaning. Thus literature (it would be better, henceforth, to say writing), by refusing to assign to the text (and to the world as text) a "secret," that is, an ultimate meaning, liberates an activity which we might call counter-theological, properly revolutionary, for to refuse to arrest meaning is finally to refuse God and his hypostases, reason, science, the law.

Let us return to Balzac's sentence: no one (that is, no "person") utters it: its source, its voice is not to be located; and yet it is perfectly read; this is because the true locus of writing is reading. Another very specific example can make this understood: recent investigations (J. P. Vernant) have shed light upon the constitutively ambiguous nature of Greek tragedy, the text of which is woven with words that have double meanings, each character understanding them unilaterally (this perpetual misunderstanding is precisely what is meant by "the tragic"); yet there is someone who understands each word in its duplicity, and understands further, one might say, the very deafness of the characters speaking in front of him: this someone is precisely the reader (or here the spectator). In this way is revealed the whole being of writing: a text consists of multiple writings, issuing from several cultures and entering into dialogue with each other, into parody, into contestation; but there is one place where this multiplicity is collected, united, and this place is not the author, as we have hitherto said it was, but the reader: the reader is the very space in which are inscribed, without any being lost, all the citations a writing consists of; the unity of a text is not in its origin, it is in its destination; but this destination can no longer be personal: the reader is a man without history, without biography, without psychology; he is only that *someone* who holds gathered into a single field all the paths of which the text is constituted. This is why it is absurd to hear the new writing condemned in the name of a humanism which hypocritically appoints itself the champion of the reader's rights. The reader has never been the concern of classical criticism; for it, there is no other man in literature but the one who writes. We are now beginning to be the dupes no longer of such antiphrases, by which our society proudly champions precisely what it dismisses, ignores, smothers or destroys; we know that to restore to writing its future, we must reverse its myth: the birth of the reader must be ransomed by the death of the author.

Translated by Richard Howard

3

Excerpt from *For a New Novel*

Alain Robbe-Grillet

STORY

A novel, for most readers—and critics—is primarily a "story." A true novelist is one who knows how to "tell a story." The felicity of "telling," which sustains him from one end of his work to the other, is identified with his vocation as a writer. To invent thrilling, moving, dramatic vicissitudes constitutes both his delight and his justification.

Hence to criticize a novel often comes down to reporting its anecdote, more or less briefly, depending on whether one has six columns or two to fill, with more or less emphasis on the essential passages: the climaxes and denouements of the plot. The judgment made on the book will consist chiefly in an appreciation of this plot, of its gradual development, its equilibrium, the expectations or surprises it affords the panting reader. A loophole in the narrative, a clumsily introduced episode, a lag in interest will be the major defects of the book; vivacity and spontaneity its highest virtues.

The writing itself will never be in question. The novelist will merely be praised for expressing himself in correct language, in an agreeable, striking, evocative manner. . . . Thus the style will be no more than a means, a manner; the basis of the novel, its *raison d'être,* what is inside it, is simply the story it tells.

Yet from serious people (those who admit that literature need not be a mere diversion) to the enthusiasts of the worst sentimental, detective, or exotic junk, everyone is in the habit of demanding a particular quality from the anecdote. It is not enough that it be entertaining, or extraordinary, or enthralling; to have its measure of human truth, it must also succeed in convincing the reader that the adventures he is hearing about have really happened to real characters, and that the novelist is confining himself to reporting, to transmitting events of which he has been the witness. A tacit convention is established between the reader and the author: the latter will pretend to believe in what he is telling, the former will forget that everything is invented and will pretend to be dealing with a document, a biography, a real-life story. To tell a story well is therefore to make what one writes resemble the prefabricated schemas people are used to, in other words, their ready-made idea of reality.

Thus, whatever the unexpected nature of the situations, the accidents, the fortuitous reactions, the narrative must flow without jolts, as though of its own accord, with that irrepressible *élan* which immediately wins our adherence. The least hesitation, the slightest oddity (two contradictory elements, for example, or two that do not exactly match), and unexpectedly the current of the novel ceases to sustain the reader, who suddenly wonders if he is not being "told a story" and who threatens to return to authentic testimonies, about which at least he will not have to ask himself questions as to the verisimilitude of things. Even more than to divert, the issue here is to reassure him.

Lastly, if he wants the illusion to be complete, the novelist is always supposed to know more than he says; the notion of a "slice of life" shows the extent of the knowledge he is supposed to have about what happened before and after. In the very interior of the duration he describes, he must give the impression of offering only the essentials, but of being able, if the reader insisted, to tell much more. The substance of the novel, in the image of reality, must appear inexhaustible.

Lifelike, spontaneous, limitless, the story must, in a word, be natural. Unfortunately, even while admitting that there is still something "natural" in the relations of man and the world, it turns out that writing, like any form of art, is on the contrary an intervention. What constitutes the novelist's strength is precisely that he invents, that he invents quite freely, without a model. The remarkable thing about modern fiction is that it asserts this characteristic quite deliberately, to such a degree that invention and imagination become, at the limit, the very subject of the book.

And no doubt such a development constitutes only one of the aspects of the general change in the relations man sustains with the world in which he lives. The narrative, as our academic critics conceive it—and many readers after them—represents an order. This order, which we may in effect qualify as natural, is linked to an entire rationalistic and organizing system, whose flowering corresponds to the assumption of power by the middle class. In that first half of the nineteenth century which saw the apogee—with *The Human Comedy*—of a narrative form which understandably remains for many a kind of paradise lost of the novel, certain important certainties were in circulation: in particular the confidence in a logic of things that was just and universal.

All the technical elements of the narrative—systematic use of the past tense and the third person, unconditional adoption of chronological development, linear plots, regular trajectory of the passions, impulse of each episode toward a conclusion, etc.—everything tended to impose the image of a stable, coherent, continuous, unequivocal, entirely decipherable universe. Since the intelligibility of the world was not even questioned, to tell a story did not raise a problem. The style of the novel could be innocent.

But then, with Flaubert, everything begins to vacillate. A hundred years later, the whole system is no more than a memory; and it is to that memory, to that dead system, that some seek with all their might to keep the novel fettered. Yet here, too, it is enough to read the great novels of the beginning of our century to realize that, while the disintegration of the plot has become insistently clearer in the course of the last few years, the plot itself had long since ceased to constitute the armature of the narrative. The demands of the anecdote are doubtless less constraining for Proust than for Flaubert, for Faulkner than for Proust, for Beckett than for Faulkner. . . . Henceforth, the issue is elsewhere. To tell a story has become strictly impossible.

Yet it is wrong to claim that nothing happens any longer in modern novels. Just as we must not assume man's absence on the pretext that the traditional character has disappeared, we must not identify the search for new narrative structures with an attempt to suppress any event, any passion, any adventure. The books of Proust and Faulkner are, in fact, crammed with stories; but in the former, they dissolve in order to be recomposed to the advantage of a mental architecture of time; whereas, in the latter, the development of themes and their many associations overwhelms all chronology to the point of seeming to bury again, to drown in the course of the novel what the narrative has just revealed. Even in Beckett, there is no lack of events, but these are constantly in the process of contesting themselves, jeopardizing themselves, destroying themselves, so that the same sentence may contain an observation and its immediate negation. In short, it is not the anecdote that is lacking, it is only its character of certainty, its tranquillity, its innocence.

And if I may cite my own works after these illustrious precursors, I should like to point out that *The Erasers* and *The Voyeur* both contain a plot, an "action" quite readily detectable, rich moreover in elements generally regarded as dramatic. If they at first seem without action to certain readers, is this not simply because the movement of the style is more important to them than that of passions and crimes? But I can readily imagine that in a few decades—sooner, perhaps—when this kind of writing, assimilated, becoming academic, will pass unnoticed in its turn, and when the young novelists, of course, will be doing something else, the criticism of the day, finding once again that nothing happens in their books, will reproach them for their lack of imagination and point to our novels as an example: "Look," they will say, "look how, back in the fifties, people knew how to invent stories!"

Translated by Richard Howard

4

Three Dialogues

Samuel Beckett and Georges Duthuit

I. TALCOAT

B— Total object, complete with missing parts, instead of partial object. Question of degree.

D— More. The tyranny of the discreet overthrown. The world a flux of movements partaking of living time, that of effort, creation, liberation, the painting, the painter. The fleeting instant of sensation given back, given forth, with context of the continuum it nourished.

B— In any case a thrusting towards a more adequate expression of natural experience, as revealed to the vigilant coenaesthesia. Whether achieved through submission or through mastery, the result is a gain in nature.

D— But that which this painter discovers, orders, transmits, is not in nature. What relation between one of these paintings and a landscape seen at a certain age, a certain season, a certain hour? Are we not on a quite different plane?

B— By nature I mean here, like the naivest realist, a composite of perceiver and perceived, not a datum, an experience. All I wish to suggest is that the tendency and accomplishment of this painting are fundamentally those of previous painting, straining to enlarge the statement of a compromise.

D— You neglect the immense difference between the significance of perception for Tal Coat and its significance for the great majority of his predecessors, apprehending as artists with the same utilitarian servility as in a traffic jam and improving the result with a lick of Euclidian geometry. The global perception of Tal Coat is disinterested, committed neither to truth nor to beauty, twin tyrannies of nature. I can see the compromise of past painting, but not that which you deplore in the Matisse of a certain period and in the Tal Coat of today.

B— I do not deplore. I agree that the Matisse in question, as well as the Franciscan orgies of Tal Coat, have prodigious value, but a value cognate with those already accumulated. What we have to consider in the case of Italian painters is not that they surveyed the world with the eyes of building contractors, a mere means like any other, but that they never stirred from the field of the possible, however much they may have enlarged it. The only thing disturbed by the revolutionaries Matisse and Tal Coat is a certain order on the plane of the feasible.

D— What other plane can there be for the maker?

B— Logically none. Yet I speak of an art turning from it in disgust, weary of its puny exploits, weary of pretending to be able, of being able, of doing a little better the same old thing, of going a little further along a dreary road.

D— And preferring what?

B— The expression that there is nothing to express, nothing with which to express, nothing from which to express, no power to express, no desire to express, together with the obligation to express.

D— But that is a violently extreme and personal point of view, of no help to us in the matter of Tal Coat.

B—

D— Perhaps that is enough for today.

II. MASSON

B— In search of the difficulty rather than in its clutch. The disquiet of him who lacks an adversary.

D— That is perhaps why he speaks so often nowadays of painting the void, "in fear and trembling." His concern was at one time with the creation of a mythology; then with man, not simply in the universe, but in society; and now . . . "inner emptiness, the prime condition, according to Chinese esthetics, of the act of painting." It would thus seem, in effect, that Masson suffers more keenly than any living painter from the need to come to rest, i.e. to establish the data of the problem to be solved, the Problem at last.

B— Though little familiar with the problems he has set himself in the past and which, by the mere fact of their solubility or for any other reason, have lost for him their legitimacy, I feel their presence not far behind these canvases veiled in consternation, and the scars of a competence that must be most painful to him. Two old maladies that should no doubt be considered separately: the malady of wanting to know what to do and the malady of wanting to be able to do it.

D— But Masson's declared purpose is now to reduce these maladies, as you call them, to nothing. He aspires to be rid of the servitude of space, that his eye may "frolic among the focusless fields, tumultuous with incessant creation." At the same time he demands the rehabilitation of the "vaporous." This may seem strange in one more fitted by temperament for fire than for damp. You of course will reply that it is the same thing as before, the same reaching towards succour from without. Opaque or transparent, the object remains sovereign. But how can Masson be expected to paint the void?

B— He is not. What is the good of passing from one untenable position to another, of seeking justification always on the same plane? Here is an artist who seems literally skewered on the ferocious dilemma of expression. Yet he continues to wriggle. The void he speaks of is perhaps simply the obliteration of an unbearable presence, unbearable because neither to be wooed nor to be stormed. If this anguish of helplessness is never stated as such, on its own merits and for its own sake, though perhaps very occasionally admitted as spice to the "exploit" it jeopardised, the reason is doubtless, among others, that it seems to contain in itself the impossibility of statement. Again an exquisitely logical attitude. In any case, it is hardly to be confused with the void.

D— Masson speaks much of transparency—"openings, circulations, communications, unknown penetrations"—where he may frolic at his ease, in freedom. Without renouncing the objects, loathsome or delicious, that are our daily bread and wine and poison, he seeks to break through their partitions to that continuity of being which is absent from the ordinary experience of living. In this he approaches Matisse (of the first period needless to say) and Tal Coat, but with this notable difference, that Masson has to contend with his own technical gifts, which have the richness, the precision, the density and balance of the high classical manner. Or perhaps I should say rather its spirit, for he has shown himself capable, as occasion required, of great technical variety.

B— What you say certainly throws light on the dramatic predicament of this artist. Allow me to note his concern with the amenities of ease and freedom. (*The stars are undoubtedly superb,* as Freud remarked on reading Kant's cosmological proof of the existence of God.) With such preoccupations it seems to me impossible that he should ever do anything different from that which the best, including himself, have done already. It is perhaps an impertinence to suggest that he wishes to. His so extremely intelligent remarks on space breathe the same possessiveness as the notebooks of Leonardo who, when he speaks of *disfazione,* knows that for him not one fragment will be lost. So forgive me if I relapse, as when we spoke of the so different Tal Coat, into my dream of an art unresentful of its insuperable indigence and too proud for the farce of giving and receiving.

D— Masson himself, having remarked that western perspective is no more than a series of traps for the capture of objects, declares that their possession does not interest him. He congratulates Bonnard for having, in his last works, "gone beyond possessive space in every shape and form, far from surveys and bounds, to the point where all possession is dissolved." I agree that there is a long cry from Bonnard to that impoverished painting, "authentically fruitless, incapable of any image whatsoever," to which you aspire, and towards which too, who knows, unconsciously perhaps, Masson tends. But must we really deplore the painting that admits "the things and creatures of spring, resplendent with desire and affirmation, ephemeral no doubt, but immortally reiterant," not in order to benefit by them, not in order to enjoy them, but in order that what is tolerable and radiant in the world may continue? Are we really to deplore the painting that is a rallying among the things of time that pass and hurry us away, towards a time that endures and gives increase?

B— (Exit weeping.)

III. BRAM VAN VELDE

B— Frenchman, fire first.

D— Speaking of Tal Coat and Masson you invoked an art of a different order, not only from theirs, but from any achieved up to date. Am I right in thinking that you had van Velde in mind when making this sweeping distinction?

B— Yes. I think he is the first to accept a certain situation and to consent to a certain act.

D— Would it be too much to ask you to state again, as simply as possible, the situation and act that you conceive to be his?

B— The situation is that of him who is helpless, cannot act, in the event cannot paint, since he is obliged to paint. The act is of him who, helpless, unable to act, acts, in the event paints, since he is obliged to paint.

D— Why is he obliged to paint?

B— I don't know.

D— Why is he helpless to paint?

B— Because there is nothing to paint and nothing to paint with.

D— And the result, you say, is art of a new order?

B— Among those whom we call great artists, I can think of none whose concern was not predominantly with his expressive possibilities, those of his vehicle, those of humanity. The assumption underlying all painting is that the domain of the maker is the domain of the feasible. The much to express, the little to express, the ability to express much, the ability to express little, merge in the common anxiety to express as much as possible, or as truly as possible, or as finely as possible, to the best of one's ability. What—

D— One moment. Are you suggesting that the painting of van Velde is inexpressive?

B— (A fortnight later) Yes.

D— You realise the absurdity of what you advance?

B— I hope I do.

D— What you say amounts to this: the form of expression known as painting, since for obscure reasons we are obliged to speak of painting, has had to wait for van Velde to be rid of the misapprehension under which it had laboured so long and so bravely, namely, that its function was to express by means of paint.

B— Others have felt that art is not necessarily expression. But the numerous attempts made to make painting independent of its occasion have only succeeded in enlarging its repertory. I suggest that van Velde is the first whose painting is bereft, rid if you prefer, of occasion in every shape and form, ideal as well as material, and the first whose hands have not been tied by the certitude that expression is an impossible act.

D— But might it not be suggested, even by one tolerant of this fantastic theory, that the occasion of his painting is his predicament, and that it is expressive of the impossibility to express?

B— No more ingenious method could be devised for restoring him, safe and sound, to the bosom of Saint Luke. But let us for once, be foolish enough not to turn tail. All have turned wisely tail, before the ultimate penury, back to the mere misery where destitute virtuous mothers may steal stale bread for their starving brats. There is more than a difference of degree between being short, short of the world, short of self, and being without these esteemed commodities. The one is a predicament, the other not.

D— But you have already spoken of the predicament of van Velde.

B— I should not have done so.

D— You prefer the purer view that here at last is a painter who does not paint, does not pretend to paint. Come, come, my dear fellow, make some kind of connected statement and then go away.

B— Would it not be enough if I simply went away?

D— No. You have begun. Finish. Begin again and go on until you have finished. Then go away. Try and bear in mind that the subject under discussion is not yourself, nor the Sufist Al-Haqq, but a particular Dutchman by name van Velde, hitherto erroneously referred to as an *artiste peintre*.

B— How would it be if I first said what I am pleased to fancy he is, fancy he does, and then that it is more than likely that he is and does quite otherwise? Would not that be an excellent issue out of all our afflictions? He happy, you happy, I happy, all three bubbling over with happiness.

D— Do as you please. But get it over.

B— There are many ways in which the thing I am trying in vain to say may be tried in vain to be said. I have experimented, as you know, both in public and in private, under duress, through faintness of heart, through weakness of mind, with two or three hundred. The pathetic antithesis possession-poverty was perhaps not the most tedious. But we begin to weary of it, do we not? The realisation that art has always been bourgeois, though it may dull our pain before the achievements of the socially progressive, is finally of scant interest. The analysis of the relation between the artist and his occasion, a relation always regarded as indispensable, does not seem to have been very productive either, the reason being perhaps that it lost its way in disquisitions on the nature of occasion. It is obvious that for the artist obsessed with his expressive vocation, anything and everything is doomed to become occasion, including, as is apparently to some extent the case with Masson, the pursuit of occasion, and the every man his own wife experiments of the spiritual Kandinsky. No painting is more replete than Mondrian's.

But if the occasion appears as an unstable term of relation, the artist, who is the other term, is hardly less so, thanks to his warren of modes and attitudes. The objections to this dualist view of the creative process are unconvincing. Two things are established, however precariously: the aliment, from fruits on plates to low mathematics and self-commiseration, and its manner of dispatch. All that should concern us is the acute and increasing anxiety of the relation itself, as though shadowed more and more darkly by a sense of invalidity, of inadequacy, of existence, of reaction at the expense of all that it excludes, all that it blinds to. The history of painting, here we go again, is the history of its attempts to escape from this sense of failure, by means of more authentic, more ample, less exclusive relations between representer and representee, in a kind of tropism towards a light as to the nature of which the best opinions continue to vary, and with a kind of Pythagorean terror, as though the irrationality of pi were an offence against the deity, not to mention his creature. My case, since I am in the dock, is that van Velde is the first to desist from this estheticised automatism, the first to submit wholly to the incoercible absence of relation in the absence of terms or, if you like, in the presence of unavailable terms, the first to admit that to be an artist is to fail, as no other dare fail, that failure is his world and the shrink from it desertion, art and craft, good housekeeping, living. No, no, allow me to expire. I know that all that is required now, in order to bring even this horrible matter to an acceptable conclusion, is to make of this submission, this admission, this fidelity to failure, a new occasion, a new term of relation, and of the act which, unable to act, obliged to act, he makes, an expressive act, even if only of itself, of its impossibility, of its obligation. I know that my inability to do so places myself, and perhaps an innocent, in what I think is still called an unenviable situation, familiar to psychiatrists. For what is this coloured plane, that was not there before? I don't know what it is, having never seen anything like it before. It seems to have nothing to do with art, in any case, if my memories of art are correct. (Prepares to go.)

D— Are you not forgetting something?

B— Surely that is enough?

D— I understood your number was to have two parts. The first was to consist in your saying what you—er—thought. This I am prepared to believe you have done. The second—

B— (Remembering, warmly) Yes, yes, I am mistaken, I am mistaken.

5

The Icon and the Absurd

Jan Kott

I

In the casinos of Las Vegas the black-jack tables and roulette wheels stand silent from five to seven A.M. Slotmachines alone remain for the stragglers unconquered by night and fatigue. These slotmachines do not give their players even the illusion of control, for the game consists only of throwing in money and moving the metal arms. Fate is blind and completely encased in the mechanism. The player merely sets fate in motion, and fate in turn brings either a loss of the stake or its manifold increase. The slotmachines are closed structures: the player and the mechanism—no one and nothing beyond that. "Others" in this structure do not exist. No one stands between the player and fate. "God," who arranges the mechanism, repairs it, takes out the money, is invisible. He doesn't exist, at least not for the player.

All the elements of the Theatre of the Absurd are present. Alienation is complete. Man is reduced to a player, has the face of a player, the reflexes of a player, the movements of a player; even his money is a badge, a stake in the game. Man is "thrown" (here we can use a favorite term of the existentialists) into a world which does not belong to him and which is stronger than he is. Man is a "stranger," so far as the slotmachine is concerned. But the machine is also a "stranger," so far as man is concerned. Their relationship is absurd. The machine controls the player rather than the player the machine. What's more, the slotmachine makes an automaton of the player. And of these two machines, the slotmachine-player, seemingly endowed with a free will and intelligence, is in reality a much less complicated entity than the slotmachine-fate. The slotmachine-player throws money into the opening and presses the handle; the slotmachine-fate executes a much more complicated act. Time alone encompasses them. But as in Theatre of the Absurd we have here two different times: the "time" of the player—one-way, present, and restricted; and the "time" of the mechanism, which is at once past, present, and future. The "time" of the slotmachine for the player is eternal; the community of players must lose, since the machines have a limitless amount of time in which to perform.

This spectacle takes place in something like absolute silence. One hears only the sound of the money thrown in and occasionally the unexpected chord of hope, like the trumpets at the Last Judgment, a shrill ringing, a sign that in one of the machines the jackpot has appeared. The vocal music is quite definite: the players are able to speak to the machines, but are unable to come to an understanding with the machines. In this kind of theatre words are useless; they cannot manage to change anything. Here, language does not serve to effect understanding. It is difficult to say what purpose it serves. It is no longer necessary. Sometimes it even seems superfluous.

II

At five o'clock in the morning Las Vegas is probably one of the most perfect visions of hell. But the Theatre of the Absurd has recurrently suggested just such a vision of hell. For example, in at least three recent works this absurd, anti-human element has been shown as a mechanism: in Beckett's *Act Without Words,* in Pinter's *The Dumbwaiter,* and Mrozek's *Striptease*. In Beckett, metaphysics is reduced to a super-slotmachine, in Pinter and Mrozek this silent slotmachine is politics and the social scene. The Absurd in each of these three plays is different; yet it is theatricalized in quite similar ways.

These three plays, like the French avant-garde of the fifties and the entire spectrum of plays coming under the heading of the Theatre of the Absurd, are only one division of the theatricalization of the theatre in the twentieth century. It seems that by the use of certain basic notions of semiotics and theories of symbols, both the theatricalization process as a whole and the character of particular theatrical styles can be presented more precisely than before.

In every symbol we distinguish between "designated" and "implied," *signifié* and *signifiant,* appearance and meaning, "icon" and "content." According to the simplest theories of semantics, signs are divided into the literal, mimetic, and symbolic. In the literal sign the icon and meaning are the same; in the symbolic sign the "code" underscores the meaning of the icon. For example, in a system of road-signs all three types are used: a lowered barrier at a railroad-crossing is a literal sign, a cow or a deer on a sign is a mimetic or imitative symbol, a red light or the word "stop" is a symbolic sign.

A theatrical production is also a collection of signs, but such a collection by its very nature is ambivalent and inconsistent. A chair in a "normal" theatre is a literal sign, simply a chair, but painted wood on canvas or hanging loose from the canvas is a mimetic sign. The sign, "Forest of Arden," is a symbolic sign. A lighted candle on the stage is a literal sign. Change of lighting is a mimetic sign: bright light denotes day, murky light signifies evening, and so on. But lighted lanterns carried onstage when lights are up in the Chinese theatre (Peter Brook used this trick in *King Lear*) can also be symbolic signs of night. In each of the various elements of any production these three types of signs are intermixed. Walking on the stage is a literal sign, but running is a mimetic sign. In the naturalistic theatre, gestures are imitative of real gestures, but these real gestures are also literal, mimetic, and symbolic signs. This semiotics of theatrical signs can be presented in a systematic way, and such attempts have already been made several times. It doesn't seem, however, that they have led to interesting results; rather they have proved to be quite an empty intellectual game. Another point is important: the analysis of icons and of the relations between icons and their meanings permits a designation of theatrical styles.

In the theatre the basic icon is the body and voice of the actor. Every art, Eric Bentley once wrote, is a laying bare of the human soul, but only in the theatre does this laying bare of the soul take place through the physical presence of human flesh onstage. When we say that Mrs. Z. was a magnificent Juliet, but bowlegged, we are making a judgment concerning the icon and the "designated," about the appearance of the sign and about that which this sign designates.

No one has matched Brecht for revealing this basic structural paradox of the theatre: the actor is himself, the actor, at the same time that he depicts someone else. In a related manner, the director measures the time of a performance according to the same time units as does the audience. Yet meanwhile, on the stage, the play's time span is left fluid and can be speeded or slowed, can be directed back into the past or thrust forward into the future. Similarly, action takes place in a designated part of a building, the theatre—on the stage, in an arena, or on a scaffold. Yet simultaneously the stage locale can accommodate every place that the text calls for. The Chinese Opera, the Japanese Noh and Kabuki, the theatre of Bali are for the viewer who does not know the "code," that is, the symbolic language, almost pure icons. The color white in itself is neither a sign of wedding or funeral. A duel between two actors in black and red make-up, dressed in armor with four banners attached is simply a display of acrobatics, and not a battle of two armies of the North and South. The circus is also a play of pure icons. The dancer dancing on a tight-rope under the big top is a circus acrobat. Everything in the circus really happens because each icon is a literal sign. Brecht, Artaud, and Witkiewicz went through a period of double fascination—for the circus and the theatre of the East. But the conclusions which they arrived at for their own visions of the theatre were varied.

Verfremdungseffekt, not quite fortuitously translated into English as "alienation" and into French as *"distantiation,"* is the key to Brecht's theatrical aesthetics and practice. In theory, *Verfremdungseffekt* was to have served to strengthen the cognitive, didactic, anti-Aristotelian function of the theatre; in practice—it strengthened the theatricalization of the theatre. The theory raises some doubts. Practice unveiled a new style of theatre. The body and costume of the actor are an icon, and therefore, if the actor plays himself—that is, an actor—the icon is a literal sign; if he plays a person from a play, a mimetic or symbolic sign—it is illusion. *Verfremdungseffekt,* the destruction of illusion, a consciously executed leap from the created character to the actor, from theatrical time to real time, from an imagined place to the real scene, can be designated as utilization of this same icon: first as a literal sign, second as a mimetic or symbolic sign. We are in the theatre—that means everything. What is happening is not "really" happening, because it really is theatre.

Brecht, didactic and rationalistic, was raised on Marxism and the cabaret. With complete subtlety he began to cultivate a kind of play based on icons and meanings. In *Galileo,* the actor in a white sheet literally represents one single thing; but when he dons a pontifical robe and a tiara, he emblemizes not just a pope, but the entire papacy, the Office itself. The ambiguous icon is not only flesh and costume; it is also a property. The hanger with the tiara, cowl, and chasuble is a literal sign. Yet, at the same time, it is a symbolic one: the Office is a costume; the pope is a mannequin.

Brecht's scene designs and methods of using masks and Eastern make-up are based on the same law of ambiguity of the icon. The actor in the mask is more theatrical than one without a mask. He is more theatrical because he is not pretending that the role he is playing is "real." The mask in Brecht's theatre is a literal icon, or a symbolic one; never, on the other hand, is it a mimetic icon. Brecht also employed a measure which the Russian formalists in the early twenties called "laying bare the device." The revolving panoramic backdrop in *Mother Courage,* turning in the opposite direction from the movement of the wagon, is a laying bare of theatrical machinery; its use is an icon of a literal sign. Similarly, in *King Lear,* Brook made use of an old theatrical device to produce thunder: three huge vibrating sheets of tin lowered onto the stage were simultaneously a literal icon—a machine—and a symbolic sign of the storm.

For Artaud this theatricalization of the stage took the form of Theatre of Cruelty: "I shall answer," he wrote in *Letters on Language,* "that if we are clearly so incapable today of giving an idea of Aeschylus, Sophocles, or Shakespeare that is worthy of them, it is probably because we have lost the sense of their theatre's physics. It is because the directly human and active aspect of their way of speaking and moving, their whole scenic rhythms, escapes us, an aspect which ought to have as much if not more importance than the admirable spoken dissection of their heroes' psychology." Artaud's understanding of "cruelty" was interchangeably connected with his understanding of "rigor" ("severity"). "Cruelty is rigor," he wrote. In French, in the word *"cruauté,"* the element "cru"—raw—sounds even more distinct. *"Une viande crue"*—raw meat. This raw meat of the theatre was not an area of meanings and "discourse" for Artaud, but the "physics," that which happens in the theatre: movement, the presence of bodies and objects, the material value of the voice. It was to be a theatre of literal signs, like the theatre of the East for an audience which does not know the Orient's symbolic language. But Artaud knew that the Balinese theatre used symbolic language. The Theatre of Cruelty was to have been a theatre of pure icons and at the same time of liturgy, ritual, and magic. Witkiewicz, whose formulations are sometimes startlingly similar to Artaud's, wrote about the theatre of "Pure Form," which was to bring a metaphysical impact that religion was not now in the position to deliver.

How is this contemporary icon of a "metaphysical" sign or ritual in the theatre supposed to look? To this question neither Artaud nor Witkiewicz was able to offer an answer. In his own dramatic works, Witkiewicz was one of the greatest and the most original precursor of the Theatre of the Absurd. And undoubtedly one of the answers to the question of theatrical identity, at any rate the historical answer, was the Theatre of the Absurd.

III

Drama after Artaud deals with the same issues of theatrical iconography. In Ionesco's *Amédée,* for instance, mushrooms sprout up in the room and the feet of the corpse slowly take up the whole stage. What do this growing corpse and these poison mushrooms represent? Perhaps suppressed remembrances, concealed betrayal, time destroying love, or approaching death. The icons of these signs are defined with extreme precision, their theatrical expressiveness is unmistakable. On the other hand, their symbolic meaning remains unclear. The empty chairs and the stammering of the Speaker, in surely the most splendid of Ionesco's plays, theatrically are again examples of symbols, which understood literally organize the action. Such emblems lead to the Theatre of Cruelty and Severity; they undoubtedly have their own "metaphysical" value, but it is not manifest here. The icon is richer and more startling than all of its meanings.

In Beckett's *Endgame,* Hamm is blind and cannot rise from his own armchair on wheels. Clov cannot sit down. Nell and Nagg can merely stick out their heads from the ash cans. In the first part of *Happy Days,* Winnie is buried in the ground up to her waist; in the second part up to her neck. In Beckett's plays the author's remarks are extremely detailed and often take up half the text. The dramatic situation is contained almost completely in the artistic icon. What does it mean? The impossibility of understanding? Life understood as growing old and decay? Awareness, which for existentialists is a "hole" in the world of essence? *Vanitas vanitatum?* If Beckett could say this or wanted to, he would have used a different type of medium.

Before the war, during the years of my Parisian youth, a favorite game of my friends was the thinking up of so-called surrealistic objects. The first prize was given once for an iron with a nail stuck into its base. The idea of the iron as an useful object was in this way completely annihilated. At another time the prize was awarded for an object called

"Paganini's Violin." Today it can be found in the Louvre. It consisted of a small violin hermetically tied by a bandage. In both instances, the prizes were offered for processes which destroyed the efficacy of the icon concerned. But what does this iron stuck with a nail or the bandaged violin mean? They were then and are now understood as symbolic signs of the Absurd. Collage is the pasting up of pieces of newspaper, illustrations, and fragments of various objects. Collages thus are similar to "surrealistic objects" made absurd; their "gestalt," inner structure, has been destroyed; they are now merely pure icons. But from their mutual clash, from their arrangement, a new icon is formed, which no longer is only a literal sign or symbol. It has or at any rate could have symbolic value. It can also be a sign of the Absurd or Senselessness.

In the plays of Różewicz, Mrozek, Ionesco, and especially Beckett, the basic artistic icon of the dramatic situation rests on the law of surrealistic collage. The shoes which Vladimir and Estragon take off and put on, the tree which blossoms, Krapp's tape, the mirror, the revolver, and all the objects which Winnie takes out of her bag are literal signs. From their clash and arrangement a symbolic sign is formed. This is a contemporary icon of human existence. More and more it takes on supraverbal character.

To a certain degree a similar process of "iconization" appeared in the language structure of the Theatre of the Absurd. What is understood when one says: "two times two is blue"? To understand this is to classify it as nonsense. ("Two times two is five" is a false statement, although it makes sense.) Understanding takes place on the highest level of linguistic awareness. It does not concern the contents because this answer does not mean anything; it is only a classification of form, structure, and the icon. The characters in *Jack, or The Submission* and *The Bald Soprano* have trouble understanding each other, but we understand them without any difficulty; and we accurately classify their answers as agglomerations, distortions, clichés, and jests, or senseless statements. They are icons for us. We put them in quotation marks; we understand them metaphorically, when they are meant literally; or else we accept them just literally, when their proper meaning is metaphorical. They could have been examples from a general theory of linguistics, from a theory of communication and its breakdown.

The problem is after all much broader and encompasses means of utilizing the language not only in the Theatre of the Absurd. Beginning with Chekhov and the later plays of Strindberg, the audience is often in the position of a cryptographer who decodes the message. Or the viewer is placed in the position of a psychoanalyst who listens to the confession of a patient. For Lacan, psychoanalysis is already really a part of structural linguistics. Everything that we know about Freud's *id* is language communication. Dreams, not only when we relate them but even when we recall them to ourselves, have a verbal form: the Freudian slip is a breakdown of communication, the associations connected with the icon of the ink-blot are also verbal answers. But this is coded communication in which every icon has two or more meanings—the obvious and the hidden, the literal and symbolic. The *id* speaks in meta- or infra-language. But in a language. There is no rendering of a non-language. The roar of the sea is unrenderable in any human language.

IV

Each avant-garde dramatist today has developed his own iconographic method, as we have seen. Genet's theatre is called the theatre of ceremony, liturgy, ritual. The correct repetition of *form* is necessary for the importance of ritual. Liturgy—traversing Artaud—is discipline. For Genet, the icon, not the intention, is important. The unbelieving priest, who repeats the words of the canon, changes bread and wine into Body and Blood. But if the words are not rendered exactly, transubstantiation does not take place. Ritual and liturgy are symbolic signs; they can even be accepted as magical signs. Ritual is initiation, the crossover of one group of society to another, a transubstantiation, a transition. A young man is accepted into a group of men, a pagan becomes a Christian, the layman receives holy orders. I repeat "I do" and raise two fingers: I become a President, a Judge, a sworn Witness, or a marriage is contracted. The icon is a verbal formula, gestures between the person leading the ceremony—the shaman—and the subject of the ritual. But the subject of the ritual can also be present symbolically, can also be represented by an object or acted out. Conventional magic depends either on the law of resemblance or on the law of temporal and spatial contiguity; in linguistic terms, as formulated by Jacobson, magic relies on the law either of metaphor or metonymy. The photograph of an unfaithful lover—an effigy which is supposed to represent him—is burned. This is magic which depends on the law of resemblance or metaphor. But in the tricks of magic one can also use the hair of another person, her dress, every object with which her body has come in contact. Such is magic based on the law of contiguity or metonymy.

In *The Maids* Genet utilizes both types of magic. Claire plays Madame, and therefore imagines her; both sisters put on the dress of Madame, admire themselves in her mirror, use her perfume. But all the magical tricks are merely icons of literal signs; the sisters are *really* only imitating Madame and can only sleep with and poison one another. Ritual is the repetition of form. In a ritual all are actors; they must repeat the words and gestures or act out the icon. But what happens when the ritual is performed on the stage? Marriage is not valid, an oath is not binding, the bishop has not been consecrated. Transubstantiation has not taken place; the Mass has merely been reflected in the mirror. Ritual repeated on the stage is only appearance and sham, a mock-ritual and a fake. It is in reality an unmasking of ritual. The performed ritual is a mirrored reflection of the true ritual, but in reality ritual is also merely a mirrored reflection, a play. In this theatre of mirrors there is only the repetitious reflection of icons. Genet's theatre is the most consistent realization of the Theatre of Cruelty and Severity. At the same time it is its most complete denial. The icon of the "metaphysical" sign repeated in the theatre becomes the icon of the literal sign. And "the natural and magic equivalent of the dogmas in which we no longer believe" does not exist. Grotowski is the last man who still believes in such dogmas.

V

In theatre, when the icon becomes completely that of the literal symbol, we have a "happening." In a happening all the signs are literal: a pyramid of chairs is only a pile of chairs placed one on top of the other; a stream of water which drenches the audience is merely a stream of water which drenches the viewers. In reality there is not even a partition between the viewers and actors, and in this the happening differs from sports events, from the circus, or from athletic contests. In the best circumstances there are only those provoking and those provoked. Judith Malina formulated this logically: "I don't want to be Antigone," she declared. "I am and want to be Judith Malina." The audience cannot go on the stage and take the hand of the actress playing Antigone because the stage is a symbol of Thebes, and the flesh of the actress is the icon of the imitating sign. But in the technique of the happening used by the Living Theatre, Judith Malina is only an icon of Judith Malina. She is the same kind of concrete sign as the audience. ("Action is the only reality" was one of the slogans hung over the Sorbonne during the May revolution.) Brecht demanded that the actor at the same time depict the character in the play and himself, that is, the actor on the stage. But in the happening there is no longer an actor: one can only be himself. Yet, what does it mean to be "oneself"? According to Gombrowicz and Genet, and according to psychoanalysis and contemporary radical criticism of personality, it is quite difficult to accept the fact that one can simply be "oneself" on the stage. Besides, we are always onstage. The face is also only a mask—or in the terminology of Gombrowicz, a "mouth" (*"gueule"*)—put on us or which was chosen by us. Every change of clothes is a theatrical costume, a disguise. We can only be "ourselves" when we are naked. "Are naked women intelligent," Stanislaw Jerzy Lec wrote in one of his aphorisms. Nakedness, it seemed to us, will mean nothing but nakedness. It is the one icon really *naked,* literally in the absolute sense. The effect of nakedness, which more and more tempts even the most distinguished directors, is not only the result of change in customs and the appeasement of censorship in a permissive society. Nakedness in the theatre is also the final consequence of a long search for concrete signs which have completely changed the character of the theatre in the twentieth century. But let us repeat another of Lec's aphorisms: "When you arrive at the very bottom, you will hear knocking from below." Nakedness as a literal sign also proved to be an illusion. "Naked as worms," says one of the characters in Sartre's *No Exit*. "Naked as the gods," Nietzsche once wrote. Perhaps, simply, naked as people. A literal and concrete sign once again proved to be a symbolic sign, perhaps even more so—one of those universal and "metaphysical" signs, which Antonin Artaud desperately dreamed about.

Translated by E. J. Czerwinski

6

Indirect Impact of the Epic Theatre

(Extracts from the Notes to *Die Mutter*)

Bertolt Brecht

I

Written in the style of the didactic pieces, but requiring actors, *Die Mutter* is a piece of anti-metaphysical, materialistic, non-aristotelian drama. This makes nothing like such a free use as does the aristotelian of the passive empathy of the spectator; it also relates differently to certain psychological effects, such as catharsis. Just as it refrains from handing its hero over to the world as if it were his inescapable fate, so it would not dream of handing the spectator over to an inspiring theatrical experience. Anxious to teach the spectator a quite definite practical attitude, directed towards changing the world, it must begin by making him adopt in the theatre a quite different attitude from what he is used to. The following are a few of the means employed in the first production of *Die Mutter* in Berlin.

II

Indirect Impact of the Epic Stage— In the first production of *Die Mutter* the stage (Caspar Neher) was not supposed to represent any real locality: it as it were took up an attitude itself towards the incidents shown; it quoted, narrated, prepared and recalled. Its sparse indication of furniture, doors, etc. was limited to objects that had a part in the play, i.e. those without which the action would have been altered or halted. A firm arrangement of iron piping slightly higher than a man was erected at varying intervals perpendicularly to the stage; other moveable horizontal pipes carrying canvasses could be slotted into it, and this allowed of quick changes. There were doors in frames hanging inside this, which could be opened and shut. A big canvas at the back of the stage was used for the projection of texts and pictorial documents which remained throughout the scene, so that this screen was also virtually part of the setting. Thus the stage not only used allusions to show actual rooms but also texts and pictures to show the great movement of ideas in which the events were taking place. The projections are in no way pure mechanical aids in the sense of being extras, they are no *pons asinorum;* they do not set out to help the spectator but to block him; they prevent his complete empathy, interrupt his being automatically carried away. They turn the impact into an *indirect* one. Thus they are organic parts of the work of art.

IV

Epic Method of Portrayal— The epic theatre uses the simplest possible groupings, such as express the event's overall sense. No more "casual," "life-like," "unforced" grouping; the stage no longer reflects the "natural" disorder of things. The opposite of natural disorder is aimed at: natural order. This order is determined from a social-historical point of view. The point of view to be adopted by the production can be made more generally intelligible, though not properly characterized, if we call it that of the genre painter and the historian.

[*Specific incidents in the second scene of the play are then listed, which were brought out by the production and presented separately.* These, says Brecht], must be portrayed as emphatically and significantly as any well-known historical episodes, though without sentimentalizing them. In this epic theatre serving a non-aristotelian type of drama the actor will at the same time do all he can to make himself observed standing between the spectator and the event. This making-oneself-observed also contributes to the desired indirect impact.

V

For Example: a Description of the First Portrayal of the Mother — Here are a few examples of what epic acting brought out, as shown by the actress who created the part (Helene Weigel):

1. In the first scene the actress stood in a particular characteristic attitude in the centre of the stage, and spoke the sentences as if they were in the third person; and so she not only refrained from pretending in fact to be or to claim to be Vlassova (the Mother), and in fact to be speaking those sentences, but actually prevented the spectator from transferring himself to a particular room, as habit and indifference might demand, and imagining himself to be the invisible eye-witness and eavesdropper of a unique intimate occasion. Instead what she did was openly to introduce the spectator to the person whom he would be watching acting and being acted upon for some hours.

5. The May Day demonstration was spoken as if the participants were before a police-court, but at the end the actor playing Smilgin indicated his collapse by going down on his knees; the actress playing the Mother then stooped during her final words and picked up the flag that had slipped from his hands.

6. . . . The scene where the Mother and other workers learn to read and write is one of the most difficult for the actor. The audience's laughter at one or two sentences must not prevent him from showing how difficult learning is for the old and unadaptable, thus achieving the stature of the real historical event, the fact that a proletariat which had been exploited and restricted to physical work was able to socialize knowledge and expropriate the bourgeois intellectually. This event is not to be read "between the lines"; it is directly stated. A lot of our actors, when something has to be stated directly in a scene, get restless and at once look there for something less direct which they can represent. They fall on whatever is "inexpressible," between the lines, because it calls for their gifts. Such an approach makes what they can and do express seem banal, and is therefore harmful. . . .

7. The Mother has to discuss her revolutionary work with her son under the enemy's nose: she deceives the prison warder by displaying what seems to him the moving, harmless attitude of the average mother.

She encourages his own harmless sympathy. So this example of a quite new and active kind of mother-love is herself exploiting her knowledge of the old familiar out-of-date kind. The actress showed that the Mother is quite aware of the humour of the situation. . . .

9. In every case she picked, out of all conceivable characteristics, those whose awareness promoted the most comprehensive political treatment of the Vlassovas (i.e. special, individual and unique ones), and such as help the Vlassovas themselves in their work. It was as if she was acting to a group of politicians—but none the less an actress for that, and within the framework of art.

VII

Is Non-aristotelian Drama Primitive, as Typified by Die Mutter? — The spectator is here considered to be faced with images of men whose originals he has to deal with—i.e. make speak and act—in real life, and cannot treat as finally and exactly determined phenomena. His duty to his fellow-men consists in ranging himself with the determining factors. In this duty the drama must support him. The determining factors, such as social background, special events, etc., must be shown as alterable. By means of a certain interchangeability of circumstances and occurrences the spectator must be given the possibility (and duty) of assembling, experimenting and abstracting. Among the differences that distinguish individuals from each other, there are quite specific ones that interest the political being who mixes with them, struggles with them and has to deal with them (e.g. those which the leaders of the class-struggle need to know). There is no point for him in stripping a given man of all his peculiarities until he stands there as Man (with a capital M), i.e. as a being who cannot be altered further. Man has to be understood in his role as man's (the spectator's) own fate. It has to be a workable definition.

VIII

"Direct," Flattening, Impact— In calling for a direct impact, the aesthetics of the day call for an impact that flattens out all social and other distinctions between individuals. Plays of the aristotelian type still manage to flatten out class conflicts in this way although the individuals themselves are becoming increasingly aware of class differences. The same result is achieved even when class conflicts are the subject of such plays, and even in cases where they take sides for a particular class. A collective entity is created in the auditorium for the *duration of the entertainment,* on the basis of the "common humanity" shared by all spectators alike. Non-aristotelian drama of *Die Mutter*'s sort is not interested in the establishment of such an entity. It divides its audience.

X

Resistance to Learning and Contempt for the Useful— One of the chief objections made by bourgeois criticism to non-aristotelian plays like *Die Mutter* is based on an equally bourgeois distinction between the concepts "entertaining" and "instructive." In this view *Die Mutter* is possibly instructive (if only for a small section of the potential audience, the argument goes) but definitely not entertaining (not even for this small section). There is a certain pleasure to be got out of looking more closely at this distinction. Surprising as it may seem, the object is to discredit learning by presenting it as not enjoyable. But in fact of course it is enjoyment that is being discredited by this deliberate suggestion that one learns nothing from it. One only needs to look around and see the function allotted to learning in bourgeois society. It amounts to the buying of materially useful items of knowledge. The purchase has to take place before the individual enters the process of production. Its field is immaturity. To admit that I am still incapable of something that is part of my profession, in other words to allow myself to be caught learning, is equivalent to confessing that I am unfit to meet competition and that I must not be allowed credit. The man who comes to the theatre for "entertainment" refuses to let himself be "treated like a schoolboy" once again because he remembers the fearful torments with which "knowledge" used to be hammered into the youth of the bourgeoisie. Libellous things are being said about the learner's attitude.

In the same way most people have taken to despising the useful and the instinct for the useful ever since men first took to making use of one another exclusively by means of underhand tricks. Nowadays utility derives only from abuse of one's fellow men.

Translated by John Willett

7

Excerpt from *Notes and Counter Notes: Writings on the Theatre**

Eugène Ionesco

All my plays have their origin in two fundamental states of consciousness: now the one, now the other is predominant, and sometimes they are combined. These basic states of consciousness are an awareness of evanescence and of solidity, of emptiness and of too much presence, of the unreal transparency of the world and its opacity, of light and of thick darkness. Each of us has surely felt at moments that the substance of the world is dreamlike, that the walls are no longer solid, that we seem to be able to see through everything into a spaceless universe made up of pure light and color; at such a moment the whole of life, the whole of history of the world, becomes useless, senseless and impossible. When you fail to go beyond this first stage of *dépaysement*—for you really do have the impression you are waking to a world unknown—the sensation of evanescence gives you a feeling of anguish, a form of giddiness. But all this may equally well lead to euphoria: the anguish suddenly turns into release; nothing counts now except the wonder of being, that new and amazing consciousness of life in the glow of a fresh

* Opening remarks from a talk given at Lausanne in November 1954.

dawn, when we have found our freedom again; the fact of being astonishes us, in a world that now seems all illusion and pretense, in which all human behavior tells of absurdity and all history of absolute futility; all reality and all language appear to lose their articulation, to distintegrate and collapse, so what possible reaction is there left, when everything has ceased to matter, but to laugh at it all? I myself at one such moment felt so completely free, so released, that I had the impression I could do anything I wished with the language and the people of a world that no longer seemed to me anything but a baseless and ridiculous sham.

Of course this state of consciousness is very rare; this joy and wonder at being alive, in a universe that troubles me no more and *is* no more, can only just hold; more commonly the opposite feeling prevails: what is light grows heavy, the transparent becomes dense, the world oppresses, the universe is crushing me. A curtain, an impassable wall stands between me and the world, between me and myself; matter fills every corner, takes up all the space and its weight annihilates all freedom; the horizon closes in and the world becomes a stifling dungeon. Language breaks down in a different way and words drop like stones or dead bodies; I feel I am invaded by heavy forces, against which I can only fight a losing battle.

This was definitely the starting point of those of my plays that are generally considered the more dramatic: *Amédée* and *Victims of Duty*. Given such a state of mind, words, their magic gone, are obviously replaced by objects, by properties: countless mushrooms sprout in the flat of Amédée and Madeleine; a dead body suffering from geometrical progression grows there too and turns the tenants out; in *Victims of Duty,* when coffee is to be served to three of the characters, there is a mounting pile of hundreds of cups; the furniture in *The New Tenant* first blocks up every staircase in the building, then clutters the stage, and finally entombs the character who came to take a room in the house; in *The Chairs* the stage is filled with dozens of chairs for invisible guests; and in *Jack* several noses appear on the face of a young girl. When words are worn out, the mind is worn out. The universe, encumbered with matter, is then empty of presence: "too much" links up with "not enough" and objects are the materialization of solitude, of the victory of the anti-spiritual forces, of everything we are struggling against. But in this anxious situation I do not quite give up the fight, and if, as I hope, I manage in spite of the anguish to introduce into the anguish, humor —which is a happy symptom of the other presence—this humor is my outlet, my release and my salvation.

I have no intention of passing judgment on my plays. It is not for me to do so. I have simply tried to give some indication of what emotional material went into their making, of what was at their source: a mood and not an ideology, an impulse not a program; the cohesive unity that grants formal structure to emotions in their primitive state satisfies an inner need and does not answer the logic of some structural order imposed from without; not submission to some predetermined action, but the exteriorization of a dynamism of the psyche.

The Bald Soprano is the only one of my plays the critics consider to be "purely comic." And yet there again the comic seems to me to be an expression of the unusual. But in my view the unusual can spring only from the dullest and most ordinary daily routine and from our everyday prose, when pursued beyond their limits. To feel the absurdity or improbability of everyday life and language is already to have transcended it; in order to transcend it, you must first saturate yourself in it. The comic is the unusual pure and simple; nothing surprises me more than banality; the "surreal" is there, within our reach, in our daily conversation.

• I MAN IN THE DISCONTINUOUS UNIVERSE

PART II

8

Experimental Music

John Cage

Formerly, whenever anyone said the music I presented was experimental, I objected. It seemed to me that composers knew what they were doing, and that the experiments that had been made had taken place prior to the finished works, just as sketches are made before paintings and rehearsals precede performances. But, giving the matter further thought, I realized that there is ordinarily an essential difference between making a piece of music and hearing one. A composer knows his work as a woodsman knows a path he has traced and retraced, while a listener is confronted by the same work as one is in the woods by a plant he has never seen before.

Now, on the other hand, times have changed; music has changed; and I no longer object to the word "experimental." I use it in fact to describe all the music that especially interests me and to which I am devoted, whether someone else wrote it or I myself did. What has happened is that I have become a listener and the music has become something to hear. Many people, of course, have given up saying "experimental" about this new music. Instead, they either move to a halfway point and say "controversial" or depart to a greater distance and question whether this "music" is music at all.

For in this new music nothing takes place but sounds: those that are notated and those that are not. Those that are not notated appear in the written music as silences, opening the doors of the music to the sounds that happen to be in the environment. This openness exists in the fields of modern sculpture and architecture. The glass houses of Mies van der Rohe reflect their environment, presenting to the eye images of clouds, trees, or grass, according to the situation. And while looking at the constructions in wire of the sculptor Richard Lippold, it is inevitable that one will see other things, and people too, if they happen to be there at the same time, through the network of wires. There is no such thing as an empty space or an empty time. There is always something to see, something to hear. In fact, try as we may to make a silence, we cannot. For certain engineering purposes, it is desirable to have as silent a situation as possible. Such a room is called an anechoic chamber, its six walls made of special material, a room without echoes. I entered one at Harvard University several years ago and heard two sounds, one high and one low. When I described them to the engineer in charge, he informed me that the high one was my nervous system in operation, the low one my blood in circulation. Until I die there will be sounds. And they will continue following my death. One need not fear about the future of music.

But this fearlessness only follows if, at the parting of the ways, where it is realized that sounds occur whether intended or not, one turns in the direction of those he does not intend. This turning is psychological and seems at first to be a giving up of everything that belongs to humanity—for a musician, the giving up of music. This psychological turning leads to the world of nature, where, gradually or suddenly, one sees that humanity and nature, not separate, are in this world together; that nothing was lost when everything was given away. In fact, everything is gained. In musical terms, any sounds may occur in any combination and in any continuity.

And it is a striking coincidence that just now the technical means to produce such a free-ranging music are available. When the Allies entered Germany towards the end of World War II, it was discovered that improvements had been made in recording sounds magnetically such that tape had become suitable for the high-fidelity recording of music. First in France with the work of Pierre Schaeffer, later here, in Germany, in Italy, in Japan, and perhaps, without my knowing it, in other places, magnetic tape was used not simply to record performances of music but to make a new music that was possible only because of it. Given a minimum of two tape recorders and a disk recorder, the following processes are possible: 1) a single recording of any sound may be made; 2) a rerecording may be made, in the course of which, by means of filters and circuits, any or all of the physical characteristics of a given recorded sound may be altered; 3) electronic mixing (combining on a third machine sounds issuing from two others) permits the presentation of any number of sounds in combination; 4) ordinary splicing permits the juxtaposition of any sounds, and when it includes unconventional cuts, it, like rerecording, brings about alterations of any or all of the original physical characteristics. The situation made available by these means is essentially a total sound-space, the limits of which are ear-determined only, the position of a particular sound in this space being the result of five determinants: frequency or pitch, amplitude or loudness, overtone structure or timbre, duration, and morphology (how the sound begins, goes on, and dies away). By the alteration of any one of these determinants, the position of the sound in sound-space changes. Any sound at any point in this total sound-space can move to become a sound at any other point. But advantage can be taken of these possibilities only if one is willing to change one's musical habits radically. That is, one may take advantage of the appearance of images without visible transition in distant places, which is a way of saying "television," if one is willing to stay at home instead of going to a theatre. Or one may fly if one is willing to give up walking.

Musical habits include scales, modes, theories of counterpoint and harmony, and the study of the timbres, singly and in combination of a limited number of sound-producing mechanisms. In mathematical terms these all concern discrete steps. They resemble walking—in the case of pitches, on steppingstones twelve in number. This cautious stepping is not characteristic of the possibilities of magnetic tape, which is revealing to us that musical action or existence can occur at any point or along any line or curve or what have you in total sound-space; that we are, in fact, technically equipped to transform our contemporary awareness of nature's manner of operation into art.

Again there is a parting of the ways. One has a choice. If he does not wish to give up his attempts to control sound, he may complicate his musical technique towards an approximation of the new possibilities and awareness. (I use the word "approximation" because a measuring mind can never finally measure nature.) Or, as before, one may give up the desire to control sound, clear his mind of music, and set about discovering means to let sounds be themselves rather than vehicles for man-made theories or expressions of human sentiments.

This project will seem fearsome to many, but on examination it gives no cause for alarm. Hearing sounds which are just sounds immediately sets the theorizing mind to theorizing, and the emotions of human beings are continually aroused by encounters with nature. Does not a mountain unintentionally evoke in us a sense of wonder? otters along a stream a sense of mirth? night in the woods a sense of fear? Do not rain falling and mists rising up suggest the love binding heaven and earth? Is not decaying flesh loathsome? Does not the death of someone we love bring sorrow? And is there a greater hero than the least plant that grows? What is more angry than the flash of lightning and the sound of thunder? These responses to nature are mine and will not necessarily correspond with another's. Emotion takes place in the person who has it. And sounds, when allowed to be themselves, do not require that those who hear them do so unfeelingly. The opposite is what is meant by response ability.

New music: new listening. Not an attempt to understand something that is being said, for, if something were being said, the sounds would be given the shapes of words. Just an attention to the activity of sounds.

Those involved with the composition of experimental music find ways and means to remove themselves from the activities of the sounds they make. Some employ chance operations, derived from sources as ancient as the Chinese *Book of Changes,* or as modern as the tables of random numbers used also by physicists in research. Or, analogous to the Rorschach tests of psychology, the interpretation of imperfections in the paper upon which one is writing may provide a music free from one's memory and imagination. Geometrical means employing spatial superimpositions at variance with the ultimate performance in time may be used. The total field of possibilities may be roughly divided and the actual sounds within these divisions may be indicated as to number but left to the performer or to the splicer to choose. In this latter case, the composer resembles the maker of a camera who allows someone else to take the picture.

Whether one uses tape or writes for conventional instruments, the present musical situation has changed from what it was before tape came into being. This also need not arouse alarm, for the coming into being of something new does not by that fact deprive what was of its proper place. Each thing has its own place, never takes the place of something else; and the more things there are, as it said, the merrier.

But several effects of tape on experimental music may be mentioned. Since so many inches of tape equal so many seconds of time, it has become more and more usual that notation is in space rather than in symbols of quarter, half, and sixteenth notes and so on. Thus where on a page a note appears will correspond to when in a time it is to occur. A stop watch is used to facilitate a performance; and a rhythm results which is a far cry from horse's hoofs and other regular beats.

Also it has been impossible with the playing of several separate tapes at once to achieve perfect synchronization. This fact has led some towards the manufacture of multiple-tracked tapes and machines with a corresponding number of heads; while others—those who have accepted the sounds they do not intend—now realize that the score, the requiring that many parts be played in a particular togetherness, is not an accurate representation of how things are. These now compose parts but not scores, and the parts may be combined in any unthought ways. This means that each performance of such a piece of music is unique, as interesting to its composer as to others listening. It is easy to see again the parallel with nature, for even with leaves of the same tree, no two are exactly alike. The parallel in art is the sculpture with moving parts, the mobile.

It goes without saying that dissonances and noises are welcome in this new music. But so is the dominant seventh chord if it happens to put in an appearance.

Rehearsals have shown that this new music, whether for tape or for instruments, is more clearly heard when the several loudspeakers of performers are separated in space rather than grouped closely together. For this music is not concerned with harmoniousness as generally understood, where the quality of harmony results from a blending of several elements. Here we are concerned with the coexistence of dissimilars, and the central points where fusion occurs are many: the ears of the listeners wherever they are. This disharmony, to paraphrase Bergson's statement about disorder, is simply a harmony to which many are unaccustomed.

Where do we go from here? Towards theatre. That art more than music resembles nature. We have eyes as well as ears, and it is our business while we are alive to use them.

And what is the purpose of writing music? One is, of course, not dealing with purposes but dealing with sounds. Or the answer must take the form of paradox: a purposeful purposelessness or a purposeless play. This play, however, is an affirmation of life—not an attempt to bring order out of chaos nor to suggest improvements in creation, but simply a way of waking up to the very life we're living, which is so excellent once one gets one's mind and one's desires out of its way and lets it act of its own accord.

9

The Aesthetics of Silence

Susan Sontag

I

Every era has to reinvent the project of "spirituality" for itself. (Spirituality = plans, terminologies, ideas of deportment aimed at resolving the painful structural contradictions inherent in the human situation, at the completion of human consciousness, at transcendence.)

In the modern era, one of the most active metaphors for the spiritual project is "art." The activities of the painter, the musician, the poet, the dancer, once they were grouped together under that generic name (a relatively recent move), have proved a particularly adaptable site on which to stage the formal dramas besetting consciousness, each individual work of art being a more or less astute paradigma for regulating or reconciling these contradictions. Of course, the site needs continual refurbishing. Whatever goal is set for art eventually proves restrictive, matched against the widest goals of consciousness. Art, itself a form of mystification, endures a succession of crises of demystification; older artistic goals are assailed and, ostensibly, replaced; outworn maps of consciousness are redrawn. But what supplies all these crises with their energy—an energy held in common, so to speak—is the very unification of numerous, quite disparate activities into a single genus. At the moment when "art" comes into being, the modern period of art begins. From then on, any of the activities therein subsumed becomes a profoundly *problematic* activity, all of whose procedures and, ultimately, whose very right to exist can be called into question.

From the promotion of the arts into "art" comes the leading myth about art, that of the absoluteness of the artist's activity. In its first, more unreflective version, the myth treated art as an *expression* of human consciousness, consciousness seeking to know itself. (The evaluative standards generated by this version of the myth were fairly easily arrived at: some expressions were more complete, more ennobling, more informative, richer than others.) The later version of the myth posits a more complex, tragic relation of art to consciousness. Denying that art is mere expression, the later myth rather relates art to the mind's need or capacity for self-estrangement. Art is no longer understood as consciousness expressing and therefore, implicitly, affirming itself. Art is not consciousness per se, but rather its antidote—evolved from within consciousness itself. (The evaluative standards generated by this version of the myth proved much harder to get at.)

The newer myth, derived from a post-psychological conception of consciousness, installs within the activity of art many of the paradoxes involved in attaining an absolute state of being described by the great religious mystics. As the activity of the mystic must end in a *via negativa,* a theology of God's absence, a craving for the cloud of unknowing beyond knowledge and for the silence beyond speech, so art must tend toward anti-art, the elimination of the "subject" (the "object," the "image"), the substitution of chance for intention, and the pursuit of silence.

In the early, linear version of art's relation to consciousness, a struggle was discerned between the "spiritual" integrity of the creative impulses and the distracting "materiality" of ordinary life, which throws up so many obstacles in the path of authentic sublimation. But the newer version, in which art is part of a dialectical transaction with consciousness, poses a deeper, more frustrating conflict. The "spirit" seeking embodiment in art clashes with the "material" character of art itself. Art is unmasked as gratuitous, and the very concreteness of the artist's tools (and, particularly in the case of language, their historicity) appears as a trap. Practiced in a world furnished with second-hand perceptions, and specifically confounded by the treachery of words, the artist's activity is cursed with mediacy. Art becomes the enemy of the artist, for it denies him the realization—the transcendence—he desires.

Therefore, art comes to be considered something to be overthrown.

A new element enters the individual artwork and becomes constitutive of it: the appeal (tacit or overt) for its own abolition—and, ultimately, for the abolition of art itself.

II

The scene changes to an empty room.

Rimbaud has gone to Abyssinia to make his fortune in the slave trade. Wittgenstein, after a period as a village schoolteacher, has chosen menial work as a hospital orderly. Duchamp has turned to chess. Accompanying these exemplary renunciations of a vacation, each man has declared that he regards his previous achievements in poetry, philosophy, or art as trifling, of no importance.

But the choice of permanent silence doesn't negate their work. On the contrary, it imparts retroactively an added power and authority to what was broken off—disavowal of the work becoming a new source of its validity, a certificate of unchallengeable seriousness. That seriousness consists in not regarding art (or philosophy practiced as an art form: Wittgenstein) as something whose seriousness lasts forever, an "end," a permanent vehicle for spiritual ambition. The truly serious attitude is one that regards art as a "means" to something that can perhaps be achieved only by abandoning art; judged more impatiently, art is a false way or (the word of the Dada artist Jacques Vaché) a stupidity.

Though no longer a confession, art is more than ever a deliverance, an exercise in asceticism. Through it, the artist becomes purified—of himself and, eventually, of his art. The artist (if not art itself) is still engaged in a progress toward "the good." But whereas formerly the artist's good was mastery of and fulfillment in his art, now the highest good for the artist is to reach the point where those goals of excellence become insignificant to him, emotionally and ethically, and he is more satisfied by being silent than by finding a voice in art. Silence in this sense, as termination, proposes a mood of ultimacy antithetical to the mood informing the self-conscious artist's traditional serious use of silence (beautifully described by Valéry and Rilke): as a zone of meditation, preparation for spiritual ripening, an ordeal that ends in gaining the right to speak.

So far as he is serious, the artist is continually tempted to sever the dialogue he has with an audience. Silence is the furthest extension of that reluctance to communicate, that ambivalence about making contact with the audience which is a leading motif of modern art, with its tireless commitment to the "new" and/or the "esoteric." Silence is the artist's ultimate other-worldly gesture: by silence, he frees himself from servile bondage to the world, which appears as patron, client, consumer, antagonist, arbiter, and distorter of his work.

Still, one cannot fail to perceive in this renunciation of "society" a highly social gesture. The cues for the artist's eventual liberation from the need to practice his vocation come from observing his fellow artists and measuring himself against them. An exemplary decision of this sort can be made only after the artist has demonstrated that he possesses genius and exercised that genius authoritatively. Once he has surpassed his peers by the standards which he acknowledges, his pride has only one place left to go. For, to be a victim of the craving for silence is to be, in still a further sense, superior to everyone else. It suggests that the artist has had the wit to ask more questions than other people, and that he possesses stronger nerves and higher standards of excellence. (That the artist *can* persevere in the interrogation of his art until he or it is exhausted scarcely needs proving. As René Char has written, "No bird has the heart to sing in a thicket of questions.")

III

The exemplary modern artist's choice of silence is rarely carried to this point of final simplification, so that he becomes literally silent. More typically, he continues speaking, but in a manner that his audience can't hear. Most valuable art in our time has been experienced by audiences as a move into silence (or unintelligibility or invisibility or inaudibility); a dismantling of the artist's competence, his responsible sense of vocation—and therefore as an aggression against them.

Modern art's chronic habit of displeasing, provoking, or frustrating its audience can be regarded as a limited, vicarious participation in the ideal of silence which has been elevated as a major standard of "seriousness" in contemporary aesthetics.

But it is also a contradictory form of participation in the ideal of silence. It is contradictory not only because the artist continues making works of art, but also because the isolation of the work from its audience never lasts. With the passage of time and the intervention of newer, more difficult works, the artist's transgression becomes ingratiating, eventually legitimate. Goethe accused Kleist of having written his plays for an "invisible theatre." But eventually the invisible theatre becomes "visible." The ugly and discordant and senseless become "beautiful." The history of art is a sequence of successful transgressions.

The characteristic aim of modern art, to be *unacceptable* to its audience, inversely states the unacceptability to the artist of the very presence of an audience—audience in the modern sense, an assembly of voyeuristic spectators. At least since Nietzsche observed in *The Birth of Tragedy* that an audience of spectators as we know it, those present whom the actors ignore, was unknown to the Greeks, a good deal of contemporary art seems moved by the desire to eliminate the audience from art, an enterprise that often presents itself as an attempt to eliminate "art" altogether. (In favor of "life"?)

Committed to the idea that the power of art is located in its power to *negate,* the ultimate weapon in the artist's inconsistent war with his audience is to verge closer and closer to silence. The sensory or conceptual gap between the artist and his audience, the space of the missing or ruptured dialogue, can also constitute the grounds for an ascetic affirmation. Beckett speaks of "my dream of an art unresentful of its insuperable indigence and too proud for the farce of giving and receiving." But there is no abolishing a minimal transaction, a minimal exchange of gifts—just as there is no talented and rigorous asceticism that, whatever its intention, doesn't produce a gain (rather than a loss) in the capacity for pleasure.

And none of the aggressions committed intentionally or inadvertently by modern artists has succeeded in either abolishing the audience or transforming it into something else, a community engaged in a common activity. They cannot. As long as art is understood and valued as an "absolute" activity, it will be a separate, elitist one. Elites presuppose masses. So far as the best art defines itself by essentially "priestly" aims, it presupposes and confirms the existence of a relatively passive, never fully initiated, voyeuristic laity that is regularly convoked to watch, listen, read, or hear—and then sent away.

The most the artist can do is to modify the different terms in this situation vis-à-vis the audience and himself. To discuss the idea of silence in art is to discuss the various alternatives within this essentially unalterable situation.

IV

How literally does silence figure in art?

Silence exists as a *decision*—in the exemplary suicide of the artist

(Kleist, Lautréamont), who thereby testifies that he has gone "too far"; and in the already cited model renunciations by the artist of his vocation.

Silence also exists as a *punishment*—self-punishment, in the exemplary madness of artists (Hölderlin, Artaud) who demonstrate that sanity itself may be the price of trespassing the accepted frontiers of consciousness; and, of course, in penalties (ranging from censorship and physical destruction of artworks to fines, exile, prison for the artist) meted out by "society" for the artist's spiritual nonconformity or subversion of the group sensibility.

Silence doesn't exist in a literal sense, however, as the *experience* of an audience. It would mean that the spectator was aware of no stimulus or that he was unable to make a response. But this can't happen; nor can it even be induced programmatically. The non-awareness of any stimulus, the inability to make a response, can result only from a defective presence on the part of the spectator, or a misunderstanding of his own reactions (misled by restrictive ideas about what would be a "relevant" response). As long as audiences, by definition, consist of sentient beings in a "situation," it is impossible for them to have no response at all.

Nor can silence, in its literal state, exist as the *property* of an artwork—even of works like Duchamp's readymades or Cage's *4′33″*, in which the artist has ostentatiously done no more to satisfy any established criteria of art than set the object in a gallery or situate the performance on a concert stage. There is no neutral surface, no neutral discourse, no neutral theme, no neutral form. Something is neutral only with respect to something else—like an intention or an expectation. As a property of the work of art itself, silence can exist only in a cooked or non-literal sense. (Put otherwise: if a work exists at all, its silence is only one element in it.) Instead of raw or achieved silence, one finds various moves in the direction of an ever receding horizon of silence—moves which, by definition, can never be fully consummated. One result is a type of art that many people characterize pejoratively as dumb, depressed, acquiescent, cold. But these privative qualities exist in a context of the artist's objective intention, which is always discernible. Cultivating the metaphoric silence suggested by conventionally lifeless subjects (as in much of Pop Art) and constructing "minimal" forms that seem to lack emotional resonance are in themselves vigorous, often tonic choices.

And, finally, even without imputing objective intentions to the artwork, there remains the inescapable truth about perception: the positivity of all experience at every moment of it. As Cage has insisted, "There is no such thing as silence. Something is always happening that makes a sound." (Cage has described how, even in a soundless chamber, he still heard two things: his heartbeat and the coursing of the blood in his head.) Similarly, there is no such thing as empty space. As long as a human eye is looking, there is always something to see. To look at something which is "empty" is still to be looking, still to be seeing something—if only the ghosts of one's own expectations. In order to perceive fullness, one must retain an acute sense of the emptiness which marks it off; conversely, in order to perceive emptiness, one must apprehend other zones of the world as full. (In *Through the Looking Glass,* Alice comes upon a shop "that seemed to be full of all manner of curious things—but the oddest part of it all was that whenever she looked hard at any shelf, to make out exactly what it had on it, that particular shelf was always quite empty, though the others round it were crowded full as they could hold.")

"Silence" never ceases to imply its opposite and to depend on its presence: just as there can't be "up" without "down" or "left" without "right," so one must acknowledge a surrounding environment of sound or language in order to recognize silence. Not only does silence exist in a world full of speech and other sounds, but any given silence has its identity as a stretch of time being perforated by sound. (Thus, much of the beauty of Harpo Marx's muteness derives from his being surrounded by manic talkers.)

A genuine emptiness, a pure silence are not feasible—either conceptually or in fact. If only because the artwork exists in a world furnished with many other things, the artist who creates silence or emptiness must produce something dialectical: a full void, an enriching emptiness, a resonating or eloquent silence. Silence remains, inescapably, a form of speech (in many instances, of complaint or indictment) and an element in a dialogue.

V

Programs for a radical reduction of means and effects in art—including the ultimate demand for the renunciation of art itself—can't be taken at face value, undialectically. Silence and allied ideas (like emptiness, reduction, the "zero degree") are boundary notions with a very complex set of uses, leading terms of a particular spiritual and cultural rhetoric. To describe silence as a rhetorical term is, of course, not to condemn this rhetoric as fraudulent or in bad faith. In my opinion, the myths of silence and emptiness are about as nourishing and viable as might be devised in an "unwholesome" time—which is, of necessity, a time in which "unwholesome" psychic states furnish the energies for most superior work in the arts. Yet one can't deny the pathos of these myths.

This pathos appears in the fact that the idea of silence allows, essentially, only two types of valuable development. Either it is taken to the point of utter self-negation (as art) or else it is practiced in a form that is heroically, ingeniously inconsistent.

VI

The art of our time is noisy with appeals for silence.

A coquettish, even cheerful nihilism. One recognizes the imperative of silence, but goes on speaking anyway. Discovering that one has nothing to say, one seeks a way to say *that*.

Beckett has expressed the wish that art would renounce all further projects for disturbing matters on "the plane of the feasible," that art would retire, "weary of puny exploits, weary of pretending to be able, of being able, of doing a little better the same old thing, of going further along a dreary road." The alternative is an art consisting of "the expression that there is nothing to express, nothing from which to express, no power to express, no desire to express, together with the obligation to express." From where does this obligation derive? The very aesthetics of the death wish seems to make of that wish something incorrigibly lively.

Apollinaire says, *"J'ai fait des gestes blancs parmi les solitudes."* But he *is* making gestures.

Since the artist can't embrace silence literally and remain an artist, what the rhetoric of silence indicates is a determination to pursue his activity more deviously than before. One way is indicated by Breton's notion of the "full margin." The artist is enjoined to devote himself to filling up the periphery of the art space, leaving the central area of usage blank. Art becomes privative, anemic—as suggested by the title of Duchamp's only effort at film-making, *Anemic Cinema,* a work from 1924–26. Beckett projects the idea of an "impoverished painting," painting which is "authentically fruitless, incapable of any image whatsoever." Jerzy Grotowski's manifesto for his Theatre Laboratory in Poland is called "Plea for a Poor Theatre." These programs for art's impoverishment must not be understood simply as terroristic admonitions to audiences, but rather as strategies for improving the audience's experience. The notions of silence, emptiness, and reduction sketch out new prescriptions for looking, hearing, etc.—which either promote a more immediate, sensuous experience of art or confront the artwork in a more conscious, conceptual way.

VII

Consider the connection between the mandate for a reduction of means and effects in art, whose horizon is silence, and the faculty of attention. In one of its aspects, art is a technique for focusing attention, for teaching skills of attention. (While the whole of the human environment might be so described—as a pedagogic instrument—this description particularly applies to works of art.) The history of the arts is tantamount to the discovery and formulation of a repertory of objects on which to lavish attention. One could trace exactly and in order how the eye of art has panned over our environment, "naming," making its limited selection of things which people then become aware of as significant, pleasurable, complex entities. (Oscar Wilde pointed out that people didn't see fogs before certain nineteenth-century poets and painters taught them how to; and surely, no one saw as much of the variety and subtlety of the human face before the era of the movies.)

Once the artist's task seemed to be simply that of opening up new areas and objects of attention. That task is still acknowledged, but it has become problematic. The very faculty of attention has come into question, and been subjected to more rigorous standards. As Jasper Johns says: "Already it's a great deal to see anything *clearly,* for we don't see *anything* clearly."

Perhaps the quality of the attention one brings to bear on something will be better (less contaminated, less distracted), the less one is offered. Furnished with impoverished art, purged by silence, one might then be able to begin to transcend the frustrating selectivity of attention, with its inevitable distortions of experience. Ideally, one should be able to pay attention to everything.

The tendency is toward less and less. But never has "less" so ostentatiously advanced itself as "more."

In the light of the current myth, in which art aims to become a "total experience," soliciting total attention, the strategies of impoverishment and reduction indicate the most exalted ambition art could adopt. Underneath what looks like a strenuous modesty, if not actual debility, is to be discerned an energetic secular blasphemy: the wish to attain the unfettered, unselective, total consciousness of "God."

VIII

Language seems a privileged metaphor for expressing the mediated character of art-making and the artwork. On the one hand, speech is both an immaterial medium (compared with, say, images) and a human activity with an apparently essential stake in the project of transcendence, of moving beyond the singular and contingent (all words being abstractions, only roughly based on or making reference to concrete particulars). On the other hand, language is the most impure, the most contaminated, the most exhausted of all the materials out of which art is made.

This dual character of language—its abstractness, and its "fallenness" in history—serves as a microcosm of the unhappy character of the arts today. Art is so far along the labyrinthine pathways of the project of transcendence that one can hardly conceive of it turning back, short of the most drastic and punitive "cultural revolution." Yet at the same time, art is foundering in the debilitating tide of what once seemed the crowning achievement of European thought: secular historical consciousness. In little more than two centuries, the consciousness of history has transformed itself from a liberation, an opening of doors, blessed enlightenment, into an almost insupportable burden of self-consciousness. It's scarcely possible for the artist to write a word (or render an image or make a gesture) that doesn't remind him of something already achieved.

As Nietzsche says: "Our pre-eminence: we live in the age of comparison, we can verify as has never been verified before." Therefore "we enjoy differently, we suffer differently: our instinctive activity is to compare an unheard number of things."

Up to a point, the community and historicity of the artist's means are implicit in the very fact of intersubjectivity: each person is a being-in-a-world. But today, particularly in the arts using language, this normal state of affairs is felt as an extraordinary, wearying problem.

Language is experienced not merely as something shared but as something corrupted, weighed down by historical accumulation. Thus, for each conscious artist, the creation of a work means dealing with two potentially antagonistic domains of meaning and their relationships.

One is his own meaning (or lack of it); the other is the set of second-order meanings that both extend his own language and encumber, compromise, and adulterate it. The artist ends by choosing between two inherently limiting alternatives, forced to take a position that is either servile or insolent. Either he flatters or appeases his audience, giving them what they already know, or he commits an aggression against his audience, giving them what they don't want.

Modern art thus transmits in full the alienation produced by historical consciousness. Whatever the artist does is in (usually conscious) alignment with something else already done, producing a compulsion to be continually checking his situation, his own stance against those of his predecessors and contemporaries. To compensate for this ignominious enslavement to history, the artist exalts himself with the dream of a wholly ahistorical, and therefore unalienated, art.

IX

Art that is "silent" consitutes one approach to this visionary, ahistorical condition.

Consider the difference between *looking* and *staring*. A look is voluntary; it is also mobile, rising and falling in intensity as its foci of interest are taken up and then exhausted. A stare has, essentially, the character of a compulsion; it is steady, unmodulated, "fixed."

Traditional art invites a look. Art that is silent engenders a stare. Silent art allows—at least in principle—no release from attention, because there has never, in principle, been any soliciting of it. A stare is perhaps as far from history, as close to eternity, as contemporary art can get.

X

Silence is a metaphor for a cleansed, non-interfering vision, appropriate to artworks that are unresponsive before being seen, unviolable in their essential integrity by human scrutiny. The spectator would approach art as he does a landscape. A landscape doesn't demand from the spectator his "understanding," his imputations of significance, his anxieties and sympathies; it demands, rather, his absence, it asks that he not add anything to *it*. Contemplation, strictly speaking, entails self-forgetfulness on the part of the spectator: an object worthy of contemplation is one which, in effect, annihilates the perceiving subject.

Toward such an ideal plenitude to which the audience can add nothing, analogous to the aesthetic relation to nature, a great deal of contemporary art aspires—through various strategies of blandness, of reduction, of deindividuation, of alogicality. In principle, the audience may not even add its thought. All objects, rightly perceived, are already full. This is what Cage must mean when, after explaining that there is no such thing as silence because something is always happening that makes a sound, he adds, "No one can have an idea once he starts really listening."

Plenitude—experiencing all the space as filled, so that ideas cannot enter—means impenetrability. A person who becomes silent becomes opaque for the other; somebody's silence opens up an array of possibilities for interpreting that silence, for imputing speech to it.

The way in which this opaqueness induces spiritual vertigo is the theme of Bergman's *Persona*. The actress's deliberate silence has two aspects: Considered as a decision apparently relating to herself, the refusal to speak is apparently the form she has given to the wish for ethical purity; but it is also, as behavior, a means of power, a species of sadism, a virtually inviolable position of strength from which she manipulates and confounds her nurse-companion, who is charged with the burden of talking.

But the opaqueness of silence can be conceived more positively, as free from anxiety. For Keats, the silence of the Grecian urn is a locus of spiritual nourishment: "unheard" melodies endure, whereas those that pipe to "the sensual ear" decay. Silence is equated with arresting time ("slow time"). One can stare endlessly at the Grecian urn. Eternity, in the argument of Keats' poem, is the only interesting stimulus to thought and also the sole occasion for coming to the end of mental activity, which means interminable, unanswered questions ("Thou, silent form, dost tease us out of thought/ As doth eternity"), in order to arrive at a final equation of ideas ("Beauty is truth, truth beauty") which is both absolutely vacuous and completely full. Keats' poem quite logically ends in a statement that will seem, if the reader hasn't followed his argument, like empty wisdom, a banality. As time, or history, is the medium of definite, determinate thought, the silence of eternity prepares for a thought beyond thought, which must appear from the perspective of traditional thinking and the familiar uses of the mind as no thought at all—though it may rather be the emblem of new, "difficult" thinking.

XI

Behind the appeals for silence lies the wish for a perceptual and cultural clean slate. And, in its most hortatory and ambitious version, the advocacy of silence expresses a mythic project of total liberation. What's envisaged is nothing less than the liberation of the artist from himself, of art from the particular artwork, of art from history, of spirit from matter, of the mind from its perceptual and intellectual limitations.

As some people know now, there are ways of thinking that we don't yet know about. Nothing could be more important or precious than that knowledge, however unborn. The sense of urgency, the spiritual restlessness it engenders, cannot be appeased, and continues to fuel the radical art of this century. Through its advocacy of silence and reduction, art commits an act of violence upon itself, turning art into a species of auto-manipulation, of conjuring—trying to bring these new ways of thinking to birth.

Silence is a strategy for the transvaluation of art, art itself being the herald of an anticipated radical transvaluation of human values. But the success of this strategy must mean its eventual abandonment, or at least its significant modification.

Silence is a prophecy, one which the artist's actions can be understood as attempting both to fulfill and to reverse.

As languague points to its own transcendence in silence, silence points to its own transcendence—to a speech beyond silence.

But can the whole enterprise become an act of bad faith if the artist knows *this,* too?

XII

A famous quotation: "Everything that can be thought at all can be thought clearly. Everything that can be said at all can be said clearly. But not everything that can be thought can be said."

Notice that Wittgenstein, with his scrupulous avoidance of the psychological issue, doesn't ask why, when, and in what circumstances someone would *want* to put into words "everything that can be thought" (even if he could), or even to utter (whether clearly or not) "everything that could be said."

XIII

Of everything that's said, one can ask: *why?* (Including: why should I say *that?* And: why should I say anything at all?)

Moreover, strictly speaking, nothing that's *said* is true. (Though a person can *be* the truth, one can't ever say it.)

Still, things that are said can sometimes be helpful—which is what people ordinarily mean when they regard something *said* as being true. Speech can enlighten, relieve, confuse, exalt, infect, antagonize, gratify, grieve, stun, animate. While language is regularly used to inspire to action, some verbal statements, either written or oral, are themselves the performing of an action (as in promising, swearing, bequeathing). Another use of speech, if anything more common than that of provoking actions, is to provoke further speech. But speech can silence, too. This indeed is how it must be: without the polarity of silence, the whole system of language would fail. And beyond its generic function as the dialectical opposite of speech, silence—like speech—also has more specific, less inevitable uses.

One use for silence: certifying the absence or renunciation of thought. Silence is often employed as a magical or mimetic procedure in repressive social relationships, as in the Jesuit regulations about speaking to superiors and in the disciplining of children. (This should not be confused with the practice of certain monastic disciplines, such as the Trappist order, in which silence is both an ascetic act and bears witness to the condition of being perfectly "full."

Another, apparently opposed, use for silence: certifying the completion of thought. In the words of Karl Jaspers, "He who has the final answers can no longer speak to the other, breaking off genuine communication for the sake of what he believes in."

Still another use for silence: providing time for the continuing or exploring of thought. Notably, speech closes off thought. (An example: the enterprise of criticism, in which there seems no way for a critic not to assert that a given artist is *this,* he's *that,* etc.) But if one decides an issue isn't closed, it's not. This is presumably the rationale behind the voluntary experiments in silence that some contemporary spiritual athletes, like Buckminster Fuller, have undertaken, and the element of wisdom in the otherwise mainly authoritarian, philistine silence of the orthodox Freudian psychoanalyst. Silence keeps things "open."

Still another use for silence: furnishing or aiding speech to attain its maximum integrity or seriousness. Everyone has experienced how, when punctuated by long silences, words weigh more; they become almost palpable. Or how, when one talks less, one begins feeling more fully one's physical presence in a given space. Silence undermines "bad speech," by which I mean dissociated speech—speech dissociated from the body (and, therefore, from feeling), speech not organically informed by the sensuous presence and concrete particularity of the speaker and by the individual occasion for using language. Unmoored from the body, speech deteriorates. It becomes false, inane, ignoble, weightless. Silence can inhibit or counteract this tendency, providing a kind of ballast, monitoring and even correcting language when it becomes inauthentic.

Given these perils to the authenticity of language (which doesn't depend on the character of any isolated statement or even group of statements, but on the relation of speaker, utterance, and situation), the imaginary project of saying clearly "everything that can be said" suggested by Wittgenstein's remarks looks fearfully complicated. (How much time would one have? Would one have to speak quickly? The philosopher's hypothetical universe of clear speech (which assigns to silence only "that whereof one cannot speak") would seem to be a moralist's, or a psychiatrist's, nightmare—at the least a place no one should lightheartedly enter. Is there anyone who *wants* to say "everything that could be said"? The psychologically plausible answer would seem to be no. But yes is plausible, too—as a rising ideal of modern culture. Isn't that what many people *do* want today—to say everything that can be said? But this aim cannot be maintained without inner conflict. In part inspired by the spread of the ideals of psychotherapy, people are yearning to say "everything" (thereby, among other results, further undermining the crumbling distinction between public and private endeavors, between information and secrets). But in an overpopulated world being connected by global electronic communication and jet travel at a pace too rapid and violent for an organically sound person to assimilate without shock, people are also suffering from a revulsion at any further proliferation of speech and images. Such different factors as the unlimited "technological reproduction" and near universal diffusion of printed language and speech as well as images (from "news" to "art objects"), and the degeneration of public language within the realms of politics and advertising and entertainment, have produced, especially among the better-educated inhabitants of modern mass society, a devaluation of language. (I should argue, contrary to McLuhan, that a devaluation of the power and credibility of images has taken place no less profound than, and essentially similar to, that afflicting language.) And, as the prestige of language falls, that of silence rises.

I am alluding, at this point, to the sociological context of the contemporary ambivalence toward language. The matter, of course, goes much deeper than this. In addition to the specific sociological determinants, one must recognize the operation of something like a perennial discontent with language that has been formulated in each of the major civilizations of the Orient and Occident, whenever thought reaches a certain high, *excruciating* order of complexity and spiritual seriousness.

Traditionally, it has been through the religious vocabulary, with its meta-absolutes of "sacred" and "profane," "human" and "divine," that the disaffection with language itself has been charted. In particular, the antecedents of art's dilemmas and strategies are to be found in the radical wing of the mystical tradition. (Cf., among Christian texts, the *Mystica Theologia* of Dionysius the Areopagite, the anonymous *Cloud of Unknowing,* the writings of Jakob Boehme and Meister Eckhart; and parallels in Zen, Taoist, and Sufi texts.) The mystical tradition has always recognized, in Norman Brown's phrase, "the neurotic character of language." (According to Boehme, Adam spoke a language different from all known languages. It was "sensual speech," the unmediated expressive instrument of the senses, proper to beings integrally part of sensuous nature—that is, still employed by all the animals except that sick animal, man. This, which Boehme calls the only "natural language," the sole language free from distortion and illusion, is what man will speak again when he recovers paradise.) But in our time, the most striking developments of such ideas have been made by artists (and certain psychotherapists) rather than by the timid legatees of the religious traditions.

Explicitly in revolt against what is deemed the desiccated, categorized life of the ordinary mind, the artist issues his own call for a revision of language. A good deal of contemporary art is moved by this quest for a consciousness purified of contaminated language and, in some versions, of the distortions produced by conceiving the world exclusively in conventional verbal (in their debased sense, "rational" or "logical") terms. Art itself becomes a kind of counterviolence, seeking to loosen the grip upon consciousness of the habits of lifeless, static verbalization, presenting models of "sensual speech."

If anything, the volume of discontent has been turned up since the arts inherited the problem of language from religious discourse. It's not just that words, ultimately, are inadequate to the highest aims of consciousness; or even that they get in the way. Art expresses a double discontent. We lack words, and we have too many of them. It raises two complaints about language. Words are too crude. And words are also too busy—inviting a hyperactivity of consciousness that is not only dysfunctional, in terms of human capacities of feeling and acting, but actively deadens the mind and blunts the senses.

Language is demoted to the status of an event. Something takes place in time, a voice speaking which points to the before and to what comes after an utterance: silence. Silence, then, is both the precondition of speech and the result or aim of properly directed speech. On this model, the artist's activity is the creating or establishing of silence; the efficacious art-work leaves silence in its wake. Silence, administered by the artist, is part of a program of perceptual and cultural therapy, often on the model of shock therapy rather than of persuasion. Even if the artist's medium is words, he can share in this task: language can be employed to check language, to express muteness. Mallarmé thought it was the job of poetry, using words, to clean up our word-clogged reality—by creating silences around things. Art must mount a full-scale attack on language itself, by means of language and its surrogates, on behalf of the standard of silence.

XIV

In the end, the radical critique of consciousness (first delineated by the mystical tradition, now administered by unorthodox psychotherapy and high modernist art) always lays the blame on language. Consciousness, experienced as a burden, is conceived of as the memory of all the words that have ever been said.

Krishnamurti claims that we must give up psychological, as distinct from factual, memory. Otherwise, we keep filling up the new with the old, closing off experience by hooking each experience onto the last.

We must destroy continuity (which is insured by psychological memory), by going to the *end* of each emotion or thought.

And after the end, what supervenes (for a while) is silence.

XV

In his Fourth Duino Elegy, Rilke gives a metaphoric statement of the problem of language and recommends a procedure for approaching as near the horizon of silence as he considers feasible. A prerequisite of "emptying out" is to be able to perceive what one is "full of," what words and mechanical gestures one is stuffed with, like a doll; only then, in polar confrontation with the doll, does the "angel" appear, a figure representing an equally inhuman though "higher" possibility, that of an entirely unmediated, translinguistic apprehension. Neither doll nor angel, human beings remain situated within the kingdom of language. But for nature, then things, then other people, then the textures of ordinary life to be experienced from a stance other than the crippled one of mere spectatorship, language must regain its chastity. As Rilke describes it in the Ninth Elegy, the redemption of language (which is to say, the redemption of the world through its interiorization in consciousness) is a long, infinitely arduous task. Human beings are so "fallen" that they must start with the simplest linguistic act: the naming of things. Perhaps no more than this minimal function can be preserved from the general corruption of discourse. Language may very well have to remain within a permanent state of reduction. Though perhaps, when this spiritual exercise of confining language to naming is perfected, it may be possible to pass on to other, more ambitious uses of language, nothing must be attempted which will allow consciousness to become reestranged from itself.

For Rilke the overcoming of the alienation of consciousness is conceivable; and not, as in the radical myths of the mystics, through transcending language altogether. It suffices to cut back drastically the scope and use of language. A tremendous spiritual preparation (the contrary of "alienation") is required for this deceptively simple act of naming. It is nothing less than the scouring and harmonious sharpening of the senses (the very opposite of such violent projects, with roughly the same end and informed by the same hostility to verbal-rational culture, as "systematically deranging the senses").

Rilke's remedy lies halfway between exploiting the numbness of language as a gross, fully installed cultural institution and yielding to the suicidal vertigo of pure silence. But this middle ground of reducing language to naming can be claimed in quite another way than his. Contrast the benign nominalism proposed by Rilke (and proposed and practiced by Francis Ponge) with the brutal nominalism adopted by many other artists. The more familiar recourse of modern art to the aesthetics of the inventory is not made—as in Rilke—with an eye to "humanizing" things, but rather to confirming their inhumanity, their impersonality, their indifference to and separateness from human concerns. (Examples of the "inhumane" preoccupation with naming: Roussel's *Impressions of Africa;* the silk-screen paintings and early films of Andy Warhol; the early novels of Robbe-Grillet, which attempt to confine the function of language to bare physical description and location.)

Rilke and Ponge assume that there *are* priorities: rich as opposed to vacuous objects, events with a certain allure. (This is the incentive for trying to peel back language, allowing the "things" themselves to speak.) More decisively, they assume that if there are states of false (language-clogged) consciousness, there are also authentic states of consciousness—which it's the function of art to promote. The alternative view denies the traditional hierarchies of interest and meaning, in which some things have more "significance" than others. The distinction between true and false experience, true and false consciousness is also denied: in principle, one should desire to pay attention to everything. It's this view, most elegantly formulated by Cage though its practice is found everywhere, that leads to the art of the inventory, the catalogue, surfaces; also "chance." The function of art isn't to sanction any specific experience, except the state of being open to the multiplicity of experience—which ends in practice by a decided stress on things usually considered trivial or unimportant.

The attachment of contemporary art to the "minimal" narrative principle of the catalogue or inventory seems almost to parody the capitalist world-view, in which the environment is atomized into "items" (a category embracing things and persons, works of art and natural organisms), and in which every item is a commodity—that is, a discrete, portable object. A general leveling of value is encouraged in the art of inventory, which is itself only one of the possible approaches to an ideally uninflected discourse. Traditionally, the effects of an artwork have been unevenly distributed, to induce in the audience a certain sequence of experience: first arousing, then manipulating, and eventually fulfilling emotional expectations. What is proposed now is a discourse without emphases in this traditional sense. (Again, the principle of the stare as opposed to the look.)

Such art could also be described as establishing great "distance" (between spectator and art object, between the spectator and his emotions). But, psychologically, distance often is linked with the most intense state of feeling, in which the coolness or impersonality with which something is treated measures the insatiable interest that thing has for us. The distance that a great deal of "anti-humanist" art proposes is actually equivalent to obsession—an aspect of the involvement in "things" of which the "humanist" nominalism of Rilke has no intimation.

XVI

"There is something strange in the acts of writing and speaking," Novalis wrote in 1799. "The ridiculous and amazing mistake people make is to believe they use words in relation to things. They are unaware of the nature of language—which is to be its own and only concern, making it so fertile and splendid a mystery. When someone talks just for the sake of talking he is saying the most original and truthful thing he can say."

Novalis' statement may help explain an apparent paradox: that in the era of the widespread advocacy of art's silence, an increasing number of works of art babble. Verbosity and repetitiveness are particularly noticeable in the temporal arts of prose fiction, music, film, and dance, many of which cultivate a kind of ontological stammer—facilitated by their refusal of the incentives for a clean, anti-redundant discourse supplied by linear, beginning-middle-and-end construction. But actually, there's no contradiction. For the contemporary appeal for silence has never indicated merely a hostile dismissal of language. It also signifies a very high estimate of language—of its powers, of its past health, and of the current dangers it poses to a free consciousness. From this intense and ambivalent valuation proceeds the impulse for a discourse that appears both irrepressible (and, in principle, interminable) and strangely inarticulate, painfully reduced. Discernible in the fictions of Stein, Burroughs, and Beckett is the subliminal idea that it might be possible to out-talk language, or to talk oneself into silence.

This is not a very promising strategy, considering what results might reasonably be anticipated from it. But perhaps not so odd, when one observes how often the aesthetic of silence appears alongside a barely controlled abhorrence of the void.

Accommodating these two contrary impulses may produce the need to fill up all the spaces with objects of slight emotional weight or with large areas of barely modulated color or evenly detailed objects, or to spin a discourse with as few possible inflections, emotive variations, and risings and fallings of emphasis. These procedures seem analogous to the behavior of an obsessional neurotic warding off a danger. The acts of such a person must be repeated in the identical form, because the danger remains the same; and they must be repeated endlessly, because the danger never seems to go away. But the emotional fires feeding the art-discourse analogous to obsessionalism may be turned down so low one can almost forget they're there. Then all that's left to the ear is a kind of steady hum or drone. What's left to the eye is the neat filling of a space with things, or, more accurately, the patient transcription of the surface detail of things.

In this view, the "silence" of things, images, and words is a prerequisite for their proliferation. Were they endowed with a more potent, individual charge, each of the various elements of the artwork would claim more psychic space and then their total number might have to be reduced.

XVII

Sometimes the accusation against language is not directed against all of language but only against the written word. Thus Tristan Tzara urged the burning of all books and libraries to bring about a new era of oral legends. And McLuhan, as everyone knows, makes the sharpest distinction between written language (which exists in "visual space") and oral speech (which exists in "auditory space"), praising the psychic and cultural advantages of the latter as the basis for sensibility.

If written language is singled out as the culprit, what will be sought is not so much the reduction as the metamorphosis of language into something looser, more intuitive, less organized and inflected, nonlinear (in McLuhan's terminology) and—noticeably—more verbose. But, of course, it is just these qualities that characterize many of the great prose narratives of our time. Joyce, Stein, Gadda, Laura Riding, Beckett, and Burroughs employ a language whose norms and energies come from oral speech, with its circular repetitive movements and essentially first-person voice.

"Speaking for the sake of speaking is the formula of deliverance," Novalis said. (Deliverance from what? From speaking? From art?)

In my opinion, Novalis has succinctly described the proper approach of the writer to language and offered the basic criterion for literature as an art. But to what extent oral speech is the privileged model for the speech of literature as an art is still an open question.

XVIII

A corollary of the growth of this conception of art's language as autonomous and self-sufficient (and, in the end, self-reflective) is a decline in "meaning" as traditionally sought in works of art. "Speaking for the sake of speaking" forces us to relocate the meaning of linguistic or para-linguistic statements. We are led to abandon meaning (in the sense of references to entities outside the artwork) as the criterion for the language of art in favor of "use." (Wittgenstein's famous thesis, "the meaning is the use," can and should be rigorously applied to art.)

"Meaning" partially or totally converted into "use" is the secret behind the widespread strategy of *literalness,* a major development of the aesthetics of silence. A variant on this: hidden literality, exemplified by such different writers as Kafka and Beckett. The narratives of Kafka and Beckett seem puzzling because they appear to invite the reader to ascribe high-powered symbolic and allegorical meanings to them and, at the same time, repel such ascriptions. Yet when the narrative is examined, it discloses no more than what it literally means. The power of their language derives precisely from the fact that the meaning is so bare.

The effect of such bareness is often a kind of anxiety—like the anxiety produced when familiar things aren't in their place or playing their accustomed role. One may be made as anxious by unexpected literalness as by the Surrealists' "disturbing" objects and unexpected scale and condition of objects conjoined in an imaginary landscape. Whatever is wholly mysterious is at once both psychically relieving and anxiety-provoking. (A perfect machine for agitating this pair of contrary emotions: the Bosch drawing in a Dutch museum that shows trees furnished with two ears at the sides of their trunks, as if they were listening to the forest, while the forest floor is strewn with eyes.) Before a fully conscious work of art, one feels something like the mixture of anxiety, detachment, pruriency, and relief that a physically sound person feels when he glimpses an amputee. Beckett speaks favorably of a work of art which would be a "total object, complete with missing parts, instead of partial object. Question of degree."

But exactly what is a totality and what constitutes completeness in art (or anything else)? That problem is, in principle, unresolvable. Whatever way a work of art is, it could have been—could be—different. The necessity of *these* parts in this order is never given; it is conferred.

The refusal to admit this essential contingency (or openness) is what inspires the audience's will to confirm the closedness of a work by interpreting it, and what creates the feeling common among reflective artists and critics that the artwork is always somehow in arrears of or inadequate to its "subject." But unless one is committed to the idea that art "expresses" something, these procedures and attitudes are far from inevitable.

XIX

This tenacious concept of art as "expression" has given rise to the most common, and dubious, version of the notion of silence—which invokes the idea of "the ineffable." The theory supposes that the province of art is "the beautiful," which implies effects of unspeakableness, indescribability, ineffability. Indeed, the search to express the inexpressible is taken as the very criterion of art; and sometimes becomes the occasion for a strict—and to my mind untenable—distinction between prose literature and poetry. It is from this position that Valéry advanced his famous argument (repeated in a quite different context by Sartre) that the novel is not, strictly speaking, an art form at all. His reason is that since the aim of prose is to communicate, the use of language in prose is perfectly straightforward. Poetry, being an art, should have quite different aims: to express an experience which is essentially ineffable; using language to express muteness. In contrast to prose writers, poets are engaged in subverting their own instrument and seeking to pass beyond it.

This theory, so far as it assumes that art is concerned with beauty, is not very interesting. (Modern aesthetics is crippled by its dependence upon this essentially vacant concept. As if art were "about" beauty, as science is "about" truth!) But even if the theory dispenses with the notion of beauty, there is still a more serious objection. The view that expressing the ineffable is an essential function of poetry (considered as a paradigm of all the arts) is naïvely unhistorical. The ineffable, while surely a perennial category of consciousness, has certainly not always made its home in the arts. Its traditional shelter was in religious discourse and, secondarily (as Plato relates in his 7th Epistle), in philosophy. The fact that contemporary artists are concerned with silence—and, therefore, in one extension, with the ineffable—must be understood historically, as a consequence of the prevailing contemporary myth of the "absoluteness" of art. The value placed on silence doesn't arise by virtue of the *nature* of art, but derives from the contemporary ascription of certain "absolute" qualities to the art object and to the activity of the artist.

The extent to which art *is* involved with the ineffable is more specific, as well as contemporary: art, in the modern conception, is always connected with systematic transgressions of a formal sort. The systematic violation of older formal conventions practiced by modern artists gives their work a certain aura of the unspeakable—for instance, as the audience uneasily senses the negative presence of what else could be, but isn't being, said; and as any "statement" made in an aggressively new or difficult form tends to seem equivocal or merely vacant. But these features of ineffability must not be acknowledged at the expense of one's awareness of the positivity of the work of art. Contemporary art, no matter how much it has defined itself by a taste for negation, can still be analyzed as a set of assertions of a formal kind.

For instance, each work of art gives us a form or paradigm or model of *knowing* something, an epistemology. But viewed as a spiritual project, a vehicle of aspirations toward an absolute, what any work of art supplies is a specific model for meta-social or meta-ethical *tact,* a standard of decorum. Each artwork indicates the unity of certain preferences about what can and cannot be said (or represented). At the same time that it may make a tacit proposal for upsetting previously consecrated rulings on what can be said (or represented), it issues its own set of limits.

XX

Contemporary artists advocate silence in two styles: loud and soft.

The loud style is a function of the unstable antithesis of "plenum" and "void." The sensuous, ecstatic, translinguistic apprehension of the plenum is notoriously fragile: in a terrible, almost instantaneous plunge it can collapse into the void of negative silence. With all its awareness of risk-taking (the hazards of spiritual nausea, even of madness), this advocacy of silence tends to be frenetic and overgeneralizing. It is also frequently apocalyptic and must endure the indignity of all apocalyptic thinking: namely, to prophesy the end, to see the day come, to outlive it, and then to set a new date for the incineration of consciousness and the definitive pollution of language and exhaustion of the possibilities of art-discourse.

The other way of talking about silence is more cautious. Basically, it presents itself as an extension of a main feature of traditional classicism: the concern with modes of propriety, with standards of seemliness. Silence is only "reticence" stepped up to the nth degree. Of course, in the translation of this concern from the matrix of traditional classical art, the tone has changed—from didactic seriousness to ironic open-mindedness. But while the clamorous style of proclaiming the rhetoric of silence may seem more passionate, its more subdued advocates (like Cage, Johns) are saying something equally drastic. They are reacting to the same idea of art's absolute aspirations (by programmatic disavowals of art); they share the same disdain for the "meanings" established by bourgeois-rationalist culture, indeed for culture itself in the familiar sense. What is voiced by the Futurists, some of the Dada artists, and Burroughs as a harsh despair and perverse vision of apocalypse is no less serious for being proclaimed in a polite voice and as a sequence of playful affirmations. Indeed, it could be argued that silence is likely to remain a viable notion for modern art and consciousness only if deployed with a considerable, near systematic irony.

XXI

It is in the nature of all spiritual projects to tend to consume themselves—exhausting their own sense, the very meaning of the terms in which they are couched. (This is why "spirituality" must be continually reinvented.) All genuinely ultimate projects of consciousness eventually become projects for the unraveling of thought itself.

Art conceived as a spiritual project is no exception. As an abstracted and fragmented replica of the positive nihilism expounded by the radical religious myths, the serious art of our time has moved increasingly toward the most excruciating inflections of consciousness. Conceivably, irony is the only feasible counterweight to this grave use of art as the arena for the ordeal of consciousness. The present prospect is that artists will go on abolishing art, only to resurrect it in a more retracted version. As long as art bears up under the pressure of chronic interrogation, it would seem desirable that some of the questions have a certain playful quality.

But this prospect depends, perhaps, on the viability of irony itself.

From Socrates on, there are countless witnesses to the value of irony for the private individual: as a complex, serious method of seeking and holding one's truth, and as a means of saving one's sanity. But as irony becomes the good taste of what is, after all, an essentially collective activity—the making of art—it may prove less serviceable.

One need not judge as categorically as Nietzsche, who thought the spread of irony throughout a culture signified the floodtide of decadence and the approaching end of that culture's vitality and powers. In the post-political, electronically connected cosmopolis in which all serious modern artists have taken out premature citizenship, certain organic connections between culture and "thinking" (and art is certainly now, mainly, a form of thinking) appear to have been broken, so that Nietzsche's diagnosis may need to be modified. But if irony has more positive resources than Nietzsche acknowledged, there still remains a question as to how far the resources of irony can be stretched. It seems unlikely that the possibilities of continually undermining one's assumptions can go on unfolding indefinitely into the future, without being eventually checked by despair or by a laugh that leaves one without any breath at all.

10

Chance-Imagery

George Brecht

> Art is not the most precious manifestation of life.
> Art has not the celestial and universal value
> that people like to attribute to it. Life is far more interesting.
>
> *Tristan Tzara* (1)
>
> Knowledge is the source of all mystery.
>
> *Shen-hui.*

The purpose of this article is to encourage insight regarding chance-imagery, especially certain less intuitively obvious formal aspects. Every statement of opinion is as wrong in one sense as it is right in some other, for every distinction is an artificial one, an arbitrary subdivision of what is actually a unified whole. This is one of the reasons that words about art are so infinitely inferior to the art itself. Art unites us with the whole; words only permit us to handle a unified reality by maneuvering arbitrarily excised chunks.

With this apology for juggling words at all, let us indicate how we intend to approach an infinitely broad and complex subject, chance and its relation to the arts. ("Arts" here is taken in a broadly historical, but actually no longer appropriate, sense.)

First, a working definition (*Chance*).
Some background (*Dada and Surrealism*).
A focal point in development (*Jackson Pollock*).
Some parallel developments in our culture (*Historical Concurrences: Statistics, Science and Philosophy*).
Randomness.
Some methodology (*Ways of Invoking Chance*).
Coda.

CHANCE

The word "chance" (with a Latin root relating to the falling of dice) can conveniently be taken to mean that the cause, or system of causes, responsible for a given effect is unknown or unlooked-for or, at least, that we are unable to completely specify it. Of course, in the real world, causes are also effects, and effects causes. The fall of a die, for example, is the effect of an infinite number of (largely unknown) causes (among which we can imagine resilience of the die, hardness of the table, angle of contact to be included), and this effect, in turn, may be the cause of my winning a certain amount of money.

It is sometimes possible to specify only the universe of possible characteristics which a chance event may have. For example, a toss of a normal die will be expected to give a number from one to six. Any particular face will be expected to turn up in about one-sixth of a great many throws. But the outcome of any one toss remains unknown until the throw has been made. It is often useful to keep in mind this "universe of possible results," even when that universe is hypothetical, for this clarifies for us the nature of our chance event as a selection from a limited universe. We should note here that events are defined as due to chance in a relative way. There is no absolute chance or random event, for chance and randomness are aspects of the way in which we structure our universe. These are elementary considerations with many ramifications, but I hope they will serve as a conceptual base-line for the discussion to follow, which should clarify the nature of chance. We shall later discuss the random event, as a special type of bias-free chance event.

In connection with art, and the affective image, we shall indicate two aspects of chance, one where the origin of images is unknown because it lies in deeper-than-conscious levels of the mind, and the second where images derive from mechanical processes not under the artist's control. Both of these processes have in common a lack of conscious design.

DADA AND SURREALISM

In the sense that there is a certain lack of conscious control in everything we do, the use of chance in art could be traced (academically) to the cave drawings of prehistoric man; but the first explicit use of chance in painting seems to have come shortly before World War I. If we admit automatism as chance, then the improvisations of Kandinsky (1911), painted "rather subconsciously in a state of strong inner tension," would take precedence over the first *papiers colles* of Picasso (1912), in which were incorporated fortuitous scraps of newspaper and cardboard.

(The question of the chance nature of automatism might be endlessly debated. It seems to me that the answer lies in the distinction between our seeking immediate causes or ultimate causes of automatic actions. It takes little reflection to see that ultimate causes might readily and reasonably be ascribed to chance, but psychoanalytic theory has taught us to expect "conscious ignorance and unconscious knowledge of the motivation of psychic accidentalness" (2), and it does not always take very deep or lengthy probing to reveal immediate causes for the physically accidental. At any rate, it is practical to consider chance as being defined by *consciously* unknown causes, and by this definition, at least, automatism is a chance process.)

Since we are restricting ourselves to the generation of chance-images, and not to their appreciation, we shall indicate only the place of the unconscious (including the subconscious, or fore-conscious) as a source of significant images. The importance of chance to the unconscious has manifold facets, not only in modern psychology, but also (and particularly) in oriental thought (such as that manifested in the *I Ching* or in Zen).

The Dadaists considered the unconscious to be a source of images free from the biases engrained in us by parents, social custom and all the other artificial restrictions on intellectual freedom:

> We are now in a position to formulate the problem of art, more accurately the problem of expression, as it appeared to the writers of and Literature group [Aragon, Breton, Soupault]: only the unconscious does not lie, it alone is worth bringing to light. All deliberate and conscious efforts, composition, logic are futile. The celebrated French lucidity is nothing but a cheap lantern. At best the "poet" can prepare traps (as a physician might do in treating a patient), with which to catch the unconscious by surprise and to prevent it from cheating.
>
> Marcel Raymond (3)

> The unconscious is inexhaustible and uncontrollable. Its force surpasses us. It is as mysterious as the last particle of a brain cell. Even if we knew it, we could not reconstruct it. Tristan Tzara (1)

As far as affective form is concerned, chance is an aspect of the universe made significant by unconscious interactions, but it is not the only aspect. When the largely iconoclastic displays of Dada were superseded by the more systematic researches of the Surrealists, Breton, for one, in the "First Surrealist Manifesto" (1924), made this general interest in the unconscious explicit:

> During the course of Surrealist development, outside all forms of idealism, outside the opiates of religion, the marvelous comes to light within *reality*. It comes to light in dreams, obsessions, preoccupations, in sleep, fear, love, chance, in hallucinations, pretended disorders, follies, ghostly apparitions, escape mechanisms and evasions; in fancies, idle wanderings, poetry, the supernatural and the unusual; in empiricism, in *superreality*. (4)

(This statement, written in 1924, followed *The Interpretation of Dreams* by 24 years, and *Psychopathology of Everyday Life* by 20.)

It is useful practically to include automatism in a consideration of chance in art, and it is only our viewpoint which makes it a chance process, but there is actually no reason why the others of Breton's categories could not also be included. We exclude them arbitrarily from this discussion only to preserve a certain tightness in our consideration of the methodological resources of the contemporary research "artist," which we will take up further on. Automatism is also an aspect of chance in the sense that we accept its product as something which it really is not. In all of Breton's manifestations of the marvelous (a handy summary) we read into phenomena characteristics which they do not possess in an absolute way. Duchamp called this "irony" ("a playful way of accepting something"), and the concept is a critical one in understanding the vector through Dada, Pollock, the present-day chance-imagists, and the future. The idea will appear again in the section on Pollock, and shows up particularly as a method I've called the "irrelevant process" (also discussed later).

We are more interested, though, in the mechanically chance process, and here Duchamp did the pioneer work. In 1913 he undertook what seems to be the first explicit use of chance for the creation of an affective image, in the "3 stoppages etalon." He made these images by holding a thread one meter long, "straight and horizontal," one meter above a blank canvas. After letting it fall onto the canvas, it was fixed with a trickle of varnish into the chance convolution in which it fell. This process was repeated to give three such canvases.

Duchamp seems to consider three phenomena basic to his exploitation of chance: wind, gravity and aim. (This discussion is based largely on an article about Duchamp by Harriet and Sidney Janis; see reference 5.) The "3 stoppages etalon" illustrate gravity; wind was used to create the cloud formations for "La Mariee mise a nu par ses celibataires, meme" (1915–1923): "Air currents blowing a piece of mesh gauze against a screen, imprinted a limpid rectangle upon it. The experiment repeated three times gave three chance images, variations on the square. . . . The third device in allowing shapes to create themselves and thus void the responsibility of the hand, is termed by Duchamp *adresse,* that is, skill in aiming. Nine marks were made upon the glass by the impact of shots of matches dipped in paint, from a toy cannon. . . . Aiming nine shots at a given point, these formed a polygram as a result of variation in the aim-control and accompanying conditions. He then converted the flat polygram or floor plan into an elevation plan. Here the nine points became the locations for the nine malic forms in perspective." (5)

Duchamp's theories on the use of chance seem highly developed, but not exhaustive. Other Dadaists, especially Arp. Ernst and Tzara, later developed other important applications of chance:

> Arp composed collages by picking up chance scraps of paper, shuffling them, and gluing them down just as they fell (example: the "Squares arranged according to the laws of chance," a collage of 1916).
>
> Ernst developed the "decalcomania of chance" (5), wherein, for example, ink was spread between two sheets of paper, which were then pulled apart (example: "Decalcomania, 1936" by Oscar Dominguez, illus. in ref. 4, p. 161).
>
> Tzara composed poems by drawing words from a hat. ("To make a dadaist poem / Take a newspaper. / Take a pair of scissors. / Choose an article as long as you are planning to make your poem. / Cut out the article. / Then cut out each of the words that make up this article and put them in a bag. / Shake it gently. / Then take out the scraps one after the other in the order in which they left the bag. / Copy conscientiously. / The poem will be like you. / And here you are a writer, infinitely original and endowed with a sensibility that is charming though beyond the understanding of the vulgar." (6)
>
> *Frottage* was a "semi-automatic process for obtaining patterns or designs by rubbing canvas or paper which has been placed over a

> rough surface such as planking, embossing, a brick wall, etc." (7) (example: Ernst, "The Horde," ca. 1927). This is an example of a technique for which we shall later have a more general term—the "irrelevant process."
>
> A very interesting technique of the Surrealists, which permitted the cause of an event to be lost, so to speak, in multiplicity, was that of the *cadavre exquis,* wherein several persons each made part of a picture, folding the paper to cover his addition, before passing the drawing to the next participant. (An example is the "Figure," 1926–1927, by Yves Tanguy, Joan Miro, Max Morise and Man Ray, illus. in ref. 4, p. 251.)

The ability of the unconscious to reconcile opposites is nowhere so evident as in Dada, for within a periphery of nonsense the ridiculous and the profound were made to evince each other: "Dada wished to destroy the reasonable frauds of men and recover the natural, unreasonable order. Dada wished to replace the logical nonsense of the men of today with an illogical nonsense. That is why we beat the Dadaist bass drum with all our might and trumpeted the praises of unreason. . . . Dada like nature is without meaning. Dada is for infinite meaning and finite means." (Gabrielle Buffet-Picabia, 1949, ref. 8.) Within such a (frameless) framework, chance played a major part, as testified by Arp himself (9): "Chance opened up perceptions to me, immediate spiritual insights. Intuition led me to revere the law of chance as the highest and deepest of laws, the law that rises from the fundament. An insignificant word might become a deadly thunderbolt. One little sound might destroy the earth. One little sound might create a new universe." The almost incredibly incisive mind of Tristan Tzara, as early as 1922, even recognized the relationship of all this to Oriental philosophy (in one of the most convincing of Dada documents, the "Lecture on Dada"): "Dada is not at all modern. It is more in the nature of a return to an almost Buddhist religion of indifference." (10) Such aspects of reality as Oriental thought—scientific thought—Dada—chance become somewhat clearer in such a light. Perhaps chance is the most allusive of the phenomena studied by the Dadaists and Surrealists because it is capable of being most widely generalized. We shall see.

The Second World War helped to disperse the European Dadaists and Surrealists, and many of the most original artists—Breton, Ernst, Tanguy, Masson—regrouped in New York, particularly around two New York galleries, the Julien Levy Gallery and Peggy Guggenheim's Art of This Century.

JACKSON POLLOCK

Jackson Pollock's first show was held at Peggy Guggenheim's gallery in 1943. Here he was able to associate with the proponents of that "sacred disorder" which was later to become the key to his own original style. "To them Pollock owed his radical new sense of freedom, and he spoke more than once of his debt to their unpremeditated and automatic methods. By elevating the appeal to chance and accident into a first principle of creation, the Surrealists had circumvented the more rigid formalisms of modern art." (11) It is not difficult to find their influence in Pollock's paintings of the war years (for example, *Guardians of the Secret,* 1943). Pollock achieved a profound, sustained and irrational synthesis of all the principles which had preceded him in Dada, and in a way consistent with his contemporary world. His paintings seem much less manifestations of one of a group of techniques for releasing the unconscious (as the Dada experiments seemed), than they do of a single, integrated use of chance as a means of unlocking the deepest possible grasp of nature in its broadest sense.

Not to get lost in conjecture, let us briefly give evidence for two points, first that Pollock's calligraphy was truly automatic and second that there is a considerable element of chance in the ultimate arrangement of pigment in the chance-paintings of roughly 1947–1951.

First, part of a statement by Pollock (12), made in 1947:

> When I am in my painting, I'm not aware of what I'm doing. It is only after a sort of "get acquainted" period that I see what I have been about.

Again, from an earlier statement (13):

> . . . the fact that good European moderns are now here is very important, for they bring with them an understanding of the problems of modern painting. I am particularly impressed with their concept of the source of art being the unconscious. This idea interests me more than these specific painters do . . . .

Aside from the lack of conscious control of paint application in these paintings, there are technical reasons for looking at this complex of interdependent forms as predominantly chance events. For one thing, the infinite number of variables involved in determining the flow of fluid paint from a source not in contact with the canvas cannot possibly be simultaneously taken into account with sufficient omniscience that the exact configuration of the paint when it hits the canvas can be predicted. Some of these variables, for example, are the paint viscosity, density, rate of flow at any instant; and direction, speed and configuration of the applicator, to say nothing of non-uniformity in the paint. Even if we deny automatism, and claim omniscience for an unconscious molded by a long learning period, it is obvious that in some of Pollock's paintings of this period (in *One, 1950,* for example) differently colored streams of paint have flowed into each other after application, resulting in a commingling completely out of the artist's hands. Never before Pollock were chance processes used with such primacy, consistency and integrity, as valuable sources of affective imagery.

Paintings get to be what they are physically through an interaction of method and material, and they have their effect in an interaction between painting and observer. As far as the observer is concerned, Pollock has demonstrated that the ability of humans to appreciate complex chance-images is almost unlimited. Here I would like to introduce the general term "chance-imagery" to apply to our formation of images resulting from chance, wherever these occur in nature. (The word "imagery" is intentionally ambiguous enough, I think, to apply either to the physical act of creating an image out of real materials, or to the formation of an image in the mind, say by abstraction from a more complex system.) One reason for doing this is to place the painter's, musician's, poet's, dancer's chance images in the same conceptual category as natural chance-images (the configuration of meadow grasses, the arrangement of stones on a brook bottom), and to get away from the idea that an artist makes something "special" and beyond the world of ordinary things. An Alpine peak or an iris petal can move us at times with all the subtle power of a *Night Watch* or one of the profound themes of Opus 131. There is no a priori reason why moving images should originate only with artists.

This leaves "art" to mean something *constructed,* from a starting point of pre-conceived notions, with the corollary that as art approaches chance-imagery, the artist enters a oneness with all of nature. This idea has in essence been well expressed by Suzuki:

> There is something divine in being spontaneous and not being hampered by human conventionalities and their artificial hypocrisies. There is something direct and fresh in this lack of restraint by anything human, which suggests a divine freedom and creativity. Nature never deliberates; it acts directly out of its own heart, whatever this may mean. In this respect Nature is divine. Its "irrationality" transcends human doubts or ambiguities, and in our submitting to it, or rather accepting it, we transcend ourselves. (14)

> Our inner life is complete when it merges into Nature and becomes one with it. (15)

When an artist achieves this essential oneness with all of nature, everything he creates illuminates nature, as well as himself.

> *Reason has cut man off from nature.*
>
> Hans Arp (16)

HISTORICAL CONCURRENCES: STATISTICS, SCIENCE AND PHILOSOPHY

I think it is interesting to look at these developments in the use of chance in painting against a background of our growing understanding of chance in other fields over the last several centuries. The conjuncture of statistical theory with mathematical physics, which occurred about 1860, resulted ultimately in a reformulation of our concept of the workings of nature; the requirements of strict causality, which classical philosophy had regarded as an a priori principle underlying the mechanics of the universe, were replaced by a measure of probability. The predominance of cause thus gave way to the predominance of chance (see ref. 17), and a climate in which chance-imagery seems an almost inevitable concomitant grew up.

The first questions regarding probability were formulated by gamblers, and perhaps this is natural, for games of chance go far back into history and prehistory (at least to the third and fourth millennia B.C.). (See, for instance, David, ref. 18.) The literature of games of chance began to collect in the sixteenth century, and about 1526 Gerolamo Cardano (who, himself, was both mathematician and gambler) wrote his *Liber de Ludo Aleae,* in which a probability was calculated by theoretical argument for the first time. In the seventeenth century, Galileo, Pascal and Fermat carried further the concepts of probability applied to gaming. In 1733 De Moivre, the English mathematician, published his formulation of the so-called "normal law," describing the distribution of events subject to a great number of independent chance influences, and these results were found to describe the distribution of errors of observation in astronomy, social science and the physical sciences, largely through the work of Laplace and Gauss, about the end of the eighteenth and beginning of the nineteenth centuries.

We now wish to trace a concurrent thread of events in physics, specifically in the kinetic theory of gases. In 1661 (two years before Cardano's *Liber de Ludo Aleae* finally appeared in print) Robert Boyle had described the relationship between the volume of a gas and the pressure exerted by it on a closed vessel, and tried to account for this behavior by comparing the gas particles to little springs lying on each other, which coil and uncoil. Twenty years later Robert Hooke suggested that the pressure of a gas was due to the impingement of hard, rapidly moving particles on the walls of the containing vessel, and this work was followed, in 1738, by the explanation of Daniel Bernoulli that Boyle's Law would be true if the particles of a gas were considered to be infinitesimal in size.

The subject of gas kinetics then lay dormant for almost a hundred years, until new progress was made in the first half of the nineteenth century, when Joule (1848) showed that the kinetic energy of gas molecules is proportional to the absolute temperature of the gas. Clausius then gave the subject both a wider and more rigorous treatment (1857), which resulted in a theoretical understanding of the simultaneous volume, pressure and temperature relationships in a gas, which had already been empirically determined. Clausius had made several simplifying assumptions, however, which turned out to be untenable, for he had held that the gas molecules were all to be considered as moving at the same speed. Since the molecules must frequently collide, changing their speeds with each collision, even if the speeds of all the molecules were initially equal, they would not be equal for long. Two years later James Clerk Maxwell set out to determine the average speed of the gas molecules (allowing for the effect of collisions), and also the distribution of speeds of individual molecules about this average.

Maxwell's conclusion was that the distribution of speeds of the molecules was described by the normal law, brought into scientific considerations by Gauss. That is, the macroscopic behavior of a gaseous mass (as exhibited, for example, by its temperature) was to be described by the average of the speeds of the individual molecules. The phenomenon of temperature as an effect, measured, for example, by the expansion of mercury in a thermometer, was therefore attributable not to *a* cause, but to a very large number of independent causes, the magnitudes of which were due to chance. Thus a change in the amount of heat energy in a body means a change in an average of many independent events. This explains why heat ordinarily travels from a hotter body to a colder, and not the opposite way. We expect an ice cube placed in a glass of water at room temperature to result in a cooler mixture; the liquid becomes cooler, and the ice melts. We do not expect the heat to travel from the ice cube to the warmer liquid, leaving a yet colder ice cube and warmer liquid. This is the essence of the so-called Second Law of Thermodynamics, and this principle is made understandable by Maxwell's statistical interpretation of gas kinetics, because this interpretation lets us form a conceptual model of a mixture of gases with different temperatures, in which high-energy molecules of the warmer gas are colliding with low-energy molecules of the cooler, imparting some of their energy in the collision. The result is a total amount of energy which, after mixture, falls somewhere between the extremes of amounts of energy possessed by the two original volumes of gases. Since the macroscopically observable variables are averages, based on summation of individual chance events, an event such as our ice-cube-in-water becoming colder becomes, not impossible by a deterministic law of nature, but only highly improbable, based on laws of probability.

We might argue that these developments do not in themselves require us to abandon strict causality, for we might hypothesize (as Laplace actually did) a superman, to whom the exact motion and speed of each molecule were known, and who would thus be capable of calculating the motion of each molecule after any specified length of time.

The resolution of these questions of strict causality versus probabilistic prediction came with Werner Heisenberg's publication of his principle of indeterminacy in 1927. Specifically, Heisenberg showed mathematically that it was not possible to determine both the position and the momentum of an electron at the same time, that is, that as the precision with which the momentum of an electron was measured was increased, the precision with which the position of the electron was measured necessarily decreased, and conversely. This was later interpreted as reflecting our inability to measure the characteristics of the smallest particles without disturbing the particles themselves, for even when the photon itself is used as the most sensitive instrument for observation of these elementary particles, it has the same order of magnitude as the objects being observed.

The causal descriptions of classical physics (and philosophy) then, (that is, such statements as: "When A happens, then B will always happen") are idealizations, or simplified models of the actual state of affairs. The best we can do is to make statements with a high degree of probability (e.g., "When A happens then B will happen in a certain proportion of cases"), for we cannot exhaustively describe the causal structure of any real system.

Thus chance became an underlying principle of our world-view.

Of course, we don't mean to imply that chance-imagery is the direct result of the artists' knowledge of these trends. We only mean that the works of great artists are products of the same complex, interacting welter of cause and effect out of which came the results of mathematical physics. If we believe history to show that art of the past has fit into the cultural matrix of the time in which it was produced, we have incentive to look for the trends in contemporary art which are consistent with analogous trends in these other fields. Unfortunately, though this must have seemed like an over-long digression, we have only been able to hint at the parallelism in these trends here.

> . . . Reason is an indispensable instrument for the organization of knowledge, without which facts of a more abstract kind could not be known. The senses do not show me that the planets move in ellipses around the sun, or that matter consists of atoms; it is sense observation in combination with reasoning that leads to such abstract truths.
>
> Hans Reichenbach (19)

RANDOMNESS

Chance images are characterized by a lack of conscious design. When these images are "hand-made," and conscious thought is evaded, so that the images have their source in deeper-than-conscious areas of the mind, we will prefer the Surrealists' term "automatic" to the word "random," though "random," in the way it is used in everyday speech, might seem appropriate (as meaning, for example, "without definite aim, direction, rule, or method," ref. 20). We will prefer this usage in order to restrict "random" to a technical meaning which it has more commonly in statistics, where it applies to special techniques for eliminating bias in sampling. The term "strict randomness" is useful for ensuring that the word random is understood in this technical sense, but, in general, we shall merely say random, and it should always be understood here that the technical meaning is implied. Chance is sometimes used in painting in such a way that the images are neither clearly automatic nor random, and here we can only refer to chance-images or chance-processes.

It remains to indicate, then, what this technical meaning comprises, recognizing that, in general, the reason for the importance of randomness for purposes of scientific inference will be the same as the reason for its importance in the arts, that is, the elimination of bias. It is not intuitively obvious that strict randomness is difficult to achieve; therefore let us indicate the general presence of bias where human choice or ordinary mechanical systems are involved. This will give us an intuitive insight into approaches capable of eliminating bias, and will lead finally to a working definition of randomness itself.

Concerning a general bias in human choice, Kendall and Smith (21) have made the following interesting statement:

> It is becoming increasingly evident that sampling left to the discretion of a human individual is not random, although he may be completely unconscious of the existence of bias, or indeed actively endeavouring to avoid it. House-to-house sampling, the sampling of crop yields, even ticket-drawing have all been found to give results widely divergent from expectation.

Yule and Kendall (22) have given an example of human bias which was detected in the course of agricultural experiments carried out in England. The heights of wheat plants were to be measured at two stages in their growth. Of the sets of eight plants sampled for measurement at each of the two stages, two were selected "at random" by eye, and the other six were selected by strictly random methods. Analysis of the measurements showed clearly that, in the samples selected by eye, there was a clear bias toward selecting taller shoots in May, before the ears of wheat had formed, while in June, after further maturation, another bias toward selecting plants of more like average height, and avoiding the extremely tall or short plants, was evidenced.

I have attempted some one-hand typing of series of random digits, and found not only a bias toward a greater frequency of higher digits (regardless of the hand used for the typing), but also peculiar patterns in the series; digits being followed unusually often by certain other digits, for example. (For an interesting discussion of chance numbers, and further references on this subject, see section 12 of Freud's *Psychopathology of Everyday Life in The Basic Writings of Sigmund Freud.*)

One might expect to avoid human bias by using mechanical systems, but experience has shown that it is not easy to find simple unbiased mechanical systems. Perfectly balanced coins and roulette wheels, like perfectly cubical and homogeneous dice, seem to occur rarely in nature, if at all. Weldon (23), for example, threw twelve dice 4,096 times. For unbiased dice the probability of a 4, 5 or 6 is ½, so that he should have obtained one of these faces 24,576 times. These three faces actually occurred 25,145 times, which is a statistically significant bias. Even an electronic analog of a roulette wheel, built by the RAND Corporation for the generation of random digits, after careful engineering and re-engineering to eliminate bias, was found again to have statistically significant biases, after running continuously for a month, in spite of the fact that tests showed the electronic equipment itself to be in good order (24).

How can bias be avoided? First, it can be reduced by resorting to compound chance events, and, formally, it can be eliminated by the use of random numbers.

By making the chance-event a compound of two or more independent events, elements in the compound event can be made more nearly independent of each other, and thus biases can be avoided. For example, in the Surrealist *cadavre exquis,* it was made impossible for any one person to foresee the overall result of combining the independently contributed parts of the drawing, so that bias in the relationship of elements in the compound chance-event (drawing) was avoided. John Cage has also used this technique in his "Music for Four Pianos," wherein four pianists play independently of each other, the resulting rhythmic and melodic pattern being thus freed of personal bias. In fact, this technique has been used, in a much-refined way, to generate a table of strictly random numbers (those published by the Interstate Commerce Commission, ref. 25). Independent columns of digits from waybills received by the commission deriving from numerical data such as shipment weight, revenue, car serial number, etc., were used as a basic set from which the final set was derived.

Tables of random numbers provide a convenient and reliable means of avoiding bias in selection; convenient because they allow random selection of anything which can be numbered, reliable because they can be verified to be statistically random. Tests for randomness in random number tables are described in references 21 and 26. The use of tables of random numbers is briefly described in the following section on methodology.

Randomness, then, implies an independence of each individual choice from every other choice, plus an aggregate impartiality toward the characteristic being sampled. In tables of random digits, for example, a state of randomness implies both that the occurrence of any particular digit at a particular point in the table is independent of the occurrence of all the other digits, and that the proportional occurrence of that digit in the long run is arbitrarily close to some pre-established value. Practically speaking, this means that in a table such as the RAND table, the digit 5 in a certain place is just as likely to be followed by a 6, 7, 8 or 9 as it is to be followed by a 0, 1, 2, 3 or 4, and also that in the table as a whole, the proportion of digits 5 should be reasonably close to one-tenth.

WAYS OF INVOKING CHANCE

The technique chosen for making random or chance selections in the arts is largely determined by the number and nature of the elements from which the selection is to be made. In addition, the degree of randomness of the finished image can be made as great as the artist's desires and capabilities allow. For example, a coin can simply be tossed to determine whether a pre-selected image shall be painted in black-on-white or white-on-black, or, at the other extreme, random number tables can be used to determine the field material (canvas, paper, etc.), size and shape of the field, medium, colors, method of application of the medium (brush, drip, etc.), components of the method (brush width, applicator dimensions, etc.), and any other characteristics of interest.

It is practical to use coins, dice, or a roulette wheel where only a limited number of elements are available for selection. Where the number of elements is large, these techniques become unwieldy, and others must be found. Where the elements can be numbered, tables of random numbers are relatively easy to use, otherwise automatism, or a very flexible approach, which (for want of a better name) I have called the "irrelevant process," can be used.

For convenience, I have listed these techniques below, with some examples. Readers may be able to add to the list.

Coins— One coin can fall either heads or tails. Two coins can fall in three different ways: both heads, one head and one tail, or both tails, and in general n coins can fall in n + 1 ways, without regard to order. With more than one coin, however, the different combinations are not equally likely. We are six times as likely to get two tails and two heads in a toss of four coins, as we are to get all tails, for example. If we desire to consider HT different from TH, then two coins can fall in four different ways (HH, HT, TH, TT), three coins in eight different ways, and n coins in 2^n ways. When coins are used for making chance selections, therefore, it is necessary to know the nature of the possible outcomes (events) which can occur, in order to avoid prejudice due to the characteristics of the chance process.

Dice— The ordinary six-sided dice are somewhat limited with respect to flexibility, having only up to six spots per face. Two or more dice used at once lead to the same complications as met with in the use of coins, that is, the necessity either of knowing the probability of various outcomes, or of using sophisticated devices to obtain the situation desired with respect to probabilities. Two dice of different colors, for example, may be used, in order to make 4:3 distinguishable from 3:4, or the dice can be thrown one after the other instead of together.

Though a die is now by definition cubical, analogous devices can be (and have been) constructed with other than six faces. David (18), for example, describes a rock crystal polyhedron of twenty numbered faces which dates back to ancient Greece.

Numbered Wheels— Small roulette wheels with 36 compartments are readily available, but are not likely to be unbiased. The device is very convenient to use, however, and gives quite usable chance series. Allan Kaprow has used the roulette wheel to arrange the elements in a composition for five voices, bell, flute, match-box, and scroll.

Another form of the numbered wheel is that sometimes found in children's games, a card with a circular series of numbers, and a pointer which can be spun. Paul Taylor has used this method to determine direction of motion in the dance.

Cards— Card shuffling must be very thoroughly done in order to approach randomness. Earle Brown has used the technique analogically in his "25 Pages" (of musical notation), designed to be played in any page order.

Bowl Drawing— Metal-bordered paper tags in a bowl provide a very convenient universe of chance instructions, if the tags are carefully and thoroughly mixed after having had the original set of instructions written on them. Some elements lend themselves to being drawn directly, without coding; for example, magnetic tapes containing a population of sounds can be cut into lengths, mixed in a bowl and drawn directly. A poem of Tzara's arranged in this way is printed in the Motherwell anthology (6).

Automatism— A chance-process by definition, and probably the most commonly used among "action-painters."

Random Numbers— Eight tables of random digits have been published, that I know of, but one or two of these are no longer in print. Two of those most readily available have been cited in references 24 and 25. After numbering the elements from which a random choice is to be made, the table is consulted, starting at any point and reading in any direction. Numbers with the requisite number of digits are taken in the same order as they occur in the table, discarding those too large for use and those previously selected (if unusable for that reason). For example, nine points are chosen on a field, and numbered 1 to 9:

1	2	3
4	5	6
7	8	9

A random block of digits from the RAND table is:

25412
49703
72007
32309
02069

Reading left-to-right and top-to-bottom, and connecting the points above in order, we obtain the random pattern:

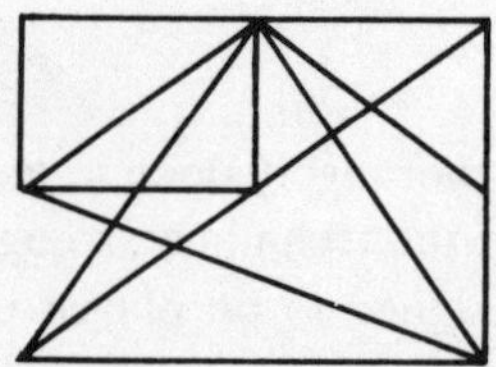

Less naive approaches suggest themselves; placing the points unevenly (at will) (Brecht: "Random Form R3"), using consecutive sets of two random numbers as sets of Cartesian coordinates (Brecht: "Random Form R4"), and so forth. Such systems for obtaining visual forms can be elaborated almost indefinitely. A special random process for the dancer exists in the "Random Walk," a theoretical model developed in statistics to describe (among other things) the random motion (Brownian movement) of small particles suspended in a liquid, and acquiring their motion from numerous chance impacts. (See reference 27.)

The Irrelevant Process— In general, bias in the selection of elements for a chance-image can be avoided by using a method of selection of those elements which is independent of the characteristics of interest in the elements themselves. The method should preferably give an irregular and unforeseen pattern of selection.

John Cage has used this approach in a composition for orchestra, ruling a staff on a sheet of paper, and placing notes on the staff at points where certain minute imperfections in the paper occur. Inked marbles rolled over an irregular surface trace a pattern determined by unforeseen imperfections in the surface and chance rebounds of the marbles from each other (Brecht: "7-57").

More remotely, significant images occur as the result of processes over which we exercise no selection at all. The most moving collage I ever experienced was the 4 x 24 foot side of a truck carrying boilers, a piece of canvas patched irregularly with other pieces of canvas of various shades of gray. Map patterns, and the classical *objets trouvés,* would also seem includible within this principle.

CODA

Chance in the arts provides a means for escaping the biases engrained in our personality by our culture and personal past history, that is, it is a means of attaining greater generality. The result is a method of approach with wide application. The methods of chance and randomness can be applied to the selection and arrangement of sounds by the composer, to movement and pace by the dancer, to three-dimensional form by the sculptor, to surface form and color by the painter, to linguistic elements by the poet. Science tells us that the universe is what we conceive it to be, and chance enables us to determine what we conceive it to be (for the conception is only partly conscious). The receptacle of forms available to the artist thus becomes open-ended, and eventually embraces all of nature, for the recognition of significant form becomes limited only by the observer's self. It must be obvious too that the infinite range of application of these methods is compounded when the matter of materials is also considered, and this is a subject we have only incidentally touched on here. One hopes that so-called avant-garde painters will some day look beyond the classical oil medium with the same open-minded receptivity that, say, Pierre Schaeffer did in his field, in 1948. ("Quand on s'êntete contre toute logique, c'est qu'on attend quelque chose d'un hasard, que cette logique n'aurait pas su prevoir. Mon mérite est d'avoir aperçu, entre cent experiences, celle, apparement aussi decevant que les autres, qui creait l'évasion. Encore fallait-il avoir l'audace de generaliser.") (28)

I doubt that an increase in our ability to recognize significance in the chance-images which nature presents all about us will mean an end of the personal activities which we have been calling art. The artist will probably continue to make significant images, both because some such images rarely occur in nature, and because of a personal release which comes about from such activity:

> The painter makes paintings in the urgent need to discharge his own emotions and visions. Pablo Picasso (29)
>
> Pictures are vehicles of passion, of all kinds and orders, not pretty luxuries like sports cars. In our society, the capacity to give and to receive passion is limited. For this reason, the act of painting is a deep human necessity, not the production of a hand-made commodity. Robert Motherwell (30)

But it seems to me that we fall short of the infinite expansion of the human spirit for which we are searching, when we recognize only images which are artifacts. We are capable of more than that.

AN AFTER-NOTE

In 1957, when this article was written, I had only recently met John Cage and had not yet seen clearly that the most important implications of chance lay in his work rather than in Pollock's. Nor could I have foreseen the resolution of the distinction between choice and chance which was to occur in my own work.

We are eight years farther on the spiral, and I prefer work to rework. "Chance-Imagery" is presented in the form in which it was originally written.

November, 1965

NOTE

1 Rigorously proved by Lorentz in 1887, following a method developed by Boltzmann in 1868.

REFERENCES

1 Tristan Tzara. "Lecture on Dada" (1922). *The Dada Painters and Poets: An Anthology*. Edited by Robert Motherwell. The Documents of Modern Art series, Wittenborn, Schultz, Inc., 1951, p. 248. We will hereafter abbreviate this anthology to "Motherwell."

2 Sigmund Freud. *Psychopathology of Everyday Life. The Basic Writings of Sigmund Freud*. English translation by A. A. Brill. The Modern Library, Random House, New York, 1938, p. 164.

3 Marcel Raymond. *From Baudelaire to Surrealism*. Quoted in Motherwell, p. xxix of the Introduction.

4 Andre Breton. "First Surrealist Manifesto." Quoted by Georges Hugnet in one of his two introductory essays for *Fantastic Art, Dada, Surrealism*. Edited by Alfred H. Barr, Jr. Third edition, The Museum of Modern Art, New York, 1947. Hereafter this book is referred to as "Barr."

5 Harriet and Sidney Janis. "Marcel Duchamp: Anti-Artist" (1945). Motherwell, Appendix C. p. 306.

6 Tristan Tzara. "Manifesto on feeble love and bitter love." Motherwell, p. 92.

7 A. H. Barr, Jr. "A list of devices, techniques, media." Barr, p. 65.

8 Gabrielle Buffet-Picabia. "Some Memories of Pre-Dada: Picabia and Duchamp" (1949). Motherwell, p. 266.

9 Jean (Hans) Arp. "Dada Was Not a Farce" (1949). Motherwell, p. 294.

10 Tristan Tzara. "Lecture on Dada" (1922). Motherwell, p. 247.

11 Sam Hunter. Catalog of the 1956 Pollock retrospective show. *Bulletin*, vol. xxiv, no. 2 of the Museum of Modern Art.

12 Jackson Pollock. "My Painting." *Possibilities* (N.Y.), no. 1:79, *Winter* 1947–48, pp. 78–83.

13 Jackson Pollock. "Jackson Pollock" (a questionnaire). *Arts and Architecture*, vol. 61, no. 2, February 1944, p. 14.

14 D. T. Suzuki. "Zen Buddhism." *Selected Writings of D. T. Suzuki*. Edited by William Barrett. Doubleday & Co., Inc., New York Anchor edition, 1956, p. 234. Used by permission of Hutchinson & Co., Ltd., London.

15 D. T. Suzuki. Ibid., p. 256.

16 Jean (Hans) Arp. "Notes from a Dada Diary." Motherwell, p. 222.

17 Max Born. *Natural Philosophy of Cause and Chance*. Oxford University Press, London, 1949, p. 92.

18 F. N. David. "Studies in the history of probability and statistics: I. Dicing and Gaming." *Biometrika*. University College London, vol. 42, parts 1 and 2, June 1955, p. 1.

19 Hans Reichenbach. *The Rise of Scientific Philosophy*. University of California Press, Berkeley, Cal.

20 *Webster's New International Dictionary*, Second edition, copyright 1959 by G. & C. Merriam Co., publishers of the Merriam-Webster Dictionaries. Used by permission.

21 M. G. Kendall and B. Babington Smith. "Randomness and Random Sampling Numbers." *Journal of the Royal Statistical Society*. London, vol. CI, pt. 1, 1938, pp. 147–166.

22 G. Udny Yule and M. G. Kendall. *An Introduction to the Theory of Statistics*. 14th edition, Hafner Publishing Co., New York, 1950.

23 Cited in M. G. Kendall. *The Advanced Theory of Statistics*. Fifth edition, Hafner Publishing Co., New York, vol. I, p. 199.

24 The RAND Corporation. *A Million Random Digits with 100,000 Normal Deviates*. The Free Press, Glencoe, Illinois, 1955. A description of the method used for production of the random digits is contained in the introduction.

25 Interstate Commerce Commission, Bureau of Transport Economics

and Statistics. *Table of 105,000 Random Decimal Digits.* Washington, D.C., May 1949. Copies are available free from the Commission. Refer to Statement No. 4914, File No. 261-A-1.

26 G. Udny Yule. "A Test of Tippett's Random Sampling Numbers." *Journal of the Royal Statistical Society,* vol. CI, pt. 1, 1938, p. 167.

27 W. Feller. *Probability Theory and its Applications.* John Wiley & Sons, Inc., New York, 1950, vol. 1, chapter 14.

28 Pierre Schaeffer. *A la recherche d'une musique concrete.* Editions du Seuil, 1952, p. 16.

29 Quoted by Frank Elgar; in Elgar and Maillard. *Picasso.* Frederick A. Praeger, Inc., New York, 1956.

30 Statement by Robert Motherwell; in "The New Decade" exhibition catalog. Edited by John I. H. Baur. Whitney Museum of American Art, New York, 1955.

ADDITIONAL READING

The Growth of Physical Science. Sir James Jeans. Cambridge University Press. 1948.

11

Excerpts from *For a New Novel*

Alain Robbe-Grillet

Is there not, first of all, a certain fraudulence in this word *human* which is always being thrown in our faces? If it is not a word quite devoid of meaning, what meaning does it really have?

It seems that those who use it all the time, those who make it the sole criterion of all praise as of all reproach, identify—deliberately, perhaps—a precise (and limited) reflection on man, his situation in the world, the phenomena of his existence, with a certain anthropocentric atmosphere, vague but imbuing all things, giving the world its so-called *signification,* that is, investing it from within by a more or less disingenuous network of sentiments and thoughts. Simplifying, we can summarize the position of our new inquisitors in two sentences; if I say, "The world is man," I shall always gain absolution; while if I say, "Things are things, and man is only man," I am immediately charged with a crime against humanity.

The crime is the assertion that there exists something in the world which is not man, which makes no sign to him, which has nothing in common with him. The crime, above all, according to this view, is to remark this separation, this distance, without attempting to effect the slightest sublimation of it.

What could be, in other words, an "inhuman" work? How, in particular, could a novel which deals with a man, and follows his steps from page to page, describing only what he does, what he sees, or what he imagines, how could such a novel be accused of turning away from man? And it is not the character himself, let us make that clear at once, who is involved in this judgment. As a "character," as an individual animated by torments and passions, no one will ever reproach him with being inhuman, even if he is a sadistic madman and a criminal—the contrary, it would seem.

But now suppose the eyes of this man rest on things without indulgence, insistently: he sees them, but he refuses to appropriate them, he refuses to maintain any suspect understanding with them, any complicity; he asks nothing of them; toward them he feels neither agreement nor dissent of any kind. He can, perhaps, make them the prop of his passions, as of his sense of sight. But his sense of sight is content to take their measurements; and his passion, similarly, rests on their surface, without attempting to penetrate them since there is nothing inside, without feigning the least appeal since they would not answer.

To condemn, in the name of the human, the novel which deals with such a man is therefore to adopt the *humanist* point of view, according to which it is not enough to show man where he is: it must further be proclaimed that man is everywhere. On the pretext that man can achieve only a subjective knowledge of the world, humanism decides to elect man the justification of everything. A true bridge of souls thrown between man and things, the humanist outlook is preeminently a pledge of solidarity.

In the literary realm, the expression of this solidarity appears chiefly as the investigation, worked up into a system, of analogical relations.

Metaphor, as a matter of fact, is never an innocent figure of speech. To say that the weather is "capricious" or the mountain "majestic," to speak of the "heart" of the forest, of a "pitiless" sun, of a village "huddled" in the valley, is, to a certain degree, to furnish clues as to the things themselves: shape, size, situation, etc. But the choice of an analogical vocabulary, however simple, already does something more than account for purely physical data, and what this *more* is can scarcely be ascribed only to the credit of belles-lettres. The height of the mountain assumes, willy-nilly, a moral value; the heat of the sun becomes the result of an intention. . . . In almost the whole of our contemporary literature, these anthropomorphic analogies are repeated too insistently, too coherently not to reveal an entire metaphysical system.

More or less consciously, the goal for the writers who employ such a terminology can only be to establish a constant relation between the universe and the being who inhabits it. Thus man's sentiments will seem alternately to derive from his contacts with the world and to find in that world their natural correspondence if not their fulfillment.

Metaphor, which is supposed to express only a comparison, without any particular motive, actually introduces a subterranean communication, a movement of sympathy (or of antipathy) which is its true *raison d'être*. For, as comparison, metaphor is almost always a useless comparison which contributes nothing new to the description. What would the village lose by being merely "situated" in the valley? The word "huddled" gives us no complementary information. On the other hand it transports the reader (in the author's wake) into the imagined soul of the village; if I accept the word "huddled," I am no longer entirely a spectator; I myself become the village, for the duration of a sentence, and the valley functions as a cavity into which I aspire to disappear.

Taking this possible adherence as their basis, the defenders of metaphor reply that it thereby possesses an advantage: that of making apparent an element which was not so. Having himself become the village, they say, the reader participates in the latter's situation, hence understands it better. Similarly in the case of the mountain: I shall make it easier to see the mountain by saying it is majestic than by measuring the apparent angle from which my gaze registers its height. . . . And this is true sometimes, but it always involves a more serious reversal: it is precisely this participation which is problematical, since it leads to the notion of a hidden unity.

It must even be added that the gain in descriptive value is here no more than an alibi: the true lovers of metaphor seek only to impose the idea of a communication. If they did not possess the verb "huddle," they would not even mention the position of the village. The height of the mountain would be nothing to them, if it did not offer the moral spectacle of "majesty."

To reject our so-called "nature" and the vocabulary which perpetuates its myth, to propose objects as purely external and superficial, is not—as has been claimed—to deny man; but it is to reject the "pananthropic" notion contained in traditional humanism, and probably in all humanism. It is no more in the last analysis than to lay claim, quite logically, to my freedom.

Therefore nothing must be neglected in this mopping-up operation. Taking a closer look, we realize that the anthropocentric analogies (mental or visceral) are not the only ones to be arraigned. *All* analogies are just as dangerous. And perhaps the most dangerous ones of all are the most secret, those in which man is not named.

Let us give some examples, at random. To discover the shape of a horse in the heavens may, of course, derive from a simple process of description and not be of any consequence. But to speak of the "gallop" of the clouds, or of their "flying mane," is no longer entirely innocent. For if a cloud (or a wave or a hill) possesses a mane, if later on the mane of a stallion "Flings arrows," if the arrow . . . etc., the reader of such images will emerge from the universe of forms to find himself plunged into a universe of significations. Between the wave and the horse, he will be tempted to conceive an undifferentiated profundity: passion, pride, power, wildness. . . . The idea of a nature leads infallibly to that of a nature common to all things, that is a *superior* or *higher* nature. The idea of an interiority always leads to the idea of a transcendence.

And the task extends step by step: from the bow to the horse, from the horse to the wave—and from the sea to love. A common nature, once again, must be the eternal answer to the *single question* of our Greco-Christian civilization; the Sphinx is before me, questions me, I need not even try to understand the terms of the riddle being asked, there is only one answer possible, only one answer to everything: man.

This will not do.

There are *questions,* and *answers.* Man is merely, from his own point of view, the only witness.

Man looks at the world, and the world does not look back at him. Man sees things and discovers, now, that he can escape the metaphysical pact others had once concluded for him, and thereby escape servitude and terror. That he can . . . that he *may,* at least, some day.

He does not thereby refuse all contact with the world; he consents on the contrary to utilize it for material ends: a utensil, *as* a utensil, never possesses "depth"; a utensil is entirely form and matter—and purpose.

Man grasps his hammer (or a stone he has selected) and pounds on a stake he wants to drive into the ground. While he uses it in this way, the hammer (or the stone) is merely form and substance: its weight, the striking surface, the other extremity which allows him to hold it. Afterward, man sets the tool down in front of him; if he no longer needs it, the hammer is no more than a thing among things: outside of his use, it has no signification.

And man today (or tomorrow) no longer experiences this absence of signification as a lack, or as a laceration. Confronting such a void, he henceforth feels no dizziness. His heart no longer needs an abyss in which to lodge.

For if he rejects communion, he also rejects tragedy.

Tragedy may be defined, here, as an attempt to "recover" the distance which exists between man and things as a new value; it would be then a test, an ordeal in which victory would consist in being vanquished. Tragedy therefore appears as the last invention of humanism to permit nothing to escape: since the correspondence between man and things has finally been denounced, the humanist saves his empire by immediately instituting a new form of solidarity, the divorce itself becoming a major path to redemption.

There is still almost a communion, but a *painful* one, perpetually in doubt and always deferred, its effectiveness in proportion to its inaccessible character. Divorce-as-a-form-of-marriage is a trap—and it is a falsification.

We see in effect to what degree such a union is perverted: instead of being the quest for a good, it is now the benediction of an evil. Unhappiness, failure, solitude, guilt, madness—such are the accidents of our existence which we are asked to entertain as the best pledges of our salvation. To entertain, not to accept: it is a matter of feeding them at our expense while continuing to struggle against them. For tragedy involves neither a true acceptance nor a true rejection. It is the sublimation of a difference.

Let us retrace, as an example, the functioning of "solitude." I call out. No one answers me. Instead of concluding that there is no one there—which could be a pure and simple observation, dated and localized in space and time—I decide to act as if there *were* someone there, but someone who, for one reason or another, will not answer. The silence which follows my outcry is henceforth no longer a *true* silence; it is charged with a content, a meaning, a depth, a soul—which immediately sends me back to my own. The distance between my cry, to my own ears, and the mute (perhaps deaf) interlocutor to whom it is addressed becomes an anguish, my hope and my despair, a meaning in my life. Henceforth nothing will matter except this false void and the problems it raises for me. Should I call any longer? Should I shout louder? Should I utter different words? I try once again. . . . Very quickly I realize that no one will answer; but the invisible presence I continue to create by my call obliges me to hurl my wretched cries into the silence forever. Soon the sound they make begins to stupefy me. As though bewitched, I call again . . . and again. My solitude, aggravated, is ultimately transmuted into a superior necessity for my alienated consciousness, a promise of my redemption. And I am obliged, if this redemption is to be fulfilled, to persist until my death, crying out for nothing.

According to the habitual process, my solitude is then no longer an accidental, momentary datum of my existence. It becomes part of me, of the entire world, of all men: it is our nature, once again. It is a solitude forever.

Wherever there is distance, separation, doubling, cleavage, there is the possibility of experiencing them as suffering, then of raising this suffering to the height of a sublime necessity. A path toward a metaphysical Beyond, this pseudo-necessity is at the same time the closed door to a realistic future. Tragedy, if it consoles us today, forbids any solider conquest tomorrow. Under the appearance of a perpetual motion, it actually petrifies the universe in a sonorous malediction. There can no longer be any question of seeking some remedy for our misfortune, once tragedy convinces us to love it.

We are in the presence of an oblique maneuver of contemporary humanism, which may deceive us. Since the effort of recuperation no longer bears on things themselves, we might suppose, at first sight, that the divorce between them and man is in any case consummated. But we soon realize that nothing of the kind is the case: whether the pact is concluded with things or with their distance from us comes down to the same thing; the "bridge of souls" subsists between them and us; in fact it is actually reinforced from the operation.

This is why the tragic sense of life never seeks to suppress the distances: it multiplies them, on the contrary, at will. Distance between man and other men, distance between man and himself, between man and the world, between the world and itself—nothing remains intact: everything is lacerated, fissured, divided, displaced. Within the most homogeneous objects as in the least ambiguous situations appears a kind of secret distance. But this is precisely an *interior distance,* a false distance, which is in reality a well-marked path, that is, already a reconciliation.

Everything is contaminated. It seems, though, that the favorite domain of tragedy is the narrative complication, the romanesque. From all mistresses-turned-nuns to all detective-gangsters, by way of all tormented criminals, all pure-souled prostitutes, all the just men constrained by conscience to injustice, all the sadists driven by love, all the madmen pursued by logic, a good "character" in a novel must above all be *double*. The plot will be "human" in proportion to its *ambiguity*. Finally the whole book will be true in proportion to its contradictions.

It is easy to ridicule. It is less so to free oneself from the tragic conditioning our mental civilization imposes upon us. One might even say that the rejection of the ideas of "nature" and of predestination lead *first* to tragedy. There is no important work in contemporary literature that does not contain at the same time the assertion of our freedom and the "tragic" germ of its abandonment.

Two great works at least, in recent decades, have offered us two new forms of the fatal complicity: absurdity and nausea.

Translated by Richard Howard

12

Two or Three Ideas

Wallace Stevens

My first proposition is that the style of a poem and the poem itself are one.

One of the better known poems in *Fleurs du Mal* is the one (XII) entitled "La Vie Antérieure" or "Former Life." It begins with the line

> *J'ai longtemps habité sous de vastes portiques*

or

> A long time I lived beneath tremendous porches.

It continues:

> Which the salt-sea suns tinged with a thousand fires
> And which great columns, upright and majestic,
> At evening, made resemble basalt grottoes.

The poem concerns the life among the images, sounds and colors of those calm, sensual presences.

> At the center of azure, of waves, of brilliances,

and so on. I have chosen this poem to illustrate my first proposition, because it happens to be a poem in which the poem itself is immediately recognizable without reference to the manner in which it is rendered. If the style and the poem are one, one ought to choose, for the purpose of illustration, a poem that illustrates this as, for example, Yeats' *Lake-Isle of Innisfree*. To choose a French poem which has to be translated is to choose an example in which the style is lost in the paraphrase of translation. On the other hand, Baudelaire's poem is useful because it identifies what is meant by the poem itself. The idea of an earlier life is like the idea of a later life, or like the idea of a different life, part of the classic repertory of poetic ideas. It is part of one's inherited store of poetic subjects. Precisely, then, because it is traditional and because we understand its romantic nature and know what to expect from it, we are suddenly and profoundly touched when we hear it declaimed by a voice that says:

> I lived, for long, under huge porticoes.

It is as if we had stepped into a ruin and were startled by a flight of birds that rose as we entered. The familiar experience is made unfamiliar and from that time on, whenever we think of that particular scene, we remember how we held our breath and how the hungry doves of another world rose out of nothingness and whistled away. We stand looking at a remembered habitation. All old dwelling-places are subject to these transmogrifications and the experience of all of us includes a succession of old dwelling-places: abodes of the imagination, ancestral or memories of places that never existed. It is plain that when, in this world of weak feeling and blank thinking, in which we are face to face with the poem every moment of time, we encounter some integration of the poem that pierces and dazzles us, the effect is an effect of style and not of the poem itself or at least not of the poem alone. The effective integration is not a disengaging of the subject. It is a question of the style in which the subject is presented.

Although I have limited myself to an instance of the relation between style and the familiar, one gets the same result in considering the relation between style and its own creations, that is between style and the unfamiliar. What we are really considering here are the creations of modern art and modern literature. If one keeps in mind the fact that most poets who have something to say are content with what they say and that most poets who have little or nothing to say are concerned primarily with the way in which they say it, the importance of this discussion becomes clear. I do not mean to imply that the poets who have something to say are the poets that matter; for obviously if it is true that the style of a poem and the poem itself are one, it follows that, in considering style and its own creations, that is to say, the relation between style and the unfamiliar, it may be, or become, that the poets who have little or nothing to say are, or will be, the poets that matter. Today, painters who have something to say are less admired than painters who seem to have little or nothing to say but who do at least believe that style and the painting are one. The inclination toward arbitrary or schematic constructions in poetry is, from the point of view of style, very strong; and certainly if these constructions were effective it would be true that the style and the poem were one.

In the light of this first idea the prejudice in favor of plain English, for instance, comes to nothing. I have never been able to see why what is called Anglo-Saxon should have the right to higgle and haggle all over the page, contesting the right of other words. If a poem seems to require a hierophantic phrase, the phrase should pass. This is a way of saying that one of the consequences of the ordination of style is not to limit it, but to enlarge it, not to impoverish it, but to enrich and liberate it.

The second idea relates to poetry and the gods, both ancient and modern, both foreign and domestic. To simplify, I shall speak only of the ancient and the foreign gods. I do not mean to refer to them in their religious aspects but as creations of the imagination; and I suppose that as with all creations of the imagination I have been thinking of them from the point of view of style, that is to say of their style. When we think of Jove, while we take him for granted as the symbol of omnipotence, the ruler of mankind, we do not fear him. He does have a superhuman size, but at least not so superhuman as to amaze and intimidate us. He has a large head and a beard and is a relic, a relic that makes a kindly impression on us and reminds us of stories that we have heard about him. All of the noble images of all of the gods have been profound and most of them have been forgotten. To speak of the origin and end of gods is not a light matter. It is to speak of the origin and end of eras of human belief. And while it is easy to look back on those that have disappeared as if they were the playthings of cosmic make-believe, and on those that made petitions to them and honored them and received their benefits as legendary innocents, we are bound, nevertheless, to concede that the gods were personae of a peremptory elevation and glory. It would be wrong to look back to them as if they had existed in some indigence of the spirit. They were in fact, as we see them now, the clear giants of a vivid time, who in the style of their beings made the style of the gods and the gods themselves one.

This brings me to the third idea, which is this: In an age of disbelief, or, what is the same thing, in a time that is largely humanistic, in one sense or another, it is for the poet to supply the satisfactions of belief, in his measure and in his style. I say in his measure to indicate that the figures of the philosopher, the artist, the teacher, the moralist and other figures, including the poet, find themselves, in such a time, to be figures of an importance greatly enhanced by the requirements both of the individual and of society; and I say in his style by way of confining the poet to his role and thereby of intensifying that role. It is this that I want to talk about today. I want to try to formulate a conception of perfection in poetry with reference to the present time and the near future and to speculate on the activities possible to it as it deploys itself throughout the lives of men and women. I think of it as a role of the utmost seriousness. It is, for one thing, a spiritual role. One might stop to draw an ideal portrait of the poet. But that would be parenthetical. In any case, we do not say that the philosopher, the artist or the teacher is to take the place of the gods. Just so, we do not say that the poet is to take the place of the gods.

To see the gods dispelled in mid-air and dissolve like clouds is one of the great human experiences. It is not as if they had gone over the horizon to disappear for a time; nor as if they had been overcome by other gods of greater power and profounder knowledge. It is simply that they came to nothing. Since we have always shared all things with them and have always had a part of their strength and, certainly, all of their knowledge, we shared likewise this experience of annihilation. It was their annihilation, not ours, and yet it left us feeling that in a measure, we, too, had been annihilated. It left us feeling dispossessed and alone in a solitude, like children without parents, in a home that seemed deserted, in which the amicable rooms and halls had taken on a look of hardness and emptiness. What was most extraordinary is that they left no mementos behind, no thrones, no mystic rings, no texts either of the soil or of the soul. It was as if they had never inhabited the earth. There was no crying out for their return. They were not forgotten because they had been a part of the glory of the earth. At the same time, no man ever muttered a petition in his heart for the restoration of those unreal shapes. There was always in every man the increasingly human self, which instead of remaining the observer, the nonparticipant, the delinquent, became constantly more and more all there was or so it seemed; and whether it was so or merely seemed so still left it for him to resolve life and the world in his own terms.

Thinking about the end of the gods creates singular attitudes in the mind of the thinker. One attitude is that the gods of classical mythology were merely aesthetic projections. They were not the objects of belief.

They were expressions of delight. Perhaps delight is too active a word. It is true that they were engaged with the future world and the immortality of the soul. It is true, also, that they were the objects of veneration and therefore of religious dignity and sanctity. But in the blue air of the Mediterranean these white and a little colossal figures had a special propriety, a special felicity. Could they have been created for that propriety, that felicity? Notwithstanding their divinity, they were close to the people among whom they moved. Is it one of the normal activities of humanity, in the solitude of reality and in the unworthy treatment of solitude, to create companions, a little colossal as I have said, who, if not superficially explicative, are, at least, assumed to be full of the secret of things and who in any event bear in themselves even, if they do not always wear it, the peculiar majesty of mankind's sense of worth, neither too much nor too little? To a people of high intelligence, whose gods have benefited by having been accepted and addressed by the superior minds of a superior world, the symbolic paraphernalia of the very great becomes unnecessary and the very great become the very natural. However all that may be, the celestial atmosphere of these deities, their ultimate remote celestial residences are not matters of chance. Their fundamental glory is the fundamental glory of men and women, who being in need of it create it, elevate it, without too much searching of its identity.

The people, not the priests, made the gods. The personages of immortality were something more than the conceptions of priests, although they may have picked up many of the conceits of priests. Who were the priests? Who have always been the high priests of any of the gods? Certainly not those officials or generations of officials who administered rites and observed rituals. The great and true priest of Apollo was he that composed the most moving of Apollo's hymns. The really illustrious archimandrite of Zeus was the one that made the being of Zeus people the whole of Olympus and the Olympian land, just as the only marvelous bishops of heaven have always been those that made it seem like heaven. I said a moment ago that we had not forgotten the gods. What is it that we remember of them? In the case of those masculine do we remember their ethics or is it their port and mien, their size, their color, not to speak of their adventures, that we remember? In the case of those feminine do we remember, as in the case of Diana, their fabulous chastity or their beauty? Do we remember those masculine in any way differently from the way in which we remember Ulysses and other men of supreme interest and excellence? In the case of those feminine do we remember Venus in any way differently from the way in which we remember Penelope and other women of much mark and feeling? In short, while the priests helped to realize the gods, it was the people that spoke of them and to them and heard their replies.

Let us stop now and restate the ideas which we are considering in relation to one another. The first is that the style of a poem and the poem itself are one; the second is that the style of the gods and the gods themselves are one; the third is that in an age of disbelief, when the gods have come to an end, when we think of them as the aesthetic projections of a time that has passed, men turn to a fundamental glory of their own and from that create a style of bearing themselves in reality. They create a new style of a new bearing in a new reality. This third idea, then, may be made to conform to the way in which the other two have been expressed by saying that the style of men and men themselves are one. Now, if the style of a poem and poem itself are one; if the style of the gods and the gods themselves are one; and if the style of men and men themselves are one; and if there is any true relation between these propositions, it might well be the case that the parts of these propositions are interchangeable. Thus, it might be true that the style of a poem and the gods themselves are one; or that the style of the gods and the style of men are one; or that the style of a poem and the style of men are one. As we hear these things said, without having time to think about them, it sounds as if they might be true, at least as if there might be something to them. Most of us are prepared to listen patiently to talk of the identity of the gods and men. But where does the poem come in? And if my answer to that is that I am concerned primarily with the poem and that my purpose this morning is to elevate the poem to the level of one of the major significances of life and to equate it, for the purpose of discussion, with gods and men, I hope it will be clear that it comes in as the central interest, the fresh and foremost object.

If in the minds of men creativeness was the same thing as creation in the natural world, if a spiritual planet matched the sun, or if without any question of a spiritual planet, the light and warmth of spring revitalized all our faculties, as in a measure they do, all the bearings one takes, all the propositions one formulates would be within the scope of that particular domination. The trouble is, however, that men in general do not create in light and warmth alone. They create in darkness and coldness. They create when they are hopeless, in the midst of antagonisms, when they are wrong, when their powers are no longer subject to their control. They create as the ministers of evil. Here in New England at this very moment nothing but good seems to be returning; and in that good, particularly if we ignore the difference between men and the natural world, how easy it is suddenly to believe in the poem as one has never believed in it before, suddenly to require of it a meaning beyond what its words can possibly say, a sound beyond any giving of the ear, a motion beyond our previous knowledge of feeling. And, of course, our three ideas have not only to be thought of as deriving what they have in common from the intricacies of human nature as distinguished from what the things of the natural world have in common, derived from strengths like light and warmth. They have to be thought of with reference to the meaning of style. Style is not something applied. It is something inherent, something that permeates. It is of the nature of that in which it is found, whether the poem, the manner of a god, the bearing of a man. It is not a dress. It may be said to be a voice that is inevitable. A man has no choice about his style. When he says I am my style the truth reminds him that it is his style that is himself. If he says, as my poem is, so are my gods and so am I, the truth remains quiet and broods on what he has said. He knows that the gods of China are always Chinese; that the gods of Greece are always Greeks and that all gods are created in the images of their creators; and he sees in these circumstances the operation of a style, a basic law. He observes the uniform enhancement of all things within the category of the imagination. He sees, in the struggle between the perfectible and the imperfectible, how the perfectible prevails, even though it falls short of perfection.

It is no doubt true that the creative faculties operate alike on poems, gods and men up to a point. They are always the same faculties. One might even say that the things created are always the same things. In case of a universal artist, all of his productions are his peculiar own. When we are dealing with racial units of the creative faculties all of the productions of one unit resemble one another. We say of a painting that it is Florentine. But we say the same thing and with equal certainty of a piece of sculpture. There is no difficulty in arguing about the poems, gods and men of Egypt or India that they look alike. But if the gods of India disappeared would not the poems of India and the men of India still remain alike? And if there were no poems, a new race of poets would produce poems that would take the place of the gods that had disappeared. What, then, is the nature of poetry in a time of disbelief? The truistic nature of some of the things that I have said shows how the free-will of the poet is limited. They demonstrate that the poetry of the future can never be anything purely eccentric and dissociated. The poetry of the present cannot be purely eccentric and dissociated. Eccentric and dissociated poetry is poetry that tries to exist or is intended to exist separately from the poem, that is to say in a style that is not identical with the poem. It never achieves anything more than a shallow mannerism, like something seen in a glass. Now, a time of disbelief is precisely a time in which the frequency of detached styles is greatest. I am not quite happy about the word detached. By detached, I mean the unsuccessful, the ineffective, the arbitrary, the literary, the nonumbilical, that which in its highest degree would still be words. For the style of the poem and the poem itself to be one there must be a mating and a marriage, not an arid love-song.

Yes: but the gods—now they come into it and make it a delicious subject, as if we were here together wasting our time on something that appears to be whimsical but turns out to be essential. They give to the subject just that degree of effulgence and excess, no more, no less, that the subject requires. Our first proposition, that the style of a poem and the poem itself are one was a definition of perfection in poetry. In the presence of the gods, or of their images, we are in the presence of perfection in created beings. The gods are a definition of perfection in ideal creatures. These remarks expound the second proposition that the style of the gods and the gods themselves are one. The exhilaration of their existence, their freedom from fate, their access to station, their liberty to command fix them in an atmosphere which thrills us as we share it with them. But these are merely attributes. What matters is their manner, their style, which tells us at once that they are as we wished them to be, that they have fulfilled us, that they are us but purified, magnified, in an expansion. It is their style that makes them gods, not merely privileged beings. It is their style most of all that fulfills themselves. If they lost all their privileges, their freedom from fate, their liberty to command, and yet still retained their style, they would still be gods, however destitute. That alone would destroy them, which deprived them of their style. When the time came for them to go, it was a time when their aesthetic had become invalid in the presence not of a greater aesthetic of the same kind, but of a different aesthetic, of which from the point of view of greatness, the difference was that of an intenser humanity. The style of the gods is derived from men. The style of the gods is derived from the style of men.

One has to pierce through the dithyrambic impressions that talk of the gods makes to the reality of what is being said. What is being said must be true and the truth of it must be seen. But the truth about the poet in a time of disbelief is not that he must turn evangelist. After all, he shares the disbelief of his time. He does not turn to Paris or Rome for relief from the monotony of reality. He turns to himself and he denies that reality was ever monotonous except in comparison. He asserts that the source of comparison having been eliminated, reality is returned, as if a shadow had passed and drawn after it and taken away whatever coating had concealed what lay beneath it. Yet the revelation of reality is not a part peculiar to a time of disbelief or, if it is, it is so in a sense singular to that time. Perhaps, the revelation of reality takes on a special meaning, without effort or consciousness on the part of the poet, at such a time. Why should a poem not change in sense when there is a fluctuation of the whole of appearance? Or why should it not change when we realize that the indifferent experience of life is the unique experience, the item of ecstasy which we have been isolating and reserving for another time and place, loftier and more secluded? There is inherent in the words *the revelation of reality* a suggestion that there is a reality of or within or beneath the surface of reality. There are many such realities through which poets constantly pass to and fro, without noticing the imaginary lines that divide one from the other. We were face to face with such a transition at the outset, for Baudelaire's line

> A long time I passed beneath an entrance roof

opens like a voice heard in a theatre and a theatre is a reality within a reality. The most provocative of all realities is that reality of which we never lose sight but never see solely as it is. The revelation of that particular reality or of that particular category of realities is like a series of paintings of some natural object affected, as the appearance of any natural object is affected, by the passage of time, and the changes that ensue, not least in the painter. That the revelation of reality has a character or quality peculiar to this time or that or, what is intended to be the same thing, that it is affected by states of mind, is elementary. The line from Baudelaire will not have the same effect on everyone at all times, any more than it will continue to have the same effect on the same person constantly. I remember that when a friend of mine in Ireland quoted the line, a few years ago, in a letter, my feeling about it was that it was a good instance of the value of knowing people of different educations. The chances are that my friend in Dublin and I have done much the same reading. The chances are, also, that we have retained many different things. For instance, this man had chosen Giorgione as the painter that meant most to him. For my own part, Giorgione would not have occurred to me. I should like you to be sure that in speaking of the revelation of reality I am not attempting to forecast the poetry of the future. It would be logical to conclude that, since a time of disbelief is also a time of truth-loving and since I have emphasized that I recognize that what I am trying to say is nothing unless it is true and that the truth of it must be seen, I think that the main characteristic of the poetry of the future or the near future will be an absence of the poetic. I do not think that. I cannot see what value it would have if I did, except as a value to me personally. If there is a logic that controls poetry, which everything that I have been saying may illustrate, it is not the narrow logic that exists on the level of prophecy. That there is a larger logic I have no doubt. But certainly it has to be large enough to allow for a good many irrelevancies.

One of the irrelevancies is the romantic. It looks like something completely contemptible in the light of literary intellectualism and cynicism. The romantic, however, has a way of renewing itself. It can be said of the romantic, just as it can be said of the imagination, that it can never effectively touch the same thing twice in the same way. It is partly because the romantic will not be what has been romantic in the past that it is preposterous to think of confining poetry hereafter to the relevation of reality. The whole effort of the imagination is toward the production of the romantic. When, therefore, the romantic is in abeyance, when it is discredited, it remains true that there is always an unknown romantic and that the imagination will not be forever denied. There is something a little romantic about the idea that the style of a poem and the poem itself are one. It seems to be a much more broadly romantic thing to say that the style of the gods and the gods themselves are one. It is completely romantic to say that the style of men and men themselves are one. To collect and collate these ideas of disparate things may seem to pass beyond the romantic to the fantastic. I hope, however, that you will agree that if each one of these ideas is valid separately, or more or less valid, it is permissible to have brought them together as a collective source of suppositions. What is romantic in all of them is the idea of style which I have not defined in any sense uniformly common to all three. A poem is a restricted creation of the imagination. The gods are the creation of the imagination at its utmost. Men are a part of reality. The gradations of romance noticeable as the sense of style is used with reference to these three, one by one, are relevant to the difficulties of the imagination in a truth-loving time. These difficulties exist only as one foresees them. They may never exist at all. An age in which the imagination might be expected to become part of time's *rejectamenta* may behold it established and protected and enthroned on one of the few ever-surviving thrones; and, to our surprise, we may find posted in the portico of its eternal dwelling, on the chief portal, among the morning's ordinances, three regulations which if they were once rules of art will then have become rules of conduct. By that time the one that will matter most is likely to be the last, that the style of man is man himself, which is about what we have been saying.

It comes to this that we use the same faculties when we write poetry that we use when we create gods or when we fix the bearing of men in reality. That this is obvious does not make the statement less. On the contrary, it makes the statement more, because its obviousness is that of the truth. The three ideas are sources of perfection. They are of such a nature that they are instances of aesthetic ideas tantamount to moral ideas, a subject precious in itself but beyond our scope today. For today, they mean that however one time may differ from another, there are always available to us the faculties of the past, but always vitally new and strong, as the sources of perfection today and tomorrow. The unity of style and the poem itself is a unity of language and life that exposes both in a supreme sense. Its collation with the unity of style and the gods and the unity of style and men is intended to demonstrate this.

13

Is There Any Poetic Writing?
from *Writing Degree Zero*

Roland Barthes

In the classical period, prose and poetry are quantities, their difference can be measured; they are neither more nor less separated than two different numbers, contiguous like them, but dissimilar because of the very difference in their magnitudes. If I use the word prose for a minimal form of speech, the most economical vehicle for thought, and if I use the letters a, b, c for certain attributes of language, which are useless but decorative, such as metre, rhyme or the ritual of images, all the linguistic surface will be accounted for in M. Jourdain's * double equation:

Poetry = Prose + a + b + c
Prose = Poetry − a − b − c

whence it clearly follows that Poetry is always different from Prose. But this difference is not one of essence, it is one of quantity. It does not, therefore, jeopardize the unity of language, which is an article of classical dogma. One may effect a different dosage in manner of speech, ac-

* Molière's *Bourgeois Gentilhomme*.

cording to the social occasion: here, prose or rhetoric, there, poetry or precosity, in accordance with a whole ritual of expression laid down by good society, but there remains everywhere a single language, which reflects the eternal categories of the mind. Classical poetry is felt to be merely an ornamental variation of prose, the fruit of an *art* (that is, a technique), never a different language, or the product of a particular sensibility. Any poetry is then only the decorative equation, whether allusive or forced, of a possible prose which is latent, virtually and potentially, in any conceivable manner of expression. "Poetic," in the days of classicism, never evokes any particular domain, any particular depth of feeling, any special coherence, or separate universe, but only an individual handling of a verbal technique, that of "expressing oneself" according to rules more artistic, therefore more sociable, than those of conversation, in other terms, the technique of projecting out an inner thought, springing fully armed from the Mind, a speech which is made more socially acceptable by virtue of the very conspicuousness of its conventions.

We know that nothing of this structure remains in modern poetry, which springs not from Baudelaire but from Rimbaud, unless it is in cases where one takes up again, in a revised traditional mode, the formal imperatives of classical poetry: henceforth, poets give to their speech the status of a closed Nature, which covers both the function and the structure of language. Poetry is then no longer a Prose either ornamental or shorn of liberties. It is a quality *sui generis* and without antecedents. It is no longer an attribute but a substance, and therefore it can very well renounce signs, since it carries its own nature within itself, and does not need to signal its identity outwardly: poetic language and prosaic language are sufficiently separate to be able to dispense with the very signs of their difference.

Furthermore, the alleged relations between thought and language are reversed; in classical art, a ready-made thought generates an utterance which "expresses" or "translates" it. Classical thought is devoid of duration, classical poetry has it only in such degree as is necessary to its technical arrangement. In modern poetics, on the contrary, words produce a kind of formal continuum from which there gradually emanates an intellectual or emotional density which would have been impossible without them; speech is then the solidified time of a more spiritual gestation, during which the "thought" is prepared, installed little by little by the contingency of words. This verbal luck, which will bring down the ripe fruit of a meaning, presupposes therefore a poetic time which is no longer that of a "fabrication," but that of a possible adventure, the meeting-point of a sign and an intention. Modern poetry is opposed to classical art by a difference which involves the whole structure of language, without leaving between those two types of poetry anything in common except the same sociological intention.

The economy of classical language (Prose and Poetry) is relational, which means that in it words are abstracted as much as possible in the interest of relationships. In it, no word has a density by itself, it is hardly the sign of a thing, but rather the means of conveying a connection. Far from plunging into an inner reality consubstantial to its outer configuration, it extends, as soon as it is uttered, towards other words, so as to form a superficial chain of intentions. A glance at the language of mathematics will perhaps enable us to grasp the relational nature of classical prose and poetry: we know that in mathematical language, not only is each quantity provided with a sign, but also that the relations between these quantities are themselves transcribed, by means of a sign expressing operative equality or difference. It may be said that the whole movement of mathematical flow derives from an explicit reading of its relations. The language of classicism is animated by an analogous, although of course less rigid, movement: its "words", neutralized, made absent by rigorous recourse to a tradition which desiccates their freshness, avoid the phonetic or semantic accident which would concentrate the flavour of language at one point and halt its intellectual momentum in the interest of an unequally distributed enjoyment. The classical flow is a succession of elements whose density is even; it is exposed to the same emotional pressure, and relieves those elements of any tendency towards an individual meaning appearing at all invented. The poetic vocabulary itself is one of usage, not of invention: images in it are recognizable in a body; they do not exist in isolation; they are due to long custom, not to individual creation. The function of the classical poet is not therefore to find new words, with more body or more brilliance, but to follow the order of an ancient ritual, to perfect the symmetry or the conciseness of a relation, to bring a thought exactly within the compass of a metre. Classical conceits involve relations, not words: they belong to an art of expression, not of invention. The words, here, do not, as they later do, thanks to a kind of violent and unexpected abruptness, reproduce the depth and singularity of an individual experience; they are spread out to form a surface, according to the exigencies of an elegant or decorative purpose. They delight us because of the formulation which brings them together, not because of their own power or beauty.

True, classical language does not reach the functional perfection of the relational network of mathematics: relations are not signified, in it, by any special signs, but only by accidents of form and disposition. It is the restraint of the words in itself, their alignment, which achieves the relational nature of classical discourse. Overworked in a restricted number of ever-similar relations, classical words are on the way to becoming an algebra where rhetorical figures of speech, clichés, function as virtual linking devices; they have lost their density and gained a more interrelated state of speech; they operate in the manner of chemical valences, outlining a verbal area full of symmetrical connections, junctions and networks from which arise, without the respite afforded by wonder, fresh intentions towards signification. Hardly have the fragments of classical discourse yielded their meaning than they become messengers or harbingers, carrying ever further a meaning which refuses to settle within the depths of a word, but tries instead to spread widely enough to become a total gesture of intellection, that is, of communication.

Now the distortion to which Hugo tried to subject the Alexandrine, which is of all meters the most interrelational, already contains the whole future of modern poetry, since what is attempted is to eliminate the intention to establish relationships and to produce instead an explosion of words. For modern poetry, since it must be distinguished from classical poetry and from any type of prose, destroys the spontaneously functional nature of language, and leaves standing only its lexical basis. It retains only the outward shape of relationships, their music, but not their reality. The Word shines forth above a line of relationships emptied of their content, grammar is bereft of its purpose, it becomes prosody and is no longer anything but an inflection which lasts only to present the Word. Connections are not properly speaking abolished, they are merely reserved areas, a parody of themselves, and this void is necessary for the density of the Word to rise out of a magic vacuum, like a sound and a sign devoid of background, like "fury and mystery."

In classical speech, connections lead the word on, and at once carry it towards a meaning which is an ever-deferred project; in modern poetry, connections are only an extension of the word, it is the Word which is "the dwelling place," it is rooted like a *fons et origo* in the prosody of functions, which are perceived but unreal. Here, connections only fascinate, and it is the Word which gratifies and fulfills like the sudden revelation of a truth. To say that this truth is of a poetic order is merely to say that the Word in poetry can never be untrue, because it is a whole; it shines with an infinite freedom and prepares to radiate towards innumerable uncertain and possible connections. Fixed connections being abolished, the word is left only with a vertical project, it is like a monolith, or a pillar which plunges into a totality of meanings, reflexes and recollections: it is a sign which stands. The poetic word is here an act without immediate past, without environment, and which holds forth only the dense shadow of reflexes from all sources which are associated with it. Thus under each Word in modern poetry there lies a sort of existential geology, in which is gathered the total content of the Name, instead of a chosen content as in classical prose and poetry. The Word is no longer guided *in advance* by the general intention of a socialized discourse; the consumer of poetry, deprived of the guide of selective connections, encounters the Word frontally, and receives it as an absolute quantity, accompanied by all its possible associations. The Word, here, is encyclopaedic, it contains simultaneously all the acceptations from which a relational discourse might have required it to choose. It therefore achieves a state which is possible only in the dictionary or in poetry—places where the noun can live without its article—and is reduced to a sort of zero degree, pregnant with all past and future specifications. The word here has a generic form; it is a category. Each poetic word is thus an unexpected object, a Pandora's box from which fly out all the potentialities of language; it is therefore produced and consumed with a peculiar curiosity, a kind of sacred relish. This Hunger of the Word, common to the whole of modern poetry, makes poetic speech terrible and inhuman. It initiates a discourse full of gaps and full of lights, filled with absences and overnourishing signs, without foresight or stability of intention, and thereby so opposed to the social function of language that merely to have recourse to a discontinuous speech is to open the door to all that stands above Nature.

For what does the rational economy of classical language mean, if not that Nature is a plenum, that it can be possessed, that it does not shy away or cover itself in shadows, but is in its entirety subjected to the toils of language? Classical language is always reducible to a persuasive continuum, it postulates the possibility of dialogue, it establishes a universe in which men are not alone, where words never have the terrible weight of things, where speech is always a meeting with the others. Classical language is a bringer of euphoria because it is immediately social. There is no genre, no written work of classicism which does not suppose a collective consumption, akin to speech; classical literary art is an object which circulates among several persons brought together on a class basis; it is a product conceived for oral transmission, for a consumption regulated by the contingencies of society: it is essentially a spoken language, in spite of its strict codification.

We have seen that on the contrary modern poetry destroyed relationships in language and reduced discourse to words as static things. This implies a reversal in our knowledge of Nature. The interrupted flow of the new poetic language initiates a discontinuous Nature, which is revealed only piecemeal. At the very moment when the withdrawal of functions obscures the relations existing in the world, the object in discourse assumes an exalted place: modern poetry is a poetry of the object. In it, Nature becomes a fragmented space, made of objects solitary and terrible, because the links between them are only potential. Nobody chooses for them a privileged meaning, or a particular use, or some service; nobody imposes a hierarchy on them, nobody reduces them to the manifestation of a mental behaviour, or of an intention, of some evidence of tenderness, in short. The bursting upon us of the poetic word then institutes an absolute object; Nature becomes a succession of verticalities, of objects, suddenly standing erect, and filled with all their possibilities: one of these can be only a landmark in an unfulfilled, and thereby terrible, world. These unrelated objects—words adorned with all the violence of their irruption, the vibration of which, though wholly mechanical, strangely affects the next word, only to die out immediately—these poetic words exclude men: there is no humanism of modern poetry. This erect discourse is full of terror, that is to say, it relates man not to other men, but to the most inhuman images in Nature: heaven, hell, holiness, childhood, madness, pure matter, etc.

At such a point, it is hardly possible to speak of a poetic mode of writing, for this is a language in which a violent drive towards autonomy destroys any ethical scope. The verbal gesture here aims at modifying Nature, it is the approach of a demiurge; it is not an attitude of the conscience but an act of coercion. Such, at least, is the language of those modern poets who carry their intention to the limit, and assume Poetry not as a spiritual exercise, a state of the soul or a placing of oneself in a situation, but as the splendour and freshness of a dream language. For such poets, it is as vain to speak about a mode of writing as of poetic feeling. Modern Poetry, in Char, for instance, is beyond this diffuse tone, this precious *aura,* which *are,* indeed, a mode of writing, usually termed poetic feeling. There is no objection to speaking of a poetic mode of writing concerning the classical writers and their epigones, or even concerning poetic prose in the manner of Gide's *Fruits of the Earth,* in which Poetry is in fact a certain linguistic ethos. In both cases, the mode of writing soaks up the style, and we can imagine that for people living in the seventeenth century, it was not easy to perceive an *immediate* difference between Racine and Pradon (and even less a difference of a poetic kind), just as it is not easy for a modern reader to pass judgment on those contemporary poets who use the same uniform and indecisive poetic mode of writing, because for them Poetry is a *climate* which means, essentially, a linguistic convention. But when the poetic language radically questions Nature by virtue of its very structure, without any resort to the content of the discourse and without falling back on some ideology, there is no mode of writing left, there are only styles, thanks to which man turns his back on society and confronts the world of objects without going through any of the forms of History or of social life.

Translated by Annette Lavers
and Colin Smith

14

The Representation of Nature in Contemporary Physics

Werner Heisenberg

The problems of modern art, so frequently and passionately discussed in our time, force us to examine those foundations which form the presupposition for every development of art, foundations which at other times are taken as self-evident. Indeed, the question has been raised whether the relation of modern man toward nature differs so fundamentally from that of former times that this difference alone is responsible for a completely different point of departure for the fine arts in contemporary culture. Certainly the relation of our period toward nature hardly finds its expression, as it did in earlier centuries, in a developed natural philosophy; rather, it is determined mainly by modern science and technology.

For this reason it is worthwhile to consider the view of nature held by modern science, and in particular by contemporary physics. From the start, however, a reservation must be made: there is little ground for believing that the current world view of science has directly influenced the development of modern art or could have done so. Yet we may believe that the changes in the foundations of modern science are an indication of profound transformations in the fundamentals of our existence, which on their part certainly have their effects in all areas of human experience. From this point of view it may be valuable for the artist to consider what changes have occurred during the last decade in the scientific view of nature.

I

First, let us consider the historical roots of recent science. When this science was being established in the seventeenth century by Kepler, Galileo, and Newton, the medieval image was at first still unbroken: man saw in nature God's creation. Nature was thought of as the work of God. It would have seemed senseless to people of that time to ask about the material world apart from its dependence on God. The words with which Kepler concluded the last volume of his *Harmony of the World* may be cited as a document of that era:

> I thank thee, O Lord, our Creator, that thou hast permitted me to look at the beauty in thy work of creation; I exult in the works of thy hands. See, I have here completed the work to which I felt called; I have earned interest from the talent that thou hast given me. I have proclaimed the glory of thy works to the people who will read these demonstrations, to the extent that the limitations of my spirit would allow.

In the course of a few decades, however, this relation of man toward nature altered fundamentally. As the scientist immersed himself in the details of natural processes, he recognized that it was in fact possible, following Galileo's example, to separate out individual processes of nature from their environment, describe them mathematically, and thus "explain" them. At the same time, it certainly became clear to him what an endless task was thus presented to the infant science. Newton could no longer see the world as the work of God, comprehensible only as a whole. His position toward nature is most clearly circumscribed by his well-known statement that he felt like a child playing at the seashore, happy whenever he found a smoother pebble or a more beautiful sea shell than usual, while the great ocean of truth lay unexplored before him. This transformation in the attitude of the scientist toward nature may perhaps be better understood when we consider that, to some Christian thought of the period, God in heaven seemed so far removed from earth that it became meaningful to view the earth apart from God. Thus there may even be justification in speaking of a specifically Christian form of godlessness in connection with modern science. This would explain why such a development has not taken place in other cultures. It is certainly no coincidence that precisely in that period, nature becomes the object of representation in the arts independent of religious themes. The same tendency comes to expression in science when nature is considered not only independent of God, but also independent of man, so that there is formed the ideal of an "objective" description or explanation of nature. Nevertheless, it must be emphasized that for Newton the sea shell is significant only because it comes from the great ocean of truth. Observing it is not yet an end in itself; rather, its study receives meaning through its relation to the whole.

In the subsequent era, the method of Newton's mechanics was successfully applied to ever wider realms of nature. This period attempted to separate out details of nature by means of experiments, to observe them objectively, and to understand the laws underlying them. It attempted to formulate interrelations mathematically and thus to arrive at "laws" that hold without qualification throughout the cosmos. By this path it finally succeeded in making the forces of nature serve our purposes through technology. The magnificent development of mechanics in the eighteenth century and of optics, heat theory, and heat technology in the nineteenth century bears witness to the power of this innovation.

In proportion to the success of this kind of science, it spread beyond the realm of daily experience into remote regions of nature that could only be disclosed with the aid of technology, which developed in conjunction with science. Newton's decisive realization was that the laws which govern the fall of a stone also determine the orbit of the moon around the earth and thus are applicable in cosmic dimensions also. In the years that followed, natural science began its victory march on a broad front into those remote regions of nature about which we may obtain information only by the detour of technology—that is, by using more or less complicated apparatus. Astronomy used the improved telescope to master ever more remote cosmic regions. Chemistry attempted to understand processes at the atomic level from the behavior of substances in chemical reactions. Experiments with the induction machine and the Voltaic pile gave the first insight into electrical phenomena that were still hidden from the daily life of that era. Thus the meaning of the word "nature" as an object of scientific research slowly changed; it became a collective concept for all those areas of experience into which man can penetrate through science and technology, whether or not they are given to him "naturally" in direct experience. The term *description* of nature also progressively lost its original significance as a representation intended to convey the most alive and imaginable picture possible of nature; instead, in increasing measure a mathematical description of nature was implied—that is, a collection of data concerning interrelations according to law in nature, precise and brief yet also as comprehensive as possible.

The expansion of the concept of nature that had half unconsciously been completed in this development did not yet have to be considered as a fundamental departure from the original aims of science; the decisive basic concepts were still the same for the expanded area of experience and for the original direct experience of nature. To the nineteenth century, nature appeared as a lawful process in space and time, in whose description it was possible to ignore as far as axioms were concerned, even if not in practice, both man and his interference in nature.

The permanent in the flux of phenomena was taken to be matter unchangeable in mass and capable of being moved by forces. Since chemical phenomena from the eighteenth century on had been successfully organized and interpreted through the atomistic hypothesis taken over from antiquity, it seemed plausible to consider the atoms, in the sense of classical natural philosophy, as the truly real, as the unchangeable building stones of matter. As in the philosophy of Democritus, sensual qualities of matter were taken as appearance; smell and color, temperature and toughness were not intrinsic properties of matter, but originated as interactions between matter and our senses and thus had to be explained through the arrangement and motion of the atoms and the effects of this arrangement on our senses. In this way the all-too-simple world view of nineteenth-century materialism was formed: the atoms, as intrinsically unchangeable beings, move in space and time and, through their mutual arrangement and motion, call forth the colorful phenomena of our sense world.

A first inroad into this simple world picture, though one not too dangerous, occurred in the second half of the last century through the development of electrical theory in which not matter but rather the force field had to be taken as the intrinsically real. Interactions between fields of force without a substance as carrier of the forces were less easily understandable than the materialistic conception of reality in atomic physics. An element of abstraction and lack of visualizability was brought into the otherwise apparently so obvious world view. That is why there was no dearth of attempts to return to the simple conception of matter in materialistic philosophy through the detour of a material ether that would carry these fields of force as elastic tensions. Such attempts, however, never quite managed to succeed. Nevertheless it was possible to be consoled by the fact that changes in fields of force could be considered as occurrences in space and time, describable objectively—that is, without consideration of the means of observation. Thus they corresponded to the generally accepted ideal of a process operating according to law in space and time. It was further possible to think of the force fields, since they can only be observed through their interaction with atoms, as called forth by the atoms, and thus to use them in a certain sense only in explaining the motions of atoms. To that extent, the atoms remained after all the intrinsically real; between them was empty space, which at most possessed a certain kind of reality as carrier of the force fields and of geometry.

For this world view it was not too significant that after the discovery of radioactivity near the end of the last century, the atoms of chemistry could no longer be taken as the final indivisible building blocks of matter but were themselves found to be composed of three types of basic building blocks, which we today call protons, neutrons, and electrons. This realization led in its practical consequences to the transmutation of the elements and to nuclear technology, and thus became tremendously important. As far as fundamental questions are concerned, however, nothing has changed now that we have recognized protons, neutrons, and electrons as the smallest building blocks of matter and interpret these as the intrinsically real. For the materialistic world view, it is important only that the possibility remains of taking these smallest constituents of the atoms as the final objective reality. On this foundation rested the coherent world view of the nineteenth and early twentieth centuries. Because of its simplicity it preserved for several decades its full powers of persuasion.

Precisely at this point profound changes in the foundations of atomic physics occurred in our century which lead away from the reality concept of classical atomism. It has turned out that the hoped-for objective reality of the elementary particles represents too rough a simplification of the true state of affairs and must yield to much more abstract conceptions. When we wish to picture to ourselves the nature of the existence of the elementary particles, we may no longer ignore the physical processes by which we obtain information about them. When we are observing objects of our daily experience, the physical process transmitting the observation of course plays only a secondary role. However, for the smallest building blocks of matter every process of observation causes a major disturbance; it turns out that we can no longer talk of the behavior of the particle apart from the process of observation. In consequence, we are finally led to believe that the laws of nature which we formulate mathematically in quantum theory deal no longer with the particles themselves but with our knowledge of the elementary particles. The question whether these particles exist in space and time "in themselves" can thus no longer be posed in this form. We can only talk about the processes that occur when, through the interaction of the particle with some other physical system such as a measuring instrument, the behavior of the particle is to be disclosed. The conception of the objective reality of the elementary particles has thus evaporated in a curious way, not into the fog of some new, obscure, or not yet understood reality concept, but into the transparent clarity of a mathematics that represents no longer the behavior of the elementary particles but rather our knowledge of this behavior. The atomic physicist has had to come to terms with the fact that his science is only a link in the endless chain of discussions of man with nature, but that it cannot simply talk of nature "as such." Natural science always presupposes man, and we must become aware of the fact that, as Bohr has expressed it, we are not only spectators but also always participants on the stage of life.

II

Before we can speak of the general implications arising out of this new situation in modern physics, it is necessary to discuss a development which is more important for practical purposes, namely the expansion of technology which has proceeded hand in hand with the growth of science. This technology has carried natural science from its origin in the West over the face of the earth and helped it to a central position in the thought of our time. In this process of development during the last two hundred years technology has always been both presupposition and consequence of natural science. It is presupposition because an extension and deepening of science often can take place only through a refinement of the means of observation. The invention of the telescope and microscope and the discovery of X-rays are examples. Technology, on the other hand, is also a consequence of science, since the technical exploitation of the forces of nature is in general only possible on the basis of a thorough knowledge of the natural laws of that particular realm of science.

Thus in the eighteenth and early nineteenth centuries there first developed a technology based on the utilization of mechanical processes. The machine at that stage often only imitated the actions of man's hand, whether in spinning and weaving or in the lifting of loads or the forging of large pieces of iron. Hence this form of technology was initially seen as an extension of the old crafts. It was understandable and obvious to the onlooker in the same way as the work of the craftsman, whose fundamental principles everyone knew even if the detailed techniques could not be copied by all. Even the introduction of the steam engine did not fundamentally change this character of technology; however, from this time on the expansion of technology could progress at a formerly unknown rate, for it now became possible to place the natural forces stored in coal in the service of man to perform his manual work for him.

A decisive transformation in the character of technology probably began with the technical utilization of electricity in the second half of the last century. It was hardly possible to speak any longer of a direct connection with the earlier crafts. Natural forces were now exploited that were almost unknown to people in direct experience of nature. For many people, even today, electricity has something uncanny about it; at the least it is often considered incomprehensible, though it is all around us. The high-voltage lines which one must not approach admittedly give us a kind of conceptual lesson concerning the force field employed by science, but basically this realm of nature remains foreign to us. Viewing the interior of a complicated electrical apparatus is sometimes unpleasant in the same way as watching a surgical operation.

Chemical technology also might be seen as a continuation of old crafts such as dyeing, tanning, and pharmacy. But here also the extent of the newly developed chemical technology from about the turn of the century no longer permits comparison with the earlier circumstances. Nuclear technology, finally, is concerned with the exploitation of natural forces to which every approach from the world of natural experience is lacking. Perhaps this technology, too, in the end will become as familiar to modern man as electricity, without which man can no longer conceive his environment. But the things that are daily around us do not for that reason become a part of nature in the original sense of the word. Perhaps, in the future, the many pieces of technical apparatus will as inescapably belong to man as the snail's house to the snail or the web to the spider. Even then, however, these machines would be more parts of our human organism than parts of surrounding nature.

Technology thus fundamentally interferes with the relation of nature to man, in that it transforms his environment in large measure and thereby incessantly and inescapably holds the scientific aspect of the world before his eyes. The claim of science to be capable of reaching out into the whole cosmos with a method that always separates and clarifies individual phenomena, and thus goes forward from relationship to relationship, is mirrored in technology which step by step penetrates new realms, transforms our environment before our eyes, and impresses our image upon it. In the same sense in which every detailed question in science is subordinate to the major task of understanding nature as a whole, so also does the smallest technical advance serve the general goal, that of enlarging the material power of man. The value of this goal is as little questioned as the value of natural knowledge in science, and the two aims coalesce in the banal slogan "Knowledge is Power." Probably it is possible to demonstrate in the cause of every technical process its subservience to this common goal; it is, on the other hand, characteristic for the whole development that the individual technical process is bound to the common goal in such an indirect way that one can hardly view it as part of a conscious plan for the accomplishment of this goal. Technology almost ceases to appear at such times as the product of conscious human effort for the spreading of material power. Instead it appears as a biological process on a large scale, in which the structures that are part of the human organism are transferred in ever larger measure to man's environment. Such a biological process would be outside man's control, for man can indeed do what he wills, but he cannot will what he wills.

III

It has often been said that the profound changes in our environment and our way of life in the technical age have also transformed our thinking in a dangerous way. Here, we are told, is the root of the crises by which our era is shaken—and by which modern art is shaped. But this objection is older than the technology and science of our time; technology and machines in a more primitive form have existed in much earlier times, so that men were forced to think about such questions in periods long past. Two and a half thousand years ago, the Chinese sage Chang Tsu spoke of the dangers to man of using machines. I would like to quote a section from his writings that is important for our subject:

> When Tsu-Kung came into the region north of the river Han, he saw an old man busy in his vegetable garden. He had dug ditches for watering. He himself climbed into the well, brought up a container full of water in his arms, and emptied it. He exerted himself to the utmost, but achieved very little.
>
> Tsu-Kung spoke: "There is an arrangement with which it is possible to fill a hundred ditches with water every day. With little effort

much is accomplished. Wouldn't you like to use it?" The gardener rose up, looked at him and said, "What would that be?"

Tsu-Kung said, "A lever is used, weighted at one end and light at the other. In this way water can be drawn, so that it gushes out. It is known as a draw-well."

At that, anger rose up in the face of the old man and he laughed, saying, "I have heard my teacher say: 'When a man uses a machine he carries on all his business in a machine-like manner. Whoever does his business in the manner of a machine develops a machine heart. Whoever has a machine heart in his breast loses his simplicity. Whoever loses his simplicity becomes uncertain in the impulses of his spirit. Uncertainty in the impulses of the spirit is something that is incompatible with truth.' Not that I am unfamiliar with such devices; I am ashamed to use them."

That this ancient tale contains a considerable amount of truth, everyone of us will agree; "uncertainty in the impulses of the spirit" is perhaps one of the most telling descriptions we can give to the condition of man in the present crisis. Nevertheless, although technology, the machine, has spread over the world to an extent that the Chinese sage could not have imagined, two thousand years later the world's finest works of art are still being created and the simplicity of the soul of which the philosopher spoke has never been completely lost. Instead, in the course of the centuries it has shown itself, sometimes weakly, sometimes powerfully, and it has borne fruit again and again. Finally, the ascent of man has, after all, occurred through the development of tools; thus technology cannot carry the whole blame for the fact that the consciousness of this interconnection has in many places been lost.

Perhaps we will come nearer the truth if the sudden and—measured by earlier changes—unusually swift diffusion of technology in the last fifty years is held responsible for the many difficulties. The speed of technological transformation, in contrast to that of earlier centuries, leaves no time to mankind in which to adjust to the new conditions of life. But even this is probably not the correct or the complete explanation of why our time seems to face a new situation, hardly without analogy in history.

We have already mentioned that the changes in the foundations of modern science may perhaps be viewed as symptoms of shifts in the fundamentals of our existence which then express themselves simultaneously in many places, be it in changes in our way of life or our usual thought forms, be it in external catastrophes, wars, or revolutions. When one attempts to grope one's way from the situation in modern science to the fundamentals that have begun to shift, one has the impression that it is not too crude a simplification of the state of affairs to assert that for the first time in the course of history man on earth faces only himself, that he finds no longer any other partner or foe. This observation applies first of all in a commonplace way in the battle of man against outward dangers. In earlier times he was endangered by wild animals, disease, hunger, cold, and other forces of nature, and in this strife every extension of technology represented a strengthening of his position and therefore progress. In our time, when the earth is becoming ever more densely settled, the narrowing of the possibilities of life and thus the threat to man's existence originates above all from other people, who also assert their claim to the goods of the earth. In such a confrontation, the extension of technology need no longer be an indication of progress.

The statement that in our time man confronts only himself is valid in the age of technology in a still wider sense. In earlier epochs man saw himself opposite nature. Nature, in which dwelt all sorts of living beings, was a realm existing according to its own laws, and into it man somehow had to fit himself. We, on the other hand, live in a world so completely transformed by man that, whether we are using the machines of our daily life, taking food prepared by machines, or striding through landscapes transformed by man, we invariably encounter structures created by man, so that in a sense we always meet only ourselves. Certainly there are parts of the earth where this process is nowhere near completion, but sooner or later the dominion of man in this respect will be complete.

This new situation becomes most obvious to us in science, in which it turns out, as I have described earlier, that we can no longer view "in themselves" the building blocks of matter which were originally thought of as the last objective reality; that they refuse to be fixed in any way in space and time; and that basically we can only make our knowledge of these particles the object of science. The aim of research is thus no longer knowledge of the atoms and their motion "in themselves," separated from our experimental questioning; rather, right from the beginning, we stand in the center of the confrontation between nature and man, of which science, of course, is only a part. The familiar classification of the world into subject and object, inner and outer world, body and soul, somehow no longer quite applies, and indeed leads to difficulties. In science, also, the object of research is no longer nature in itself but rather nature exposed to man's questioning, and to this extent man here also meets himself.

Our time has clearly been given the task of coming to terms with this new situation in all aspects of life, and only when this is accomplished will man be able to regain that "certainty in the impulses of the spirit" talked of by the Chinese sage. The way to this goal will be long and arduous, and we do not know what stations of the cross are still ahead. But if indications are sought as to the nature of the way, it may be permissible to consider once more the example of the exact sciences.

In quantum theory, we accepted the described situation when it became possible to represent it mathematically and when, therefore, in every case we could say clearly and without danger of logical contradiction how the result of an experiment would turn out. We thus resigned ourselves to the new situation the moment the ambiguities were removed. The mathematical formulas indeed no longer portray nature, but rather our knowledge of nature. Thus we have renounced a form of natural description that was familiar for centuries and still was taken as the obvious goal of all exact science even a few decades ago. It could also be said for the present that we have accepted the situation in the realm of modern atomic physics only because our experience can in fact be correctly represented in that area. As soon as we look at the philosophical interpretations of quantum theory, we find that opinions still differ widely; the view is occasionally heard that this new form of natural description is not yet satisfying since it does not correspond to the earlier ideal of scientific truth, and hence is to be taken only as another symptom of the crisis of our time, and in any case is not the final formulation.

It will be useful to discuss in this connection the concept of scientific truth in somewhat more general terms and to ask for criteria as to when an item of scientific knowledge can be called consistent and final. For the moment, a more external criterion: As long as any realm of the intellectual life is developing steadily and without inner break, specific detailed questions are presented to the individual working in this area, questions that are in a sense problems of technique, whose solution is certainly not an end in itself but appears valuable in the interest of the larger relationship that alone is important. These detailed problems are presented to us, they do not have to be sought, and working on them is the presupposition for collaborating at the larger relationship. In the same sense, medieval stone masons endeavored to copy as accurately as possible the folds of garments, and the solution of their special problem was necessary because the folds of the garments of the saints were part of the large religious relationship that was the real aim. In a similar way, special problems have always presented themselves in modern science, and work on these is the presupposition for the understanding of the large relationship. These questions presented themselves, also, in the development of the last fifty years; they did not have to be sought. And the aim was always the same: the large interrelatedness of the laws of nature. In this sense, purely from the outside, there seems to be no basis for any break in the continuity of exact science.

With respect to the finality of the results, however, we should remember that in the realm of exact science final solutions are continually being found for certain delimited areas of experience. The problems, for instance, which could be studied with the concepts of Newtonian mechanics found their final answer for all time through Newton's laws and the mathematical deductions drawn from them. These solutions, to be sure, do not extend beyond the concepts and questions of Newtonian mechanics. Thus electrical theory, for instance, was not accessible to analysis by these concepts. New systems of concepts emerged in the exploration of this new realm of experience with whose help the laws of electricity could be mathematically formulated in their final form. The word "final" in connection with exact science evidently means that we will always find closed, mathematically describable systems of concepts and laws that fit certain areas of experience, are valid in them anywhere in the universe, and are incapable of modification or improvement. It cannot, however, be expected that these concepts and laws will later be suitable for the representation of new realms of experience. Only in this limited sense, therefore, can the concepts and laws of quantum theory be designated as final, and only in this limited sense can it ever happen that scientific knowledge finds its final fixation in mathematical or any other language.

Similarly, certain philosophies of justice assume that justice always exists but that, in general, in every new legal case justice must be found anew, that at all events the written law always covers only limited areas of life and therefore cannot be everywhere binding. Exact science also goes forward in the belief that it will be possible in every new realm of experience to understand nature, but what the word "understand" might signify is not at all predetermined. The natural knowledge of earlier epochs, fixed in mathematical formulas, might be "final," but not in any sense always applicable. This state of affairs makes it impossible to base articles of belief that are to be binding for one's bearing in life on scientific knowledge alone. The establishment of such articles of faith could only be based on such "fixed" scientific knowledge, a knowledge only applicable to limited realms of experience. The assertion often found at the beginning of creeds originating in our time that they deal not with belief but with scientifically based knowledge, thus contains an inner contradiction and rests on a self-deception.

Nevertheless, this realization must not mislead us into underestimating the firmness of the ground on which the edifice of exact science has been built. The concept of scientific truth basic to natural science can bear many kinds of natural understanding. Not only the science of past centuries but also modern atomic physics is based on it. Hence it follows that one can come to terms with a knowledge situation in which an objectification of the process of nature is no longer possible, and that one should be able to find our relation to nature within it.

When we speak of a picture of nature provided by contemporary exact science, we do not actually mean any longer a picture of nature, but rather a picture of our relation to nature. The old compartmentalization of the world into an objective process in space and time, on the one hand, and the soul in which this process is mirrored, on the other—that is, the Cartesian differentiation of *res cogitans* and *res extensa*—is no longer suitable as the starting point for the understanding of modern science. In the field of view of this science there appears above all the network of relations between man and nature, of the connections through which we as physical beings are dependent parts of nature and at the same time, as human beings, make them the object of our thought and actions. Science no longer is in the position of observer of nature, but rather recognizes itself as part of the interplay between man and nature. The scientific method of separating, explaining, and arranging becomes conscious of its limits, set by the fact that the employment of this procedure changes and transforms its object; the procedure can no longer keep its distance from the object. The world view of natural science thus ceases to be a view of "natural" science in its proper sense.

The clarification of these paradoxes in a narrow segment of science has certainly not achieved much for the general situation of our time, in which, to repeat a simplification used earlier, we suddenly and above all confront ourselves. The hope that the extension of man's material and spiritual power always represents progress thus finds a limit, even though it may not yet be clearly visible. The dangers are the greater, the more violently the wave of optimism engendered by the belief in progress surges against this limit. Perhaps the nature of the danger here discussed can be made clearer by another metaphor. With the seemingly unlimited expansion of his material might, man finds himself in the position of a captain whose ship has been so securely built of iron and steel that the needle of his compass no longer points to the north, but only toward the ship's mass of iron. With such a ship no destination can be reached; it will move aimlessly and be subject in addition to winds and ocean currents. But let us remember the state of affairs of modern physics: the danger only exists so long as the captain is unaware that his compass does not respond to the earth's magnetic forces. The moment the situation is recognized, the danger can be considered as half removed. For the captain who does not want to travel in circles but desires to reach a known—or unknown—destination will find ways and means for determining the orientation of his ship. He may start using modern types of compasses that are not affected by the iron of the ship, or he may navigate, as in former times, by the stars. Of course we cannot decree the visibility or lack of visibility of the stars, and in our time perhaps they are only rarely visible. In any event, awareness that the hopes engendered by the belief in progress will meet a limit implies the wish not to travel in circles but to reach a goal. To the extent that we reach clarity about this limit, the limit itself may furnish the first firm hold by which we can orient ourselves anew.

Perhaps from this comparison with modern science we may draw hope that we may here be dealing with a limit for certain forms of expansion of human activity, not, however, with a limit to human activity as such. The space in which man as spiritual being is developing has more dimensions than the one within which he has moved forward in the preceding centuries. It follows that in the course of long stretches of time the conscious acceptance of this limit will perhaps lead to a certain stabilization in which the thoughts of men will again arrange themselves around a common center. Such a development may perhaps also supply a new foundation for the development of art; but to speak about that does not behoove the scientist.

Translated by O. T. Benfey

15

The Instrumentally Extended World

P. W. Bridgman

[Let us] examine to what extent the instrumentally extended World is similar to the world of direct sense perception. The situation with regard to length is fairly straightforward, and I have examined it at some length in *The Logic of Modern Physics*. The most important property of the space of ordinary perception is its Euclidean character. This property continues a long way toward the very small, perhaps even as far as the dimensions of the nucleus, 10^{-13} centimeters in diameter. Of course the operational meaning of microscopic length continually changes, and eventually the only meaning is that certain equations are satisfied when complicated functions of macroscopically measured quantities are substituted into them. Beyond the dimensions of the nucleus the resemblance to the geometric world of experience gets vaguer and vaguer, until with the minimum lengths of Heisenberg of 10^{-23} cm or the characteristic lengths of Eddington of 10^{-43} cm all immediate physical significance would seem to be lost.

When it comes to time, the instrumentally extended time loses contact with the time of perception much earlier. Instrumentally extended time behaves like the time of perception so long as the time of perception is also the time of mechanics, that is, for intervals as short as 10^{-8} seconds, or perhaps even shorter. In this range we can construct crystal clocks whose vibrations satisfy the ordinary mechanical equations of elasticity theory, and which have an accuracy greater than that of most timepieces. The accuracy of atomic clocks, in which the time is the time of the equations of electrodynamics, is even greater.

The question whether small-scale instrumental time is the same sort of thing as large-scale instrumental time is in some respects equivalent to asking whether there are clocks for small-scale time. Now the question of what is a clock for even large-scale time is not altogether simple. In the first instance the time of ordinary experience is a nebulous sort of thing, characterized only by the relations "earlier than" and "later than," but without any obvious basis for making it more precisely numerical. The situation is much the same is it is with regard to temperature. Here we start with a physiological temperature, characterized only by the relations hotter than and colder than, and eventually are able to turn this into something more precise by coupling temperature to other sorts of phenomena which are capable of exact numerical specification. For temperature the additional requirement is provided by the second law of thermodynamics—temperature is presently defined so that the second law holds in terms of it. The definition is not a mere convention as it would be if the second law were formulated with respect to a unique set of phenomena (for example, the thermal phenomena in gaseous hydrogen), but the character of convention is eliminated by the fact that the second law is universal for all substances. In the same way with time and clocks, Newtonian mechanics holds for time measured with a "clock", the clock being, I think, otherwise undefined. If one wants a formal definition the scheme has to be inverted and a clock defined as such an instrument that Newtonian mechanics holds when time is measured with it. Again, because of the universal validity of Newtonian mechanics, we are not dealing with a pure convention—a clock constructed to make Newtonian mechanics hold for one particular system would at the same time make it hold for all mechanical systems.

At first glance it would seem that we are here defining a physical concept in terms of its properties, something forbidden operationally, but closer examination will show that this is only apparent. For the prescription, "Construct the clock so that Newtonian mechanics holds," can be turned into a specific prescription with each step uniquely determined. For instance, the clock may be a body falling from rest, the indicated time to be determined by the position of the falling body on scale. The scale is then to be graduated to give the time calculated by the ordinary laws for a falling body, that is, graduated so that $s = \frac{1}{2}gt^2$, where s is the distance of fall in centimeters. With a clock so constructed *any* mechanical phenomenon may be measured, and *all* will be found to satisfy the Newtonian equations.

It would seem that the same sort of attack must be made on the problem of short times. Can an instrument be made which will give numbers to short intervals of time in such a way that Newtonian mechanics holds in these short intervals? We have seen that the answer would certainly seem to be yes for times as short as 10^{-8} seconds. But for much shorter times one will probably have to change the definition of clock from "an instrument determined by Newtonian mechanics" to "an instrument determined by classical electrodynamics." We have such an instrument in the so-called atomic clocks. The consistency of short-wave phenomena down to wave lengths at least as short as 1 centimeter is another indication of the large-scale significance of times extended to at least the order of 10^{-10}. To give meaning to times still shorter one will probably be driven to lean on the indirect results of theory and be satisfied if one can develop a consistent theory of atomic and nuclear action that reproduces experiment. The time so accessible cannot well be less than the time required by light to travel across the diameter of the nucleus, or say times of the order of 10^{-23} seconds. As long as theory is successful we probably will be justified in continuing to handle time in the same way as we do the time of ordinary experience, which means using it formally in the same way in our equations. But what about times very much shorter? What about Eddington, who had a natural unit of time of 1.3×10^{-43} seconds and a unit of length of 4×10^{-33} centimeters, and who declares with regard to the unit of length: "But it is evident that this length must be the key to some essential structure." And what about Heisenberg, who talks about a minimum length and a discrete structure of space?

In any event it would seem that the question of the nature of time in the small cannot be separated from other sorts of thing—perhaps most generally, for very short times, the structure of the mathematical equations. This is, however, not different from what we find on the scale of everyday life—there is no such thing as time in and for itself—it gets its meaning and its measurability in conjunction with other things.

Among the properties of mechanically extended time are transitivity and additivity. That is, if event A is earlier than B and B is earlier than C, then A is earlier than C. Or, the time interval from A to B plus that from B to C is equal to that from A to C. In the world of direct perception this sort of thing by no means corresponds to direct experience when we deal with short times, but we are stopped by the "psychological present." Within this we have such phenomena as A being simultaneous with B and B simultaneous with C but A not simultaneous with C. It is typical of the intellectual temper of the times that we have no hesitation in giving priority to the time of instrumental extension and in seeking for an explanation of the phenomena of the psychological present within the framework suggested by our instrumentation. There is one respect, however, in which I am unable to divorce myself from the involvement of my concept of time with my introspectional experience. For me it is meaningless to talk of time going backward, although it is possible to set up a formal description of circumstances under which other people say that they would speak of time going backward.

There has been considerable discussion recently of time flowing backward (Margenau, Feynman, Reichenbach, Grünbaum). The meaning of a backward flow may be made a matter of pure definition, if one cares to, but such discussions seem to me to overlook the fact that the clock time of physics is concerned with only part of the temporal aspects of experience. It seems to me that the full time of experience has to be treated as an unanalyzable—our descriptions are in terms of it and there is nothing which we can recognize as more fundamental or which is capable of replacing it. What possible sort of experience can we formulate which we would describe as meaning that time had reversed its flow and was going backward? Would we not say that it was our clocks which were going backward in time, or that events were occurring again in the inverse order in time? If we are asked to explain why it is that time flows forward, and if we accept the view that "explanation" consists in reducing a situation to elements with which we are so familiar that we accept them without question, and if we take seriously the thesis that time is unanalyzable, then we must say that no explanation is possible of the forward flight of time because *there is nothing to explain*. To say that time flows forward is, in this context, a convention. This time of direct experience may be called psychological or introspectional time. As it emerges in consciousness it can only be accepted. It is essentially private, yet we all can talk together about it, just as we can talk together about our toothaches. It seems to me that the persistent endeavor of many people to ascribe a meaning to the backward flow of introspectional time, and their no less persistent failure, is a striking example of the nearly universal urge to get away from ourselves and of the impossibility of doing it. The "time" of the physicists above, for which it makes sense of sorts to flow backward, is a different sort of thing.

These remarks all apply to local time as distinguished from the extended time of general relativity theory. In the fuller context of extended time many other questions arise—some of these have been touched on in my *Logic of Modern Physics*.

Our world is essentially the world of our perceptions, and the nature of this world is indelibly colored by the nature of the psychological present. But this psychological present is essentially different from the present of an idealized extension of our world of instruments. The psychological present is a smeared-out totality in which we grasp whole visual fields in a single glance as units, and *see* objects moving at a single instant of time, whereas instrumentally we find structure in this temporal amorphousness of a fineness of scale presumably limited only by the frequencies of the atoms of our nervous systems. These frequencies are of the order of 10^{13} per second, so that if we take the duration of the psychological present as of the order of 0.01 second, we have here the possibility of instrumental detail nearly a million million times finer than that accessible to direct perception. There is room here for all the complexities of conscious experience, and for complexities not yet suspected. On a scale of this fineness the coherent wholes of conscious perception will get broken down into a succession of discretenesses, just as happens on a television screen. In fact, a due consideration of the implications of the movie or television screen might well have revolutionary repercussions on our outlook on the world around us. Even without the suggestion of the movie and television, a sufficiently acute analysis of our ordinary perceptions might have prepared us for this, because we can sometimes see that the apparently homogeneous scene which we take in at a glance is built up by the rapid shifting of attention from detail to detail.

The suggestion is not infrequently made by reputable physicists, Heisenberg, for example, that space and time may be discontinuous. This is usually taken to imply the existence of a minimum length and a minimum interval of time. Closely related to this is the view that there may be natural standards of length and time to be found in the direction of the very small, as, for example, by L. L. Whyte. Such natural standards, when found, would play something of the role of minimum lengths or times. The question for us is: what is the meaning of all this, and, in particular, if there are such things, how shall we recognize them experimentally?

Consider the discontinuities first. Under what experimental conditions would we want to speak of a discontinuous space? Now the concept of space is not to be disassociated from the positional aspects of the bodies which occupy it—in fact it may be defined in terms of those positional aspects. Discontinuous space therefore means something about our experience with bodies that occupy space. Imagine an apparatus as follows: a length-measuring apparatus, which consists of an optical projecting system by which any arbitrary body to be measured can be projected, enormously magnified, on a screen with a scale. The length of the body is then calculated from the position of the images of its end points and the optical magnification. If it should turn out that the manifold of numbers which we get in this way for the length of all possible objects under all possible circumstances was a discrete set with missing ranges of numbers, then we would probably want to say that space is discontinuous. Furthermore, we would probably want to say that the minimum differences between the numbers in our discrete manifold, if there is such, is the minimum length. But what a strange situation, and how shall we rationalize it? Shall we say that it is a matter of experiment that the end points of a body, or its other points too, for that matter, can occupy only certain discrete positions? And can we avoid asking *where* these discrete positions are, or what it is that determines that we have one particular set of discrete positions and not another, displaced with respect to it by half the minimum distance, say? The set of discrete positions must obviously be the same in all reference systems, and what does this mean except that the old absolute frame of reference has come back, with a fantastically fine granular structure and with the traditional difficulties of the classical ether enormously magnified? How shall we describe the motion of a body in such a system? Its points must jump from one position to the next—what determines when they shall jump, or when shall we say that they have jumped? The difficulties here appear enormous, but perhaps they are not insuperable.

The upshot would seem to be that if one wants to connote by space merely an aspect of the complex of all experimental happenings, then one can specify conditions which one would describe as discontinuous space, at least without running into self-contradiction. But if one wants to include in the concept of space the mental operations by which one correlates or thinks about the experimental findings, then discontinuous space does involve self-contradictory operations, that is, so long as we correlate the manifold of real numbers to the points of a line. So long as we tie together the concept of space and the fact that we can always think of a number between any two given numbers, no matter how close, we cannot admit a discontinuous space, simply because it is unthinkable.

How now with discontinuous time? The discontinuity of time is evidently connected with the measurement of time. Time is measured with clocks. If the intervals of time which we obtained with clocks, that is, the numbers which we obtained from our readings of the position of the hands of a clock, formed a discontinuous manifold, then we might conceivably want to say that time is discontinuous. But is this what we would probably say? If we assume that space is already discontinuous we know that the hands of the clock can occupy only certain discrete positions. Would we say that time is discontinuous or that the appearance of discontinuity is due to the discontinuity of space? We would doubtless want to speak of a discontinuity of time if the discrete jump in the values of time corresponded to the jump of the hands of the clock over an interval of space much larger than the minimum interval. Such a state of affairs would obviously land us in great difficulties when we tried to use clocks with hands moving with smaller and smaller velocities. There are other conceptual difficulties in trying to imagine what a situation would be like that would make us want to say that time is discontinuous. Although the velocity of light is the upper limit to the propagation of signals or other causal effects, there is no upper limit to other possible velocities. A searchlight on the sun sweeps the orbit of Neptune with a velocity greater than the velocity of light by as much as we please. Now imagine a clock in which the hand is such a sweeping ray of light. The time of this clock is the time of arrival of the sweeping ray at the graduations along the circumference. These graduations may be separated by the minimum distance, if there is such. But there would seem to be no lower limit to the time interval between the possible arrival of the sweeping ray at one graduation and its arrival at the next graduation. For this reason I find it much more difficult to imagine circumstances under which I would want to say that time is discontinuous than circumstances for a discontinuous space. And whatever the structure of physical space turns out to be, it would appear to me that mathematics, particularly elementary mathematics, will probably continue to treat space as continuous. The length of the diagonal of a square will probably continue to be written as $\sqrt{2}$ times the side, in spite of the fact that this is inconsistent with a minimum length. The complications arising from not writing it in this way would appear to be too formidable.

If it should turn out that physically there is a discontinuous space and time, that is, a granular structure for space and time, then minimum lengths and times are logically determined incidentally as the differences between the neighboring discrete numbers that express the granularity. It is also logically possible that the differences of these numbers should not be constant, but they might vary with position and epoch. As a matter of fact, however, when the physicist talks about minimum lengths and minimum times he usually means something logically different. Such minima may be defined in terms of various combinations of atomic and other constants which have the requisite dimensions. Several different suggestions of this sort have been made by various authors—the significance of such suggestions is to be found only in a theoretical context and I shall not attempt to go into the matter further here. It is to be remarked in general, however, that the numerical magnitude of such natural minimum lengths or times, which can also serve as natural standards of length or time, is of a higher order than the minimums set by any possible discrete structure of space or time.

Not only do we use instruments to give us fineness of detail inaccessible to direct sense perception, but we also use them to extend qualitatively the range of our senses into regions where our senses no longer operate, as when we detect and measure radiation phenomena at wavelengths beyond the sensitivity of our eyes, or acoustical phenomena above the range of our hearing. More than this, we use instruments to make ourselves aware of the existence of phenomena to which our senses are totally unresponsive, as, for example, the phenomena of magnetism. In fact, there are so many phenomena beyond the range of our senses or to which our senses are totally insensitive that the world of modern physics has become predominantly the world of instruments. We have to ask ourselves how seriously we shall take the indications of our instruments. What sort of significance shall we ascribe to them? And what sort of a world can the world of instruments be, anyhow?

It can be said in the first place that the brute material of the physicist is the data of his instruments to an almost exclusive extent. The task of the physicist might be defined, in the first place, to acquire factual mastery of the data given by all possible instruments under all possible conditions, including here sometimes data given directly by the unaided senses, and then to correlate this material so far as possible into a conceptual whole. In carrying out this task the physicist will have to think about the nature of his instrumental data—it is questions concerned with this that I want to examine now. What sort of information is an instrument capable of giving us? To what extent is what the instrument gives us colored by the instrument itself, or is the instrument capable of revealing to us something "independent of the instrument?" We would not have asked this last question before the advent of quantum theory. We now know that this is a very important question indeed for a certain range of phenomena, and that in this range instrument-of-observation and object-of-observation cannot be separated from each other. On the scale of ordinary sense perception, however, where we have the possibility of getting to the same terminus by the use of several senses, the question loses its importance, and we can usually think of the object as something in itself, unaffected by the instrument, the only function of the instrument being to reveal the object to us.

To forget the instrument through which our knowledge comes constitutes an enormous simplification, a simplification without which one may well question whether men could, up to the present, have been able to cope intellectually with their surroundings at all. In most practical situations such neglect of the instrument is highly justified. The point I wish to make here, however, is that even on the scale of everyday life there are some situations in which this divorce of object from instrument is illegitimate, so that the concept of object, in and for itself, becomes meaningless.

• | TOWARD A NEW SET OF RELATIONS BETWEEN THE UNCONSCIOUS AND THE CONSCIOUS

PART III

16

Language and Eros

Norman O. Brown

If psychoanalysis represents any advance in the general theory of human nature, it must be able to advance the theory of language; and conversely, symptoms are so close to symbols that psychoanalysis cannot state its theory of neurosis without having a general theory of what Cassirer called the *animal symbolicum*. Language, like art, is one of those problems the solution of which requires a synthesis of psychoanalysis with non-psychoanalytical disciplines, a synthesis aimed at a general theory of human nature and based on a resolute commitment to the vision of culture as neurosis. Hence Freud (apart from one inadequate paragraph to be considered later) has no general theory of language; and the most significant attempt at synthesis is that of the psychoanalytically minded anthropologist Weston LaBarre.

The essential paradox in the psychoanalytical approach to language is to see it as sublimated sexuality and as a crucial instrument in that general deflection of libido from sexual to social aims which, according to psychoanalytical theory, is sublimation and is culture. Hence Freud, in his nearest approach to a general theory of language, tentatively adopted Sperber's theory of the derivation of language from the mating calls of animals, language being constituted by establishing a connection between the mating calls and work processes. "Primitive man thus made his work agreeable, so to speak, by treating it as the equivalent of and substitute for sexual activities."

Sublimation is perhaps the most difficult concept in psychoanalysis, and only later in this book * shall we be prepared to understand it. Above all, sublimation is a process involving not just the sexual instinct but also its antagonist, and therefore it cannot be understood before we understand Eros' antagonist. Quite specifically, in Freud's later theory, negation, a fundamental principle in language, is regarded as a derivative of the death instinct. We do not at this point have a theory of sublimation, and therefore do not offer a theory of language. And yet it may be worth while to make a preliminary assessment of the psychoanalytic point of view.

If language is made out of love, we must transcend the economic-rational, or operational, notion of "the origin of language from and in the process of human labor" (Engel's phrase). From the psychoanalytical point of view language is indeed inseparable from human labor; its function, in Freud's comment on Sperber, is to make work possible. But work is made possible by being made agreeable, and it is made agreeable by becoming a substitute for repressed sexuality. Over and beyond labor there is love, and labor is sustained by the energy of repressed love.

But if language is made out of (sublimated) sexuality, it can hardly be genital sexuality (the mating calls of animals), as supposed in Sperber's theory. Such a hypothesis is at odds with the psychoanalytical emphasis on infantile, pregenital sexuality as the great reservoir of Eros from which sublimations (and culture) are drawn. It is also at odds with the fact that the acquisition of the power of speech by the human child occurs during the early blossoming of infantile sexuality and as an inseparable part of it. It takes no psychoanalytical finesse, but only simple observation of childhood, to recognize that in the history of every human being language originates in the infantile life of play, pleasure, and love which centers round the mother; over this primary function is built the secondary function of organizing human energy in socially productive work. In the ontogenetic development of every human being, it is the language of love and the pleasure principle before it becomes the language of work and the reality-principle; language is an operational superstructure on an erotic base.

Freud says that ideas are libidinal cathexes, that is to say, acts of love; that conscious attention is no mere act of perception but also a li-

* *Life Against Death*. The editors.

bidinal hypercathexis; and that "affirmation, as being a substitute for union, belongs to Eros." Psychoanalysis then would have to ally itself with the theory of Rousseau and Herder, restated by the modern authority on comparative linguistics, Jespersen: "Men sang out their feelings long before they were able to speak their thoughts." Susanne Langer, following Jespersen, says of language, "Its beginnings are not natural adjustments, ways to means; they are purposeless lalling-instincts, primitive aesthetic reactions, and dream-like associations of ideas." And if language has an infantile erotic base, it must be basically a playful activity. Observation of children shows that learning to speak is for them in itself play and then serves to enrich their life of play. And the analysis of language, not a particular language but language generally, reveals its essentially playful structure. In the words of Cassirer, "Language is, by its very nature and essence, metaphorical"; and every metaphor is a play upon words. Jespersen also concludes that "language originated as play." The element of play in language is the erotic element; and this erotic element is in essence not genital, but polymorphously perverse.

If, in the history of every child, language is first of all a mode of erotic expression and then later succumbs to the domination of the reality-principle, it follows, or perhaps we should say mirrors, the path taken by the human psyche and must share the ultimate fate of the human psyche, namely neurosis. Language will then have to be analyzed as compromise-formation, produced by the conflict of the pleasure-principle and the reality-principle, like any neurotic symptom. To regard human speech, the self-evident sign of our superiority over animals, as a disease or at least as essentially diseased, is for common sense, and for the philosopher Cassirer, a monstrous hypothesis. Yet psychoanalysis, which insists on the necessary connection between cultural achievement and neurosis and between social organization and neurosis, and which therefore defines man as the neurotic animal, can hardly take any other position. On this point Freud was not aware of the implications of the line of thought he started; nineteenth-century science, with which he identified himself, was not critical of its own instruments. But if psychoanalysis is carried to the logical conclusion that language is neurotic, it can join hands with the twentieth-century school of linguistic analysis —a depth analysis of language—inspired by that man with a real genius for the psychopathology of language, Wittgenstein. He said, "Philosophy is a battle against the bewitchment [*Verbexung*] of our intelligence by means of language."

Some of these linguistic analysts have had the project of getting rid of the disease in language by reducing language to purely operational terms. From the psychoanalytic point of view, a purely operational language would be a language without a libidinal (erotic) component; and psychoanalysis would suggest that such a project is impossible because language, like man, has an erotic base, and also useless because man cannot be persuaded to operate (work) for operation's sake. Wittgenstein, if I understand him correctly, has a position much closer to that of psychoanalysis; he limits the task of philosophy to that of recognizing the inevitable insanity of language. "My aim is," he says, "to teach you to pass from a piece of disguised nonsense to something that is patent nonsense." "He who understands me finally recognizes [my propositions] as senseless." Psychoanalysis begins where Wittgenstein ends. The problem is not the disease of language, but the disease called man.

Language as disease and language as play—the two meet in the concept of neurotic play, that is to say, magic (Wittgenstein's "bewitchment"). In his essay on "Animism, Magic and Omnipotence of Thought," Freud goes beyond Frazer's notion that primitive magic is simply a system of erroneous thinking which, lacking a true ("scientific") understanding of the connections between things, posited causal interrelation on the basis of superficial association of ideas. Freud looks for a dynamic psychological factor which would explain the positive commitment to magic, and he finds it in the belief in the omnipotence of thoughts and wishes. But since the belief in the omnipotence of thoughts is also to be found in children and in adult civilized neurotics, Freud is able to make a psychoanalytic explanation of it. It is a characteristic feature in the narcissistic phase of infantile sexual development; primitive adults preserve a high degree of the narcissistic orientation, while adult civilized neurotics regress to it.

Now if we can say that language is diseased in so far as it contains magical qualities, in so far as it reflects a belief in the reality of thoughts and wishes, we are able to trace the magical quality of language to its organic connection with the narcissistic phase of infantile sexual development, the phase in which the child develops the pure pleasure-ego. For the world of the pure pleasure-ego is a dream world, a world constructed out of "neurotic currency" in which wishes are true—though for the child this currency is not neurotic, since he knows nothing of the conflict of the pleasure-principle and the reality-principle and his unreal world is his real world. And by the same token it is a world of play, in which the representation of the gratified wish is accepted as real. And in effect, says Freud, it *is* real; the child and the primitive man are satisfied with play and imitative representation not because they realize their impotence and are resigned to these substitutes, but because they so obviously place an excessive valuation on their wishes. Language as play and language as disease are the two sides of language as wish-fulfillment thinking, and wish-fulfillment thinking is a legacy of childhood indelible in our minds, carrying the secret project of the pure pleasure-ego, the search for an erotic sense of reality.

The mystical tradition long ago recognized the neurotic character of language. Jacob Boehme speaks of the language of Adam—different from all languages as we know them—as the only natural language, the only language free from distortion and illusion, the language which man will recover when he recovers paradise. According to Boehme, Adam's language was an unclouded mirror of the senses, so that he calls this ideal language "sensual speech"—*die sensualische Sprache*. It is the language appropriate to a species that is actualizing the true potentialities of its sensuous or sensual nature, and as such is in unity with all of sensuous nature and all life. Hence Boehme says that animals enjoy true self-expression, while men do not:

> No people understands any more the sensual language, and the birds in the air and the beasts in the forest do understand it according to their species. Therefore man may reflect what he has been robbed of, and what he is to recover in the second birth. For in the sensual language all spirits speak with each other, they need no other language, for it is the language of nature.

Hence that heir of the mystics and ally of psychoanalysis in the task of making the unconscious conscious, modern poetry, has envisaged the necessity of transcending language. Valéry defines the goal of art as the recovery of our sensuous and sensual nature: "The art of the superior artist is to restore by means of conscious operations the integrity [*valeur*] of sensuality and the emotional power of things." But if language is essentially a neurotic compromise between the erotic (pleasure) and operational (reality) principles, it follows that the consciousness in the artistic use of language, is subversive of its own instrument and seeks to pass beyond it. Language is, in Valéry's words, "the beautiful chains which entangle the distracted god in the flesh"—

> Belles chaînes en qui s'engage
> Le dieu dans la chair égaré.

And the goal of poetry is an experience essentially ineffable: "The Beautiful implies effects of unspeakableness, indescribableness, ineffability. . . . Now if it is desired to produce such an effect by means of things said, by language—or if such an effect is felt as a result of the use of language—it follows that language is being employed in order to make mute, is expressing muteness."

Similarly Rilke sets the goal of mute speech, "essentially natural speech by means of the body"—in Boehme's terms, sensual speech. The ineffability of beauty, and the connection between beauty and what Valéry calls the integrity of sensuality, together constitute a measure of the repression of Eros in civilization, as well as a measure of the difference between men as they are today, with their neurotic addiction to their neurotic speech, and men as they might be if they attained their proper perfection as an animal species and recovered the power of sensual speech.

17

Excerpts from *The Theatre and Its Double*

Antonin Artaud

Like the plague, the theater is a formidable call to the forces that impel the mind by example to the source of its conflicts. And it is evident that Ford's passional example * merely symbolizes a still greater and absolutely essential task.

The terrorizing apparition of Evil which in the Mysteries of Eleusis was produced in its pure, truly revealed form corresponds to the dark hour of certain ancient tragedies which all true theater must recover.

If the essential theater is like the plague, it is not because it is contagious, but because like the plague it is the revelation, the bringing forth, the exteriorization of a depth of latent cruelty by means of which all the perverse possibilities of the mind, whether of an individual or a people, are localized.

Like the plague the theater is the time of evil, the triumph of dark powers that are nourished by a power even more profound until extinction.

In the theater as in the plague there is a kind of strange sun, a light

* *'Tis Pity She's a Whore*. The editors.

of abnormal intensity by which it seems that the difficult and even the impossible suddenly become our normal element. And Ford's play, like all true theater, is within the radiance of this strange sun. His *Annabella* resembles the plague's freedom by means of which, from degree to degree, stage to stage, the victim swells his individuality and the survivor gradually becomes a grandiose and overwhelming being.

We can now say that all true freedom is dark, and infallibly identified with sexual freedom which is also dark, although we do not know precisely why. For it has been a long time since the Platonic Eros, the procreative sense, the freedom of life vanished beneath the somber veneer of the *Libido* which is identified with all that is dirty, abject, infamous in the process of living and of throwing oneself headlong with a natural and impure vigor, with a perpetually renewed strength, upon life.

And that is why all the great Myths are dark, so that one cannot imagine, save in an atmosphere of carnage, torture, and bloodshed, all the magnificent Fables which recount to the multitudes the first sexual division and the first carnage of essences that appeared in creation.

The theater, like the plague, is in the image of this carnage and this essential separation. It releases conflicts, disengages powers, liberates possibilities, and if these possibilities and these powers are dark, it is the fault not of the plague nor of the theater, but of life.

We do not see that life as it is and as it has been fashioned for us provides many reasons for exaltation. It appears that by means of the plague, a gigantic abscess, as much moral as social, has been collectively drained; and that like the plague, the theater has been created to drain abscesses collectively.

Perhaps the theater's poison, injected into the social body, disintegrates it, as Saint Augustine says, but at least it does so as a plague, as an avenging scourge a redeeming epidemic in which credulous ages have chosen to see the finger of God and which is nothing but the application of a law of nature whereby every gesture is counterbalanced by a gesture and every action by its reaction.

The theater like the plague is a crisis which is resolved by death or cure. And the plague is a superior disease because it is a total crisis after which nothing remains except death or an extreme purification. Similarly the theater is a disease because it is the supreme equilibrium which cannot be achieved without destruction. It invites the mind to share a delirium which exalts its energies; and we can see, to conclude, that from the human point of view, the action of theater, like that of plague, is beneficial, for impelling men to see themselves as they are, it causes the mask to fall, reveals the lie, the slackness, baseness, and hypocrisy of our world; it shakes off the asphyxiating inertia of matter which invades even the clearest testimony of the senses; and in revealing to collectivities of men their dark power, their hidden force, it invites them to take, in the face of destiny, a superior and heroic attitude they would never have assumed without it.

And the question we must now ask is whether, in this slippery world which is committing suicide without noticing it, there can be found a nucleus of men capable of imposing this superior notion of the theater, men who will restore to all of us the natural and magic equivalent of the dogmas in which we no longer believe.

And I ask this question:

How does it happen that in the theater, at least in the theater as we know it in Europe, or better in the Occident, everything specifically theatrical, i.e., everything that cannot be expressed in speech, in words, or, if you prefer, everything that is not contained in the dialogue (and the dialogue itself considered as a function of its possibilities for "sound" on the stage, as a function of the *exigencies* of this sonorisation) is left in the background?

How does it happen, moreover, that the Occidental theater (I say Occidental because there are fortunately others, like the Oriental theater, which have preserved intact the idea of theater, while in the Occident this idea—like all the rest—has been *prostituted*), how does it happen that the Occidental theater does not see theater under any other aspect than as a theater of dialogue?

Dialogue—a thing written and spoken—does not belong specifically to the stage, it belongs to books, as is proved by the fact that in all handbooks of literary history a place is reserved for the theater as a subordinate branch of the history of the spoken language.

I say that the stage is a concrete physical place which asks to be filled, and to be given its own concrete language to speak.

I say that this concrete language, intended for the senses and independent of speech, has first to satisfy the senses, that there is a poetry of the senses as there is a poetry of language, and that this concrete physical language to which I refer is truly theatrical only to the degree that the thoughts it expresses are beyond the reach of the spoken language.

I will be asked what these thoughts are which words cannot express and which, far more than words, would find their ideal expression in the concrete physical language of the stage.

I will answer this question a little later.

What is essential now, it seems to me, is to determine what this physical language consists of, this solidified, materialized language by means of which theater is able to differentiate itself from speech.

It consists of everything that occupies the stage, everything that can be manifested and expressed materially on a stage and that is addressed first of all to the senses instead of being addressed primarily to the mind as is the language of words. (I am well aware that words too have possibilities as sound, different ways of being projected into space, which are called *intonations*. Furthermore, there would be a great deal to say about the concrete value of intonation in the theater, about this faculty words have of creating a music in their own right according to the way they are pronounced, independently of their concrete meaning and even going counter to this meaning—of creating beneath language a subterranean current of impressions, correspondences, and analogies; but this theatrical consideration of language is already a subordinate *aspect* of language for the playwright, an accessory consideration of which, especially in our time, he takes no account in the construction of his plays. So let us pass on.)

This language created for the senses must from the outset be concerned with satisfying them. This does not prevent it from developing later its full intellectual effect on all possible levels and in every direction. But it permits the substitution, for the poetry of language, of a poetry in space which will be resolved in precisely the domain which does not belong strictly to words.

Doubtless you would prefer, for a better understanding of what I mean, a few examples of this poetry in space capable of creating kinds of material images equivalent to word images. You will find these examples a little further on.

This very difficult and complex poetry assumes many aspects: especially the aspects of all the means of expression utilizable on the stage,[1] such as music, dance, plastic art, pantomime, mimicry, gesticulation, intonation, architecture, lighting, and scenery.

Each of these means has its own intrinsic poetry, and a kind of ironic poetry as well, resulting from the way it combines with the other means of expression; and the consequences of these combinations, of their reactions and their reciprocal destructions, are easy to perceive.

I shall return a little later to this poetry which can be fully effective only if it is concrete, i.e., only if it produces something objectively from the fact of its *active* presence on the stage:—only if a sound, as in the Balinese theater, has its equivalent in a gesture and, instead of serving as a decoration, an accompaniment of a thought, instead causes its movement, directs it, destroys it, or changes it completely, etc.

One form of this poetry in space—besides the one that can be created by combinations of lines, shapes, colors, objects in their natural state, such as one finds in all the arts—belongs to sign-language. I hope I shall be allowed to speak for a moment about this other aspect of pure theatrical language which does without words, a language of signs, gestures and attitudes having an ideographic value as they exist in certain unperverted pantomimes.

By "unperverted pantomime" I mean direct Pantomime where gestures—instead of representing words or sentences, as in our European Pantomime (a mere fifty years old!) which is merely a distortion of the mute roles of Italian comedy—represent ideas, attitudes of mind, aspects of nature, all in an effective, concrete manner, i.e., by constantly evoking objects or natural details, like that Oriental language which represents night by a tree on which a bird that has already closed one eye is beginning to close the other. Another such abstract idea or attitude of mind could be represented by some of the innumerable symbols from Scripture, as the needle's eye through which the camel cannot pass.

It is plain that these signs constitute true hieroglyphs, in which man, to the extent that he contributes to their formation, is only a form like the rest, yet to which, because of his double nature, he adds a singular prestige.

This language which evokes in the mind images of an intense natural (or spiritual) poetry provides a good idea of what a poetry in space independent of spoken language could mean in the theater.

Whatever the case of this language and its poetry may be, I have noticed that in our theater which lives under the exclusive dictatorship of speech, this language of gesture and mime, this wordless pantomime, these postures, attitudes, objective intonations, in brief everything I consider specifically theatrical in the theater, all these elements when they exist apart from text are generally considered the minor part of theater; they are negligently referred to as "craft," and identified with what is understood by staging or "production," and can consider themselves fortunate if the words *mise en scène* are not applied to the idea of artistic and external sumptuousness pertaining exclusively to costumes, lighting, and set.

And in opposition to this way of looking at things, a way which seems to me entirely Occidental or rather Latin, i.e., pigheaded, I shall say that to the degree that this language derives from the stage, draws its efficacy from its spontaneous creation on the stage, to the degree that it struggles directly with the stage without passing through words (and why not conceive of a play composed directly on the stage, realized on the stage)—it is the *mise en scène* that is the theater much more than the written and spoken play. I will be asked no doubt to define what is Latin in this way of seeing opposed to mine. What is Latin is this need to use words to express ideas that are obvious. For to me obvious ideas are, in the theater as everywhere else, dead and done with.

The idea of a play made directly in terms of the stage, encountering obstacles of both production and performance, compels the discovery of an active language, active and anarchic, a language in which the customary limits of feelings and words are transcended.

In any case, and I hasten to say it at once, a theater which subordinates the *mise en scène* and production, i.e., everything in itself that is specifically theatrical, to the text, is a theater of idiots, madmen, inverts, grammarians, grocers, antipoets and positivists, i.e., Occidentals.

Furthermore, I am well aware that the language of gestures and postures, dance and music, is less capable of analyzing a character, revealing a man's thoughts, or elucidating states of consciousness clearly and precisely than is verbal language, but who ever said the theater was created to analyze a character, to resolve the conflicts of love and duty, to wrestle with all the problems of a topical and psychological nature that monopolize our contemporary stage?

Given the theater as we see it here, one would say there is nothing more to life than knowing whether we can make love skillfully, whether we will go to war or are cowardly enough to make peace, how we cope with our little pangs of conscience, and whether we will become conscious of our "complexes" (in the language of experts) or if indeed our "complexes" will do us in. Rarely, moreover, does the debate rise to a social level, rarely do we question our social and moral system. Our theater never goes so far as to ask whether this social and moral system might not by chance be iniquitous.

I believe, however, that our present social state is iniquitous and should be destroyed. If this is a fact for the theater to be preoccupied with, it is even more a matter for machine guns. Our theater is not even capable of asking the question in the burning and effective way it must be asked, but even if it should ask this question it would still be far from its purpose, which is for me a higher and more secret one.

All the preoccupations enumerated above stink unbelievably of man, provisional, material man, I shall even say *carrion man*. Such preoccupation with personal problems disgusts me, and disgusts me all the more with nearly the whole contemporary theater which, as human as it is antipoetic, except for three or four plays, seems to me to stink of decadence and pus.

The contemporary theater is decadent because it has lost the feeling on the one hand for seriousness and on the other for laughter; because it has broken away from gravity, from effects that are immediate and painful—in a word, from Danger.

Because it has lost a sense of real humor, a sense of laughter's power of physical and anarchic dissociation.

Because it has broken away from the spirit of profound anarchy which is at the root of all poetry.

It must be admitted that everything in the destination of an object, in the meaning or the use of a natural form, is a matter of convention.

Nature, in giving a tree the form of a tree, could just as well have given it the form of an animal or of a hill; we would have thought *tree* for the animal or the hill, and the trick would have been turned.

It is agreed that a beautiful woman has a melodious voice; if, since the world began, we had heard all beautiful women call to us in trumpet blasts and greet us like bellowing elephants, we would have eternally associated the idea of bellowing with the idea of a beautiful woman, and a portion of our inner vision of the world would have been radically transformed thereby.

This helps us to understand that poetry is anarchic to the degree that it brings into play all the relationships of object to object and of form to signification. It is anarchic also to the degree that its occurrence is the consequence of a disorder that draws us closer to chaos.

I shall give no further examples. One could multiply them infinitely and not only with humorous ones like those I have just used.

Theatrically these inversions of form, displacements of signification could become the essential element of that humorous poetry in space which is the exclusive province of the *mise en scène*.

In a Marx Brothers' film a man thinks he is going to take a woman in his arms but instead gets a cow, which moos. And through a conjunction of circumstances which it would take too long to analyze here, that moo, at just that moment, assumes an intellectual dignity equal to any woman's cry.

Such a situation, possible in the cinema, is no less possible in the theater as it exists: it would take very little—for instance, replace the cow with an animated manikin, a kind of monster endowed with speech, or a man disguised as an animal—to rediscover the secret of an objective poetry at the root of humor, which the theater has renounced and abandoned to the Music Hall, and which the Cinema later adopted.

A moment ago I mentioned danger. The best way, it seems to me, to realize this idea of danger on the stage is by the *objective* unforeseen, the unforeseen not in situations but in things, the abrupt, untimely transition from an intellectual image to a true image; for example, a man who is blaspheming sees suddenly and realistically materialized before him the image of his blasphemy (always on condition, I would add, that such an image is not entirely gratuitous but engenders in its turn other images in the same spiritual vein, etc.).

Another example would be the sudden appearance of a fabricated Being, made of wood and cloth, entirely invented, corresponding to nothing, yet disquieting by nature, capable of reintroducing on the stage a little breath of that great metaphysical fear which is at the root of all ancient theater.

The Balinese with their imaginary dragon, like all the Orientals, have not lost the sense of that mysterious fear which they know is one of the most stirring (and indeed essential) elements of the theater when it is restored to its proper level.

True poetry is, willy nilly, metaphysical and it is just its metaphysical bearing, I should say, the intensity of its metaphysical effect, that comprises its essential worth.

This is the second or third time I have brought up metaphysics here. I was speaking a moment ago, apropos of psychology, about dead ideas, and I expect many will be tempted to tell me that if there is one inhuman idea in the world, one ineffectual and dead idea which conveys little enough even to the mind, it is indeed the idea of metaphysics.

This is due, as René Guénon says, "to our purely Occidental way, our antipoetic and truncated way of considering principles (apart from the massive and energetic spiritual state which corresponds to them)."

In the Oriental theater of metaphysical tendencies, as opposed to the Occidental theater of psychological tendencies, this whole complex of gestures, signs, postures, and sonorities which constitute the language of stage performance, this language which develops all its physical and poetic effects on every level of consciousness and in all the senses, necessarily induces thought to adopt profound attitudes which could be called *metaphysics-in-action*.

I shall take up this point again in a moment. For the present let us return to the theater as we know it.

A few days ago, I was present at a discussion about the theater. I saw some sort of human snakes, otherwise known as playwrights, explain how to worm a play into the good graces of a director, like certain men in history who used to insinuate poison into the ears of their rivals. There was some question, I believe, of determining the future orientation of the theater and, in other terms, its destiny.

No one determined anything, and at no time was there any question of the true destiny of the theater, i.e., of what, by definition and essence, the theater is destined to represent, nor of the means at its disposal for realizing this destiny. On the contrary the theater seemed to me a sort of frozen world, its artists cramped among gestures that will never be good for anything again, brittle intonations which are already falling to pieces, music reduced to a kind of arithmetic whose figures are beginning to fade, some sort of luminous explosions, themselves congealed and responding to vague traces of movement—and around all this an extraordinary fluttering of men in black suits who quarrel over the receipts, at the threshold of a white-hot box office. As if the theatrical mechanism were henceforth reduced to all that surrounds it; and because it is reduced to what surrounds it and because the theater is reduced to everything that is not the theater, its atmosphere stinks in the nostrils of people of taste.

For me the theater is identical with its possibilities for realization when the most extreme poetic results are derived from them; the possibilities for realization in the theater relate entirely to the *mise en scène* considered as a language in space and in movement.

To derive, then, the most extreme poetic results from the means of realization is to make metaphysics of them, and I think no one will object to this way of considering the question.

And to make metaphysics out of language, gestures, attitudes, sets, and music from a theatrical point of view is, it seems to me, to consider them in relation to all the ways they can have of making contact with time and with movement.

To give objective examples of this poetry that follows upon the way a gesture, a sonority, an intonation presses with more or less insistence upon this or that segment of space at such and such a time appears to me as difficult as to communicate in words the feeling of a particular sound or the degree and quality of a physical pain. It depends upon the production and can be determined only on the stage.

I should now review all the means of expression which the theater (or the *mise en scène,* which, in the system I have just expounded, is identified with it) contains. That would carry me too far, and I shall simply select from them one or two examples.

First, the spoken language.

To make metaphysics out of a spoken language is to make the language express what it does not ordinarily express: to make use of it in a new, exceptional, and unaccustomed fashion; to reveal its possibilities for producing physical shock; to divide and distribute it actively in space; to deal with intonations in an absolutely concrete manner, restoring their power to shatter as well as really to manifest something; to turn against language and its basely utilitarian, one could say alimentary, sources, against its trapped-beast origins; and finally, to consider language as the form of *Incantation*.

Everything in this active poetic mode of envisaging expression on the stage leads us to abandon the modern humanistic and psychological meaning of the theater, in order to recover the religious and mystic preference of which our theater has completely lost the sense.

If it is enough to pronounce the words *religious* or *mystic* to be taken for a churchwarden or an illiterate priest outside a Buddhist temple, at best good only for turning prayer wheels, this merely signifies and condemns our incapacity to derive the full import from our words and our profound ignorance of the spirit of synthesis and analogy.

Perhaps it means that at the point where we are we have lost all touch with the true theater, since we confine it to the domain of what daily thought can reach, the familiar or unfamiliar domain of consciousness;—and if we address ourselves theatrically to the unconscious, it is merely to take from it what it has been able to collect (or conceal) of accessible everyday experience.

Let it be further said that one of the reasons for the physical efficacity upon the mind, for the force of the direct images of action in certain productions of the Oriental theater, such as those of the Balinese theater, is that this theater is based upon age-old traditions which have preserved intact the secrets of using gestures, intonations, and harmonies in relation to the senses and on all possible levels—this does not condemn the Oriental theater, but it condemns us, and along with us the state of things in which we live and which is to be destroyed, destroyed with diligence and malice on every level and at every point where it prevents the free exercise of thought.

It is a question of knowing what we want. If we are prepared for war, plague, famine, and slaughter we do not even need to say so, we have only to continue as we are; continue behaving like snobs, rushing en masse to hear such and such a singer, to see such and such an admirable performance which never transcends the realm of art (and even the Russian ballet at the height of its splendor never transcended the realm of art), to marvel at such and such an exhibition of painting in which exciting shapes explode here and there but at random and without any genuine consciousness of the forces they could rouse.

This empiricism, randomness, individualism, and anarchy must cease.

Enough of personal poems, benefitting those who create them much more than those who read them.

Once and for all, enough of this closed, egoistic, and personal art.

Our spiritual anarchy and intellectual disorder are a function of the anarchy of everything else—or rather, everything else is a function of this anarchy.

I am not one of those who believe that civilization has to change in order for the theater to change; but I do believe that the theater, utilized in the highest and most difficult sense possible, has the power to influence the aspect and formation of things: and the encounter upon the stage of two passionate manifestations, two living centers, two nervous magnetisms is something entire, true, even decisive, as, in life, the encounter of one epidermis with another in a timeless debauchery.

That is why I propose a theater of cruelty.—With this mania we all have for depreciating everything, as soon as I have said "cruelty," everybody will at once take it to mean "blood." But *"theater of cruelty"* means a theater difficult and cruel for myself first of all. And, on the level of performance, it is not the cruelty we can exercise upon each other by hacking at each other's bodies, carving up our personal anatomies, or, like Assyrian emperors, sending parcels of human ears, noses, or neatly detached nostrils through the mail, but the much more terrible and necessary cruelty which things can exercise against us. We are not free. And the sky can still fall on our heads. And the theater has been created to teach us that first of all.

Either we will be capable of returning by present-day means to this superior idea of poetry and poetry-through-theater which underlies the Myths told by the great ancient tragedians, capable once more of entertaining a religious idea of the theater (without meditation, useless contemplation, and vague dreams), capable of attaining awareness and a possession of certain dominant forces, of certain notions that control all others, and (since ideas, when they are effective, carry their energy with them) capable of recovering within ourselves those energies which ultimately create order and increase the value of life, or else we might as well abandon ourselves now, without protest, and recognize that we are no longer good for anything but disorder, famine, blood, war, and epidemics.

Either we restore all the arts to a central attitude and necessity, finding an analogy between a gesture made in painting or the theater, and a gesture made by lava in a volcanic explosion, or we must stop painting, babbling, writing, or doing whatever it is we do.

I propose to bring back into the theater this elementary magical idea, taken up by modern psychoanalysis, which consists in effecting a patient's cure by making him assume the apparent and exterior attitudes of the desired condition.

I propose to renounce our empiricism of imagery, in which the unconscious furnishes images at random, and which the poet arranges at random too, calling them poetic and hence hermetic images, as if the kind of trance that poetry provides did not have its reverberations throughout the whole sensibility, in every nerve, and as if poetry were some vague force whose movements were invariable.

I propose to return through the theater to an idea of the physical knowledge of images and the means of inducing trances, as in Chinese medicine which knows, over the entire extent of the human anatomy, at what points to puncture in order to regulate the subtlest functions.

Those who have forgotten the communicative power and magical mimesis of a gesture, the theater can reinstruct, because a gesture carries its energy with it, and there are still human beings in the theater to manifest the force of the gesture made.

To create art is to deprive a gesture of its reverberation in the organism, whereas this reverberation, if the gesture is made in the conditions and with the force required, incites the organism and, through it, the entire individuality, to take attitudes in harmony with the gesture.

The theater is the only place in the world, the last general means we still possess of directly affecting the organism and, in periods of neurosis and petty sensuality like the one in which we are immersed, of attacking this sensuality by physical means it cannot withstand.

If music affects snakes, it is not on account of the spiritual notions it offers them, but because snakes are long and coil their length upon the earth, because their bodies touch the earth at almost every point; and because the musical vibrations which are communicated to the earth affect them like a very subtle, very long massage; and I propose to treat the spectators like the snakecharmer's subjects and conduct them *by means of their organisms* to an apprehension of the subtlest notions.

At first by crude means, which will gradually be refined. These immediate crude means will hold their attention at the start.

That is why in the "theater of cruelty" the spectator is in the center and the spectacle surrounds him.

In this spectacle the sonorisation is constant: sounds, noises, cries are chosen first for their vibratory quality, then for what they represent.

Among these gradually refined means light is interposed in its turn. Light which is not created merely to add color or to brighten, and which brings its power, influence, suggestions with it. And the light of a green cavern does not sensually dispose the organism like the light of a windy day.

After sound and light there is action, and the dynamism of action: here the theater, far from copying life, puts itself whenever possible in communication with pure forces. And whether you accept or deny them, there is nevertheless a way of speaking which gives the name of "forces" to whatever brings to birth images of energy in the unconscious, and gratuitous crime on the surface.

A violent and concentrated action is a kind of lyricism: it summons up supernatural images, a bloodstream of images, a bleeding spurt of images in the poet's head and in the spectator's as well.

Whatever the conflicts that haunt the mind of a given period, I defy any spectator to whom such violent scenes will have transferred their blood, who will have felt in himself the transit of a superior action, who will have seen the extraordinary and essential movements of his thought illuminated in extraordinary deeds—the violence and blood having been placed at the service of the violence of the thought—I defy that spectator to give himself up, once outside the theater, to ideas of war, riot, and blatant murder.

So expressed, this idea seems dangerous and sophomoric. It will be claimed that example breeds example, that if the attitude of cure induces cure, the attitude of murder will induce murder. Everything depends upon the manner and the purity with which the thing is done. There is a risk. But let it not be forgotten that though a theatrical gesture is violent, it is disinterested; and that the theater teaches precisely the uselessness of the action which, once done, is not to be done, and the superior use of the state unused by the action and which, *restored,* produces a purification.

I propose then a theater in which violent physical images crush and hypnotize the sensibility of the spectator seized by the theater as by a whirlwind of higher forces.

A theater which, abandoning psychology, recounts the extraordinary, stages natural conflicts, natural and subtle forces, and presents itself first of all as an exceptional power of redirection. A theater that induces trance, as the dances of Dervishes induce trance, and that addresses itself to the organism by precise instruments, by the same means as those of certain tribal music cures which we admire on records but are incapable of originating among ourselves.

There is a risk involved, but in the present circumstances I believe it is a risk worth running. I do not believe we have managed to revitalize the world we live in, and I do not believe it is worth the trouble of clinging to; but I do propose something to get us out of our marasmus, instead of continuing to complain about it, and about the boredom, inertia, and stupidity of everything.

NOTE

1 To the degree that they prove capable of profiting from the immediate physical possibilities the stage offers them in order to substitute, for fixed forms of art, living and intimidating forms by which the sense of old ceremonial magic can find a new reality in the theater; to the degree that they yield to what might be called the *physical temptation* of the stage.

18

Excerpts from *The Armies of the Night*[*]

Norman Mailer

A generation of the American young had come along different from five previous generations of the middle class. The new generation believed in technology more than any before it, but the generation also believed in LSD, in witches, in tribal knowledge, in orgy, and revolution. It had no respect whatsoever for the unassailable logic of the next step: belief was reserved for the revelatory mystery of the happening where you did not know what was going to happen next; that was what was good about it. Their radicalism was in their hate for the authority—the authority was manifest of evil to this generation. It was the authority who had covered the land with those suburbs where they stifled as children while watching the adventures of the West in the movies, while looking at the guardians of dull genial celebrity on television; they had had their minds jabbed and poked and twitched and probed and finally galvanized into surrealistic modes of response by commercials cutting into dramatic narratives, and parents flipping from network to network—they were forced willy-nilly to build their idea of the space-time continuum (and therefore their nervous system) on the jumps and cracks

* Excerpts characterizing and describing the Marchers on the Pentagon. —The editors.

and leaps and breaks which every phenomenon from the media seemed to contain within it.

The authority had operated on their brain with commercials, and washed their brain with packaged education, packaged politics. The authority had presented itself as honorable, and it was corrupt, corrupt as payola on television, and scandals concerning the safety of automobiles, and scandals concerning the leasing of aviation contracts—the real scandals as everyone was beginning to sense were more intimate and could be found in all the products in all the suburban homes which did not work so well as they should have worked, and broke down too soon for mysterious reasons. The shoddiness was buried in the package, buried somewhere in the undiscoverable root of all those modern factories with their sanitized aisles and automated machines; perhaps one place the shoddiness was buried was in the hangovers of a working class finally alienated from any remote interest or attention in the process of the work itself. Work was shoddy everywhere. Even in the Warren Commission.

Finally, this new generation of the Left hated the authority, because the authority lied. It lied through the teeth of corporation executives as Cabinet officials and police enforcement officers and newspaper editors and advertising agencies, and in its mass magazines, where the subtlest apologies for the disasters of the authority (and the neatest deformations of the news) were grafted in the best possible style into the ever-open mind of the walking American lobotomy: the corporation office worker and his high school son.

The New Left was drawing its political aesthetic from Cuba. The revolutionary idea which the followers of Castro had induced from their experience in the hills was that you created the revolution first and learned from it, learned of what your revolution might consist and where it might go out of the intimate truth of the way it presented itself to your experience. Just as the truth of his material was revealed to a good writer by the cutting edge of his style (he could thus hope his style was in each case the most appropriate tool for the material of the experience) so a revolutionary began to uncover the nature of his true situation by trying to ride the beast of his revolution. The idea behind these ideas was then obviously that the future of the revolution existed in the nerves and cells of the people who created it and lived with it, rather than in the sanctity of the original idea.

Castro's Cuba was of course a mystery to Mailer. He had heard much in its favor, much he could hardly enjoy. That was not necessarily to the point. Revolutions could fail as well by Castro's method as by the most inflexible Comintern program; what seemed significant here, was the idea of a revolution which preceded ideology; the New Left had obviously adopted the idea for this March.

The aesthetic of the New Left now therefore began with the notion that the authority could not comprehend nor contain nor finally manage to control any political action whose end was unknown. They could attack it, beat it, jail it, misrepresent it, and finally abuse it, but they could not feel a sense of victory because they could not understand a movement which inspired thousands and hundreds of thousands to march without a coordinated plan. The bureaucrats of the Old Left had not been alone in their adoration of the solid-as-brickwork-logic-of-the-next-step; no, the bureaucrats of the American Center, now liked it as much, and were as aghast at any political activity which ignored it.

These Leviathan ruminations and meditations on the nature of the March coming up, and the reasons for their participation without much discussion now completed, ch-ch-ch-click! in the touch of the tea cup on Mailer's lip, let us move on to the event concerning us—that first major battle of a war which may go on for twenty years; let us even consider there is one interesting chance (one chance of a thousand) that in fifty years the day may loom in our history large as the ghosts of the Union dead.

And from the north and the east, from the direction of the White House and the Smithsonian and the Capitol, from Union Station and the Department of Justice the troops were coming in, the volunteers were answering the call. They came walking up in all sizes, a citizens' army not ranked yet by height, an army of both sexes in numbers almost equal, and of all ages, although most were young. Some were well-dressed, some were poor, many were conventional in appearance, as often were not. The hippies were there in great number, perambulating down the hill, many dressed like the legions of Sgt. Pepper's Band, some were gotten up like Arab sheiks, or in Park Avenue's doormen's greatcoats, others like Rogers and Clark of the West, Wyatt Earp, Kit Carson, Daniel Boone in buckskin, some had grown mustaches to look like *Have Gun, Will Travel*—Paladin's surrogate was here!—and wild Indians with feathers, a hippie gotten up like Batman, another like Claude Rains in *The Invisible Man*—his face wrapped in a turban of bandages and he wore a black satin top hat. A host of these troops wore capes, beat-up khaki capes, slept on, used as blankets, towels, improvised duffel bags; or fine capes, orange linings, or luminous rose linings, the edges ragged, near a tatter, the threads ready to feather, but a musketeer's hat on their head. One hippie may have been dressed like Charles Chaplin; Buster Keaton and W. C. Fields could have come to the ball; there were Martians and Moon-men and a knight unhorsed who stalked about in the weight of real armor. There were to be seen a hundred soldiers in Confederate gray, and maybe there were two or three hundred hippies in officer's coats of Union dark-blue. They had picked up their costumes where they could, in surplus stores, and Blow-your-mind shops, Digger free emporiums, and psychedelic caches of Hindu junk. There were soldiers in Foreign Legion uniforms, and tropical bush jackets, San Quentin and Chino, California striped shirt and pants, British copies of Eisenhower jackets, hippies dressed like Turkish shepherds and Roman senators, gurus, and samurai in dirty smocks. They were close to being assembled from all the intersections between history and the comic books, between legend and television, the Biblical archetypes and the movies. The sight of these troops, this army with a thousand costumes, fulfilled to the hilt our General's oldest idea of war which is that every man should dress as he pleases if he is going into battle, for that is his right, and variety never hurts the zest of the hardiest workers in every battalion (here today by thousands in plaid hunting jackets, corduroys or dungarees, ready for assault!). If the sight of such masquerade lost its usual happy connotation of masked ladies and starving children outside the ball, it was not only because of the shabbiness of the costumes (up close half of them must have been used by hippies for everyday wear) but also because the aesthetic at last was in the politics—the dress ball was going into battle. Still, there were nightmares beneath the gaiety of these middle-class runaways, these Crusaders, going out to attack the hard core of technology land with less training than armies were once offered by a medieval assembly ground. The nightmare was in the echo of those trips which had fractured their sense of past and present. If nature was a veil whose tissue had been ripped by static, screams of jet motors, the highway grid of the suburbs, smog, defoliation, pollution of streams, overfertilization of earth, anti-fertilization of women, and the radiation of two decades of near blind atom busting, then perhaps the history of the past was another tissue, spiritual, no doubt, without physical embodiment, unless its embodiment was in the cuneiform hieroglyphics of the chromosome (so much like primitive writing!) but that tissue of past history, whether traceable in the flesh, or merely palpable in the collective underworld of the dream, was nonetheless being bombed by the use of LSD as outrageously as the atoll of Eniwetok, Hiroshima, Nagasaki, and the scorched foliage of Vietnam.

The history of the past was being exploded right into the present: perhaps there were now lacunae in the firmament of the past, holes where once had been the psychic reality of an era which was gone. Mailer was haunted by the nightmare that the evils of the present not only exploited the present, but consumed the past, and gave every promise of demolishing whole territories of the future. The same villains who, promiscuously, wantonly, heedlessly, had gorged on LSD and consumed God knows what essential marrows of history, wearing indeed the history of all eras on their back as trophies of this gluttony, were now going forth (conscience-struck?) to make war on those other villains, corporation-land villains, who were destroying the promise of the present in their self-righteousness and greed and secret lust (often unknown to themselves) for some sexo-technological variety of neo-fascism.

Mailer's final allegiance, however, was with the villains who were hippies. They would never have looked to blow their minds and destroy some part of the past if the authority had not brainwashed the mood of the present until it smelled like deodorant. (To cover the odor of burning flesh in Vietnam?) So he continued to enjoy the play of costumes, but his pleasure was now edged with a hint of the sinister. Not inappropriate for battle. He and Lowell were still in the best of moods. The morning was so splendid—it spoke of a vitality in nature which no number of bombings in space nor inner-space might ever subdue; the rustle of costumes warming up for the war spoke of future redemptions as quickly as they reminded of hog-swillings from the past, and the thin air! wine of Civil War apples in the October air! edge of excitement and awe—how would this day end? No one could know. Incredible spectacle now gathering—tens of thousands traveling hundreds of miles to attend a symbolic battle. In the capital of technology land beat a primitive drum. New drum of the Left! And the Left had been until this year the secret unwitting accomplice of every increase in the power of the technicians, bureaucrats, and labor leaders who ran the governmental military-industrial complex of super-technology land.

19

The Omnipresence of the Grotesque*

Benjamin Nelson

My remarks grow out of a sense of frustration which came over me recurrently in the course of our last session at the Whitney Museum. I found everything said by all participants to be of great relevance and interest, but I did not quite see how I could apply the prevailing categories of the disciplines familiar to me—sociology, history, anthropology, psychoanalysis, more generally, the social sciences and humanities—in such a way as to throw new light on the questions under discussion. I therefore decided that it was urgent that I proceed at once to sort out the thoughts I have been having since we last met. The key results of my efforts during the interim lead me now, frankly, to avow my conviction that such discussions as we had last time—and will doubtless have again today—evidently call for a fresh look at certain familiar paradigms in the professional study of human culture and action.

* The substance of this paper was read to the Riverdale meeting of the Society for the Arts, Religion and Contemporary Culture on April 25, 1970.

I

I begin with the exceedingly suggestives clues, also noted in passing by Professor Hopper, which Mr. Robert Sowers offered in his presentation to the last session of our conference. Showing over 150 slides of every sort and description, Mr. Sowers revealed the grotesque to range across the entire universe of art and, for that matter, over almost every epoch. The great depth of illustrations was a perfect foil for the multifariousness of his categories—and both together served to goad me into strenuous efforts to ascend to new ground.

The Grotesque, Mr. Sowers said, is the *"investment of anything with a far more or far less complex, vital, animate, conscious, genial or menacing order of existence than we ordinarily attribute to it."* Mr. Sowers added that when all of his illustrations were taken together, it might be found that there were three essential forms, *archetypes,* if one preferred, which insistently recurred in them with multiple variations and idiomatic difference.

1. *The Monster*. The first form of the Grotesque to which Mr. Sowers referred he described as the *Monster,* by which he meant "some either humanoid or superhuman, *but not human,* incredibly strong, animal with a diabolical, semihuman countenance."

2. *The Orifice*. The second of Mr. Sowers' family of illustrations established the recurrence of the images of orifice: jaws, caves, and so forth. The variety and range of these illustrations were truly extraordinary.

3. *The Maelstrom*. Mr. Sowers reached perhaps his peak of analytic insight when he remarked that the images comprised under his third head essentially represented to us a "condition or a situation, full of chaos, claustrophobic jamming, nightmarish atmosphere, flashbulb lighting and dark background, all sorts of contrary, extremely unpleasant, disordered conditions which suggest *a world of depravity and disorder.*"

Mr. Sowers' next moves carried him into another sphere: he went ahead to develop a series of categories of formal devices most frequently discovered in the illustrations of the grotesque.

The first device he described under the name of *"aggressive* symmetry"; another as "overanimation"; a third, as the "obvious disintegration of form"; a fourth, as "attenuation." Mr. Sowers then spoke of "aggressive protrusions" and "highly overcharged *over*-articulation"; and then there was the reduction of all kinds of living forms of seeming *mechanism* or, as one might say, *under*-articulation. Then there was the Grotesque of "obsessions"; the Grotesque of "distinctions"; the Grotesque of "misplaced ability"—and, at this point, it seemed to me the speaker slipped into largely descriptive perspective and used a largely aesthetic vocabulary: "visual *double-entendre,*" "pure camp," the "Grotesque of Squalor," and so forth. Coming to his close, Mr. Sowers issued an important caution:

> The Grotesque is bound to be a culturally relative thing, so that what will strike a people at one time as being grotesque will not necessarily do so for others elsewhere, and so forth.

II

During the entire course of this presentation, I continued to ask myself a single set of questions: "To what sets of experiences did these images, these forms, and these devices refer? To what sets of experiences . . . could they be referred? Was there any kind of general view that one might evolve as to the sources, roots, meanings of the experience of the Grotesque? Where could one look for keys as to the issues, problems, dilemmas, displacements or whatever, which may have been roots and sources of the Grotesque? What elements or settings of sociocultural process, what aspects of group cultural experience, or the existences of individuals help explain the varieties of the grotesque?" Thus, as I must now confess, Mr. Sowers' presentation had the effect of deepening a suspicion I had from the start, namely, that far from constituting a single expression or naming a distinct species of events, the word "Grotesque" related to a mass of very different contexts and ranges of reference which spread over a wide expanse of densely tangled terrain.

And so having early lost my way on a dimly lit stretch of the road, I started on a new journey, whose results follow:

From one point of view, there is nothing more grotesque in the world than what we call "normal, everyday reality." This awareness has been illustrated with particular force by the contributors to the so-called "Theatre of the Absurd." Ionesco has been unambiguously clear on this score; he has repeatedly said that he has no intent in conjuring up works of the imagination in the conventional aesthetic sense. Nor will he allow that he considers himself a pessimist. Rather, in the idiom of our land, he has insisted on "telling it exactly as it is." Ionesco knows that when the ordinary is *re-presented,* it has a sense of total uncanniness; he feels obligated, he explains, to tell the story without adornment "so that people who feel a need for solutions can at least have something to depart from."

Are there circumstances when "normal reality" takes a more than normally grotesque appearance? The answer is yes—when times are unusually stressful; when sensitivities are exceptionally heightened; when an extraordinary shift in *consciousness* has resulted in a widened sense of a Great Awakening. Changes of this scope cause the familiar inconsistencies of the "taken-for-granted" world to appear void of reason, *absurd*.

I must admit that I am aware that strict warrant is lacking in the social sciences for some of the terms I have used in the last paragraph and some others I shall need to use from this point forward in my essay. For this reason I turn abruptly to a cluster of ticklish semantical problems associated with terms expelled or loosed from the languages of the social sciences and humanities too soon, before their older meanings and possible newer uses were fully explored. I speak first of three older terms which have long struck me as critical coordinates of a renovated theory of sociocultural process, the linked terms *Existence-Experience-Expression*. Only a few remarks about the so-called interfaces among these notions can be allowed here.

The word "existence" has long been a technical term in philosophy which has received new and vastly extended use in the "Existentialisms" of our day. Despite its roots in the classical past and its great range in present-day thought, it is not now a phrase in the working vocabulary of any of the cultural or social disciplines. As a frame of reference comprising every sort of factual situation, it can have many new uses in the study of sociocultural process. To understand the structures of cultural "experience" and expression we must surely know the effects of existential determinations.

The word "experience," dear to many philosophers since at least the times of Kant and Hegel—the Americans are especially numerous in this lot—oddly happens to be a word not in use or allowable in sociology, anthropology or psychology. There is no estimating the price paid by social scientists for the lack of this concept. I can allow myself only a few sentences to suggest some of the uses to which the term "experience" shall be put here. "Experience" in the present context refers to any trace which serves as an input in an ongoing process of response and making. Standing at the crossroads, experience is thus both a confluence and a source of change in existence and expression alike. The structure of events associated with the occasions of experience emerge at the crossroads of our journeys across life's way.

The third in my series—"expression"—seems to provoke least opposition today, at least in the generic sense in which I intend it, namely as any utterance, sign, or symbol or enactment to which a meaning can be imputed.

Our triangular perspective offers us many advantages over competing models. With its help, the social scientist and the humanist scholar are reasonably protected from falling into theoretical traps in the mapping of the links and directions of influence in sociocultural process. Our paradigm reminds us that experience cannot be described as a simple function of existence: all experience is also subject to the influence of intertemporal frames of expression. Conversely, cultural expression is never an immediate outcome of existence, individual or social; all cultural expression goes through the filter of experience. In short: if we omit the notion of experience, we omit the tides of human action and reaction; we omit the sources of innovation.

Grotesque images are the forms gestated in all the settings of our experience, against the horizon of the antecedent traditions of expression, on the basis of the existences we are fated to have. As I have written elsewhere, we all move in orbits of one sort or another. We all have the experiences of our worlds and we all, in one way or another, do actually give vent to or create expression of one or another sort. There is nothing in what I have said which would suggest that our *existences* are simple functions of our social locations, that our *experiences* are no more than the stimulus-sets of this time and place, or that our *expressions* are direct derivations of current patterns of existence or experience.

There are three other terms to which I find myself needing to have fresh access for the sake of helping to evolve an enriched vocabulary of the social sciences and humanities. I shall detail them in turn.

The word "consciousness" has no place at all in the vocabulary of current psychology, sociology, or anthropology despite the fact that it is in very frequent use, usually over on the Left, among those who want to talk about the *new consciousness* or *working-class consciousness,* the *myth of the objective consciousness,* or the relation of *consciousness* to society. Few of those who use the term normally undertake to say very much about it that is precise. (The situation is not much better for the critical word "unconscious"!)

"Civilization" is yet another critical word not now in systematic professional use at this time. There are hardly a handful of sociological colleagues across our country who would allow the words "civilization" or "civilizational" as technical terms of a responsible professional sociological language. (The latest edition of the *International Encyclopedia of the Social Sciences* does not have an entry under "Civilization"; instead, the reader is advised, "*See* Urbanization." Should he proceed to "Urbanization," he would find nothing on Civilization, nor, for that matter, would he find a great deal on Urbanization either from critical points of view that have the civilizational dimension.) In short, the sorts of distinctions that one would want to make in the area that are critical for the present purpose are not available.

How can we explain these gaps? I may not do more now than speak to this issue in a prefatory way. If we would make sense of our present maps of knowledge, we need to realize that each of our disciplines arrived at its present state in the course of a prolonged process of fission of older and more comprehensive units and unities. More recently than most historians suppose, particular sets of questions were disengaged from a primary matrix and were encouraged to claim an independent existence outside the matrix in which the questions had previously been imbedded. I have elsewhere documented the story of a sort of paradigm instance of this kind of atomization. Related processes occurred in all the social sciences.

Today, the questions which men put to themselves can only be put in terms of the specialized languages, the semantics of the individual disciplines. It is no wonder that I am taken to wander in so many areas in the effort to ask the sorts of questions central for the explorations of the grotesque.

Luckily, men committed to their specialties often do better than they *know*. This is attested by many of splendid studies, especially in anthropology, literary criticism, and so-called humanistic or literary sociology. Yet the fact is that so long as roads do not readily open out for new concepts; so long as fresh accesses to imperfectly explored old terms are lacking, it is not possible to ask questions in the proper way. I come now to a more decisive point.

III

The very large number of illustrations offered by Mr. Sowers ranged across very diverse historical periods and cultural settings, and yet they assumed a small number of forms. Shall we say that this fact proves the existence in the "collective unconscious" of a set of archetypes which are carried forth in the racial inheritance? Or shall we say that possibly there are structures of consciousness which, when triggered by some set of wider experiences in a given social or historical or cultural context, are likely to come up in almost the same fashion each time for other reasons?

Contemporary psychologists, sociologists, and anthropologists tend, in the main, to think they have ways of accounting for the symbols we are discussing without necessarily referring to any of the wider sociocultural historical frames.

All of us must recall innumerable cases of claims by men distinguished in the above mentioned disciplines, that some very fundamental and far-reaching collective alteration in structures of consciousness and expression are simple derivations of experiences *in the primary environment of family*.

This pattern of explanation is the one offered in most of the current discussions dealing with the "generation gap." It hardly matters whether authors we read are strongly committed to a strict Freudian or neo-Freudian or a social-psychological socialization model. The fact remains that for the majority of these writers the explanation which seems to have worth or relevance is the one which claims the primacy of some set of experiences within the original setting or socialization of family interaction.

Mr. Sowers appears to have felt under no special obligation to propose explanations of his examples of *Grotesque,* whether *monster, orifice,* or *maelstrom.* Even though I cannot promise to explore genetic issues in detail here, I find myself needing and wanting to make some distinctions in this sphere. Images of *monster* and *orifice* may—as a matter of fact they *do*—have a nearness to primary associations which are likely to recur in almost all peoples everywhere as a result of intense and searing experiences in the primary environments of coming into being, growth, and development. Renderings of these phenomena in the arts, especially the plastic arts, prove again and again to exhibit the workings and influence of primary process.

We are at a different horizon, however, when we seek to understand the illustrations of *maelstrom*. Here we see a much wider range of reference, and it is harder to connect with any single environment—it calls for a much wider setting of experience than either *monster* or *orifice*. The complex structures of societal or civilizational experience or, for that matter, even subsocietal, social group experience, are often of first instance in this case.

The fact is: there is no making sense of the total range of our experience without including reference to horizons and to vectors far beyond those of small groups and families. I see no reason to extend unqualified acceptance to the notion largely favored by American sociologists and psychologists, and said to derive from the fundamental work of Georg Simmel. For me sociology is a good deal more than the study or analysis of social (in the sense of *interpersonal*) interaction.[1]

Psycholologists and sociologists omit these wider frames of reference from their horizons at great loss. Philosophies of methodological individualism have worked great confusion here by casting doubt on both the reality and relevance of societal, international, civilizational and, indeed, even intercivilizational frames. Societies *do* run courses, but these courses are surely not necessarily linear; societies even exhibit *malaises,* distempers, and even functional disorders.

I have elsewhere contended that critical changes are now occurring dyschronically in central institutions and the structures of consciousness. Our society and our world are taking on the appearance of the Grotesque precisely because of the nightmarish jammings of these dyschronicities. The deep fissures traced by these jammings are leading great numbers to speak of desiring "to destroy *the system* ONCE AND FOR ALL," to cry out for a great deal more than a change of command or procedure in the way of running the economy; they demand the substitution of wholly new values for the ones now "believed to be" in the saddle. From every corner these days, calls for new heights of countercivilizational and civilizational fulfillment are coming to us from the societal depths. Civilizational, societal, sub-societal, and social group-processes continue to fuse into powerful images of maelstrom and Great Awakening.

Today the Grotesque is our everyday way of being and living, appearing and seeming, dressing and wandering forth into a demented world. Many of the most outstanding works of modern literary and visual art prove to re-present experience to us in terms of carnival or circus. A related sensibility is attested to by the use everywhere today of such terms as "scene," "put down," "put on," "camp," "laugh-in"!

The Grotesque is now revealed as the supreme vehicle for *"putting down* (and off) the old" and *"putting on* the new." *Annihilation* of the "gloomy actual," reads the scenario, is succeeded at once by total *re-creation ex nihilo;* ever pregnant Chaos engenders the Cosmos of the Everlasting Now—the Perfected Future!

IV

I allow myself a few related illustrations from the everyday life of our time. As odd as the manifestations of our time may seem, they are surely not unique.

Indeed, the Grotesque is once again an aspect of every single person's experience, just as it was in the days of Diogenes the Cynic; just as it was centuries later in the days of Dante, whose haunting visions of the Grotesque call out to us from the cantos of the *Inferno;* just as it was in the era of the Black Death and the Hundred Years' War when great numbers of men and women disported themselves too strangely for many contemporaries to understand. Everyone of us would do well to reread the chapter on "The Dance of Death," in Johan Huizinga's masterly *Waning of the Middle Ages.* Also: how forget the Ranters, Diggers, Levellers, Seekers, Families of Love in 17th-century England? The Lycanthropists and Nihilists of 19th-century France and Russia? Again and again, people—old and young alike—fashioning odd costumes and sometimes making their own flesh their only dress, ranging across the world.

There may, however, be one more aspect of our situation. The apparent anomalies of our time are general, universal; they are also deliberate. Everything undergoes the kinds of shifting that one would expect in a society which, as Kierkegaard saw, had this inexhaustible capacity to absorb any sort of dissenting innovation and turn it into some kind of form of impersonation, new life-style, new stage-setting, new points of departure for spectacle, business, or busy work.

When I walk out the door of my classroom into New York City, I always look very carefully around me and insist on trying to identify the cast of characters, *dramatis personae,* striding on the twin stages of Fifth Avenue and Fourteenth Street. Inevitably, the "actors" range all the way from the Cynics or early Christians to tomorrow's Spacemen; the hair style, garb, walk, facial and other gestures, proclaim the man. A little while ago, the 14th century was IN (*fashion*), but now it seems OUT (*of fashion*). Only yesterday one of my favorite students was very much IN—wearing the Rubens' beret. But that was *yesterday!* As for resurrections of the 19th century, they occur too often to make news. Simultaneity has not yet conquered all. Despite the apparent depth references of our acts, our perceptions remain traditional. (The collective "our" here refers to all of us, including today's artists, scholars, actors.) If we had a depth-historical relation to time-space, we would have much less trouble understanding the resurrection among us of groups of people reliving the lives of the Diggers or the Families of Love and Charlie Mansons.

Nothing that has once become history ever disappears. Anything that once was can always be. History always—and never—repeats itself. Yet it is not necessary to say, as Marx insisted we must say, that if history repeated itself it would manifest itself the first time as Tragedy and the second time as Farce. This is a notable cultural epigram but not an unexceptionable rule of history.

V

Images of the Grotesque, especially images of the maelstrom, regularly seem to multiply when large numbers of people find it impossible to function, much less thrive, in their everyday worlds. The hopes for finding a modicum of joy and meaning in ordinary life—what I prefer to call *generic succession existence*—are now felt to be choked.

Then, each one is affected in a measure by the experience of askewness. We must recall that a large number of Mr. Sowers' pungent illustrations last time attested to the passage of persons and groups through heightened states, including some of a so-called "pathological" or "psychopathological" sort. The feelings and fantasies at work in these episodes are very frequently beyond the power of even gifted men and artists to control or moderate; when these states occur they reveal a terrible insistence and sameness. This is why the symbols are so often indiscriminately ascribed to experience assumed to be prior in the biogenetic sequence: there is a blunder here, sociological no less than logical, which results from the failure to distinguish between an originative source and a proximate expression. The role played by symbols usually ascribed to primary process does not constitute proof that the originating issues root in the biological or familial frames. Much of today's evidence of primary process traces to the perturbations in societal, political, and civilizational settings. We turn now to these wider settings.[2]

Every man is ever in the midst of predicaments from which neither culture nor civilization can wholly shield him. So long, however, as human agents are able to feel that the tides of change and the streams of cues are congruent with their needs and expectations, they are generally able to achieve some meaning which will sustain them through their lives. In times of heightened strains and sensitivities, ever larger segments of experience seem empty of rhyme or reason—*Grotesque*. The various kinds of discontinuities envelop increasing numbers in a sense of maelstrom.

The fact of change is not of itself the decisive element in the grotesque. We are all able to tolerate inconsistencies, but we cannot tolerate inconsistencies that are so severe that we fail to find anywhere around us any sense of vital center or purpose or meaning or any rationale to which we can in fact offer our allegiance or loyalty. Few of us can live at ease in maelstroms.

Lastly—within our now enlarged frame of reference—there is another disjunction which implies especially deep crises in civilizational values. This occurs when the social organization seems to be working at a very high level of "productive efficiency"; when the cultural system seems to be maintaining itself with the help of vast numbers of persons who are specialists—yet many people going through their rounds in the phases of life's cycle feel let down by the incongruous evidence that the system works to provide them largely negative psychic and moral incomes. Their senses of fitness are outraged. In the language of the Existentialists, the outcomes seem arbitrary, "nauseous," absolutely *grotesque*.

Whether we be ready or not, junctures of this sort call upon us to offer more than merely reactive response to the flux of experience in the spirit of the Grotesque. We find ourselves challenged to evolve new societal structures, new structures of new consciousness and to find new patterns of meaning. We are desperate to work our way out of maelstrom.

The achievement of new structures of this scope is always difficult. Today the difficulties are doubly great because of the concurrences of confusing conjunctions and discontinuities. Extending a fertile suggestion made by an art historian in the pages of Karl Mannheim, I find myself inclined to describe these movements under the names of *"contemporaneity of the non-contemporaneous"* and *"non-contemporaneity of the contemporaneous."*

Neither of these situations is purely of the present moment, or purely modern, or purely Western. Yet there have been few eras when the sense of commingling of all events and time scales has been so powerful or when, on the other hand, the feelings of discontinuities in the senses of reality have been so rife among clashing generational groups.

Indeed, the mixed experience of *simultaneity* and *non-contemporaneity* are as general and as encompassing as they have ever been in the history of civilizations. A hundred factors conspire to extend imagination in global and cosmic directions. Arts, sciences, technologies work together to reinforce the sense that the *entire* past and present are caught up in ecstatic embrace. All history has now become material for a living theatre of ongoing spectacle. The past is felt to be wholly alive and the insurgent future is waiting in the wings for immediate appearance.

The "grotesque" new ways do not inevitably have to be mere "put-ons," or totalistic aggressions; some are experimental designs for living in a world that is only now being forged through new structures of consciousness. After new journeys—"trips"—there will come new maps. It hardly matters whether we welcome the results or not; many of the new ways of being now in the making will constitute themselves as the prevailing modes and the new social metaphysics.

The "contemporaneity of the non-contemporaneous" is a less taxing frame than the more familiar *"non-contemporaneity of the contemporaneous."* It is the latter which is cited nowadays as the *central* element in the gap of the generations. The structures of our varying sensibilities are not so much mistaken in their objects as they are differently related to the myriad changes going on in our societal experience and in our ways of life. Those who have become hardened crystals of now unlivable pasts are opposed by those who have yet to forge viable ways. Odd conjunctions and disjunctions occur at every turn. The warring forms of consciousness embroil all in a state of civil war.

We have come full circle and are back at the center from which we have never truly departed. *The omnipresence of the grotesque* is the very hallmark of our time.

NOTES

1 I am pleased to report that my long-standing conviction on this matter is now supported in a newly discovered, as yet unpublished, manuscript of Max Weber, one of our foremost sociologists and historians of culture and civilization, who declares that Georg Simmel made a serious mistake in this definition of sociology.

2 See the addendum at the end of the References.

REFERENCES

Some of the points discussed above are considered in a number of my previously published essays, which are listed below.

1951 The Moralities of Thought and the Logics of Action. (Originally written in 1951 and circulated to colleagues and students in Minneapolis, Minn.)

1956 The Future of Illusions. In *Man in Contemporary Society,* Vol. 2. New York: Columbia University Press. Pp. 958–979. (Originally in *Psychoanalysis,* Vol. 2. Summer 1954.)

1961 Introductory Comment on Norman O. Brown's "Apocalypse. The Place of Mystery in the Life of the Mind." *Harper's Magazine,* May. Pp. 46–47.

1962 Introduction to Søren Kierkegaard's *The Point of View for My Work as an Author.* New York: Harper Torchbooks. Pp. v–xxi.

1963 *The Balcony* and Parisian Existentialism. *Tulane Drama Review,* Vol. 7, No. 3. Pp. 66–79. Reprinted in Kelley Morris (Ed.), *The Theatre of the Double.* New York: Bantam Books, 1970.

Sartre, Genet, Freud. *This Review,* Vol. 50, No. 3. Pp. 156–171.

1964 Actors, Directors, Roles, Cues, Meanings, Identities: Further Thoughts on "Anomie." *Ibid.,* Vol. 51, No. 1. Pp. 135–160.

1965 The Psychoanalyst as Mediator and Double-Agent. *Ibid.,* Vol. 52, No. 3. Pp. 45–60.

Max Weber's *The Sociology of Religion:* A Review-Article. *American Sociological Review,* Vol. 30, No. 4. Pp. 595–599.

On Life's Way—Reflections on *Herzog.* In *Soundings.* New York: State University of New York at Stony Brook. Spring. Pp. 148–154.

Self-Images and Systems of Spiritual Direction in the History of European Civilization. In S. Z. Klausner (Ed.), *The Quest for Self-Control: Classical Philosophies and Scientific Research.* New York: Free Press. Pp. 49–103.

1968 The *Avant-Garde* Dramatist as Alienist and Double-Agent. *This Review,* Vol. 55, No. 3. Pp. 505–512.

1969 *Conscience* and the Making of Early Modern Cultures: *The Protestant Ethic* beyond Max Weber. *Social Research,* Vol. 36, No. 1. Pp. 4–21. (Originally presented at the session on "Sociology and History" to the American Sociological Association, August 1967, San Francisco.)

Introduction to G. Rosen's *Madness and Society.* New York: Harper Torchbooks.

1970 Psychiatry and Its Histories: From Tradition to Take-Off. In G. Mora and J. Brand (Eds.), *Psychiatry and Its History: Methodological Problems in Research.* Springfield, Ill.: Charles C. Thomas. Pp. 229–259.

Civilizations, Communities, Consciences. Four Public Lectures. University of Chicago, Spring Quarter. Sponsored by The Committee on Social Thought. (In manuscript.)

ADDENDUM

A reader of the foregoing (Marie C. Nelson) suggests that I add the following to lines 27–29 of p. 181:

> What *does* root is the need—when social chaos offers no adequate protective structure—to take refuge in disconcerting acts and alarming self-adornment as aggressive self-protection to actively ward off evil. And when this is sufficiently widespread, such grotesquerie of act and appearance assumes also the passive function of self-protective coloration. An instance of this might be the wearing of the Safari hat which proclaims at one and the same time: "I am a White Hunter *and* a harmless tourist."

In this connection, attention is called to Mrs. Nelson's previous paper, published under the name of Marie L. Coleman, "An Integrative Approach to Individual and Group Psychology." *This Review*, Vol. 36, No. 4. 1949. Pp. 389–401.

20

Excerpts from *Notes and Counter Notes: Writings on the Theatre*

Eugène Ionesco

I was dissatisfied even by the plays I had managed to read. Not all of them! For I was not blind to the merits of Sophocles, Aeschylus or Shakespeare, nor a little later to some of the plays of Kleist or Büchner. Why? Because, I thought, all these plays make extraordinary reading on account of their literary qualities, which may well not be specifically theatrical. In any case, after Shakespeare and Kleist, I do not think I have enjoyed reading a play. Strindberg seemed to me clumsy and inadequate. I was even bored by Molière. I was not interested in those stories of misers, hypocrites and cuckolds. I disliked his unmetaphysical mind. Shakespeare raised questions about the whole condition and destiny of man. In the long run Molière's little problems seemed to me of relatively minor importance, sometimes a little sad of course, dramatic even, but never tragic; for they could be resolved. The unendurable admits of no solution, and only the unendurable is profoundly tragic, profoundly comic and essentially theatrical.

On the other hand, the greatness of Shakespeare's plays seemed to me diminished in performance. No Shakespearean production ever captivated me as much as my reading of *Hamlet, Othello* and *Julius Cae-*

sar, etc. As I went so rarely to the theatre, perhaps I have never seen the best productions of Shakespeare's drama? In any case, in performance I had the impression that the unendurable had been made endurable. It was anguish tamed.

So I am really not a passionate theatregoer, still less a man of the theatre. I really hated the theatre. It bored me. And yet . . . when I was a child, I can still remember how my mother could not drag me away from the Punch and Judy show in the Luxembourg Gardens. I would go there day after day and could stay there, spellbound, all day long. But I did not laugh. That Punch and Judy show kept me there open-mouthed, watching those puppets talking, moving and cudgeling each other. It was the very image of the world that appeared to me, strange and improbable but truer than true, in the profoundly simplifed form of caricature, as though to stress the grotesque and brutal nature of the truth. And from then until I was fifteen any form of play would thrill me and make me feel that the world is very strange, a feeling so deeply rooted that it has never left me. Every live show awoke in me this feeling for the strangeness of the world, and it impressed me nowhere more than at the theatre. And yet, when I was thirteen, I wrote a play, my first piece of writing, which had nothing strange about it. It was a patriotic play: extreme youth is an excuse for anything.

When did I stop liking the theatre? From the moment when, as I began to grow more clear-sighted and acquire a critical mind, I became conscious of stage tricks, of obvious theatrical contrivance, that is to say from the moment I stopped being naïve. Where are the *monstres sacrés* of the theatre who could give us back our lost naïveté? And what possible magic could justify the theatre's claim to bind us in its spell? There is no magic now, nothing is sacred: there is no valid reason for this to be restored to us.

Besides, there is nothing more difficult than writing for the theatre. Novels and poems last well. Their appeal is not blunted even by the centuries. We still find interest in a number of minor works from the nineteenth, eighteenth and seventeenth centuries. And how many even older works do we not still find interesting? All painting and music resists the passage of time. The moving simplicity of the least significant sculptured heads on countless cathedrals still remains fresh and alive, intact; and we shall go on responding to the architectural rhythms of great monuments of the most distant civilizations, which speak to us directly through them in a language that is clear and revealing. But what of the theatre?

Today the theatre is blamed by some for not belonging to its own times. In my view it belongs only too well. This is what makes it so weak and ephemeral. I mean that the theatre *does* belong to its own times, but not quite enough. Every period needs something "out of period" and incommunicable to be introduced into what is "period" and communicable. Everything is a circumscribed moment in history, of course. But all history is contained in each moment of history: any moment in history is valid when it transcends history; in the particular lies the universal.

The themes chosen by many authors merely spring from a certain ideological fashion, which is something *less* than the period it belongs to. Or else these themes are the expression of some particular political attitude, and the plays that illustrate them will die with the ideology that has inspired them, for ideologies go out of fashion. Any Christian tomb, any Greek or Etruscan stele moves us and tells us more about the destiny of man than any number of laboriously committed plays, which are made to serve a discipline, a system of thought and language different from what is properly their own.

It is true that all authors have tried to make propaganda. The great ones are those who failed, who have gained access, consciously or not, to a deeper and more universal reality. Nothing is more precarious than a play. It may maintain its position for a very short time, but it soon falls apart, revealing nothing but contrivance.

In all sincerity, Corneille bores me. Perhaps we like him (without believing in him) only from habit. We cannot help it. He has been forced on us at school. I find Schiller unbearable. For a long time now, Marivaux's plays have seemed to me futile little comedies. Musset's are thin and Vigny's unactable. Victor Hugo's bloody dramas send us into fits of laughter; whereas it is difficult to laugh, whatever people say, at most of Labiche's funny plays. Dumas fils, with his *Dame aux Camélias,* is ridiculously sentimental. As for the others! Oscar Wilde? Facile. Ibsen? Boorish. Strindberg? Clumsy. A recent dramatist, Giraudoux, not long dead, does not always get across the footlights now; like Cocteau's, his drama seems to us superficial and contrived. It has lost its sparkle: with Cocteau the theatrical tricks are too obvious; with Giraudoux the tricks and contrivances of language, distinguished though they be, still remain tricks.

Pirandello himself has been left behind the times, for his theatre was built on theories about personality or the multiformity of truth, which now seem clear as daylight since psychoanalysis and psychology plumbed the depths. In testing the validity of Pirandello's theories, modern psychology, inevitably going further than Pirandello in its exploration of the human psyche, certainly confirms Pirandello's findings, but at the same time shows him to be limited and inadequate: for what has been said by Pirandello is now said more thoroughly and scientifically. So the value of his theatre does not rest on his contribution to psychology but on the quality of his drama, which must inevitably lie elsewhere: what interests us in this author is no longer the discovery of the antagonistic elements in human personality, but what he has made of them dramatically. The strictly theatrical interest of his work lies outside science, beyond the limits of his own ideology. All that is left of Pirandello is his dramatic technique, the mechanics of his theatre: which again proves that drama founded on ideology or philosophy, exclusively inspired by them, is built on sand and crumbles away. It is his dramatic idiom, his purely theatrical instinct that keeps Pirandello alive for us today.

In the same way, it is not Racine's psychological insight into the passions that sustains his theatre; but what Racine has made of it as a poet and man of the theatre.

If we were to go through the centuries and count the dramatists who can still move an audience, we should find about twenty . . . or at the most thirty. But the paintings, poems and novels that still mean something to us can be counted in their thousands. The naïveté essential to a work of art is lacking in the theatre. I do not say a dramatist of great simplicity will not appear; but at the moment I see no sign of him on the horizon. I mean a simplicity that is lucid, springing from the inmost depths of our being, revealing them, revealing them to ourselves, restoring our own simplicity, our secret souls. At the moment there is no naïveté, in audience or writer.

What faults are there then to be found in dramatists and their plays? Their tricks, I was saying, that is to say their too obvious contrivances. The theatre may appear to be a secondary, a minor form of literature. It always seems rather coarse-grained. There is no doubt it is an art that deals in effects. It cannot do without them, and this is the reproach leveled against it. And these effects have to be broad. One has the impression that the texture has been roughened. The textual refinement of literature is ironed out. Drama of literary subtlety soon wears thin. Half-tones are deepened or banished by light that is too brilliant. No shading, no nuance is possible. Problem plays, *pièces à thèse,* are roughhewn pieces of approximation. Drama is not the idiom for ideas. When it tries to become a vehicle for ideologies, all it can do is vulgarize them. It dangerously oversimplifies. It makes them too elementary and depreciates them. It is "naïve," but in the bad sense. All ideological drama runs the risk of being parochial. What would, not the *utility,* but the proper *function* of the theatre be, if it was restricted to the task of duplicating philosophy or theology or politics or pedagogy? Psychological drama is not psychological enough. One might as well read a psychological treatise. Ideological drama is not philosophical enough. Instead of going to see a dramatic illustration of this or that political creed I would rather read my usual daily paper or listen to the speeches of my party candidates.

Dissatisfied with the gross naïveté and rudimentary character of the theatre, philosophers, literary men, ideologists and poets of refinement, all intelligent people try to make their drama intelligent. They write with intelligence, with taste and talent. They put their thoughts into it, they express their conception of life and the world, and believe that writing a play should be like presenting a thesis in which problems find their solution on the stage. They sometimes construct their work in the form of a syllogism, with the two premises in the first two acts and the conclusion in the third.

There is no denying the construction is sometimes first-rate. And yet this does not answer the demands we make of drama, because it fails to lift the theatre out of an intermediate zone that lies somewhere between where discursive reasoning can be only one ingredient—and the higher realms of thought.

Should one give up the theatre if one refuses to reduce it to a parochial level or subordinate it to manifestations of the human spirit that impose different forms and modes of expression? Can it, like painting or music, find its own autonomous existence?

Drama is one of the oldest of the arts. And I can't help thinking we cannot do without it. We cannot resist the desire to people a stage with live characters that are at the same time real and invented. We cannot deny our need to make them speak and live before our eyes. To bring phantoms to life and give them flesh and blood is a prodigious adventure, so unique that I myself was absolutely amazed, during the rehearsals of my first play, when I suddenly saw, moving on the stage of the *Noctambules,* characters who owed their life to me. It was a terrifying experience. What right had I to do a thing like that? Was it allowed? And how could Nicolas Bataille, one of my actors, turn into Mr. Martin? . . . It was almost diabolical. And so it was only when I had written something for the theatre, quite by chance and with the intention of holding it up to ridicule, that I began to love it, to rediscover it in myself, to understand it, to be fascinated by it: and then I knew what I had to do.

I told myself that the too intelligent playwrights were not intelligent enough: that it was no use for thinkers to look to the theatre for the idiom of a philosophical treatise; that when they tried to bring too much subtlety and refinement into the theatre it was not only too much but not enough; that if the theatre was merely a deplorable enlargement of refined subtleties, which I found so embarrassing, it merely meant that the enlargement was not sufficient. The overlarge was not large enough, the unsubtle was too subtle.

So if the essence of the theatre lay in magnifying its effects, they had to be magnified still further, underlined and stressed to the maximum. To push drama out of that intermediate zone where it is neither theatre nor literature is to restore it to its own domain, to its natural frontiers. It was not for me to conceal the devices of the theatre, but rather make them still more evident, deliberately obvious, go all-out for caricature and the grotesque, way beyond the pale irony of witty drawing-room comedies. No drawing-room comedies, but farce, the extreme exaggeration of parody. Humor, yes, but using the methods of burlesque. Comic effects that are firm, broad and outrageous. No dramatic comedies either. But back to the unendurable. Everything raised to paroxysm, where the source of tragedy lies. A theatre of violence: violently comic, violently dramatic.

Avoid psychology or rather give it a metaphysical dimension. Drama lies in extreme exaggeration of the feelings, an exaggeration that dislocates flat everyday reality. Dislocation, disarticulation of language too.

Moreover, if the actors embarrassed me by not seeming natural enough, perhaps it was because they also were, or tried to be, *too* natural: by trying not to be, perhaps they will still appear natural, but in a different way. They must not be afraid of not being natural.

We need to be virtually bludgeoned into detachment from our daily lives, our habits and mental laziness, which conceal from us the strangeness of the world. Without a fresh virginity of mind, without a new and healthy awareness of existential reality, there can be no theatre and no art either; the real must be in a way dislocated, before it can be reintegrated.

To achieve this effect, a trick can sometimes be used: playing against the text. A serious, solemn, formal production or interpretation can be grafted onto a text that is absurd, wild and comic. On the other hand, to avoid the ridiculous sentimentality of the tear-jerker, a dramatic text can be treated as buffoonery and the tragic feeling of a play can be underlined by farce. Light makes shadows darker, shadows intensify light. For my part, I have never understood the difference people make between the comic and the tragic. As the "comic" is an intuitive perception of the absurd, it seems to me more hopeless than the "tragic." The "comic" offers no escape. I say "hopeless," but in reality it lies outside the boundaries of hope or despair.

Tragedy may appear to some in one sense comforting, for in trying to express the helplessness of a beaten man, one broken by fate for example, tragedy thus admits the reality of fate and destiny, of sometimes incomprehensible but objective laws that govern the universe. And man's helplessness, the futility of our efforts, can also, in a sense, appear comic.

I have called my comedies "anti-plays" or "comic dramas," and my dramas "pseudo-dramas" or "tragic farces": for it seems to me that the comic is tragic, and that the tragedy of man is pure derision. The contemporary critical mind takes nothing too seriously or too lightly. In *Victims of Duty* I tried to sink comedy in tragedy: in *The Chairs* tragedy in comedy or, if you like, to confront comedy and tragedy in order to link them in a new dramatic synthesis. But it is not a true synthesis, for these two elements do not coalesce, they coexist: one constantly repels the other, they show each other up, criticize and deny one another and, thanks to their opposition, thus succeed dynamically in maintaining a balance and creating tension. The two plays that best satisfy this condition are, I believe: *Victims of Duty* and *The New Tenant.*

Similarly, one can confront the prosaic and the poetic, the strange and the ordinary. That is what I wanted to do in *Jack, or the Submission,* which I called "*a naturalistic* comedy" too, because after starting off in a naturalistic tone I tried to go beyond naturalism.

In the same way *Amédée, or How to Get Rid of It,* where the scene is laid in the flat of a petit bourgeois couple, is a realistic play into which fantastic elements have been introduced, a contrast intended at one and the same time to banish and recall the "realism."

In my first play, *The Bald Soprano,* which started off as an attempt to parody the theatre, and hence a certain kind of human behavior, it was by plunging into banality, by draining the sense from the hollowest clichés of everyday language that I tried to render the strangeness that seems to pervade our whole existence. The tragic and the farcical, the prosaic and the poetic, the realistic and the fantastic, the strange and the ordinary, perhaps these are the contradictory principles (there is no theatre without conflict) that may serve as a basis for a new dramatic structure. In this way perhaps the unnatural can by its very violence appear natural, and the too natural will avoid the naturalistic.

The theatre (or what is called theatre) taken to pieces.

The Bald Soprano, like *The Lesson,* among other things attempts to make the mechanics of drama function in a vacuum. An experiment in abstract or nonrepresentational drama. Or, on the contrary, concrete drama if you like, since it consists only of what can be seen, since it comes to life on the stage, since it is play acting, playing with words, with scenes and images, giving concrete expression to symbols. And so made of nonrepresentational forms. The interest does not lie in any kind of plot, in any particular action which may play a subordinate part, but must do no more than canalize a dramatic tension it supports, sustains and punctuates. The aim is to release dramatic tension without the help of any proper plot or any special subject. But it still leads, in the end, to the revelation of something monstrous: this is essential, moreover, for in the last resort drama is a revelation of monstrosity or of some monstrous formless state of being or of monstrous forms that we carry within ourselves. The task is to arrive at this exaltation or these revelations without a theme or subject that justifies or motivates, for this would be ideological and so false and hypocritical.

The progression of purposeless passion, a rising crescendo that is all the more natural, dramatic and exciting because it is not hampered by content, and by that I mean any *apparent* content or subject which conceals the *genuine* subject from us: the particular meaning of a dramatic plot hides its essential significance.

Abstract theatre. Pure drama. Anti-thematic, anti-ideological, anti-social-realist, anti-philosophical, anti-boulevard-psychology, anti-bourgeois, the rediscovery of a new free theatre. And by free I mean liberated, without prejudice, exploratory: the only theatre that can be a sincere and precise witness and uncover fresh evidence.

The Bald Soprano: characters without character. Puppets. Faceless creatures. Or rather empty frames, which the actors can fill with their own faces, their own shapes, souls, flesh and blood. Into the disconnected and meaningless words that they utter they can put what they like, express what they like: comedy, drama, humor, themselves, what they have in them that is more than themselves. They have no need to slip into the skins of their characters, into other people's skins, all they have to do is to slip straight into their own skins. This is not so easy as it looks. It is not so easy to be oneself, to play one's own character.

And yet the young cast of *The Bald Soprano* really succeeded in being themselves. Or rather a part of themselves. Hollow, purely social characters: for there is no such thing as a social soul.

They were full of grace, the young actors in Nicolas Bataille's company in *The Bald Soprano:* a void in Sunday-clothes, a charming void, a blossoming void, a void of phantom figures, a youthful void, a contemporary void. Beyond the emptiness, there still remained their charm.

Push burlesque to its extreme limits, then, with a flick of the finger, an imperceptible transition, and you are back in tragedy. It is a conjuring trick. The public should not notice the passage from burlesque to tragedy. Neither perhaps should the actors, or only slightly. The light changes. That is what I tried in *The Lesson*.

> A burlesque text, play it dramatic.
> A dramatic text, play it burlesque.
> Make words say things they never meant.

One cannot always take credit for everything: an author's comic writing is very often the expression of a certain confusion. His own nonsense is exploited, it makes people laugh. It also makes many dramatic critics say that what one writes is extremely intelligent.

Every period has its own special commonplaces, apart from the more ordinary ones that belong to every period. Every ideology, I mean every ideological cliché, will one day look pretty silly . . . and comical.

If I understood everything, I would obviously not be comic.

21

Self-consciousness*

R. D. Laing

Self-consciousness, as the term is ordinarily used, implies two things: an awareness of oneself by oneself, and *an awareness of oneself as an object of someone else's observation.*

These two forms of awareness of the self, as an object in one's own eyes and as an object in the other's eyes, are closely related to each other. In the schizoid individual both are enhanced and both assume a somewhat compulsive nature. The schizoid individual is frequently tormented by the compulsive nature of his awareness of his own processes, and also by the equally compulsive nature of his sense of his body as an object in the world of others. The heightened sense of being always seen, or at any rate of being always potentially seeable, may be principally referable to the body, but the preoccupation with being seeable may be condensed with the idea of the mental self being penetrable, and vulnerable, as when the individual feels that one can look right through him into his "mind" or "soul." Such "plate-glass" feelings are usually spoken about in terms of metaphor or simile, but in psychotic conditions the gaze or scrutiny of the other can be experienced as an actual penetration into the core of the "inner" self.

* From *The Divided Self.* The editors.

The heightening or intensifying of the awareness of one's own being, both as an object of one's own awareness and of the awareness of others, is practically universal in adolescents, and is associated with the well-known accompaniments of shyness, blushing, and general embarrassment. One readily invokes some version of "guilt" to account for such awkwardness. But to suggest, say, that the individual is self-conscious "because" he has guilty secrets (e.g. masturbation) does not take us far. Most adolescents masturbate, and not uncommonly they are frightened that it will show in some way in their faces. But why, if "guilt" is the key to this phenomenon, does guilt have these particular consequences and not others, since there are many ways of being guilty, and a heightened sense of oneself as an embarrassed or ridiculous object in the eyes of others is not the only way. "Guilt" in itself is inadequate to help us here. Many people with profound and crushing guilt do not feel unduly self-conscious. Moreover, it is possible, for instance, to tell a lie and feel guilt at doing so without being frightened that the lie will show in one's face, or that one will be struck blind. It is indeed an important achievement for the child to gain the assurance that the adults have no means of knowing what he does, if they do not see him; that they cannot do more than guess at what he thinks to himself if he does not tell them; that actions that no one has seen and thoughts that he has "kept to himself" are in no way accessible to others unless he himself "gives the show away." The child who *cannot* keep a secret or who *cannot* tell a lie because of the persistence of such primitive magical fears has not established his full measure of autonomy and identity. No doubt in most circumstances good reasons can be found against telling lies, but the *inability* to do so is not one of the best reasons.

The self-conscious person feels he is more the object of other people's interest than, in fact, he is. Such a person walking along the street approaches a cinema queue. He will have to "steel himself" to walk past it: preferably, he will cross to the other side of the street. It is an ordeal to go into a restaurant and sit down at a table by himself. At a dance he will wait until two or three couples are already dancing before he can face taking the floor himself, and so on.

Curiously enough, those people who suffer from intense anxiety when performing or acting before an audience are by no means necessarily "self-conscious" in general, and people who are usually extremely self-conscious may lose their compulsive preoccupations with this issue when they are performing in front of others—the very situation, on first reflection, one might suppose would be most difficult for them to negotiate.

Further features of such self-consciousness may seem again to point to guilt being the key to the understanding of the difficulty. The look that the individual expects other people to direct upon him is practically always imagined to be unfavourably critical of him. He is frightened that he will look a fool, or he is frightened that other people will think he wants to show off. When a patient expresses such phantasies it is easy to suppose that he has a secret unacknowledged desire to show off, to be the centre of attraction, to be superior, to make others look fools beside him, and that this desire is charged with guilt and anxiety and so is unable to be experienced as such. Situations, therefore, which evoke phantasies of this desire being gratified lose all pleasure. The individual would then be a concealed exhibitionist, whose body was unconsciously equated with his penis. Every time his body is on show, therefore, the neurotic guilt associated with this potential avenue of gratification exposes him to a form of castration anxiety which "presents" phenomenologically as "self-consciousness."

An understanding of self-consciousness in some such terms eludes, I believe, the central issue facing the individual whose basic existential position is one of ontological insecurity and whose schizoid nature is partly a direct expression of, and occasion for, his ontological insecurity, and partly an attempt to overcome it; or, putting the last remark in slightly different terms, partly an attempt to defend himself against the dangers to his being that are the consequences of his failure to achieve a secure sense of his own identity.

Self-consciousness in the ontologically insecure person plays a double role:

1. Being aware of himself and knowing that other people are aware of him are a means of assuring himself that he exists, and also that they exist. Kafka clearly demonstrates this in his story called "Conversation with a Suppliant": the suppliant starts from the existential position of ontological insecurity. He states, "There has never been a time in which I have been convinced from within myself that I am alive." The need to gain a conviction of his own aliveness and the realness of things is, therefore, the basic issue in his existence. His way of seeking to gain such conviction is by feeling himself to be an object in the real world; but, since *his* world is unreal, he must be an object in the world of someone else, for objects to other people seem to be real, and even calm and beautiful. At least, ". . . it must be so, for I often hear people talking about them as though they were." Hence it is that he makes his confession ". . . don't be angry if I tell you that *it is the aim of my life to get people to look at me*" (italics mine).

A further factor is the discontinuity in the temporal self. When there is uncertainty of identity in time, there is a tendency to rely on spatial means of identifying oneself. Perhaps this goes some way to account for the frequently pre-eminent importance to the person of being *seen*. However, sometimes the greatest reliance may be placed on the awareness of oneself in time. This is especially so when time is experienced as a succession of moments. The loss of a section of the linear temporal series of moments through inattention to one's time-self may be felt as a catastrophe. Dooley (1941) gives various examples of this temporal self-awareness arising as part of the person's "struggle against fear of obliteration" and his attempt at the preservation of his integrity "against threats of being engulfed, crushed, of losing . . . identity. . . ." One of her patients said: "I forgot myself at the Ice Carnival the other night. I was so absorbed in looking at it that I forgot what time it was and who and where I was. When I suddenly realized I hadn't been thinking about myself I was frightened to death. The unreality feeling came. I must never forget myself for a single minute. I watch the clock and keep busy, or else I won't know who I am" (p. 17).

2. In a world full of danger, to be a potentially seeable object is to be constantly exposed to danger. Self-consciousness, then, may be the apprehensive awareness of oneself as potentially exposed to danger by the simple fact of being visible to others. The obvious defence against such a danger is to make oneself invisible in one way or another.

In an actual instance, the issue is thus always necessarily complex. Kafka's suppliant makes it the aim of his life to get people to look at him, since thereby he mitigates his state of depersonalization and derealization and inner deadness. He needs other people to experience him as a real live person because he has never been convinced from within himself that he was alive. This, however, implies a trust in the benign quality of the other person's apprehension of him which is not always present. Once he becomes aware of something it becomes unreal, although "I always feel that they were once real and are now flitting away." One would not be surprised to find that such a person would have in some measure a distrust of other people's awareness of him. What, for instance, if they had, after all, the same "fugitive awareness" of him as he had of them? Could he place any more reliance on their consciousness than on his own to lend him a conviction that he was alive? Quite often, in fact, the balance swings right over so that the individual feels that his greatest risk is to be the object of another person's awareness. The myth of Perseus and the Medusa's head, the "evil eye," delusions of death rays and so on are I believe referable to this dread.

Indeed, considered biologically, the very fact of being visible exposes an animal to the risk of attack from its enemies, and no animal is without enemies. Being visible is therefore a basic biological risk; being invisible is a basic biological defence. We all employ some form of camouflage. The following is a written description given by a patient who employed a form of magical camouflage to help her over her anxiety when she was twelve years old.

> I was about twelve, and had to walk to my father's shop through a large park, which was a long, dreary walk. I supposed, too, that I was rather scared. I didn't like it, especially when it was getting dark. I started to play a game to help to pass the time. You know how as a child you count the stones or stand on the crosses on the pavement—well, I hit on this way of passing the time. *It struck me that if I stared long enough at the environment that I would blend with it and disappear just as if the place was empty and I had disappeared. It is as if you get yourself to feel you don't know who you are or where you are.* To blend into the scenery so to speak. Then, you are scared of it because it begins to come on without encouragement. I would just be walking along and felt that I had blended with the landscape. Then I would get frightened and repeat my name over and over again to bring me back to life, so to speak.

It may be that here is a biological analogue for many anxieties about being obvious, being out of the ordinary, being distinctive, drawing attention to oneself, where the defences employed against such dangers so often consist in attempts to merge with the human landscape, to make it as difficult as possible for anyone to see in what way one differs from anyone else. Oberndorf (1950), for instance, has suggested that depersonalization is a defence analogous to "playing possum." We shall consider these defences in some detail in the case of Peter (Chapter 8).

Being like everyone else, being someone other than oneself, playing a part, being incognito, anonymous, being nobody (psychotically, pretending to have no body), are defences that are carried through with great thoroughness in certain schizoid and schizophrenic conditions.

The above patient became frightened when she had blended with the landscape. Then, in her words: "I would repeat my name over and over again to bring me back to life, so to speak." This raises an important issue. I think that it would be a correct conjecture to suppose that the particular form of defence against anxiety in this little girl could only have arisen from a shaky ontological foundation. A securely established sense of identity is not easily lost, not as readily as this girl of twelve was able to lose hers in her game. It is, therefore, probable that this very ontological insecurity at least partly occasioned her anxiety in the first place and that she then used her source of weakness as her avenue of escape. This principle has been seen operating already in the cases of James, David, Mrs. D., and others. In blending with the landscape, she lost her autonomous identity, in fact she lost her self and it was just her "self" that was endangered by being alone in the gathering dusk in an empty expanse.

The most general expression of this principle is that when the risk is loss of being, the defence is to lapse into a state of non-being with, however, all the time the inner reservation that this lapsing into non-being is just a game, just pretending.

As Tillich (1952, p. 62) writes: "Neurosis is the way of avoiding non-being by avoiding being." [1] The trouble is that the individual may find that the pretence has been in the pretending and that, in a more real way than he had bargained for, he has actually lapsed into that very state of non-being he has so much dreaded, in which he has become stripped of his sense of autonomy, reality, life, identity, and from which he may not find it possible to regain his foothold "in" life again by the simple repetition of his name. In fact this little girl's game got out of hand in this way. When the patient wrote her account of her life, from which the above quotation is taken, she had remained severely depersonalized for a number of years.

In this region everything is paradoxical. In Chapter 5 we stated that the self dreads as well as longs for real aliveness. The self dreads to become alive and real because it fears that in so doing the risk of annihilation is immediately potentiated. "Self-consciousness" is implicated in this paradox.

Our little girl blended with the landscape. Now, someone who only too easily blends with other people (we have described ways in which this occurs in the previous chapter), and is frightened of losing his identity thereby, uses his awareness of his self as a means of remaining detached and aloof. Self-consciousness comes to be relied upon to help sustain the individual's precarious ontological security. This insistence on awareness, especially awareness of the self, ramifies in many directions. For instance, whereas the hysteric seems only too glad to be able to forget and to "repress" aspects of his being, the schizoid individual characteristically seeks to make his awareness of himself as intensive and extensive as possible.

Yet it has been remarked how charged with hostility is the self-scrutiny to which the schizoid subjects himself. The schizoid individual (and this applies still more to the schizophrenic) does not bask in the warmth of a loving self-regard. Self-scrutiny is quite improperly regarded as a form of narcissism. Neither the schizoid nor the schizophrenic is narcissistic in this sense. As a schizophrenic put it (see p. 204), she was scorched under the glare of a black sun. The schizoid individual exists under the black sun, the evil eye, of his own scrutiny. The glare of his awareness kills his spontaneity, his freshness; it destroys all joy. Everything withers under it. And yet he remains, although profoundly *not* narcissistic, compulsively preoccupied with the sustained observation of his own mental and/or bodily processes. In Federn's language, he cathects his ego-as-object with mortido.

A very similar point was made in different terms when it was said earlier that the schizoid individual depersonalizes his relationship with himself. That is to say, he turns the living spontaneity of his being into something dead and lifeless by inspecting it. This he does to others as well, and fears their doing it to him (petrification).

We are now in a position to suggest that whereas he is afraid *not* to be dead and lifeless—as stated, he dreads real aliveness—so also he is afraid *not* to continue being aware of himself. Awareness of his self is still a guarantee, an assurance of his continued existence, although he may have to live through a death-in-life. Awareness of an object lessens its potential danger. Consciousness is then a type of radar, a scanning mechanism. The object can be felt to be under control. As a death ray, consciousness has two main properties: its power to petrify (to turn to stone: to turn oneself or the other into things); and its power to penetrate. Thus, if it is in these terms that the gaze of others is experienced, there is a constant dread and resentment at being turned into someone else's thing, of being penetrated by him, and a sense of being in someone else's power and control. Freedom then consists in being inaccessible.

The individual may attempt to forestall these dangers by turning the other into stone. Unfortunately, since one cannot be seen by a stone, one becomes, in so far as others have been successfully reduced to things in one's own eyes, the only person who can see oneself. The process now swings in the reverse direction, culminating in the longing to be rid of the deadening and intolerable self-awareness so that the prospect of being a passive thing penetrated and controlled by the other may come as a welcome relief. Within such oscillation there is no position of peace, since the individual has no choice between feasible alternatives.

The compulsive preoccupation with being seen, or simply with being visible, suggests that we must be dealing with underlying phantasies of not being seen, of being invisible. If, as we saw, being visible can be both in itself persecutory and also a reassurance that one is still alive, then being invisible will have equally ambiguous meanings.

The "self-conscious" person is caught in a dilemma. He may *need* to be seen and recognized, in order to maintain his sense of realness and identity. Yet, at the same time, the other represents a threat to his identity and reality. One finds extremely subtle efforts expended in order to resolve this dilemma in terms of the secret inner self and the behavioral false-self systems already described. James, for instance, feels that "other people provide me with my existence." On his own, he feels that he is empty and nobody. "I can't feel real unless there is someone there. . . ." Nevertheless, he cannot feel at ease with another person, because he feels as "in danger" with others as by himself.

He is, therefore, driven compulsively to seek company, but never allows himself to "be himself" in the presence of anyone else. He avoids social anxiety by never really *being with* others. He never quite says what he means or means what he says. The part he plays is always not quite himself. He takes care to laugh when he thinks a joke is *not* funny, and look bored when he is amused. He makes friends with people he does not really like and is rather cool to those with whom he would "really" like to be friends. No one, therefore, really knows him, or understands him. He can be *himself* in safety only in isolation, albeit with a sense of emptiness and unreality. With others, he plays an elaborate game of pretence and equivocation. His social self is felt to be false and futile. What he longs for most is the possibility of "a moment of recognition," but whenever this by chance occurs, when he has by accident "given himself away," he is covered in confusion and suffused with panic.

The more he keeps his "true self" in hiding, concealed, unseen, and the more he presents to others a false front, the more compulsive this false presentation of himself becomes. He appears to be extremely narcissistic and exhibitionistic. In fact he hates himself and is terrified to reveal himself to others. Instead, he compulsively exhibits what he regards as mere extraneous trappings to others; he dresses ostentatiously, speaks loudly and insistently. He is constantly drawing attention to himself, and at the same time drawing attention *away* from his self. His behaviour is compulsive. All his thoughts are occupied with being seen. His longing is to be known. But this is also what is most dreaded.

Here the "self" has become an invisible transcendent entity, known only to itself. The body in action is no longer the expression of the self. The self is not actualized in and through the body. It is distinct and dissociated. The implicit meaning of Mrs. R.'s (p. 54) actions was: "I am only what other people regard me as being." James played on the opposite possibility. "I am not what anyone can see." His apparent exhibitionism was, therefore, a way of avoiding people discovering what or who he felt he really was.

The adult is not able to use either being seen or being invisible as a stable defence against the other, since each holds dangers of its own as well as affording its own form of safety. How complicated are the issues at stake can be gauged by considering the complexity even of the earliest and simplest infantile situations.

It is a common game for children to play at being invisible and at being seen. This game has several variations. It can be played alone; in front of a mirror; or with the collusion of adults.

In a footnote to his famous description (1920) of the little boy's play with the reel and string, Freud gives a description of one version of this game. It is worth while recalling the whole passage although it is to the footnote that I wish to direct particular attention.

> The child was not at all precocious in his intellectual development. At the age of one and a half he could say only a few comprehensible words; he could also make use of a number of sounds which expressed a meaning intelligible to those around him. He was, however, on good terms with his parents and their one servant-girl, and tributes were paid to his being a "good boy." He did not disturb his parents at night, he conscientiously obeyed orders not to touch certain things or go into certain rooms, and above all he never cried when his mother left him for a few hours. At the same time, he was greatly attached to his mother, who had not only fed him herself but had also looked after him without any outside help. This good little boy, however, had an occasional disturbing habit of taking any small objects he could get hold of and throwing them away from him into a corner, under the bed, and so on, so that hunting for his toys and picking them up was often quite a business. As he did this he gave vent to a loud, long-drawn-out "o–o–o–o," accompanied by an expression of interest and satisfaction. His mother and the writer of the present account were agreed in thinking that this was not a mere interjection but represented the German word *fort* (gone). I eventually realized that it was a game and that the only use he made of any of his toys was to play "gone" with them. One day I made an observation which confirmed my view. The child had a wooden reel with a piece of string tied round it. It never occurred to him to pull it along the floor behind

> him, for instance, and play at its being a carriage. What he did was to hold the reel by the string and very skilfully throw it over the edge of his curtained cot, so that it disappeared into it, at the same time uttering his expressive "o–o–o–o." He then pulled the reel out of the cot again by the string and hailed its reappearance with a joyful "da" (there). This then was the complete game: disappearance and return. As a rule one only witnessed the first act which was repeated untiringly as a game in itself though there is no doubt that greater pleasure was attached to the second act.

Freud adds this significant footnote to his account of this game:

> A further observation subsequently confirmed this interpretation fully. One day, the child's mother had been away for several hours and on her return was met with the words, "Baby o–o–o–o!" which was at first incomprehensible. It soon turned out, however, that during this long period of solitude *the child had found a method of making himself disappear* [italics mine]. He had discovered his reflection in a full-length mirror which did not quite reach to the ground so that by crouching down he could make his mirror-image "gone."

Thus, this little boy not only plays at making his mother disappear, but plays also at making himself disappear. Freud suggests that both games are to be understood as attempts to master the anxiety of a danger situation by repeating it again and again in play.

If this is so, the fear of being invisible, of disappearing, is closely associated with the fear of his mother disappearing. It seems that loss of the mother, at a certain stage, threatens the individual with loss of his self. The mother, however, is not simply a *thing* which the child can see, but a *person* who sees the child. Therefore, we suggest that a necessary component in the development of the self is the experience of oneself as a person under the loving eye of the mother. The ordinary infant lives almost continually under the eyes of adults. But being seen is simply one of innumerable ways in which the infant's total being is given attention. He is attended to, by being noticed, petted, rocked, cuddled, thrown in the air, bathed: his body is handled to an extent that it never will be again. Some mothers can recognize and respond to the child's "mental" processes but cannot responsively accept its concrete bodily actuality and vice versa. It may be that a *failure of responsiveness* on the mother's part to one or other aspect of the infant's being will have important consequences.

A further consideration of what this boy was achieving by his game suggests that he was able, as Freud presumes, to make *himself* disappear by not being able to see his reflection in the mirror. That is to say, if he could not see himself *there,* he himself would be "gone"; thus he was employing a schizoid presupposition by the help of the mirror, whereby there were two "hims," one *there* and the other *here*. That is to say, in overcoming or attempting to overcome the loss or absence of the real other in whose eyes he lived and moved and had his being, he becomes another person to himself who could look at him from the mirror.

However, although the "person" whom *he* could see in the mirror was neither his own self nor another person but only a reflection of his own person, when he could no longer see that other reflected image of his own person in the mirror he himself disappeared, possibly in the way he felt that he disappeared when he could no longer feel that he was under scrutiny or in the presence of his mother. Now, whether the threat from the real other arises out of the contingency of the fact that the other may at any time go away or die or not reciprocate one's feelings for him, or whether the other represents more directly a threat in the form of implosion or penetration, the schizoid person seeks in the boy's way of being a mirror to himself, to turn his self, a quasi duality with an overall unity, into two selves, i.e. into an actual duality. In this little boy, of the "two selves," his own actual self outside the mirror was the one which one could imagine would most readily be identified with his mother. This *identification of the self with the phantasy of the person by whom one is seen* may contribute decisively to the characteristics of the observing self. As stated above, this observing self often kills and withers anything that is under its scrutiny. The individual has now a persecuting observer in the very core of his being. It may be that the child becomes possessed by the alien and destructive presence of the observer who has turned bad in his absence, occupying the place of the observing self, of the boy himself outside the mirror. If this happens, he retains his awareness of himself as an object in the eyes of another by observing himself as the other: he lends the other his eyes in order that he may continue to be seen; he then becomes an object in his own eyes. But the part of himself who looks into him and sees him, has developed the persecutory features he has come to feel the real person outside him to have.

The mirror game can have peculiar variants. The manifest onset of one man's illness occurred when he looked into a mirror and saw someone else there (in fact, his own reflection): "him." "He" was to be his persecutor in a paranoid psychosis. "He" (i.e. "him") was the instigator of a plot to kill him (i.e. the patient) and he (the patient) was determined to "put a bullet through 'him' " (his alienated self).

In the game of this little boy, he, in the position of the person who was perceiving him, that is, his mother, was in a sense killing himself in a magical way: he was killing the mirror image of himself. We shall have occasion to return later to this peculiar state of affairs when studying schizophrenia. Making *himself* disappear and return again must have had a similar significance to that of his other game, of making his mother (symbolically) disappear and reappear. The game makes sense in this way, however, only if we can believe that there is a danger situation for him not only in not being able to see his mother but also in not feeling himself to be seen by her. At this stage, *esse = percipi,* not only as regards others but also as regards the self.

At two years six months, one of my daughters played a similar game. I had to cover my eyes with my hands on the command, "Don't see us." Then, on the command, "See me," I had suddenly to take my hands away, and express surprise and delight at seeing her. I also had to look at her and pretend I could not see her. I have been made to play this game with other children. There is no question of not seeing them doing something naughty. The whole point seems to lie in the child experiencing himself temporarily as not being seen. It is not a question of the child not seeing *me*. One notices also that no actual physical separation occurs in the game. Neither the adult nor the child, in this game, has to hide or actually to disappear. It is a magical version of the peek-a-boo game.

The child who cries when its mother disappears from the room is threatened with the disappearance of his own being, since for him also *percipi = esse*. It is only in the mother's presence that he is able fully to *live* and *move* and *have his being*. Why do children want the light on at night, and want their parents so often to sit with them until they fall asleep? It may be that one aspect of these needs is that the child becomes frightened if he can no longer see himself, or feel himself to be seen by someone else; or to hear others and be heard by them. Going to sleep consists, phenomenologically, in a loss of one's own awareness of one's being as well as that of the world. This may be in itself frightening, so the child needs to feel seen or heard by *another* person, while he is losing his own awareness of his being in the process of falling asleep. In sleep the "inner" light that illumines one's own being is out. Leaving on the light not only provides assurance that if he wakes there are no terrors in the dark, but provides a magical assurance that during sleep he is being watched over by benign presences (parents, good fairies, angels). Even worse, perhaps, than the possible presence of bad things in the dark is the terror that in the dark is *nothing* and *no one*. Not to be conscious of oneself, therefore, may be equated with nonentity. The schizoid individual is assuring himself that he exists by always being aware of himself. Yet he is persecuted by his own insight and lucidity.

The need to be perceived is not, of course, purely a visual affair. It extends to the general need to have one's presence endorsed or confirmed by the other, the need for one's total existence to be recognized; the need, in fact, to be loved. Thus those people who cannot sustain from within themselves the sense of their own identity or, like Kafka's suppliant, have no inner conviction that they are alive, may feel that they are real live persons only when they are experienced as such by another, as was the case with Mrs. R. (p. 54), who was threatened with depersonalization when she could not be recognized or imagine herself recognized and responded to by someone who knew her sufficiently well for their recognition of and response to her to be significant. Her need to be seen was based on the equation that "I am the person that *other* people know and recognize me to be." She required the tangible reassurance of the presence of another who knew her, in whose presence her own uncertainties about whom she was could be temporarily allayed.

NOTE

1 *The Courage to Be.* The editors.

22

A New Refutation of Time

Jorge Luis Borges

Vor mir war keine Zeit, nach mir wird keine seyn,
Mit mir gebiert sie sich, mit mir geht sie auch ein.

Daniel von Czepko:
Sexcenta monodisticha sapientum, III, II (1655)

PROLOGUE

If published toward the middle of the eighteenth century, this refutation (or its name) would persist in Hume's bibliographies and perhaps would have merited a line by Huxley or Kemp Smith. Published in 1947—after Bergson—, it is the anachronistic *reductio ad absurdum* of a preterite system or, what is worse, the feeble artifice of an Argentine lost in the maze of metaphysics. Both conjectures are verisimilar and perhaps true; in order to correct them, I cannot promise a novel conclusion in exchange for my rudimentary dialectic. The thesis I shall divulge is as ancient as Zeno's arrow or the Greek king's carriage in the *Milinda Panha;* the novelty, if any, consists in applying to my purpose the classic instrument of Berkeley. Both he and his continuer David Hume abound in paragraphs which contradict or exclude my thesis; nevertheless, I believe I have deduced the inevitable consequences of their doctrine.

A New Refutation of Time

The first article (A) was written in 1944 and appeared in number 115 of the review *Sur;* the second, of 1946, is a reworking of the first. Deliberately I did not make the two into one, understanding that the reading of two analogous texts might facilitate the comprehension of an indocile subject.

A word about the title. I am not unaware that it is an example of the monster termed by the logicians *contradictio in adjecto,* because stating that a refutation time is new (or old) attributes to it a predicate of temporal nature which establishes the very notion the subject would destroy. I leave it as is, however, so that its slight mockery may prove that I do not exaggerate the importance of these verbal games. Besides, our language is so saturated and animated by time that it is quite possible there is not one statement in these pages which in some way does not demand or invoke the idea of time.

I dedicate these exercises to my forebear Juan Crisóstomo Lafinur (1797–1824), who left some memorable endecasyllables to Argentine letters and who tried to reform the teaching of philosophy, purifying it of theological shadows and expounding in his courses the principles of Locke and Condillac. He died in exile; like all men, he was given bad times in which to live.

Buenos Aires, 23 December 1946 *J. L. B.*

A

1— In the course of a life dedicated to letters and (at times) to metaphysical perplexity, I have glimpsed or foreseen a refutation of time, in which I myself do not believe, but which regularly visits me at night and in the weary twilight with the illusory force of an axiom. This refutation is found in some way or another in all my books: it is prefigured by the poems "Inscription on Any Grave" and "The Trick" from my *Fervor of Buenos Aires* (1923); it is declared by two articles in *Inquisitions* (1925), page 46 of *Evaristo Carriego* (1930), the narration "Feeling in Death" from my *History of Eternity* (1936) and the note on page 24 of *The Garden of Forking Paths* (1941). None of the texts I have enumerated satisfies me, not even the penultimate one, less demonstrative and well-reasoned than it is divinatory and pathetic. I shall try to establish a basis for all of them in this essay.

Two arguments led me to this refutation: the idealism of Berkeley and Leibniz's principle of indiscernibles.

Berkeley (*Principles of Human Knowledge, 3*) observed: "That neither our thoughts, nor passions, nor ideas formed by the imagination, exist without the mind, is what everybody will allow. And it seems no less evident that the various sensations or ideas imprinted on the sense, however blended or combined together (that is, whatever objects they compose) cannot exist otherwise than in a mind perceiving them. . . . The table I write on, I say, exists, that is, I see and feel it; and if I were out of my study I should say it existed, meaning thereby that if I was in my study I might perceive it, or that some other spirit actually does perceive it. . . . For as to what is said of the absolute existence of unthinking things without any relation to their being perceived, that seems perfectly unintelligible. Their *esse* is *percipi,* nor is it possible they should have any existence, out of the minds or thinking things which perceive them." In paragraph twenty-three he added, forestalling objections: "But say you, surely there is nothing easier than to imagine trees, for instance, in a park or books existing in a closet, and no body by to perceive them. I answer, you may so, there is no difficulty in it: but what is all this, I beseech you, more than framing in your mind certain ideas which you call *books* and *trees,* and at the same time omitting to frame the idea of any one that may perceive them? But do not you your self perceive or think of them all the while? This therefore is nothing to the purpose: it only shows you have the power of imagining or forming ideas in your mind; but it doth not shew that you can conceive it possible, the objects of your thought may exist without the mind. . . ." In another paragraph, number six, he had already declared: "Some truths there are so near and obvious to the mind, that a man need only open his eyes to see them. Such I take this important one to be, to wit, that all the choir of heaven and furniture of the earth, in a word all those bodies which compose the mighty frame of the world, have not any substance without a mind, that their being is to be perceived or known; that consequently so long as they are not actually perceived by me, or do not exist in any mind or that of any other created spirit, they must either have no existence at all, or else subsist in the mind of some eternal spirit. . . ."

Such is, in the words of its inventor, the idealist doctrine. To understand it is easy; what is difficult is to think within its limits. Schopenhauer himself, when expounding it, committed culpable negligences. In the first lines of the first volume of his *Welt als Wille und Vorstellung* —from the year 1819—he formulated this declaration which makes him worthy of the enduring perplexity of all men: "The world is my idea: this is a truth which holds good for everything that lives and knows, though man alone can bring it into reflective and abstract consciousness. If he really does this, he has attained to philosophical wisdom. It then becomes clear and certain to him what he knows is not a sun and an earth, but only an eye that sees a sun, a hand that feels an earth. . . ." In other words, for the idealist Schopenhauer, man's eyes and hands are less illusory or apparent than the earth and the sun. In 1844 he published a complementary volume. In its first chapter he rediscovers and aggravates the previous error: he defines the universe as a phenomenon of the brain and distinguishes the "world in the head" from "the world outside the head." Berkeley, however, had his Philonous say in 1713: "The brain therefore you speak of, being a sensible thing, exists only in the mind. Now, I would fain know whether you think it reasonable to suppose, that one idea or thing existing in the mind, occasions all other ideas. And if you think so, pray how do you account for the origin of that primary idea or brain itself?" Schopenhauer's dualism or cerebralism may also be licitly opposed by Spiller's monism. Spiller (*The Mind of Man,* chapter VIII, 1902) argues that the retina and the cutaneous surface invoked in order to explain visual and tactile phenomena are, in turn, two tactile and visual systems and that the room we see (the "objective" one) is no greater than the one imagined (the "cerebral" one) and does not contain it, since what we have here are two independent visual systems. Berkeley (*Principles of Human Knowledge,* 10 and 116) likewise denied the existence of primary qualities—the solidity and extension of things—and of absolute space.

Berkeley affirmed the continuous existence of objects, since when no individual sees them, God does; Hume, with greater logic, denies such an existence (*Treatise of Human Nature,* I, 4, 2). Berkeley affirmed the existence of personal identity, "I my self am not my ideas, but somewhat else, a thinking active principle that perceives . . ." (*Dialogues,* 3); Hume, the skeptic, refutes this identity and makes of every man "a bundle or collection of different perceptions, which succeed each other with an inconceivable rapidity" (*op. cit.,* I, 4, 6). Both affirm the existence of time: for Berkeley, it is "the succession of ideas in my mind, which flows uniformly, and is participated in by all beings" (*Principles of Human Knowledge,* 98); for Hume, "a succession of indivisible moments" (*op. cit.,* I, 2, 2).

I have accumulated transcriptions from the apologists of idealism, I have abounded in their canonical passages, I have been reiterative and explicit, I have censured Schopenhauer (not without ingratitude), so that my reader may begin to penetrate into this unstable world of the mind. A world of evanescent impressions; a world without matter or spirit, neither objective nor subjective; a world without the ideal architecture of space; a world made of time, of the absolute uniform time of the *Principia;* a tireless labyrinth, a chaos, a dream. This almost perfect dissolution was reached by David Hume.

Once the idealist argument is admitted, I see that it is possible—perhaps inevitable—to go further. For Hume it is not licit to speak of the form of the moon or of its color; the form and color *are* the moon; neither can one speak of the perceptions of the mind, since the mind is nothing other than a series of perceptions. The Cartesian "I think, therefore I am" is thus invalidated; to say "I think" postulates the self, is a begging of the question; Lichtenberg, in the eighteenth century, proposed that in place of "I think" we should say, impersonally, "it thinks," just as one would say "it thunders" or "it rains." I repeat: behind our faces there is no secret self which governs our acts and receives our impressions; we are, solely, the series of these imaginary acts and these errant impressions. The series? Once matter and spirit, which are continuities, are negated, once space too has been negated, I do not know what right we have to that continuity which is time. Let us imagine a present moment of any kind. During one of his nights on the Mississippi, Huckleberry Finn awakens; the raft, lost in partial darkness, continues downstream; it is perhaps a bit cold. Huckleberry Finn recognizes the soft indefatigable sound of the water; he negligently opens his eyes; he sees a vague number of stars, an indistinct line of trees; then, he sinks back into his immemorable sleep as into the dark waters.[1] Idealist metaphysics declares that to add a material substance (the object) and a spiritual substance (the subject) to those perceptions is venturesome and useless; I maintain that it is no less illogical to think that such perceptions are terms in a series whose beginning is as inconceivable as its end. To add to the river and the bank, Huck perceives the notion of another substantive river and another bank, to add another perception to that immediate network of perceptions, is, for idealism, unjustifiable; for myself, it is no less unjustifiable to add a chronological precision: the fact, for example, that the foregoing event took place on the night of the seventh of June, 1849, between ten and eleven minutes past four. In other words: I deny, with the arguments of idealism, the vast temporal series which idealism admits. Hume denied the existence of an absolute space, in which all things have their place; I deny the existence of one single time, in which all things are linked as in a chain. The denial of coexistence is no less arduous than the denial of succession.

I deny, in an elevated number of instances, the successive; I deny, in an elevated number of instances, the contemporary as well. The lover who thinks "While I was so happy, thinking of the fidelity of my love, she was deceiving me" deceives himself: if every state we experience is absolute, such happiness was not contemporary to the betrayal; the discovery of that betrayal is another state, which cannot modify the "previous" ones, though it can modify their recollection. The misfortune of today is no more real than the happiness of the past. I shall seek a more concrete example. In the first part of August, 1824, Captain Isidoro Suárez, at the head of a squadron of Peruvian hussars, decided the victory of Junín; in the first part of August, 1824, De Quincey published a diatribe against *Wilhelm Meisters Lehrjahre;* these events were not contemporary (they are now), since the two men died—one in the city of Montevideo, the other in Edinburgh—without knowing anything about each other. . . . Each moment is autonomous. Neither vengeance nor pardon nor prisons nor even oblivion can modify the invulnerable past. To me, hope and fear seem no less vain, for they always refer to future events: that is, to events that will not happen to us, who are the minutely detailed present. I am told that the present, the specious present of the psychologists, lasts from a few seconds to a minute fraction of a second; that can be the duration of the history of the universe. In other words, there is no such history, just as a man has no life; not even one of his nights exists; each moment we live exists, but not their imaginary combination. The universe, the sum of all things, is a collection no less ideal than that of all the horses Shakespeare dreamt of—one, many, none?—between 1592 and 1594. I add: if time is a mental process, how can thousands of men—or even two different men—share it?

The argument of the preceding paragraphs, interrupted and encumbered with illustrations, may seem intricate. I shall seek a more direct method. Let us consider a life in whose course there is an abundance of repetitions: mine, for example. I never pass in front of the Recoleta without remembering that my father, my grandparents and great-grandparents are buried there, just as I shall be some day; then I remember that I have remembered the same thing an untold number of times already; I cannot walk through the suburbs in the solitude of the night without thinking that the night pleases us because it suppresses idle details, just as our memory does; I cannot lament the loss of a love or a friendship without meditating that one loses only what one really never had; every time I cross one of the street corners of the southern part of the city, I think of you, Helen; every time the wind brings me the smell of eucalyptus, I think of Adrogué in my childhood; every time I remember the ninety-first fragment of Heraclitus, "You shall not go down twice to the same river," I admire its dialectical dexterity, because the ease with which we accept the first meaning ("The river is different") clandestinely imposes upon us the second ("I am different") and grants us the illusion of having invented it; every time I hear a Germanophile vituperate the Yiddish language, I reflect that Yiddish is, after all, a German dialect, scarcely colored by the language of the Holy Spirit. These tautologies (and others I leave in silence) make up my entire life. Of course, they are repeated imprecisely; there are differences of emphasis, temperature, light and general physiological condition. I suspect, however, that the number of circumstantial variants is not infinite: we can postulate, in the mind of an individual (or of two individuals who do not know of each other but in whom the same process works), two identical moments. Once this identity is postulated, one may ask: Are not these identical moments the same? Is not one single repeated term sufficient to break down and confuse the series of time? Do not the fervent readers who surrender themselves to Shakespeare become, literally, Shakespeare?

As yet I am ignorant of the ethics of the system I have outlined. I do not know if it even exists. The fifth paragraph of the fourth chapter of the treatise *Sanhedrin* of the Mishnah declares that, for God's Justice, he who kills one man destroys the world; if there is no plurality, he who annihilates all men would be no more guilty than the primitive and solitary Cain, which fact is orthodox, nor more universal in his destruction, which fact may be magical. I understand that this is so. The vociferous catastrophes of a general order—fires, wars, epidemics—are one single pain, illusorily multiplied in many mirrors. Thus Bernard Shaw sees it (*Guide to Socialism,* 86): "What you can suffer is the maximum that can be suffered on earth. If you die of starvation, you will suffer all the starvation there has been or will be. If ten thousand people die with you, their participation in your lot will not make you be ten thousand times more hungry nor multiply the time of your agony ten thousand times. Do not let yourself be overcome by the horrible sum of human sufferings; such a sum does not exist. Neither poverty nor pain are cumulative." *Cf.* also *The Problem of Pain,* VII, by C. S. Lewis.

Lucretius (*De rerum natura,* I, 830) attributes to Anaxagoras the doctrine that gold consists of particles of gold, fire of sparks, bone of tiny imperceptible bones; Josiah Royce, perhaps influenced by St. Augustine, judges that time is made of time and that "every *now* within which something happens is therefore *also* a succession" (*The World and the Individual,* II, 139). This proposition is compatible with that of this essay.

2— All language is of a successive nature; it does not lend itself to a reasoning of the eternal, the intemporal. Those who have followed the foregoing argumentation with displeasure will perhaps prefer this page from the year 1928. I have already mentioned it; it is the narrative entitled "Feeling in Death":

> I want to set down here an experience which I had some nights ago: a trifle too evanescent and ecstatic to be called an adventure, too irrational and sentimental to be called a thought. It consists of a scene and its word: a word already stated by me, but not lived with complete dedication until then. I shall now proceed to give its history, with the accidents of time and place which were its declaration.
>
> I remember it as follows. The afternoon preceding that night, I was in Barracas: a locality not visited by my habit and whose distance from those I later traversed had already lent a strange flavor to that day. The evening had no destiny at all; since it was clear, I went out to take a walk and to recollect after dinner. I did not want to determine a route for my stroll; I tried to attain a maximum latitude of probabilities in order not to fatigue my expectation with the necessary foresight of any one of them. I managed, to the imperfect degree of possibility, to do what is called walking at random; I accepted, with no other conscious prejudice than that of avoiding the wider avenues or streets, the most obscure invitations of chance. However, a kind of familiar gravitation led me farther on, in the direction of certain neighborhoods, the names of which I have every desire to recall and which dictate reverence to my heart. I do not mean by this my own neighborhood, the precise surroundings of my childhood, but rather its still mysterious environs: an area I have possessed often in words but seldom in reality, immediate and at the same time mythical. The reverse of the familiar, its far side, are for me those penultimate streets, almost as effectively unknown as the hidden foundations of our house or our invisible skeleton. My progress brought me to a corner. I breathed in the night, in a most serene holiday from thought. The view, not at all complex, seemed simplified by my tiredness. It was made unreal by its very typicality. The street was one of low houses and though its first meaning was one of poverty, its second was certainly one of contentment. It was as humble and enchanting as anything could be. None of the houses dared open itself to the street; the fig tree darkened over the corner; the little arched doorways—higher than the taut outlines of the walls—seemed wrought from the same infinite substance of the night. The sidewalk formed an escarpment over the street; the street was of elemental earth, the earth of an as yet unconquered America. Farther down, the alleyway, already

open to the pampa, crumbled into the Maldonado. Above the turbid and chaotic earth, a rose-colored wall seemed not to house the moonlight, but rather to effuse an intimate light of its own. There can be no better way of naming tenderness than that soft rose color.

I kept looking at this simplicity. I thought, surely out loud: This is the same as thirty years ago. . . . I conjectured the date: a recent time in other countries but now quite remote in this changeable part of the world. Perhaps a bird was singing and for it I felt a tiny affection, the same size as the bird; but the most certain thing was that in this now vertiginous silence there was no other sound than the intemporal one of the crickets. The easy thought "I am in the eighteen-nineties" ceased to be a few approximate words and was deepened into a reality. I felt dead, I felt as an abstract spectator of the world; an indefinite fear imbued with science, which is the best clarity of metaphysics. I did not think that I had returned upstream on the supposed waters of Time; rather I suspected that I was the possessor of a reticent or absent sense of the inconceivable word *eternity*. Only later was I able to define that imagination.

I write it now as follows: That pure representation of homogeneous objects—the night in serenity, a limpid little wall, the provincial scent of the honeysuckle, the elemental earth—is not merely identical to the one present on that corner so many years ago; it is, without resemblances or repetitions, the very same. Time, if we can intuitively grasp such an identity, is a delusion: the difference and inseparability of one moment belonging to its apparent past from another belonging to its apparent present is sufficient to disintegrate it.

It is evident that the number of such human moments is not infinite. The elemental ones—those of physical suffering and physical pleasure, those of the coming of sleep, those of the hearing of a piece of music, those of great intensity or great lassitude—are even more impersonal. Aforehand I derive this conclusion: life is too poor not to be immortal as well. But we do not even have the certainty of our poverty, since time, which is easily refutable in sense experience, is not so in the intellectual, from whose essence the concept of succession seems inseparable. Thus shall remain as an emotional anecdote the half-glimpsed idea and as the confessed irresolution of this page the true moment of ecstasy and possible suggestion of eternity with which that night was not parsimonious for me.

B

Of the many docrtines registered by the history of philosophy, perhaps idealism is the oldest and most widespread. This observation was made by Carlyle (*Novalis,* 1829); to the philosophers he alleges it is fitting to add, with no hope of completing the infinite census, the Platonists, for whom the only reality is that of the archetype (Norris, Judas Abrabanel, Gemistus, Plotinus), the theologians, for whom all that is not the divinity is contingent (Malebranche, Johannes Eckhart), the monists, who make the universe an idle adjective of the Absolute (Bradley, Hegel, Parmenides). . . . Idealism is as ancient as metaphysical restlessness itself; its most acute apologist, George Berkeley, flourished in the eighteenth century; contrary to what Schopenhauer declares (*Welt als Wille und Vorstellung,* II, i), his merit cannot be the intuition of that doctrine but rather the arguments he conceived in order to reason it; Hume applied them to the mind; my purpose is to apply them to time. But first I shall recapitulate the diverse stages of this dialectic.

Berkeley denied the existence of matter. This does not mean, one should note, that he denied the existence of colors, odors, tastes, sounds and tactile sensations; what he denied was that, aside from these perceptions, which make up the external world, there was anything invisible, intangible, called matter. He denied that there were pains that no one feels, colors that no one sees, forms that no one touches. He reasoned that to add a matter to our perceptions is to add an inconceivable, superfluous world to the world. He believed in the world of appearances woven by our senses, but understood that the material world (that of Toland, say) is an illusory duplication. He observed (*Principles of Human Knowledge,* 3): "That neither our thoughts, nor passions, nor ideas formed by the imagination, exist without the mind, is what everybody will allow. And it seems no less evident that the various sensations or ideas imprinted on the sense, however blended or combined together (that is, whatever objects they compose) cannot exist otherwise than in a mind perceiving them. . . . The table I write on, I say, exists, that is, I see and feel it; and if I were out of my study I should say it existed, meaning thereby that if I was in my study I might perceive it, or that some other spirit actually does perceive it. . . . For as to what is said of the absolute existence of unthinking things without any relation to their being perceived, that seems perfectly unintelligible. Their *esse* is *percipi,* nor is it possible they should have any existence, out of the minds or thinking things which perceive them." In paragraph twenty-three he added, forestalling objections: "But say you, surely there is nothing easier than to imagine trees, for instance, in a park or books existing in a closet, and no body by to perceive them. I answer, you may so, there is no difficulty in it: but what is all this, I beseech you, more than framing in your mind certain ideas which you call *books* and *trees* and at the same time omitting to frame the idea of any one that may perceive them? But do not you your self perceive or think of them all the while? This therefore is nothing to the purpose: it only shows you have the power of imagining or forming ideas in your mind; but it doth not shew that you can conceive it possible, the objects of your thought may exist without the mind. . . ." In another paragraph, number six, he had already declared: "Some truths there are so near and obvious to the mind, that a man need only open his eyes to see them. Such I take this important one to be, to wit, that all the choir of heaven and furniture of the earth, in a word all those bodies which compose the mighty frame of the world, have not any substance without a mind, that their being is to be perceived or known; that consequently so long as they are not actually perceived by me, or do not exist in any mind or that of any other created spirit, they must either have no existence at all, or else subsist in the mind of some eternal spirit. . . ." (The God of Berkeley is a ubiquitous spectator whose function is that of lending coherence to the world.)

The doctrine I have just expounded has been interpreted in perverse ways. Herbert Spencer thought he had refuted it (*Principles of Psychology,* VIII, 6), reasoning that if there is nothing outside consciousness, consciousness must be infinite in time and space. The first is certain if we understand that all time is time perceived by someone, but erroneous if we infer that this time must necessarily embrace an infinite number of centuries; the second is illicit, since Berkeley (*Principles of Human Knowledge,* 116; *Siris,* 266) repeatedly denied the existence of an absolute space. Even more indecipherable is the error into which Schopenhauer falls (*Welt als Wille und Vorstellung,* II, i) when he shows that for the idealists the world is a phenomenon of the brain; Berkeley, however, had written (*Dialogues between Hylas and Philonous,* II): "The brain therefore you speak of, being a sensible thing, exists only in the mind. Now, I would fain know whether you think it reasonable to suppose, that one idea or thing existing in the mind, occasions all other ideas. And if you think so, pray how do you account for the origin of this primary idea or brain itself?" The brain, in fact, is no less a part of the external world than is the constellation of the Centaur.

Berkeley denied that there was an object behind our sense impressions; David Hume, that there was a subject behind the perception of changes. The former had denied the existence of matter, the latter denied the existence of spirit; the former had not wanted us to add to the succession of impressions the metaphysical notion of matter, the latter did not want us to add to the succession of mental states the metaphysical notion of self. So logical is this extension of Berkeley's arguments that Berkeley himself had already foreseen it, as Alexander Campbell Fraser notes, and even tried to reject it by means of the Cartesian *ergo sum*. "If your principles are valid, you your self are nothing more than a system of fluctuating ideas, unsustained by any substance, since it is as absurd to speak of a spiritual substance as it is of a material substance," reasons Hylas, anticipating David Hume in the third and last of the *Dialogues*. Hume corroborates (*Treatise of Human Nature,* I, 4, 6): "We are a bundle or collection of different perceptions, which succeed each other with an inconceivable rapidity . . . . The mind is a kind of theatre, where several perceptions successively make their appearance; pass, re-pass, glide away, and mingle in an infinite variety of postures and situations . . . . The comparison of the theatre must not mislead us. They are the successive perceptions only, that constitute the mind; nor have we the most distant notion of the place, where these scenes are represented, or of the materials, of which it is compos'd."

Once the idealist argument is admitted, I see that it is possible—perhaps inevitable—to go further. For Berkeley, time is "the succession of ideas in my mind, which flows uniformly, and is participated by all beings" (*Principles of Human Knowledge,* 98); for Hume, "a succession of indivisible moments" (*Treatise of Human Nature,* I, 2, 2). However, once matter and spirit—which are continuities—are negated, once space too is negated, I do not know with what right we retain that continuity which is time. Outside each perception (real or conjectural) matter does not exist; outside each mental state spirit does not exist; neither does time exist outside each present moment. Let us take a moment of maximum simplicity: for example, that of Chuang Tzu's dream (Herbert Allen Giles: *Chuang Tzu,* 1889). Chuang Tzu, some twenty-four centuries ago, dreamt he was a butterfly and did not know, when he awoke, if he was a man who had dreamt he was a butterfly or a butterfly who now dreamt he was a man. Let us not consider the awakening; let us consider the moment of the dream itself, or one of its moments. "I dreamt I was a butterfly flying through the air and knowing nothing of Chuang Tzu," reads the ancient text. We shall never know if Chuang Tzu saw a garden over which he seemed to fly or a moving yellow triangle which no doubt was he, but we do know that the image was subjective, though furnished by his memory. The doctrine of psycho-physical parallelism would judge that the image must have been accompanied by some change in the dreamer's nervous system; according to Berkeley, the body of Chuang Tzu did not exist at that moment, save as a perception in the mind of God. Hume simplifies even more what happened. According to him, the spirit of Chuang Tzu did not exist at that moment; only the colors of the dream and the certainty of being a butterfly existed. They existed as a momentary term in the "bundle or collection of perceptions" which, some four centuries before Christ, was the mind of Chuang Tzu; they existed as a term *n* in an infinite temporal series, between $n-1$ and $n+1$. There is no other reality, for idealism, than that of mental processes; adding an objective butterfly to the butterfly which is perceived seems a vain duplication; adding a self to these processes seems no less exorbitant. Idealism judges that there was a dreaming, a perceiving, but not a dreamer or even a dream; it judges that speaking of objects and subjects is pure mythology. Now if each psychic state is self-sufficient, if linking it to a circumstance or to a self is an illicit and idle addition, with what right shall we then ascribe to it a place in time? Chuang Tzu dreamt that he was a butterfly and during that dream he was not Chuang Tzu, but a butterfly. How, with space and self abolished, shall we link those moments to his waking moments and to the feudal period of Chinese history? This does not mean that we shall never know, even in an approximate fashion, the date of that dream; it means that the chronological fixing of an event, of an event in the universe, is alien and external to it. In China the dream of Chuang Tzu is proverbial; let us imagine that of its almost infinite readers, one dreams that he is a butterfly and then dreams that he is Chuang Tzu. Let us imagine that, by a not impossible stroke of chance, this dream reproduces point for point the master's. Once this identity is postulated, it is fitting to ask: Are not these moments which coincide one and the same? Is not one repeated term sufficient to break down and confuse the history of the world, to denounce that there is no such history?

The denial of time involves two negations: the negation of the succession of the terms of a series, negation of the synchronism of the terms in two different series. In fact, if each term is absolute, its relations are reduced to the consciousness that those relations exist. A state precedes another if it is known to be prior; a state of G is contemporary to a state of H if it is known to be contemporary. Contrary to what was declared by Schopenhauer [2] in his table of fundamental truths (*Welt als Wille und Vorstellung,* II, 4), each fraction of time does not simultaneously fill the whole of space; time is not ubiquitous. (Of course, at this stage in the argument, space no longer exists.)

Meinong, in his theory of apprehension, admits the apprehension of imaginary objects: the fourth dimension, let us say, or the sensitive statue of Condillac or the hypothetical animal of Lotze or the square root of minus one. If the reasons I have indicated are valid, then matter, self, the external world, world history and our lives also belong to this same nebulous orb.

Besides, the phrase "negation of time" is ambiguous. It can mean the eternity of Plato or Boethius and also the dilemmas of Sextus Empiricus. The latter (*Adversus Mathematicos,* XI, 197) denies the existence of the past, that which already was, and the future, that which is not yet, and argues that the present is divisible or indivisible. It is not indivisible, for in such a case it would have no beginning to link it to the past nor end to link it to the future, nor even a middle, since what has no beginning or end can have no middle; neither is it divisible, for in such a case it would consist of a part that was and another that is not. *Ergo,* it does not exist, but since the past and the future do not exist either, time does not exist. F. H. Bradley rediscovers and improves this perplexity. He observes (*Appearance and Reality,* IV) that if the present is divisible in other presents, it is no less complicated than time itself, and if it is indivisible, time is a mere relation between intemporal things. Such reasoning, as can be seen, negates the parts in order then to negate the whole; I reject the whole in order to exalt each of the parts. Via the dialectics of Berkeley and Hume I have arrived at Schopenhauer's dictum: "The form of the phenomenon of will . . . is really only the *present,* not the future nor the past. The latter are only in the conception, exist only in the connection of knowledge, so far as it follows the principle of sufficient reason. No man has ever lived in the past, and none will live in the future; the *present* alone is the form of all life, and is its sure possession which can never be taken from it. . . . We might compare time to a constantly revolving sphere; the half that was always sinking would be the past, that which was always rising would be the future; but the indivisible point at the top, where the tangent touches, would be the extensionless present. As the tangent does not revolve with the sphere, neither does the present, the point of contact of the object, the form of which is time, with the subject which has no form, because it does not belong to the knowable, but is the condition of all that is knowable" (*Welt als Wille und Vorstellung,* I, 54). A Buddhist treatise of the fifth century, the *Visuddhimagga* (Road to Purity), illustrates the same doctrine with the same figure: "Strictly speaking, the duration of the life of a living being is exceedingly brief, lasting only while a thought lasts. Just as a chariot wheel in rolling rolls only at one point of the tire, and in resting rests only at one point; in exactly the same way the life of a living being lasts only for the period of one thought" (Radhakrishnan: *Indian Philosophy,* I, 373). Other Buddhist texts say that the world annihilates itself and reappears six thousand five hundred million times a day and that all men are an illusion, vertiginously produced by a series of momentaneous and solitary men. "The being of a past moment of thought—the *Road to Purity* tells us—has lived, but does not live nor will it live. The being of a future moment will live, but has not lived nor does it live. The being of the present moment of thought does live, but has not lived nor will it live" (*op. cit.,* I, 407), a dictum which we may compare with the following of Plutarch (*De E apud Delphos,* 18): "The man of yesterday has died in that of today, that of today dies in that of tomorrow."

And yet, and yet. . . . Denying temporal succession, denying the self, denying the astronomical universe, are apparent desperations and secret consolations. Our destiny (as contrasted with the hell of Swedenborg and the hell of Tibetan mythology) is not frightful by being unreal; it is frightful because it is irreversible and iron-clad. Time is the substance I am made of. Time is a river which sweeps me along, but I am the river; it is a tiger which destroys me, but I am the tiger; it is a fire which consumes me, but I am the fire. The world, unfortunately, is real; I, unfortunately, am Borges.

FOOTNOTE TO THE PROLOGUE

There is no exposition of Buddhism that does not mention the *Milinda Panha,* an apologetic work of the second century, which relates a debate whose interlocutors are the king of Bactriana, Menander, and the monk Nagasena. The latter reasons that just as the king's carriage is neither its wheels nor its body nor its axle nor its pole nor its yoke, neither is man his matter, form, impressions, ideas, instincts or consciousness. He is not the combination of these parts nor does he exist outside of them. . . . After a controversy of many days, Menander (Milinda) is converted to the Buddhist faith.

The *Milanda Panha* has been translated into English by Rhys Davids (Oxford, 1890–1894).

Translated by James E. Irby

NOTES

1. For the convenience of the reader I have selected a moment between two periods of sleep, a literary moment, not a historical one. If anyone suspects a fallacy, he may substitute another example, one from his own life if he so chooses.
2. And, earlier, by Newton, who maintained: "Each particle of space is eternal, each indivisible moment of duration is everywhere" (*Principia,* III, 42).

23

The Existential Analysis School of Thought*

Ludwig Binswanger

I. EXISTENTIAL ANALYSIS—ITS NATURE AND GOALS

By "EXISTENTIAL ANALYSIS" we understand an anthropological [1] type of scientific investigation—that is, one which is aimed at the essence of being human. Its name as well as its philosophical foundation are derived from Heidegger's Analysis of Being, "*Daseins* Analytics." It is his—not yet properly recognized—merit to have uncovered a fundamental structure of existence and to have described it in its essential parts, that is, the structure of being-in-the-world. By identifying the basic condition or structure of existence with being-in-the-world, Heidegger intends to say something about the condition of the possibility for existence. The formulation "being-in-the-world" as used by Heidegger is, therefore, in the nature of an ontological thesis, a statement about an essential condition that determines existence in general. From the discovery and presentation of this essential condition, existential

* From *Existence: A New Dimension in Psychiatry and Psychology*. The editors.

analysis received its decisive stimulation, its philosophical foundation and justification, as well as its methodological directives. However, existential analysis itself is neither an ontology nor a philosophy and therefore must refuse to be termed a *philosophical anthropology;* as the reader will soon realize, only the designation of *phenomenological anthropology* meets the facts of the situation.

Existential analysis does not propose an ontological thesis about an essential condition determining existence, but makes *ontic statements* —that is, statements of factual findings about actually appearing forms and configurations of existence. In this sense, existential analysis is an empirical science, with its own method and particular ideal of exactness, namely with the method and the ideal of exactness of the *phenomenological* empirical sciences.

Today we can no longer evade recognition of the fact that there are two types of empirical scientific knowledge. One is the *discursive inductive* knowledge in the sense of describing, explaining, and controlling "natural events," whereas the second is the *phenomenological empirical* knowledge in the sense of a methodical, critical exploitation or interpretation of phenomenal contents. It is the old disagreement between Goethe and Newton which today—far from disturbing us—has changed by virtue of our deepened insight into the nature of experience from an "either/or" into an "as well as." The same phenomenological empirical knowledge is used regardless of whether we deal with the interpretation of the aesthetic content of an artistic style-period, with the literary content of a poem or a drama, or with the self-and-world content of a Rorschach response or of a psychotic form of existence. In phenomenological experience, the discursive taking apart of natural objects into characteristics or qualities and their inductive elaboration into types, concepts, judgments, conclusions, and theories is replaced by giving expression to the content of what is purely phenomenally given and therefore is not part of "nature as such" in any way. But the phenomenal content can find expression and, in being expressed, can unfold itself only if we approach and question it by the phenomenological method —or else we shall receive not a scientifically founded and verifiable answer but just an accidental *aperçu*. In this, as in every science, everything depends upon the method of approach and inquiry—*i.e.,* on the ways and means of the phenomenological method of experience.

Over the last few decades the concept of phenomenology has changed in some respects. Today, we must strictly differentiate between Husserl's pure or eidetic phenomenology as a transcendental discipline, and the phenomenological interpretation of human forms of existence as an empirical discipline. But understanding the latter is not possible without knowledge of the former.

In this we should be guided, to mention only one factor, by abstinence from what Flaubert calls *la rage de vouloir conclure,* that is, by overcoming our passionate need to draw conclusions, to form an opinion, or to pass judgment—a task which in the light of our one-sided natural-scientific intellectual training cannot be considered an easy one. In short, instead of reflecting on something we should let the something speak for itself or, to quote Flaubert again, "express the thing as it is." However, the "as it is" contains one more fundamental ontological and phenomenological problem; for we finite human beings can acquire information on the "how" of a thing only according to the "world-design" which guides our understanding of things. Therefore, I have to return once more to Heidegger's thesis of existence as "being-in-the-world."

The ontological thesis that the basic constitution or structure of existence is being-in-the-world is not a philosophical *aperçu* but rather represents an extremely consistent development and extension of fundamental philosophical theories, namely of Kant's theory about the conditions of the possibility of experience (in the natural-scientific sense) on the one hand, and of Husserl's theory of transcendental phenomenology on the other. I shall not elaborate on these connections and developments. What I want to emphasize here is only the identification of being-in-the-world and transcendence; for it is through this that we can understand what "being-in-the-world" and "world" signify in their anthropological application. The German word for transcendence or transcending is *Ueberstieg* (Climbing over or above, mounting). An *Ueberstieg* requires, first, that toward which the *Ueberstieg* is directed and, secondly, that which is *ueberstiegen* or transcended; the first, then, toward which the transcendence occurs, we call "world," whereas the second, which is transcended, is the being itself (*das Seiende selbst*) and especially that in the form of which a human existence itself "exists." In other words, not only "world" constitutes itself in the act of transcending—be it as a mere dawn of world or as objectifying knowledge—but the self also does so.

Why do I have to mention these seemingly complicated matters?

Only because through the concept of being-in-the-world as transcendence has the fatal defect of all psychology been overcome and the road cleared for anthropology, the fatal defect being the theory of a dichotomy of world into subject and object. On the basis of that theory, human existence has been reduced to a mere subject, to a worldless rump subject in which all sorts of happenings, events, functions occur, which has all sorts of traits and performs all sorts of acts, without anybody, however, being able to say (notwithstanding theoretical constructs) how the subject can ever meet an "object" and can communicate and arrive at an understanding with other subjects. In contrast, being-in-the-world implies always being in the world with beings such as I, with coexistents. Heidegger, in his concept of being-in-the-world as transcendence, has not only returned to a point prior to the subject-object dichotomy of knowledge and eliminated the gap between self and world, but has also elucidated the structure of subjectivity as transcendence. Thus he has opened a new horizon of understanding for, and given a new impulse to, the scientific exploration of human existence and its specific modes of being. The split of Being into subject (man, person) and object (thing, environment) is now replaced by the unity of existence and "world," secured by transcendence.[2]

Transcending, therefore, implies far more, and something much more original, than knowing, even more than "intentionality" in Husserl's sense, since "world" becomes accessible to us first and foremost already through our "key" (*Stimmung*). If for a moment we remember the definition of being-in-the-world as transcendence and view from this point our psychiatric analysis of existence, we realize that by investigating the structure of being-in-the-world we can also approach and explore psychoses; and realize furthermore that we have to understand them as specific modes of transcending. In this context we do not say: mental illnesses are diseases of the brain (which, of course, they remain from a medical-clinical viewpoint). But we say: in the mental diseases we face modifications of the fundamental or essential structure and of the structural links of being-in-the-world as transcendence. It is one of the tasks of psychiatry to investigate and establish these variations in a scientifically exact way.

As can be seen from all our analyses published so far, spatialization and temporalization of existence play an important part in existential analysis. I shall confine myself here to the still more central problem of time. What makes this problem so central is the fact that transcendence is rooted in the very nature of time, in its unfolding into future, "having been" (*Gewesenheit*), and present. This will help to explain why, in our anthropological analyses of psychotic forms of being-human, we are not satisfied with our investigation unless we gain at least some insight into the respective variations of the structure of our patients' time. . . .

In those forms of being-in-the-world which are generally called "psychotic" we have so far found two types of modifications of "world" formation, one characterized by "leaping" (ordered flight of ideas) and by a "whirl" (disorderly flight of ideas), and the other characterized by a shrinking and simultaneous narrowing of existence along with its turning into swamp and earth (*Verweltlichung*). We may describe the latter also in the following terms: the freedom of letting "world" occur is replaced by the unfreedom of being overwhelmed by a certain "world-design." In the case of Ellen West, for instance, the freedom of forming an "ethereal" world was replaced more and more by the unfreedom of sinking into the narrow world of the grave and the swamp. "World," however, signifies not only world-formation and predesign of world, but —on the basis of the predesign and model-image—also the *how* of being-*in*-the-world and the attitude *toward* world. Thus, the transformation of the ethereal into a grave-world could also be established in the change of the existence as expressed by an exultingly soaring bird to an existence in the form of a slowly crawling, blind earthworm.

All this takes us only to the outermost gate of Heidegger's fundamental ontology or "*Daseins* Analytics" and just to the gates of anthropological or existential analysis which has been inspired by and founded on the former. But I hasten to outline the method of existential analysis and the area of its scientific function. At this point, I have to mention that my positive criticism of Heidegger's theory has led me to its extension: being-in-the-world as being of the existence for the sake of *myself* (designated by Heidegger as "care") has been juxtaposed with "being-beyond-the-world" as being of the existence for the sake of *ourselves* (designated by me as "love"). This transformation of Heidegger's system has to be considered especially in the analysis of psychotic forms of existence where we frequently observe modifications of transcendence in the sense of the "overswing" [3] of love, rather than in the sense of the "overclimb" of care. Let us only remember the enormously complex shrinkage of the existential structure which we so summarily call "autism."

II. THE DIFFERENTIATION BETWEEN HUMAN EXISTENCE AND ANIMAL BEING

"World" in Its Existential Analytical, and "World Around" (Umwelt) in Its Biological Meaning— However sketchy and incomplete my statements have been so far, I hope they have indicated why in our analyses, the concept of "world"—in the sense of world-formation or of "world-design" (Husserl's "mundanization" [*Mundanisierung*])—represents one of the most important basic concepts and is even used as a methodological clue. For the *what* of the respective world-design always furnishes information about the *how* of the being-in-the-world and the *how* of being oneself. In order to clarify the nature of the world-design, I shall now confront it with some world-concepts of a biological nature. First comes to mind Von Uexküll's biological world-concept, particularly because it shows, in spite of its differences, a certain similarity in its methodological application. I shall start with the methodological agreement.

Von Uexküll distinguishes a perception world (*Merkwelt*), an inner world, and an action world of the animal and combines perception world and action world under the name environment (*Unwelt* or "world-around"). The "circular interaction" occurring between these worlds he designates as *function-circle*. And just as we would say that it is not possible to describe the psychosis of a person without having fully encompassed (*umschritten*) his "worlds," so Von Uexküll states: "It is not possible to describe the biology of an animal unless one has fully encompassed its function-circles." And as we would continue by saying: "Therefore, we are fully justified in assuming the existence of as many worlds as there are psychotics," so Von Uexküll continues: "Therefore, one is fully justified in assuming the existence of as many environments (*Umwelten*) as there are animals." He comes similarly close to our viewpoint when he says: "Also, to understand each person's actions, we have to visit his 'special stage.' "

Von Uexküll's concept of environment however is much too narrow to be applied to man, because he understands by this term merely the "island of the senses"—*i.e.,* of sensory perceptions which "surround man like a garment." Hence it does not surprise us that in his brilliant descriptions of his friends' environments he continuously transgresses that narrow concept and demonstrates throughout how these friends are really "in-the-world" as *human beings*.

We further agree, for the present, with Von Uexküll's statement: "It is nothing but mental inertness to assume the existence of a single objective world [we psychiatrists naïvely call it reality] which one tailors as closely as possible to one's own environment, and which one has extended in all directions in space and time." [4]

However, Von Uexküll overlooks the fact that man, in contrast to animal, has his own world as well as an objective one which is common to all. This was known already to Heraclitus, who said that in the state of wakefulness we all have a common world, while in our sleep, as in passion, emotional states, sensuous lust, and drunkenness, each of us turns away from the common world toward his own. That common world—and Heraclitus recognized this, too—is one of phronesis, or rational deliberation and thinking. We psychiatrists have paid far too much attention to the deviations of our patients from life in the world which is common to all, instead of focusing primarily upon the patients' own or private world, as was first systematically done by Freud.

There is, however, one factor which not only differentiates our existential analytical concept of world from Von Uexküll's biological concept but places it even in diametrical opposition. It is true that, in Von Uexküll's theory, the animal and its environment form at times a genuine structure within the function-circle and that they appear there as "made to order for each other." However, Von Uexküll still considers the animal as subject and its environment as an object separated from it. Unity of animal and environment, of subject and object, is, according to Von Uexküll, guaranteed by the respective "blueprints" (action-plans, but also perception-plans) of the animal which, in turn, are part of an "overwhelmingly vast planful system." It now becomes clear that in order to proceed from Von Uexküll's theory to existential analysis, one must perform the Kantian-Copernican turn; instead of starting with nature and its planful system and dealing in natural science, one has to start at transcendental subjectivity and to proceed to existence as transcendence. Von Uexküll still throws both into one pot, as one deduces from the following ideas (which are quite impressive in themselves):

> Let us take as an example a certain oak tree and then ask ourselves what kind of an environmental object will that oak tree be, in the environment of an owl that perches in its hollow trunk; in the environment of a singing bird that nests in its branches; of a fox which has its hole under its roots; of a woodpecker which goes after wood-fretters in its bark; in the environment of such a wood-fretter itself; of an ant which runs along its trunk, etc. And, eventually, we ask ourselves what the role of the oak tree is in the environment of a hunter, of a romantic young girl, and of a prosaic wood-merchant. The oak, being a closed planful system itself, is woven into ever new plans on numerous environment stages, the tracing of which is a genuine task for the science of nature.

Von Uexküll is a natural scientist and not a philosopher. So it should not be held against him that he, like most natural scientists, makes light of the essential difference between animal and man and does not "keep sacred" (Spemann) the division between them. And yet, just at this point, this division becomes almost tangible. In the first place, the animal is tied to its "blueprint." It cannot go beyond it, whereas human existence not only contains numerous possibilities of modes of being but is precisely rooted in this multifold potentiality of being. Human existence affords the possibility of being a hunter, of being romantic, of being in business, and thus is free to design itself toward the most different potentialities of being; in other words, existence can "transcend" the being—in this case the being which is called "oak" —or make it accessible to itself, through the most diverse world-designs.

Secondly, we remember—now departing completely from the biological point of view—that transcendence implies not only world-design but, at the same time, self-design, potential modes of being for the self. Human existence is a very different being for the self, according to whether it designs its world as a hunter and *is* a hunter or, as a young girl, is a romantic self, or as a wood trader is a prosaic-calculating self. All these are different ways of being in the world and of potential modes of the self which are joined by numerous others, particularly that of the genuine potentiality of being oneself, and of the potentiality of being *we* in the sense of love.[5]

The animal, not being able to be an *I-you-we-self* (since it is kept from even saying *"I-you-we"*) does not have any world. For self and world are, indeed, reciprocal concepts. When we speak of the environment (*Umwelt*) the paramecium, the earthworm, the cephalopod, the horse, and even man *has,* this *"has"* possesses a very different meaning from the one we use when saying that man *"has"* a world. In the first case, the *"has"* signifies the establishment of a "blueprint," especially of the perception-and-action-organization, limited by nature to quite definite possibilities of stimulation and reaction. The animal has its environment by the grace of nature, not by the grace of freedom to transcend the situation. That means, it can neither design world nor open up world nor decide independently in and for a situation. It is, and always has been, in a once and for all determined "situational circle."[6] On the other hand, the "having" of a "world" on the part of man implies that man, although he has not laid his own foundation himself but was thrown into being and, insofar as that, has an environment like the animal, still has the possibility of transcending this being of his, namely, of climbing above it in care and of swinging beyond it in love.

Somewhat closer to our viewpoint than Von Uexküll's theory is Von Weizsaecker's concept of the "gestalt-circle" as a self-contained biological act.

"In so far as a living being through its movement and perception integrates itself into an environment, these movements and perceptions form a unit—a biological act."

Like Von Uexküll, Von Weizsaecker also prides himself on "having consciously introduced the *subject* as a matter of biological research and on having obtained recognition for it as such." That which produces the relation between subject and object is now no longer named "function-circle" but "gestalt-circle." According to Von Weizsaecker, the fundamental condition is "subjectivity" (which already shows a deeper view than the reference to the subject). But that fundamental condition cannot be recognized explicitly because it cannot in itself become the object; it is the "court of highest appeal," a power that "can be experienced either as unconscious dependency or as freedom." Von Weizsaecker, then, rejects the "external substantial dualism of Psyche and Physis"; he believes in replacing it by "the polar unity of subject and object." "But," he explains very rightly, "the subject is not a stable property; one has continuously to acquire it in order to possess it." Actually, it is only noticed when in a "crisis" one is threatened with losing it and later is able to rally again, thanks to its strength and resilience. "Simultaneously with each subject-jump, an object-jump, too, takes place and although the unity of the world is questionable, still each subject gathers at least his environmental world (*Umwelt*) whose objects he binds together into a little universe in a monadic unit."

All these theories are not only of the greatest interest to psychology and psychopathology but in addition bring clearly into focus the fact that only the concept of being-in-the-world as transcendence is genuinely consistent and penetrating; at the same time, they demonstrate that this concept can be applied consistently only to *human* existence.

Finally, I would like to remind the reader of Goldstein's world-concept, which proves so fruitful for the understanding of organic disturbances of the brain. Even where he uses the expression "milieu" in place of "world," we are still dealing with a genuine biological world-concept. As we know, it is one of his fundamental propositions that "a defective organism . . . can produce organized behavior only by such limitation of its milieu as corresponds to its defect." At other times he speaks of a "loss of freedom" and of a "tightening of the tie to the environment" on account of a defect. We remember the fact that certain organic patients are no longer able to orient and conduct themselves in the world of "ideas," while being perfectly able to do so in the world of action or of practice where, as Goldstein put it more recently, "effects can come about through concrete acts in handling material presently at hand." In speaking, like Head, of a "disturbance of the symbolic expression" or, jointly with Gelb, of a "disturbance of categorical behavior," Goldstein in both instances formulates only a modification of "being-in-the-world" as transcending.

This chapter has tried to demonstrate the degree to which biological thinking today endeavors to view and investigate organism and world as a unity in a unitary gestalt, symbolized by the circle. What prevails is the insight that everything here is connected with everything, that no partial change within the circle can occur without a change of the whole and that, in general, no isolated facts exist anymore. This, however, carries with it also a change in the concept of *fact,* of the fact itself, and of the methods in studying facts. For the goal is now no longer to arrive at conclusions by induction through mere accumulation of facts but to delve lovingly into the nature and content of the single phenomenon. Goldstein is well aware of this when he says: "In the formation of biological knowledge, the single links that are integrated into the whole cannot simply be evaluated quantitatively, as though the insight became the more certain the more links we establish. Rather, all the single facts are of a greater or lesser qualitative value." And he continues: "If in biology we see a science dealing with phenomena that can be established by analytical natural-scientific methods alone, we have to forego all insight which grasps the organism as a whole, and with it actually any insight into the life processes at all."

This already carries us close to a phenomenological view of life in the widest sense, a view, that is, which aims at the grasping of the life-content of phenomena and not at their factual meaning within a precisely circumscribed object-area.[7]

III. THE EXISTENTIAL-ANALYTICAL SCHOOL OF THOUGHT IN PSYCHIATRY

As compared with biological research, which exhausts or interprets the life-content of the phenomena, existential-analytical research has a double advantage. Firstly, it does not have to deal with so vague a "concept" as that of life, but with the widely and completely uncovered *structure of existence* as "being-in-the-world" and "beyond-the-world." Secondly, it can let existence actually speak up about itself —let it have its say. In other words, the phenomena to be interpreted are largely language phenomena. We know that the content of existence can nowhere be more clearly seen or more securely interpreted than through language; because it is in language that our world-designs actually ensconce and articulate themselves and where, therefore, they can be ascertained and communicated.

As to the first advantage, knowledge of the structure or basic constitution of existence provides us with a systematic clue for the practical existential-analytical investigation at hand. We know, now, what to focus on in the exploration of a psychosis, and how to proceed. We know that we have to ascertain the kind of spatialization and temporalization, of lighting and coloring; the texture, or materiality and motility, of the world-design toward which the given form of existence or its individual configuration casts itself. Such a methodical clue can be furnished only by the structure of being-in-the-world because that structure places a norm at our disposal and so enables us to determine deviations from this norm in the manner of the exact sciences. Much to our surprise it has turned out that, in the psychoses which were so far investigated, such deviations could not be understood merely negatively as abnormalities, but that they, in turn, represent a new norm, a new *form* of being-in-the-world. If, for example, we can speak of a manic form of life or, rather, of existence, it means that we could establish a norm which embraces and governs all modes of expression and behavior designated as "manic" by us. It is this *norm* which we call the "world" of the manic. The same holds true for the far more complicated, hitherto incalculably manifold world-designs of the schizophrenic. To explore and ascertain the world of these patients means, here as everywhere, to explore and ascertain in what way everything that is—men as well as things—is accessible to these forms of existence. For we know well enough that that-which-is as such never becomes accessible to man, except in and through a certain world-design.

As to the second advantage, the possibility of exploring language phenomena, it is the essence of speech and speaking that they express and communicate a *certain content of meaning*. This content of meaning is, as we know, an infinitely manifold one. Everything, therefore, depends upon the precise criteria by which we explore the language manifestations of our patients. We do not—as the psychoanalyst systematically does—focus merely upon the historical content, upon references to an experienced or conjectured pattern of the inner life-history. And we do not at all watch the content for all possible references to facts pertaining to life function, as does the psychopathologist in focusing on disturbances of speech or thinking functions. What attracts our attention in existential-analysis is rather the content of language expressions and manifestations insofar as they point to the world-design or designs in which the speaker lives or has lived or, in one word, their world-content. By world-content, then, we mean the content of facts pertaining to worlds; that is, of references to the way in which the given form or configuration of existence discovers world designs and opens up world—and is, or exists, in the respective world. There are, furthermore, indications of the way in which the existence is *beyond-the-world;* that is, how it *is,* or *is not,* at home in the eternity (*Ewigkeit*) and haven (*Heimat*) of love.

In "The Case of Ellen West," my first study planned as an example of existential analysis as applied to psychiatry, conditions were particularly favorable for existential analysis. In this case I had at my disposal an unusual abundance of spontaneous and immediately comprehensible verbal manifestations such as self-descriptions, dream accounts, diary entries, poems, letters, autobiographical drafts, whereas usually, and especially in cases of deteriorated schizophrenics, we have to obtain the material for existential analysis by persistent and systematic exploration of our patients over months and years. First and foremost it is our task to assure ourselves, over and over again, of what our patients really mean by their verbal expressions. Only then can we dare to approach the scientific task of discerning the "worlds" in which the patients are or, in other words, to understand how all partial links of the existential structure become comprehensible through the total structure, just as the total structure constitutes itself, without incongruity, from the partial links. In this, as in any other scientific investigation, there do occur errors, dead ends, premature interpretations; but, also as in any other, there are ways and means of correcting and rectifying these errors. It is one of the most impressive achievements of existential analysis to have shown that even in the realm of subjectivity "nothing is left to chance," but that a certain organized structure can be recognized from which each word, each idea, drawing, action, or gesture receives its peculiar imprint—an insight of which we make continuous use in existential-analytical interpretations of the Rorschach test and recently also in the Word Association Test. It is always the same world-design which confronts us in a patient's spontaneous verbal manifestations, in the systematic exploration of his Rorschach and Word Association responses, in his drawings, and also, frequently, in his dreams. And only after having encompassed (*umschritten*) these worlds—to speak in Von Uexküll's words—and brought them together can we understand the form of our patient's existence in the sense of what we call "neurosis" or "psychosis." Only then may we dare to attempt to understand single, partial links of those forms of world and existence (clinically evaluated as symptoms) from the modes and ways of the patient's total being-in-the-world.

Naturally, the connections of the life-history, too, here play an important part but, as we shall soon realize, by no means in the same way as in psychoanalysis. Whereas for the latter they are the goal of the investigation, for existential analysis they merely provide material for that investigation.

The following examples will illustrate the kind of world-designs with which we have to deal in psychopathology; but the number of such deviations is infinite. We are still at the beginning of describing and investigating them.

For my first clinical illustration I shall report the case of a young girl who at the age of five experienced a puzzling attack of anxiety and fainting when her heel got stuck in her skate and separated from her shoes. Ever since, the girl—now twenty-one years of age—suffered spells of irresistible anxiety whenever a heel of one of her shoes appeared to loosen or when someone touched the heel or only spoke of heels. (Her own had to be nailed to her soles.) On such occasions, if she could not get away in time, she would faint.

Psychoanalysis proved clearly and convincingly that hidden behind the fear of loose or separating heels were birth phantasies, both about being born herself and therefore separated from mother and about giving birth to a child of her own. Of the various disruptions of continuity which psychoanalysis revealed as being frightening to the girl, the one between mother and child was fundamental and most feared. (I am omitting completely, in this context, the masculine component.) Before the period of Freud, one would have stated that the skating accident, harmless as it was per se, had "caused" the "heel phobia." Freud demonstrated subsequently that the pathogenic effect is produced by phantasies connected with and preceding such an accident. Yet in both periods still another explanation would be drawn upon to account for the fact that a specific event or phantasy had such a far-reaching effect precisely upon this person—namely, the explanation of "constitution" or predisposition." For each of us has experienced the "birth trauma," but some lose their heels without developing a hysterical phobia.

We do not, of course, propose to unfold, let alone solve, the problem of "predisposition" in all its aspects; but I dare say that we can throw some more light on it when we view it from an "anthropological" angle. In later studies we were able to demonstrate that we could reach even *behind* the phantasies insofar as we could trace and investigate the world-design which made possible those phantasies and phobias in the first place.

What serves as a clue to the world-design of our little patient is the category of *continuity,* of continuous connection and containment. This entails a tremendous constriction, simplification, and depletion of the "world content," of the extremely complex totality of the patient's contexts of reference. Everything that makes the world significant is submitted to the rule of that *one* category which alone supports her "world" and being. This is what causes the great anxiety about any disruption of continuity, any gap, tearing or separating, being separated or torn. This is why separation from the mother, experienced by everyone as the arch-separation in human life, had to become so prevalent that any event of separation served to symbolize the fear of separation from the mother and to invite and activate those phantasies and daydreams.

We should, therefore, not explain the emergence of the phobia by an overly strong "pre-oedipal" tie to the mother, but rather realize that such an overly strong filial tie is only possible on the premise of a world-design exclusively based on connectedness, cohesiveness, continuity. Such a way of experiencing "world"—which always implies such a "key" [8]—does not have to be "conscious"; but neither must we call it "unconscious" in the psychoanalytical sense, since it is outside the contrast of these opposites. Indeed, it does not refer to anything psychological but to something which only makes possible the psychic fact. At this point we face what is actually "abnormal" in this existence—but we must not forget that where the world-design is narrowed and constricted to such a degree, the self, too, is constricted and prevented from maturing. Everything is supposed to stay as it was before. If, however, something new does happen and continuity is disrupted, it can only result in catastrophe, panic, anxiety attack. For then the world actually collapses, and nothing is left to hold it up. The inner or existential maturation and the genuine time-orientation toward the future are replaced by a preponderance of the past, of "already having-been-in." The world must stop here, nothing must happen, nothing must change. The context must be preserved as it has always been. It is this type of temporal orientation that permits the element of *suddenness* to assume such enormous significance; because suddenness is the time quality that explodes continuity, hacks it and chops it to pieces, throws the earlier existence out of its course, and exposes it to the Dreadful,[9] to the naked horror. This is what in psychopathology we term, in a most simplifying and summarizing manner, anxiety attack.

Neither the loss of the heel nor the womb and birth phantasies are "explanations" of the emergence of the phobia. Rather, they became so significant because holding on to mother meant to this child's existence —as is natural for the small child—having a hold on the world. By the same token, the skating incident assumed its traumatic significance because, in it, the world suddenly changed its face, disclosed itself from the angle of suddenness, of something totally different, new, and unexpected. For that there was no place in this child's world; it could not enter into her world-design; it stayed, as it were, always outside; it could not be mastered. In other words, instead of being accepted by the inner life so that its meaning and content could be absorbed, it appeared and reappeared over and over again without having any meaning for the existence, in an ever-recurring invasion by the Sudden into the motionlessness of the world-clock. This world-design did not manifest itself before the traumatic event occurred; it did only on the *occasion* of that event. Just as the a priori or transcendental forms [10] of the human mind make experience only into what experience is, so the form of that world-design had first to produce the condition of the possibility for the ice-skating incident in order for it to be experienced as traumatic.

It should be mentioned that this case is not at all an isolated one. We know that anxiety can be tied to various types of disruption of continuity; *e.g.*, it may appear as horror at the sight of a loose button hanging on a thread or of a break in the thread of saliva. Whatever the life-historical events are to which these anxieties refer, we are always dealing here with the same depletion of being-in-the-world, narrowed down to include only the category of continuity. In this peculiar world-design with its peculiar being-in-the-world and its peculiar self, we see in existential terms the real key to the understanding of what is taking place. Like the biologist and neuropathologist, we do not stop at the single fact, the single disturbance, the single symptom, but we keep searching for an embracing whole within which the fact can be understood as a partial phenomenon. But this whole is neither a functional whole—a "Gestalt-circle"—nor a whole in the sense of a complex. Indeed, it is no objective whole at all but a whole in the sense of the unity of a world-design.

We have seen that we cannot progress far enough in our understanding of anxiety if we consider it only as a psychopathological symptom per se. In short, we must never separate "anxiety" from "world," and we should keep in mind that anxiety always emerges when the world becomes shaky or threatens to vanish. The emptier, more simplified, and more constricted the world-design to which an existence has committed itself, the sooner will anxiety appear and the more severe will it be. The "world" of the healthy with its tremendously varied contexture of references and compounds of circumstance can never become entirely shaky or sink. If it is threatened in one region, other regions will emerge and offer a foothold. But where the "world," as in the present case and in numerous others, is so greatly dominated by one or a few categories, naturally the threat to the preservation of that one or those few categories must result in a more intensified anxiety.

Phobia is always an attempt at safeguarding a restricted, impoverished "world," whereas anxiety expresses the loss of such a safeguard, the collapse of the "world," and thus the delivery of the existence to nothingness—the intolerable, dreadful, "naked horror." We then must strictly differentiate between the historically and situationally conditioned *point of breakthrough* of anxiety and the existential *source* of anxiety. Freud made a similar distinction when he differentiated between phobia as a symptom and the patient's own libido as the real object of anxiety. However, in our concept the theoretical construct of libido is replaced by the phenomenological-ontological structure of existence as being-in-the-world. We do not hold that man is afraid of his own libido, but we state that existence as being-in-the-world is, as such, determined by uncanniness and nothingness. The source of anxiety is existence itself.

Whereas in the preceding instance we had to deal with a static "world," as it were, a world in which nothing was supposed to "come to pass" or happen, in which everything had to remain unchanged and no separating agent was to interfere with its unity, we shall in the following example meet a torturously heterogeneous, disharmonious "world," again dating from early childhood. The patient, displaying a pseudoneurotic syndrome of polymorphous schizophrenia, suffered from all sorts of somato-, auto-, and allopsychic phobias.[11] The "world" in which that which is—everything-that-is (*alles Seiende*)—was accessible to him was a world of push and pressure, loaded with energy to the point of bursting. In that world no step could be made without running the danger of being knocked against or knocking against something, whether in real life or in phantasy. The temporality of this world was one of *urgency* (René Le Senne), its spatiality therefore one of horribly crowded narrowness and closeness, pressing upon "body and soul" of the existence. This came clearly to light in the Rorschach test. At one point the patient saw pieces of furniture "on which one might knock one's shin"; at another, "a drum that strikes one's leg"; at a third, "lobsters which squeeze you," "something you get scratched with"; and finally, "centrifugal balls of a flywheel which hit me in the face, me of all people, although for decades they had stayed fixed with the machine; only when I get there something happens."

As the world of things behaves, so does the world of one's fellow men; everywhere lurk danger and disrespect, mobs or jeering watchers. All this, of course, points to the borderline of delusions of "reference" or "encroachment."

It is very instructive to observe the patient's desperate attempts to control this disharmonious, energy-crammed, threatening world, to harmonize it artificially, and to belittle it in order to avoid the constantly imminent catastrophe. He does this by keeping himself at the greatest possible distance from the world, rationalizing this distance completely —a process which, here as everywhere, is accompanied by the devaluation and depletion of the world's abundance of life, love, and beauty. This is particularly demonstrated in his Word Association Test. His Rorschach responses, too, bear witness to the artificial rationalization of his world, to its symmetrization and mechanization. Whereas in our first case everything-that-is (*alles Seiende*) was only accessible in a world reduced to the category of continuity, in this case it is a world reduced to the mechanical category of push and pressure. We are therefore not surprised to see that in this existence and its world there is no steadiness, that its stream of life does not flow quietly along, but that everything occurs by jerks and starts, from the simplest gestures and movements to the formulation of lingual expression and the performance of thinking and volitional decisions. Everything about the patient is jagged and occurs abruptly, while between the single jerks and pushes emptiness prevails. (The reader will notice that we are describing in existential-analytical terms what would clinically be called schizoid and autistic.) Again, very typical is the patient's behavior in the Rorschach test. He feels a desire to "fold up the cards and file them away with a final effort," just as he would like to fold up and file away the world as such with a final effort, or else he would not be able to control it any more.

But these final efforts exhaust him to such a degree that he becomes increasingly inactive and dull. If in the first case it was continuity of existence that had to be preserved at all costs, in the present case it is its dynamic *balance*. Here, too, a heavy phobic armor is employed in the interest of that preservation. Where it fails, even if only in phantasy, anxiety attacks and complete desperation take over. This case, whose existential and world-structure could be only very roughly suggested here, was published as the second study on schizophrenia under the title of "Juerg Zuend."

Whereas the above case permitted us a view of the kind of world in which "delusions of reference and encroachment" [12] become possible, a third case, that of Lola Voss, gave us some insight into the world-structure which makes possible delusions of persecutions. It offered us the rare opportunity to watch the appearance of severe hallucinatory delusions of persecutions, preceded by a pronounced phobic phase. This expressed itself in a highly complicated superstitious system of consulting an oracle of words and syllables, whose positive or negative dicta guided the patient in the commission or omission of certain acts. She would feel compelled to break up the names of things into syllables, to recombine these syllables in accordance with her system and, depending on the results of these combinations, to make contact with the persons or things in question or to avoid them like the plague. Again, all this served as a safeguarding for the existence and its worlds against catastrophe. But in this case, catastrophe was not felt to be in the disruption of the world's continuity nor in the disturbance of its dynamic balance, but in the invasion by the unspeakably Uncanny and Horrid. This patient's "world" was not dynamically loaded with conflicting forces which had to be artificially harmonized; hers was not a world-design reduced to push and pressure but one reduced to the categories of familiarity and strangeness—or uncanniness (*Vertrautheit und Unvertrautheit—oder Unheimlichkeit*). The existence was constantly threatened by a prowling, as yet impersonal, hostile power. The incredibly thin and flimsy net of artificial syllable-combinations served as a safeguard against the danger of being overwhelmed by that power and against the unbearable threat of being delivered to it.

It was very informative to observe how, simultaneously with the disappearance of these safeguards, a new, quite different, because now quite unintended, safeguard made its appearance, namely the actual delusions of persecution.

The place of the impersonal power of the bottomless Uncanny (*Unheimlichen*) was now taken by the secret (*heimliche*) conspiracy of personalized enemies. Against these the patient could now consciously defend herself—with accusations, counterattacks, attempts at escape—all of which seemed like child's play compared with the constantly helpless state of being threatened by the horrible power of the incomprehensible Uncanny. But such gain in the security of existence was accompanied by the patient's complete loss of existential freedom, her complete yielding to the idea of hostility on the part of her fellow men, or, in psychopathological terms, by delusions of persecution.

I am reporting this case in order to demonstrate that we cannot understand these delusions if we begin our investigation with a study of the delusions themselves. Rather should we pay close attention to what *precedes* the delusions—be it for months, weeks, days, or only hours. We would then surely find that the delusions of persecution, similarly to the phobias, represent a protection of the existence against the invasion of something inconceivably Frightful, compared with which even the secret conspiracies of enemies are more tolerable; because the enemies, unlike the incomprehensible Frightful, can be "taken at something" [13] —by perceiving, anticipating, repelling, battling them.

In addition, the case of Lola Voss can show that we are no longer constrained by the bothersome contrast of psychic life with which we can empathize and that with which we cannot, but that we have at our disposal a method, a scientific tool, with which we can bring closer to a systematic scientific understanding even the so-called incomprehensible life of the psyche.

Of course, it still depends upon the imagination of the single researcher and physician how truly he is able to reexperience and resuffer, by virtue of his own experiential abilities, all the potential experience which existential-analytical research methodically and planfully opens to his insight.

In many cases, however, it does not suffice to consider only *one* world-design, as we have done so far for the sake of simplicity of presentation. Whereas this serves our purpose in the morbid depressions, as in mania and melancholia, in our investigations of what is clinically known as schizophrenic processes we cannot neglect the bringing into focus and the describing of the various worlds in which our patients live in order to show the changes in their "being-in-the-world" and "beyond-the-world." In the case of Ellen West, for instance, we saw the existence in the shape of a jubilant bird soaring into the sky—a flight in a world of light and infinite space. We saw the existence as a standing and walking on the ground in the world of resolute action. And, finally, we saw it in the form of a blind worm crawling in muddy earth, in the moldering grave, the narrow hole. Above all, we saw that "mental illness" really means for the "mind," how the human mind really reacts under such conditions, how its forms actually change. In this case it was a change to a precisely traceable narrowing-down, to a depletion or excavation of existence, world, and beyond-world to the point where, finally, of all the spiritual riches of the patient's world, of its abundance in love, beauty, truth, kindness, in variety, growth, and blossoming, "nothing was left except the big unfilled hole." What did remain was the animalistic compulsion to cram down food, the irresistible instinctual urge to fill the belly to the brim. All this could be demonstrated not only in the modes and changes of spatiality, of the hue, materiality, and dynamics of the various worlds, but also in the modes and changes of temporality, up to the state of the "eternal emptiness" of so-called autism.

As to manic-depressive insanity, I refer to my studies on *The Flight of Ideas* and to the investigations of the manifold forms of depressive states by E. Minkowski, Erwin Straus, and Von Gebsattel, all of which, although not existential-analytical in the full sense of the word, were definitely conducted in an empirical-phenomenological fashion. In mentioning E. Minkowski we must gratefully acknowledge that he was the first to introduce phenomenology into psychiatry for practical purposes, particularly in the area of schizophrenia where he immediately put it to fruitful use.[14] I wish to mention further the work of Erwin Straus and Von Gebsattel on compulsion and phobias, and of the late Franz Fischer on *Space and Time Structure in the Existence of the Schizophrenic*. Applications of existential-analytical thinking can be found in Von Gebsattel's excellent study, *The World of the Compulsive,* and in Roland Kuhn's study, *Interpretations of Masks in the Rorschach Test* (1945).

Apart from the deepening of our understanding of psychoses and neuroses, existential analysis is indispensable to psychology and characterology. As to characterology, I shall confine myself here to the analysis of miserliness. It has been said that miserliness consists in persisting in the state of potentiality, in "a fight against realization," and that only from this angle can the bondage to money be understood (Erwin Straus). But this is still too rationalistic an interpretation. One has rather to analyze the miser's world-design and existence; in short, to explore what world-design and what world-interpretation lie at the root of miserliness, or in what way that-which-is (*Seiende*) is accessible to the stingy.

Viewing the behavior of the miser and his description in literature (as by Molière and Balzac), we find that he is primarily interested in *filling,* namely the filling of cases and boxes, stockings and bags with "gold," and only consequently in refusing to spend and in retaining. "Filling" is the a priori or transcendental tie that allows us to combine faeces and money through a common denominator. It is only this that provides psychoanalysis with the empirical possibility of considering money-addiction as "originating" from the retention of faeces. But by no means is the retaining of faeces the "cause" of stinginess.

The above-mentioned empty spaces, however, are designed not only to be filled but, in addition, to hide their content from the eyes and hands of fellow men. The miser "sits" or "squats" on his money "like the hen on her egg." (We can learn a great deal from such phrases of idiomatic language since language has always proceeded, to a high degree, phenomenologically rather than discursively.) The pleasure of spending money, of giving it out—possible only in sympathetic contact with one's fellow men—is replaced by the pleasure of secret viewing, rummaging, touching and mental touching, and counting the gold. Such are the secret orgies of the miser, to which may be added the lust for the glittering, sparkling gold as such as the only spark of life and love which is left to the miser. The prevalence of filling-up and its worldly correlate, the cavity, points to something "Moloch-like" [15] in such a world and existence. This, naturally, carries with it (according to the unitary structure of being-in-the-world) also a certain moloch-like form of the self-world, and in this case particularly of the body-world and of body-consciousness, as rightly emphasized by psychoanalysis. As to temporality, the very saying that one can be "stingy with one's time" proves that the miser's time is here spatialized in a moloch-like sense, insofar as small portions of time are eagerly and constantly being saved, accumulated, and jealously guarded. From this follows the inability to give "of one's time." Of course all this implies at the same time the loss of the possibility of true or existential temporalization, of maturation of personality. The miser's relation to death which here, as in all existential-analytical investigations, is of the greatest importance, can in this context not be discussed. It is closely linked to his relations to his fellow men and linked also to his profound lack of love.

In the same way in which we investigate and understand a characterological trait, we investigate and understand what in psychiatry and psychopathology is so summarily termed feelings and moods. A feeling or a mood is not properly described as long as one docs not describe how the human existence that has it, or is in it, is in-the-world, "has" world and exists. (See in my studies on *The Flight of Ideas* the description of the optimistic moods and the feelings of exhilarant gaiety.) What has to be considered here is, in addition to temporality and spatiality, the shade, the lighting, the materiality and, above all, the dynamics of the given world-design. All this can be examined again through the medium of individual verbal manifestations as well as through metaphors, proverbs, idiomatic phrases in general, and through the language of writers and poets. Indeed, idiomatic language and poetry are inexhaustible sources for existential analysis.

The peculiar dynamics of the world of feelings and moods, their ascending and descending motion, their Upward and Downward, I have pointed out in my essay on "Dream and Existence." Evidence for this kind of motion can be found in waking states as well as in dreams, introspective descriptions, and Rorschach responses. Gaston Bachelard, in his *L'Air et les Songes,* gives a brilliant, comprehensive presentation of the verticality of existence, *de la vie ascensionnelle* on the one hand and *de la chute* on the other.[16]

He impressively and beautifully demonstrates the existential-analytical significance of the fundamental metaphors *de la hauteur, de l'elevation; de la profondeur, de l'abaissement, de la chute* (earlier referred to by E. Minkowski in his *Vers une Cosmologie*). Bachelard quite correctly speaks of a psychology—we would call it an anthropology—*ascensionnelle.* Without this background, neither feelings nor "keys" (*Stimmung*) nor "keyed" (*gestimmte*) Rorschach responses can be scientifically understood and described.[17] Bachelard, too, has realized what impressed itself so urgently upon us in the case of Ellen West—that the imagination obeys the "law of the four elements" and that each element is imagined according to its special dynamism. We are particularly happy to find in Bachelard insight into the fact that those forms of being which are characterized by dropping and falling, those of a descending life in general, invariably lead to an *imagination terrestre,* a turning into earth, or a bogging down of the existence. This, in turn, is of the greatest importance for the understanding of Rorschach results.

This *materialité* of the world-design, originating from the "key" (*Gestimmtheit*) of the existence is by no means confined to the environment, to the world of things, or to the universe in general, but refers equally to the world of one's fellow men (*Mitwelt*) and to the self-world (*Eigenwelt*) (as demonstrated in the cases of Ellen West and Juerg Zuend). For them, self-world and environment were only accessible in the form of the hard, energy-loaded material, while the world of their fellow men was only accessible by way of an equally energy-loaded, hard, and impenetrable resistance. When the poet speaks of the "dull resistance of the world" he demonstrates that the world of one's fellow men can be experienced in the form not just of a metaphor but of an actually and bitterly felt hard and resistant matter. The same is expressed in sayings such as "a tough guy" and "a roughneck."

Finally, what part is existential analysis equipped to play in the total picture of psychiatric investigation and research?

Existential analysis is not a psychopathology, nor is it clinical research nor any kind of objectifying research. Its results have first to be recast by psychopathology into forms that are peculiar to it, such as that of a psychic organism, or even of a psychic apparatus, in order to be projected onto the physical organism.[18] This cannot be achieved without a greatly simplifying reduction whereby the observed existential-analytical phenomena are largely divested of their phenomenal contents and reinterpreted into functions of the psychic organism, psychic "mechanisms," etc. However, psychopathology would be digging its own grave were it not always striving to test its concepts of functions against the phenomenal contents to which these concepts are applied and to enrich and deepen them through the latter. Additionally, existential analysis satisfies the demands for a deeper insight into the nature and origin of psychopathological symptoms. If in these symptoms we recognize "facts of communication"—namely, disturbances and difficulties in communication—we should do our utmost to retrace their causes—retrace them, that is, to the fact that the mentally ill live in "worlds" different from ours. Therefore, knowledge and scientific description of those "worlds" become the main goal of psychopathology, a task which it can perform only with the help of existential analysis. The much-discussed *gap* that separates our "world" from the "world" of the mentally ill and makes communication between the two so difficult is not only scientifically explained but also scientifically bridged by existential analysis. We are now no longer stopped at the so-called borderline between that psychic life with which we can, and that with which we cannot, empathize. Quite a number of case reports show that our method has succeeded beyond earlier hopes in communicating with patients, in penetrating their life-history, and in understanding and describing their world-designs even in cases where all this seemed impossible before. This applies, in my experience, particularly to cases of hypochondriacal paranoids who are otherwise hardly accessible. Thus we also comply here with a *therapeutic* demand.

This insight—that the world-designs as such distinguish the mentally ill from the healthy and hamper communication with the former—also throws new light on the problem of the projection [19] of psychopathological symptoms onto specific brain processes. Now it cannot be so important to localize single psychic symptoms in the brain but rather, primarily, to ask where and how to localize the fundamental psychic disturbance which is recognizable by the change of "being-in-the-world" as such. For indeed, the "symptom" (*e.g.,* of flight of ideas, of psychomotor inhibition, neologism, stereotypy, etc.) proves to be the expression of a spreading change of the soul, a change of the total form of existence and the total style of life.

NOTES

1 [Binswanger uses this word not in its usual American meaning, which is cultural anthropology, the comparative study of races, mores, etc., but rather in its more strictly etymological sense, that is, anthropology as the study of man ("anthropos") and specifically, as he goes on to say above, the study of the essential meaning and characteristics of being human.—TRANSLATOR.]

2 Where we speak of "world" in terms of existential analysis, there world always means that toward which the existence has climbed and according to which it has designed itself: or, in other words, the manner and mode in which that which is (*Seiende*) becomes accessible to the existence. However, we use the expression "world" not only in its transcendental but also in its "objective" sense, as, *e.g.,* when we speak of the "dull resistance of the world," of the "temptations of the world," "retiring from the world," etc., whereby we have primarily the world of our fellow men in mind. Similarly, we speak of a person's environment and of his "own world" as of particular regions of that which exists in the objective world, and not as of transcendental world designs. This is terminologically troublesome, but not open to change any more. Hence, where the meaning is not self-evident, we have to place "world" always in quotation marks, or use the term "world design."

3 [This is a literal translation for the term *Überschwung.* Binswanger means the kind of transcendence which goes with love, an emphasis he introduced and which he contrasts to the transcendence arising out of "care" (one of Heidegger's concepts). His point is that the psychotic deviates particularly in regard to the former.—Editors of *Existence.*]

4 See *Unwelt und Innenwelt der Tiere,* 2, Aufl., 1921, S. 4: "Only to the superficial observer it seems as if all sea-animals were living in a homogeneous world, common to all of them. Closer study teaches us that each of those thousands of forms of life possesses an environment peculiar to itself which is conditioned by and, in turn, conditions the 'building plan' of the animal." Also, *viz., Theoretische Biologie,* S. 232: "We now know that there is not one space and one time only, but that there are as many spaces and times as there are subjects, as each subject is contained by its own environment which possesses its own space and time. Each of these thousandfold worlds offers to the sensory perceptions a new potentiality to unfold themselves."

5 We therefore differentiate in the structure of the existence as being-in-the-world: (a) the ways in which it designs world and builds world—in short, the ways of world-design and world images; (b) the ways in which it, accordingly, exists as a self—*i.e.,* establishes itself or does not establish itself; (c) but also the ways of transcendence as such, that is, the ways in which the existence is in the world (*e.g.,* acting, thinking, creating, fancying). Thus, doing existential analysis in the area of psychiatry means to examine and describe how the various forms of the mentally ill, and each one for himself, design worlds, establish their self and—in the widest sense—act and love.

6 This was already emphasized by Herder in his essay, "On the Origin of Language": Each animal has its circle within which it belongs from its birth, in which it remains for its life time, and in which it dies.

7 *Viz.,* again Goldstein, *Der Aufbau des Organismus,* S. 242: "Biological insight is the continuous process through which we experience increasingly the idea of the organism, something of a 'ken' which is always based on the grounds of very empirical facts."

8 [Or attunement (*Gestimmheit*).—TRANSLATOR.]

9 [This adjective used as a noun, "the Dreadful," signifies the abstract quintessence of all that is dreadful, the epitome of dreadfulness. This and similar expressions which follow in this essay—such as "the Sudden," "the Uncanny," "the Horrid"—have been capitalized to indicate that the adjective has the substantive quality of a noun.—Editors of *Existence.*]

10 [Binswanger is here using Kantian expressions.—Editors of *Existence.*]

11 [A reference to concepts by Wernicke, meaning simply phobias relative to the patient's own body, to his own psyche, and to the external world.—TRANSLATOR.]

12 The Swiss School differentiates between delusions characterized by ideas of reference and being encroached upon (*Beeintraechtigung*), on the one hand, and of persecutions on the other.

13 [A Heideggerian concept which, in this context, serves to emphasize that these enemies can be "handled" by the patient.—TRANSLATOR.]

14 Also, his books *Le Temps vécu* (1932) and, particularly, *Vers une cosmologie* (Ed. Montaigne, 1936) should be mentioned. The latter is an excellent introduction into "cosmological" thinking in phenomenological terms.

15 [The author here refers not to the cruel aspects of Moloch-worship but to the hollowness of the idol which had to be filled.—Editors of *Existence.*]

16 But we also know of a horizontality of existence, particularly from Rorschach responses. This horizontality is characterized by the road, the river, the plain. It does not reveal the "key" of the existence, but the ways of its "life-itinerary," that is, the way in which it is able or unable to stay, or not stay, in life.

17 However, Bachelard's investigations are still based on imagination (*le forces imaginantes de notre esprit, viz., L'Eau et les rêves* [José Corti, 1942]; *La Psychanalyse du feu* [Gallimard, 1938]; *Lautréamont,* [Corti, 1939]). The latter book also provides an exemplary interpretation of a case interesting for the psychiatrist. What is still missing in them is an anthropological, and even more, an ontological, basis for B.'s studies. He realizes not yet that his "imagination," too, is nothing but a certain mode of being-in-the-world and being-beyond-it, especially of the latter. But he approximates this insight when he explains (*L'Air et les songes,* p. 13): *"l'imagination est une des forces de l'audace humaine,"* and when he sees in the *verticalité*—characterizing the ascending life—not a mere metaphor, but *"un principe d'ordre, une loi de filiation."* B.'s works today are indispensable for the literary critic and language scientist as well as for the psychiatrist.

18 We are speaking here of the role of psychopathology within the total frame of psychiatric medical research. We do not neglect the fact that in the psychoanalytical investigation, as well as in every purely "understanding" psychopathology, germs of existential-analytical views can always be found. But they indicate neither a methodical scientific procedure nor a knowledge of why and in what way existential analysis differs from the investigation of life-historical connections and from an "empathic" or "intuitive" entering into the patient's psychic life.

19 [The German term "projection" used here in the sense of localizing or assigning.—TRANSLATOR.]

24

Findings in a Case of Schizophrenic Depression

Eugene Minkowski

In the year 1922, a stroke of good luck—or, more exactly, life's vicissitudes—obliged me to spend two months as the personal physician of a patient. I was with him constantly, night and day. It is not difficult to imagine the unpleasant moments that such a symbiosis presents, but on the other hand it creates special conditions for the observer and gives him the possibility, by permitting him constantly to compare his own and the patient's psyche, of noting certain particularities that ordinarily escape attention.

Briefly, here is the clinical picture. The patient was a man of sixty-six who presented a depressive psychosis accompanied by delusions of persecution and extensive interpretations.

The patient expressed thoughts of guilt and ruin. A foreigner, he reproached himself for not having chosen French citizenship, seeing therein a heinous crime; he also stated that he had not paid his taxes and that he no longer had any money. An atrocious punishment awaited him as a result of his crimes. His family would have their arms and legs cut off and would then be exposed in some arid field. The same would happen to him; he would have a nail driven into his head and all sorts of garbage would be poured into his belly. Mutilated in the most horrible manner, he would be led, in the middle of a parade, to a fair and condemned to live, covered with vermin, in a cage with wild beasts or with the rats of the sewers until death overtook him. All the world was cognizant of his crimes and the punishment which awaited him; for that matter, everyone, with the exception of his family, would play some role therein. People looked oddly at him in the street, his servants were paid to spy on him and betray him, every newspaper article was directed at him, and books had been printed solely against him and his family. At the head of this vast movement against him was the medical corps.

These ideas of guilt, ruin, imminent punishment, and persecution were accompanied by interpretations of a really surprising scope. This was the "residue politics" (*politique des restes*), as he called it—a political system that had been instituted especially for him. Every leftover, all residue, would be put aside to be one day stuffed into his abdomen—and this, from all over the world. Everything would be included without exception. When one smoked, there would be the burnt match, the ashes, and the cigarette butt. At meals, he was preoccupied with the crumbs, the fruit pits, the chicken bones, the wine or water at the bottom of the glasses. The egg, he said, was his worst enemy because of the shell—it was also the expression of the great anger of his persecutors. When one sewed, there would be bits of thread and needles. All the matches, strings, bits of paper, and pieces of glass that he saw while walking in the street were meant for him. After that came nail parings and hair clippings, empty bottles, letters and envelopes, subway tickets, address-bands, the dust that one brought in on one's shoes, bath water, the garbage from the kitchen and from all the restaurants of France, etc. Then it was rotten fruit and vegetables, cadavers of animals and men, the urine and feces of horses. "Whoever speaks of a clock," he would tell us, "speaks of the hands, cogs, springs, case, pendulum, etc." And all this he would have to swallow. In sum, these interpretations were boundless; they included everything, absolutely everything that he saw or imagined. In these conditions, it is not difficult to understand that the smallest thing, the most minute act of daily life, was immediately interpreted as being hostile to him.

Such was the clinical picture. Actually, it does not present anything particularly extraordinary unless it would be the scope, we would even say the universality, of his delusions of persecution and his interpretations. This universal character of the morbid manifestations is, however, an unquestionable advantage when we wish to penetrate the very nature of psychopathological phenomena. When these phenomena are limited to certain persons or objects, we first look for an explanation for this elective character. Why does the patient feel that this person persecutes him instead of another; why does he, in his delirium, attribute a particular importance to this thing instead of that one? Such are the questions that face us then. It is the *content* of the delusion of hallucination that attracts our attention, and it is there that the affective factors, the complexes and the symbolism that play such a great role in modern psychiatry, enter in. On the other hand, the cases where the content of the morbid phenomenon is in no way limited but has a universal character lend themselves better, I submit, to the study of a phenomenon as such; of the delusion, for example, as a phenomenon which is specific and unique.

Although my patient's case is relatively banal from a clinical point of view, this can hardly be said of the circumstances in which I was able to study him. I have already said that I lived with him for two months. Thus, I had the possibility of following him from day to day, not in a mental hospital or sanitarium, but in an ordinary environment. His way of reacting to the habitual external stimuli, his ability to adapt himself to the exigencies of daily life, the variability of his symptoms and their particular nuances come much more clearly to life under such conditions. To this must be added another point. We are unable to conserve a professional attitude twenty-four hours a day. We, too, react to the patient as do the other persons of his environment. Compassion, mildness, persuasion, impatience, and anger appear one by one. Thus it was that, in the above circumstances, I was not only able to observe the patient but also at almost each instant I had the possibility of comparing his psychic life and mine. It was like two melodies being played simultaneously; although these two melodies are as unharmonious as possible, nevertheless, a certain balance becomes established between the notes of the one and the other and permits us to penetrate a bit more deeply into our patient's psyche. The findings that were thus noted are on one hand psychological, on the other, phenomenological.

I. PSYCHOLOGICAL FINDINGS—ALTERNATING OF ATTITUDES AND EXTENSION OF THE DELIRIUM

We have already outlined the clinical picture. The patient, however, did not invariably present the same tableau. We are not referring here to the fact that occasionally he behaved as a normal individual, taking part in the general conversation and in no way betraying his pathology. Our attention was much more drawn by the fact that in the area of his symptoms variations and changes occurred according to the circumstances. From the first, two different attitudes could be distinguished: now the depressive element was dominant, now it was the delusional and delirious patient that we saw before us. The alternating of these two main attitudes did not come about in an entirely disorganized fashion; on the contrary, it seemed to be determined at least partially by specific factors and to be subservient to precise motives. Here it is useful to confront the two melodies that I mentioned above. When, after a more or less violent scene, one felt the need to relax, and I, personally, wanted to tell my partner, "Okay, let's make peace," he would almost invariably react with an episode of simple depression. He would pity himself, list his misfortunes, and call on our compassion; the interpretations, on the other hand, scarcely entered the picture. It was as if, in so doing, he dug out of his arsenal of pathological attitudes the one which could be used to establish a certain contact with his fellow man. As he repeated his melancholic complaints and cries of suffering, they no longer moved us; nevertheless, they remained his "contact attitude" in our symbiosis. These were, in his pathological psyche, the last-ditch defenses of his syntonism. With reference to the contact with the environment, the attitude of the delusional, interpreting patient was obviously completely different. Then, often, he accused me personally. He could not stand my perfidy; on one hand, I was as friendly as could be with his family, but on the other, I was an active conspirator in the plot being woven against him. One day that my children came to visit me, I was supposed to have purposely had them bring a coin purse with some change in it; these coins, now, would also be put into his belly; it was shameful to make one's own children take part in such inhuman goings-on. Finally, he called me a murderer and gratified me with the name of *Deibler*. At that point, everything fell apart; nothing remained except two people who could no longer understand each other and, as a result, were hostile toward one another. I became angry. He translated his anger in his personal manner, adopting an antisocial attitude. He accused me of the most evil deeds, then, as if purposely, went to the garden and picked up every string and match stick that he could find.

The alternating of symptoms and their various forms establishes thusly a sort of current which runs between normal life and the pathological psyche. It is like the ebb and flow of the sea; now it is calm and the prevalent attitude is one of contact—one cannot keep from feeling an upsurge of hope; now it is a high sea, everything tearing loose, and once again all is submerged.

Besides this alternating of attitudes, a certain intellectual activity was evident concerning his delusions, and this activity brought a hint of life into the shadows of his ill personality. It had a special character, aiming at going over absolutely every object that might be put in his belly. I carelessly took a subway ticket from my pocket. "Hey," he said, "I hadn't yet thought about tickets." Then he would talk about train tickets, streetcar tickets, tickets for buses, the subway, etc. This question would preoccupy him for several days and, afterwards, would be brought up again from time to time in his conversation as a brief reminder. This, "My, I hadn't yet thought of that," was repeated at each item that he thought he had forgotten until then. Moreover, with the same aim he named all the things that he saw around him or listed all the forms of the same general class of things. When germs happened to be mentioned, he listed all the microbes that he knew—those causing rabies, typhus, cholera, tuberculosis, and so forth. All of this would be stuffed down him. On another occasion it was acids that he ticked off—hydrochloric, sulfuric, oxalic, acetic, nitric, etc.—all with the same tone of voice. In this way, he pursued an intangible goal—to go through all the possible and imaginable objects in the universe. As he said, "That leads toward infinity." We will have occasion to bring this up again. For that matter, this activity was not limited to the above enumerations, and a certain retrospective work went on at the same time. Perhaps he might think of a hair-box in some barber shop that he once patronized; hair clippings were thrown into it, and now he was terrified to think of the mass of hair that must have been put aside for him. Another time, he might remember some dinner to which he had invited many friends; he would calculate how many eggs must have been used that day. At all costs, he wanted to know how long the "residue politics" had been in force.

There were still other problems that preoccupied him and that lent a more vivid note to the exasperating monotony of his stream of thought. Some of these problems were tinged with reality. For example, his "residue politics" would obviously necessitate enormous expenditures. All the bits of string and broken glass that had first to be put in his way and later collected again, the newspapers that had to be bought, and the books that had to be published—what a sum that must amount to! He supposed that donations were being requested all over France, as well as secret governmental funds being appropriated. He wondered, too, how they would manage to stuff all the canes and umbrellas into his stomach; "there my reasoning fails me," he would say. Then he found the solution: he would be made to absorb only a bit of each thing and the rest would be arranged around him when he was exposed to public derision in some side show.

II. PHENOMENOLOGICAL FINDINGS

So it was that our patient's daily life was spent. *But where, exactly, is the discordance between his psyche and our own?* This question leads us to a study of the phenomenological findings.

From the first glance, it is obvious that his mental processes were quite different from our own; because of the delusions, this difference may even seem so great as to make us doubt whether there can be any correlation. However, we cannot be satisfied with such an attitude of psychiatric agnosticism. Modern psychiatry, aided by the psychology of complexes, has already demonstrated that many morbid symptoms can be traced back to normal drives and thus made intelligible. However, as we have already pointed out, most of these studies have been concerned with content. Here, our aim is quite different. We are trying to gain a fuller understanding of the nature of the pathological phenomenon itself by asking, for example, what is a delusion? Is it really nothing but a disorder of perception and of judgment? This brings us back to our present problem—namely, where is the discordance between the patient's psyche and our own?

From the first day of my life with the patient, my attention was drawn to the following point. When I arrived, he stated that his execution would certainly take place that night; in his terror, unable to sleep, he also kept me awake all that night. I comforted myself with the thought that, come the morning, he would see that all his fears had been in vain. However, the same scene was repeated the next day and the next, until after three or four days I had given up hope, whereas his attitude had not budged one iota. What had happened? It was simply that I, as a normal human being, had rapidly drawn from the observed facts my conclusions about the future. He, on the other hand, had let the same facts go by him, totally unable to draw any profit from them for relating himself to the same future. I now knew that he would continue to go on, day after day, swearing that he was to be tortured to death that night, and so he did, giving no thought to the present or the past. Our thinking is essentially empirical; we are interested in facts only insofar as we can use them as a basis for planning the future. This carry-over from past and present into the future was completely lacking in him; he did not show the slightest tendency to generalize or to arrive at any empirical rules. When I would tell him, "Look here, you can believe me when I assure you that nothing is threatening you—so far, my predictions have always been fulfilled," he would reply, "I admit that so far you've always been right, but that doesn't mean that you'll be right tomorrow." This reasoning, against which one feels so futile, indicated a profound disorder in his general attitude toward the future; that time which we normally integrate into a progressive whole was here split into isolated fragments.

One objection may well be raised at this point: isn't the disorder pertaining to the future a natural consequence of the delusional belief that execution is imminent? Here lies the crux of the problem. Could we not, on the contrary, suppose that the more basic disorder is the distorted attitude toward the future, whereas the delusion is only one of its manifestations? Let us consider it more closely.

What exactly was our patient's experience of time, and how did it differ from ours? His conception might be more precisely described in the following way: monotonously and uniformly, he experienced the days following one another; he knew that time was passing and, whimpering, complained that "one more day was gone." As day after day went by, a certain rhythm became evident to him: on Mondays, the silver was polished; on Tuesday, the barber came to cut his hair; on Wednesday, the gardener mowed the lawn, etc. All of which only added to the waste which was his due—the only link which still connected him to the world. There was no action or desire which, emanating from the present, reached out to the future, spanning the dull, similar days. As a result, each day kept an unusual independence, failing to be immersed in the perception of any life continuity; each day life began anew, like a solitary island in a gray sea of passing time. What had been done, lived, and spoken no longer played the same role as in our life because there seemed to be no wish to go further; every day was an exasperating monotony of the same words, the same complaints, until one felt that this being had lost all sense of necessary continuity. Such was the march of time for him.

However, our picture is still incomplete; an essential element is missing in it—the fact that *the future was blocked* by the certainty of a terrifying and destructive event. This certainty dominated the patient's entire outlook, and absolutely all of his energy was attached to this inevitable event. Although he might pity his wife and children for the atrocious fate that awaited them, he could do no more; he could no longer follow the events of daily life, he was no more up to date and was out of tune with the fortuitous events of daily living. If he had occasion to ask about some member of the family who was ill, his attention was short-lived and he seemed unable to go beyond the most banal questions. "It's always the same old thing," said his wife, and he, too, was aware of this. "It sounds phony. Nothing I say to my wife rings true." In other words, he presented the flattening of affect which we find so often in these patients.

Such was our patient's experience of time. How does it resemble ours and how does it differ? All of us may have similar feelings in moments of discouragement or dejection or when we believe that we are dying. Then the idea of death, this prototype of empirical certainty, takes over and, blocking off the future, dominates our outlook on life. Our synthetic view of time disintegrates and we live in a succession of similar days which follow one another with a boundless monotony and sadness. With most of us, however, these are only transient episodes. Life forces, our personal impetus, lift us and carry us over such a parade of miserable days toward a future which reopens its doors widely to us; we think and act and desire beyond that death which, even so, we could not escape. The very existence of such phenomena as the desire to "do something for future generations" clearly indicates our attitude in this regard. In our patient, it was this propulsion toward the future which seemed to be totally lacking, leading, as a result, to his general attitude. Nor would anything be changed for him if, quieted after a certain time, he would accept the fact that his punishment would not be for that very night but for a later date, such as Bastille Day or Armistice Day. The future would still be blocked as before; his life impetus could not spring from the present toward such a distorted future.

One might object here that, basically, this is the outlook of a person who has been condemned to death and point out that his patient reacted in this way to thc delusion that he and his family were to be executed. I doubt this, although I have never seen anyone under a death sentence. Of course, I accept that this picture corresponds to that *idea* which we have of the feelings of someone in a death cell; but don't we draw this idea from ourselves? Don't we feel this way because all of us occasionally realize that we are sentenced to die, especially in those moments when our personal impetuses weaken and the future shuts its door in our face? Isn't it possible to admit that the patient's outlook is determined by a similar weakening of this same impetus, the complex feeling of time and of living disintegrating, with a subsequent regression to that lower rung which we all latently possess? Looked at in this light, a delusion is not something which is simply an outgrowth of phantasy but, rather, is a branch grafted onto a phenomenon which, as part of all of our lives, comes into play when our life synthesis begins to weaken. The particular form of the delusion, in this case the belief in execution, is only an effort made by the rational part of the mind (itself, remaining intact) to establish some logical connection between the various sections of a crumbling edifice.

Let us see whether or not we can look at the other delusions of this patient in the same light, beginning with his delusions of persecution.

The personal impetus is a determining factor in more than just our attitude with regard to the future; it also rules over our relationship with our environment and thus participates in that picture which we have of that environment. In this personal impetus, there is an element of expansion; we go beyond the limits of our own ego and leave a personal imprint on the world about us, creating works which sever themselves from us to live their own lives. This accompanies a specific, positive feeling which we call contentment—that pleasure which accompanies every finished action or firm decision. As a feeling, it is unique and has no exact negative counterpart where actions are concerned. In life, if we place contentment at the positive pole, that phenomenon which most closely approaches the negative pole is sensory pain. This latter, as we know, is one of the most essential factors in determining the structure of our relationship with the world about us; intrinsically bound up in pain is the feeling of some external force acting upon us to which we are compelled to submit. Seen in this light, pain evidently opposes the expansive tendency of our personal impetus; we can no longer turn ourselves outward, nor do we try to leave our personal stamp on the external world. Instead, we let the world, in all its impetuousness, come to us, making us suffer. Thus, pain is also an attitude toward the environment. Usually brief, even momentary, it becomes lasting when it no longer meets and is counteracted by its antagonist, the individual's life impetus.

When this latter fades, all of that world we live in seems to throw itself upon us, a hostile force which can only bring suffering. This is the reflection of a particular attitude toward the environment that, usually submerged by other attitudes, paints the entire universe in different colors when it emerges to rule the person. My patient would say, "Everything will be cut off of me except just what is necessary in order for me to suffer." He was aware only of pain and constructed every relationship with the external world exclusively on the model of this phenomenon of sensory pain.

It was against this hostile background that shadows came and went —silhouettes of other persons, of things, and of events. They were really only bas-reliefs growing out of the background. "Everything, everything turns against me," the patient whimpered. "Opposites all mean the same thing: the silence here makes me think of the deep and violent hatred of the people; the noise which those workers make outside reminds me of the nail that will be driven in my head; the most natural things are the most dangerous. How clever and infamous their scheme is. All one has to do is continue doing what one has always done—washing, combing one's hair, eating, going to the toilet—and all this will be turned against me." Everything spoke "the same clear and precise language"; black and white meant the same thing; everything was directed against him to make him suffer.

Here, again, he could not advance from a simple fact to a generalization. His attitude determined a precise picture of the universe which, then, was reflected on all the environment. Men were no longer perceived as individuals with their personal and individual values but became pale, distorted shadows moving against a backdrop of hostility. These were not living men who were persecuting him but men who had been transformed into persecutors and were no more than that. All the complex psychic life of human beings had disappeared; they were only schematic mannequins. All idea of chance, coincidence, of unintentional or unconscious acts was wiped out for the patient. The smallest bit of thread had been purposely laid in his way; horses were in on the plot and deliberately excreted beneath his window; the cigarette smoked by a passer-by was a signal; a failure of the electricity was caused so that people would light candles and that many more "remains" would be stuffed down him.

His thinking no longer was concerned with the usual value of an object, nor did he clearly delimit each one of them. An object was only a representative of the whole and his mind went beyond its particular meaning in ever-extending arcs. The address-band of his newspaper made him think of all the bands of all the copies of that paper which are distributed every day, which led him to all the address-bands of all the newspapers of France. A member of his family had a bronchitis and expectorated; the patient began to speak of all the sputum of all the tuberculosis sanitaria in the country and then went on to all the leavings of all the hospitals. When I shaved in front of him, he spoke of the soldiers in a nearby barracks who also shaved and then included all the soldiers of the army. "The minute that I do something," he confided while washing himself, "I must remember that forty million others do the same."

Let us remember here his way of searching to enumerate all the things which, one day, would be put into his belly. Perhaps one day we will be able to explain the genesis of delusions of enormity along these lines. What is particularly interesting to us at this point is the idea that the patient's mind had lost the ability to stop and fix itself at each object's boundaries but—as he said himself—had immediately to go further, gliding rapidly from the solitary object to infinity. This same sphere of immediate interest, which in the patient was spatially limitless, was temporally blocked in the future. Ours on the other hand, is limited in space but extends endlessly into the future. The life impetus was missing in the patient and he was unable to project it onto either men or things; the individuality of external objects did not exist for him. In short, human beings and objects seemed to merge, everything speaking, to him, "the same clear and precise language."

Another observation may confirm this point of view. His mind not only fled toward infinity, it also decomposed every object that it met. The clock, as we have already mentioned, was not just a clock but an assemblage of instruments of torture—cogs, key, hands, pendulum, etc. Every object that he saw was like the clock.

One fact must be kept in mind—as soon as he performed some action his entire attitude changed, but once the act was finished he immediately fell back into his delusions. For example, when I wanted to weigh him, this interested him. He got on the scale, shifted the weights, and correctly found his weight. However, he was no sooner finished than he began, "What use is all that? This scale is only a lot of iron and wood and all that will be put into my belly."

In these circumstances, it is obvious that the essential values of an object or another being—such as the aesthetic value—could not be appreciated by him: he was unable to adopt the appropriate attitude. "You see these roses?" he asked me. "My wife would say that they are beautiful but, as far as I can see, they are just a bunch of leaves and petals, stems and thorns."

Thus, objects merged and seemed alike. Differences, always linked to the apperception of the individuality of each object, faded, and similarity was the only point of view under which they were envisaged. Thought, proceeding by analogy, discovered similarities which usually escape us as being practically unimportant; he, however, attributed great importance to them. The number of the house where we lived was the same as that of a sanitarium where he had spent a year; my pocket calendar was identical to that of one of the nurses at the sanitarium, and I paced the room just as she used to. Therefore, we must be applying the same methods here that they had used there. These similarities were discovered with amazing speed and he found them in places that it never would have occurred to us to look for them. For example, one 13th of July (the day before Bastille Day), he noticed that a pair of shorts that he put on was embroidered with the number 13 and immediately connected the two. His shirt, on the other hand, had the number 3, which also exists in 13. That year it happened that, as the National Holiday fell next to the weekend, a three-day holiday had been declared. All of this proved that he and his family were to be executed on Bastille Day. Hundreds of similar examples could be given.

I think that the patient's attitude toward other men, events, and things concords with the view that we have taken of his delusions of persecution.

It must be pointed out that the patient's attitude toward others cannot be understood exclusively as that of a relationship of victim and persecutor. Through all this, he nevertheless attempted to safeguard a certain communion of thought with others. Although I was seen as a murderer and an executioner, he did not run from me; on the contrary, my presence helped him to a certain extent because I *knew* the same things that he knew and he could, thus, speak freely with me. If I were gone for a while, he needed to tell me all the new discoveries that he had made during my absence. Any attempt that I made to object was refused by, "Go on, you know all about this just as well as I do. You know even more about it than I do."

In summary, we arrived at the following conclusions. The individual life impetus weakening, the synthesis of the human personality disintegrates; those elements which go to make up the personality acquire more independence and act as entities; the feeling of time breaks up and is reduced to a feeling of a succession of similar days; the attitude toward the environment is determined by the phenomena of sensory pain; there remains only the person face to face with a hostile universe; the objects found in the environment insert themselves between the person and the hostile universe and are interpreted in consequence; the intellect translates this as all men being persecutors and all inanimate objects, instruments of torture. Thus, delusions should not be considered only as the products of a morbid imagination or distortions of judgment; on the contrary, they represent an attempt to translate the new and unusual situation of the disintegrating personality in terms of prior psychic mechanisms.

No matter how delusional the patient was, it seems difficult to admit that he would simply fancy such absurd and nonsensical thoughts as those that he constantly expressed. Wouldn't it help our thinking to assume that at the base of these ideas we will always find a natural phenomenon which has been more or less modified and, following a disintegration of the personality, has acquired an unusual independence? The patient attempts to express this situation by borrowing thoughts from his former life and, thus, ends by expressing delusional material. We then come along and augment this chasm by accepting the content of the verbalizations, seeing them only as aberrations of his imagination or his judgment.

So far, these are only suggestions. Perhaps it will be possible to continue along the same lines and, in so doing, to gain a better understanding of the nature of those phenomena which go to make up mental illness. Meanwhile, in the same general line, I should like to add a few more points relative to the same patient.

He expressed delusions of total ruin. Should we interpret these as ideas which just came to him? Does the depressive state alone explain the genesis of such thoughts? Sadness and emotional suffering, it would seem to us, could be attached to various other objects without giving rise to such bizarre and unrealistic feelings. Perhaps we would be closer to the truth if we conceived of such a feeling of ruin as translating what in everyday thinking is a distortion of the possession phenomenon, the phenomenon of that which is our own.[1] This sense of property is an integral part of our personality. As we have said, there is a close correlation between it and desire; we never wish for that which we already have and, on the other hand, the fulfillment of a desire in one way or another enlarges the sphere of our own possessions. Desire, in going beyond possession, always limits the boundaries of the latter. Wherever our life impetus and, conjointly, our desire dies, not only is the future shut off but also the boundaries of our possession-sphere disintegrate. The phenomenon of possession is disturbed and our ability to attribute something to ourselves is affected and altered. The person translates this both to himself and to others when he says that he is broke.[2] Ideas of negation, patients' complaints that they no longer have a stomach, intestines, or a brain, are perhaps only their way of expressing the same situation.

We may develop an analogous conception with reference to feelings of guilt. Here, too, the analysis of those phenomena which are the essentials of a human personality leads us to findings which seems to shed light on the genesis of such feelings. We must repeat our previous remarks concerning the asymmetry between good and evil. Once an error is made or a bad action committed, it remains engraved in the conscience, leaving palpable traces; from this point of view, it is static and a backward glance is enough to uncover it. On the other hand, the only remains of positive accomplishments or good acts is in the fact that we can do better in the future; such acts are really no more than bridges that we cross in our attempts to improve. Our entire individual evolution consists in trying to surpass that which has already been done. When our mental life dims, the future closes in front of us, while at the same time the feeling of positive actions of the past disappears. An intact memory remains, but everything is dominated by the static feeling of evil. Our patient would say that he was the world's greatest criminal, and he would see "concretized remorse" everywhere.

Perhaps, by more close study of those phenomena which make up the life of a human being, we may eventually gain a better understanding of the mysterious manifestations of mental illness. It is toward this goal that we have set our sights.

Translated by Barbara Bliss

NOTES

1 E. Minkowski, *Le Temps vécu,* p. 117.

2 It is useful to remember at this point that the word "poor" also means "unhappy," even when poverty is not the cause of the unhappiness. When we pity someone, we say, "poor man."

25

Challenge and Collapse: *The Nemesis of Creativity*

Marshall McLuhan

It was Bertrand Russell who declared that the great discovery of the twentieth century was the technique of the suspended judgment. A. N. Whitehead, on the other hand, explained how the great discovery of the nineteenth century was the discovery of the technique of discovery. Namely, the technique of starting with the thing to be discovered and working back, step by step, as on an assembly line, to the point at which it is necessary to start in order to reach the desired object. In the arts this meant starting with the *effect* and then inventing a poem, painting, or building that would have just that effect and no other.

But the "technique of the suspended judgment" goes further. It anticipates the effect of, say, an unhappy childhood on an adult, and offsets the effect before it happens. In psychiatry, it is the technique of total permissiveness extended as an anesthetic for the mind, while various adhesions and moral effects of false judgments are systematically eliminated.

This is a very different thing from the numbing or narcotic effect of new technology that lulls attention while the new form slams the gates of judgment and perception. For massive social surgery is needed to insert new technology into the group mind, and this is achieved by the built-in numbing apparatus discussed earlier. Now the "technique of the suspended judgment" presents the possibility of rejecting the narcotic and of postponing indefinitely the operation of inserting the new technology in the social psyche. A new stasis is in prospect.

Werner Heisenberg, in *The Physicist's Conception of Nature,* is an example of the new quantum physicist whose over-all awareness of forms suggests to him that we would do well to stand aside from most of them. He points out that technical change alters not only habits of life, but patterns of thought and valuation, citing with approval the outlook of the Chinese sage:

> As Tsu-Kung was traveling through the regions north of the river Han, he saw an old man working in his vegetable garden. He had dug an irrigation ditch. The man would descend into a well, fetch up a vessel of water in his arms and pour it out into the ditch. While his efforts were tremendous the results appeared to be very meager.
>
> Tsu-Kung said, "There is a way whereby you can irrigate a hundred ditches in one day, and whereby you can do much with little effort. Would you not like to hear of it?"
>
> Then the gardener stood up, looked at him and said, "And what would that be?"
>
> Tsu-Kung replied, "You take a wooden lever, weighted at the back and light in front. In this way you can bring up water so quickly that it just gushes out. This is called a draw-well."
>
> Then anger rose up in the old man's face, and he said, "I have heard my teacher say that whoever uses machines does all his work like a machine. He who does his work like a machine grows a heart like a machine, and he who carries the heart of a machine in his breast loses his simplicity. He who has lost his simplicity becomes unsure in the strivings of his soul. Uncertainty in the strivings of the soul is something which does not agree with honest sense. It is not that I do not know of such things; I am ashamed to use them."

Perhaps thc most interesting point about this anecdote is that it appeals to a modern physicist. It would not have appealed to Newton or to Adam Smith, for they were great experts and advocates of the fragmentary and the specialist approaches. It is by means quite in accord with the outlook of the Chinese sage that Hans Selye works at his "stress" idea of illness. In the 1920s he had been baffled at why physicians always seemed to concentrate on the recognition of individual diseases and specific remedies for such isolated causes, while never paying any attention to the "syndrome of just being sick." Those who are concerned with the program "content" of media and not with the medium proper, appear to be in the position of physicians who ignore the "syndrome of just being sick." Hans Selye, in tackling a total, inclusive approach to the field of sickness, began what Adolphe Jonas has continued in *Irritation and Counter-Irritation;* namely, a quest for the response to injury as such, or to novel impact of any kind. Today we have anesthetics that enable us to perform the most frightful physical operations on one another.

The new media and technologies by which we amplify and extend ourselves constitute huge collective surgery carried out on the social body with complete disregard for antiseptics. If the operations are needed, the inevitability of infecting the whole system during the operation has to be considered. For in operating on society with a new technology, it is not the incised area that is most affected. The area of impact and incision is numb. It is the entire system that is changed. The effect of radio is visual, the effect of the photo is auditory. Each new impact shifts the ratios among all the senses. What we seek today is either a means of controlling these shifts in the sense-ratios of the psychic and social outlook, or a means of avoiding them altogether. To have a disease without its symptoms is to be immune. No society has ever known enough about its actions to have developed immunity to its new extensions or technologies. Today we have begun to sense that art may be able to provide such immunity.

In the history of human culture there is no example of a conscious adjustment of the various factors of personal and social life to new extensions except in the puny and peripheral efforts of artists. The artist picks up the message of cultural and technological challenge decades before its transforming impact occurs. He, then, builds models or Noah's arks for facing the change that is at hand. "The war of 1870 need never have been fought had people read my *Sentimental Education,*" said Gustave Flaubert.

It is this aspect of *new* art that Kenneth Galbraith recommends to the careful study of businessmen who want to stay in business. For in the electric age there is no longer any sense in talking about the artist's being ahead of his time. Our technology is, also, ahead of its time, if we reckon by the ability to recognize it for what it is. To prevent undue wreckage in society, the artist tends now to move from the ivory tower to the control tower of society. Just as higher education is no longer a frill or luxury but a stark need of production and operational design in the electric age, so the artist is indispensable in the shaping and analysis and understanding of the life of forms, and structures created by electric technology.

The percussed victims of the new technology have invariably muttered clichés about the impracticality of artists and their fanciful preferences. But in the past century it has come to be generally acknowledged that, in the words of Wyndham Lewis, "The artist is always engaged in writing a detailed history of the future because he is the only person aware of the nature of the present." Knowledge of this simple fact is now needed for human survival. The ability of the artist to sidestep the bully blow of new technology of any age, and to parry such violence with full awareness, is age-old. Equally age-old is the inability of the percussed victims, who cannot sidestep the new violence, to recognize their need of the artist. To reward and to make celebrities of artists can, also, be a way of ignoring their prophetic work, and preventing its timely use for survival. The artist is the man in any field, scientific or humanistic, who grasps the implications of his actions and of new knowledge in his own time. He is the man of integral awareness.

The artist can correct the sense ratios before the blow of new technology has numbed conscious procedures. He can correct them before numbness and subliminal groping and reaction begin. If this is true, how is it possible to present the matter to those who are in a position to do something about it? If there were even a remote likelihood of this analysis being true, it would warrant a global armistice and period of stock-taking. If it is true that the artist possesses the means of anticipating and avoiding the consequences of technological trauma, then what are we to think of the world and bureaucracy of "art appreciation"? Would it not seem suddenly to be a conspiracy to make the artist a frill, a fribble, or a Milltown? If men were able to be convinced that art is precise advance knowledge of how to cope with the psychic and social consequences of the next technology, would they all become artists? Or would they begin a careful translation of new art forms into social navigation charts? I am curious to know what would happen if art were suddenly seen for what it is, namely, exact information of how to rearrange one's psyche in order to anticipate the next blow from our own extended faculties. Would we, then, cease to look at works of art as an explorer might regard the gold and gems used as the ornaments of simple nonliterates?

At any rate, in experimental art, men are given the exact specifications of coming violence to their own psyches from their own counter-irritants or technology. For those parts of ourselves that we thrust out in the form of new invention are attempts to counter or neutralize collective pressures and irritations. But the counter-irritant usually proves a greater plague than the initial irritant, like a drug habit. And it is here that the artist can show us how to "ride with the punch," instead of "taking it on the chin." It can only be repeated that human history is a record of "taking it on the chin."

Emile Durkheim long ago expressed the idea that the specialized task always escaped the action of the social conscience. In this regard, it would appear that the artist is the social conscience and is treated accordingly! "We have no art," say the Balinese; "we do everything as well as possible."

The modern metropolis is now sprawling helplessly after the impact of the motorcar. As a response to the challenge of railway speeds the suburb and the garden city arrived too late, or just in time to become a motorcar disaster. For an arrangement of functions adjusted to one set of intensities becomes unbearable at another intensity. And a technological extension of our bodies designed to alleviate physical stress can bring on psychic stress that may be much worse. Western specialist technology transferred to the Arab world in late Roman times released a furious discharge of tribal energy.

The somewhat devious means of diagnosis that have to be used to pin down the actual form and impact of a new medium are not unlike those indicated in detective fiction by Peter Cheyney. In *You Can't Keep the Change* (Collins, London, 1956) he wrote:

> A case to Callaghan was merely a collection of people, some of whom,—all of whom—were giving incorrect information, or telling lies, because circumstances either forced them or led them into the process.
>
> But the fact that they *had* to tell lies; *had* to give false impressions, necessitated a reorientation of their own viewpoints and their own lives. Sooner or later they became exhausted or careless. Then, and not until then, was an investigator able to put his finger on the one fact that would lead him to a possible logical solution.

It is interesting to note that success in keeping up a respectable front of customary kind can only be done by a frantic scramble back of the façade. After the crime, after the blow has fallen, the façade of custom can only be held up by swift rearrangement of the props. So it is in our social lives when a new technology strikes, or in our private life when some intense and, therefore, indigestible experience occurs, and the censor acts at once to numb us from the blow and to ready the faculties to assimilate the intruder. Peter Cheyney's observations of a mode of detective fiction is another instance of a popular form of entertainment functioning as mimic model of the real thing.

Perhaps the most obvious "closure" or psychic consequence of any new technology is just the demand for it. Nobody wants a motorcar till there are motorcars, and nobody is interested in TV until there are TV programs. This power of technology to create its own world of demand is not independent of technology being first an extension of our own bodies and senses. When we are deprived of our sense of sight, the other senses take up the role of sight in some degree. But the need to use the senses that are available is as insistent as breathing—a fact that makes sense of the urge to keep radio and TV going more or less continuously. The urge to continuous use is quite independent of the "content" of public programs or of the private sense life, being testimony to the fact that technology is part of our bodies. Electric technology is directly related to our central nervous systems, so it is ridiculous to talk of "what the public wants" played over its own nerves. This question would be like asking people what sort of sights and sounds they would prefer around them in an urban metropolis! Once we have surrendered our senses and nervous systems to the private manipulation of those who would try to benefit from taking a lease on our eyes and ears and nerves, we don't really have any rights left. Leasing our eyes and ears and nerves to commercial interests is like handing over the common speech to a private corporation, or like giving the earth's atmosphere to a company as a monopoly. Something like this has already happened with outer space, for the same reasons that we have leased our central nervous systems to various corporations. As long as we adopt the Narcissus attitude of regarding the extensions of our own bodies as really *out there* and really independent of us, we will meet all technological challenges with the same sort of banana-skin pirouette and collapse.

Archimedes once said, "Give me a place to stand and I will move the world." Today he would have pointed to our electric media and said, "I will stand on your eyes, your ears, your nerves, and your brain, and the world will move in any tempo or pattern I choose." We have leased these "places to stand" to private corporations.

Arnold Toynbee has devoted much of his *A Study of History* to analyzing the kinds of challenge faced by a variety of cultures during many centuries. Highly relevant to Western man is Toynbee's explanation of how the lame and the crippled respond to their handicaps in a society of active warriors. They become specialists like Vulcan, the smith and armorer. And how do whole communities act when conquered and enslaved? The same strategy serves them as it does the lame individual in a society of warriors. They specialize and become indispensable to their masters. It is probably the long human history of enslavement, and the collapse into specialism as a counter-irritant, that have put the stigma of servitude and pusillanimity on the figure of the specialist, even in modern times. The capitulation of Western man to his technology, with its crescendo of specialized demands, has always appeared to many observers of our world as a kind of enslavement. But the resulting fragmentation has been voluntary and enthusiastic, unlike the conscious strategy of specialism on the part of the captives of military conquest.

It is plain that fragmentation or specialism as a technique of achieving security under tyranny and oppression of any kind has an attendant danger. Perfect adaptation to any environment is achieved by a total channeling of energies and vital force that amounts to a kind of static terminus for a creature. Even slight changes in the environment of the very well adjusted find them without any resource to meet new challenge. Such is the plight of the representatives of "conventional wisdom" in any society. Their entire stake of security and status is in a single form of acquired knowledge, so that innovation is for them not novelty but annihilation.

A related form of challenge that has always faced cultures is the simple fact of a frontier or a wall, on the other side of which exists another kind of society. Mere existence side by side of any two forms of organization generates a great deal of tension. Such, indeed, has been the principle of symbolist artistic structures in the past century. Toynbee observes that the challenge of a civilization set side by side with a tribal society has over and over demonstrated that the simpler society finds its integral economy and institutions "disintegrated by a rain of psychic energy generated by the civilization" of the more complex culture. When two societies exist side by side, the psychic challenge of the more complex one acts as an explosive release of energy in the simpler one. For prolific evidence of this kind of problem it is not necessary to look beyond the life of the teenager lived daily in the midst of a complex urban center. As the barbarian was driven to furious restlessness by the civilized contact, collapsing into mass migration, so the teenager, compelled to share the life of a city that cannot accept him as an adult, collapses into "rebellion without a cause." Earlier the adolescent had been provided with a rain check. He was prepared to wait it out. But since TV, the drive to participation has ended adolescence, and every American home has its Berlin wall.

Toynbee is very generous in providing examples of widely varied challenge and collapse, and is especially apt in pointing to the frequent and futile resort to futurism and archaism as strategies of encountering radical change. But to point back to the day of the horse or to look forward to the coming of antigravitational vehicles is not an adequate response to the challenge of the motorcar. Yet these two uniform ways of backward and forward looking are habitual ways of avoiding the discontinuities of present experience with their demand for sensitive inspection and appraisal. Only the dedicated artist seems to have the power for encountering the present actuality.

Toynbee urges again and again the cultural strategy of the imitation of the example of great men. This, of course, is to locate cultural safety in the power of the *will* rather than in the power of adequate *perception* of situations. Anybody could quip that this is the British trust in character as opposed to intellect. In view of the endless power of men to hypnotize themselves into unawareness in the presence of challenge, it may be argued that willpower is as useful as intelligence for survival. Today we need also the will to be exceedingly informed and aware.

Arnold Toynbee gives an example of Renaissance technology being effectively encountered and creatively controlled when he shows how the revival of the decentralized medieval parliament saved English society from the monopoly of centralism that seized the continent. Lewis Mumford in *The City in History* tells the strange tale of how the New England town was able to carry out the pattern of the medieval ideal city because it was able to dispense with walls and to mix town and country. When the technology of a time is powerfully thrusting in one direction, wisdom may well call for a countervailing thrust. The implosion of electric energy in our century cannot be met by explosion or expansion, but it can be met by decentralism and the flexibility of multiple small centers. For example, the rush of students into our universities is not explosion but implosion. And the needful strategy to encounter this force is not to enlarge the university, but to create numerous groups of autonomous colleges in place of our centralized university plant that grew up on the lines of European government and nineteenth-century industry.

In the same way the excessive tactile effects of the TV image cannot be met by mere program changes. Imaginative strategy based on adequate diagnosis would prescribe a corresponding depth or structural approach to the existing literary and visual world. If we persist in a conventional approach to these developments our traditional culture will be swept aside as scholasticism was in the sixteenth century. Had the Schoolmen with their complex oral culture understood the Gutenberg technology, they could have created a new synthesis of written and oral education, instead of bowing out of the picture and allowing the merely visual page to take over the educational enterprise. The oral Schoolmen did not meet the new visual challenge of print, and the resulting expansion or explosion of Gutenberg technology was in many respects an impoverishment of the culture, as historians like Mumford are now beginning to explain. Arnold Toynbee, in *A Study of History,* in considering "the nature of growths of civilizations," not only abandons the concept of enlargement as a criterion of real growth of society, but states: "More often geographical expansion is a concomitant of real decline and coincides with a 'time of troubles' or a universal state—both of them stages of decline and disintegration."

Toynbee expounds the principle that times of trouble or rapid change produce militarism, and it is militarism that produces empire and expansion. The old Greek myth which taught that the alphabet produced militarism ("King Cadmus sowed the dragon's teeth, and they sprang up armed men") really goes much deeper than Toynbee's story. In fact, "militarism" is just vague description, not analysis of causality at all. Militarism is a kind of visual organization of social energies that is both specialist and explosive, so that it is merely repetitive to say, as Toynbee does, that it both creates large empires and causes social breakdown. But militarism is a form of industrialism or the concentration of large amounts of homogenized energies into a few kinds of production. The Roman soldier was a man with a spade. He was an expert workman and builder who processed and packaged the resources of many societies and sent them home. Before machinery, the only massive work forces available for processing material were soldiers or slaves. As the Greek myth of Cadmus points out, the phonetic alphabet was the greatest processer of men for homogenized military life that was known to antiquity. The age of Greek society that Herodotus acknowledges to have been "overwhelmed by more troubles than in the twenty preceding generations" was the time that to our literary retrospect appears as one of the greatest of human centuries. It was Macaulay who remarked that it was not pleasant to live in times about which it was exciting to read. The succeeding age of Alexander saw Hellenism expand into Asia and prepare the course of the later Roman expansion. These, however, were the very centuries in which Greek civilization obviously fell apart.

Toynbee points to the strange falsification of history by archeology, insofar as the survival of many material objects of the past does not indicate the quality of ordinary life and experience at any particular time. Continuous technical improvement in the means of warfare occurs over the entire period of Hellenic and Roman decline. Toynbee checks out his hypothesis by testing it with the developments in Greek agriculture.

When the enterprise of Solon weaned the Greeks from mixed farming to a program of specialized products for export, there were happy consequences and a glorious manifestation of energy in Greek life. When the next phase of the same specialist stress involved much reliance on slave labor, there was spectacular increase of production. But the armies of technologically specialized slaves working the land blighted the social existence of the independent yeomen and small farmers, and led to the strange world of the Roman towns and cities crowded with rootless parasites.

To a much greater degree than Roman slavery, the specialism of mechanized industry and market organization has faced Western man with the challenge of manufacture by mono-facture, or the tackling of all things and operations one-bit-at-a-time. This is the challenge that has permeated all aspects of our lives and enabled us to expand so triumphantly in all directions and in all spheres.

PART IV

• | PATTERNS AND CONSEQUENCES OF SELF-REFLECTIVE ART

26

Toward an Unanxious Profession*

Harold Rosenberg

Changes in art have been taking place at such lightning speed that compared with even three years ago the current scene is virtually unrecognizable. Then, neo-Dadaist and Pop Art were crowding Abstract Expressionism and it seemed pertinent to discuss which was really newer and might have greater staying power. Today, both Pop and Action Painting, as well as two or three subsequent "vanguards," have passed into the swelling reservoir of modernist modes and *no* discussion seems pertinent. Works intended to shock or startle scarcely stir up a query at a provincial panel discussion. Attitudes, styles, moods, casts of character replace one another without a struggle. All the art movements of this century, and some earlier ones, have become equally up to date. It is as if art history had decided to turn over on its side and go to sleep. One is reminded of the situation in American writing fifteen years ago when the leading issue was, "Where are the issues?"

Is it, then, permissible still to speak of the work of art as an "anxious object"? Has not the ghost that haunted painting and sculpture in the forties and fifties been laid—perhaps forever? A lonely and doubt-

* From *The Anxious Object: Art Today and its Audience.*—The editors.

ing spirit can hardly be said to personify the crackling art world of the second half of the sixties. Indisputably, Josef Albers, the master of painting conceived as calculated sheets of color, had the facts on his side when he sent me the message last year that "*Angst* is dead."

The entire social basis of art is being transformed—to all appearances for the better. Instead of being, as it used to be, an activity of rebellion, despair or self-indulgence on the fringe of society, art is being normalized as a professional activity within society. For the first time, the art formerly called vanguard has been accepted *en masse* and its ideals of innovation, experiment, dissent have been institutionalized and made official. Its functions are being clarified in relation to accepted practice in decoration, entertainment and education, and the rewards to be won in art by talent and diligence are becoming increasingly predictable.

Along with changes in the social situation of art has come a metamorphosis in the temperament of the artist and in what he seeks to achieve through his work: in a word, a change in actual values, though often under cover of the old slogans. No longer does the American artist tend to be a first- or second-generation outsider lost in a metropolis or suburb and accumulating his art experience through random insights and chance meetings. Today, he is an all-American youth from farm, village or town who has been through a university art department and surveyed the treasures of art through the ages and its majestic status as the darling of power and wealth. Instead of resigning himself to a life of bohemian disorder and frustration, he may now look forward to a career in which possibilities are unlimited. In short, painting is no longer a haven for self-defeating contemplatives but a glamorous arena in which performers of talent may rival the celebrity of senators or TV stars.

Given these transformations, inner and outer, anxiety as a psychological state is today no more typical of artists than of doctors, truck drivers or physicists (though it is typical of all of them). Noting the comfortable prospects for painters and sculptors, some critics have concluded that the disturbance of art is a phenomenon of the past; it is a mood, they tell us, that belongs to the decade following the war. Anxious painting in this view is the kin of Existentialism and the Theatre of the Absurd. It is an aspect of the life style of dusty lofts, blue jeans, the Cedar Tavern (at its old address), no sales, tumescent paint letting go in drips. Today, this stereotype continues, anxiety is no longer a reality in art, which is at last properly concerned with its own development. To mention anxiety is to arouse suspicion of nostalgia or of a vested interest in the past, if not of a reactionary reversion to the middle-class notion of genius suffering in a garret.

In this capsule wisdom the problem of contemporary civilization is mistaken for an episode in the history of fashion. Only the grossest materialism, such as pervades American cultural journalism, could equate poverty with anxiety, high income with serenity. Psychologically, Action painters twenty years ago were no more anxious than Pop artists or kinetic geometers are today. All indications are that they were probably much *less* anxious. They were resigned to being who they were and where they were. Spending most of their time with other artists, they led a far more relaxed and vivacious social life than the lions rampant of today's art world. Most important, in Action Painting the act of painting is a catharsis—theoretically at least, it is able to reach the deepest knots of the artist's personality and to loosen them. By contrast, in the recent cool modes of painting and constructing, process prevails, and the unexcited artist performs the necessary steps without upsetting his normal condition of uneasiness.

The story that there was a period in American art—say, between 1942 and 1952—when anxious painters painted anxious pictures is a fable, useful mainly for the education of instant art historians. *Angst* may be dead in the minds of the majority of artists today, but the anxiety of art has nothing to do with prevailing quantities of worry about careers, rent bills, publicity or girl (boy) friends.

In connection with the pioneers of postwar New York art, I found it appropriate some fifteen years ago to denote the new spirit by quoting from one of Apollinaire's poems a line about making "empty gestures in the solitudes." In the lofts of downtown Manhattan the pathos consisted not only of the social isolation of art but of the painful awareness of the artist that art could not reach beyond the gesture on the canvas without entering into a complex of relationships alien to his deepest feelings. The artist of the 1930's had dedicated his work to movements designed to change those relationships; he had ended by finding that the ideologies of both revolution and reform led to consequences that were humanly questionable, emotionally frustrating and a drag upon creation.

Must one remind budding art historians that the uneasiness of art in the face of its own situation was not adopted by artists as a manner, in the way that one adopts a leather jacket or a hairdo that covers the eyes? Anxiety was forced upon art as the experience that accompanies the rejection of shallow or fraudulent solutions.

I have spoken, as is common, of "the artist." I mean, of course, "some artists." Already at the opening of the 1950's it seemed necessary to append underneath the verse of Apollinaire on solitude the cool verdict of Wallace Stevens: "The American will is easily satisfied in its efforts to realize itself in knowing itself." Already all but a handful of the leaders of the new art had entered into the pantheon of the "easily satisfied" and were proclaiming a revived faith in the sufficiency of art. Already the new vanguard audience, though still in the process of formation, had begun to give birth to its own species of artist happy to be the clown of its dictionary of repeated ideas.

No sector of a culture can avoid taking on to some degree the features of the culture as a whole. In the United States professions attain stability when their practices are accepted as rituals beyond the need of justification. Having reached this stage, art today resists discussion as to its content and function, as the police resist civilian review.

The anxiety of art is a peculiar kind of insight. It arises, not as a reflex to the condition of artists, but from their reflection upon the role of art among other human activities. Where this anxiety is absent, nothing that befalls the artist as a person, not even the threat of physical extinction, will bring it into being. There is a craftsman's pleasure in doing, and delight in the work of one's hands, that some people find entirely adequate to satisfy their minds. The world may fall apart, it will interest them less than the discovery of a new brand of crayon.

Albers himself excellently illustrates the type of faith in the self-sufficiency of art that excludes from painting everything but the statement and solution of its own technical problems. For him anxiety has not just now ceased to be a factor in painting; properly speaking, it never was one, however much artists might have been misled by so irrelevant a sentiment. In a recent interview in *Art News* Albers was asked about his frame of mind during the rise of the Nazis—did he, for example, feel impelled to join in the demonstrations of his fellow artists in Germany? *"Nein,"* exclaimed Albers. "I was determined not to follow anything. For me it was glass [the material he was then working with]. I was completely one-sided. I never went when the Constructivists and Surrealists assembled. It was for me just glass." For artists like Albers the "realm of art" is permanently insulated against the unrest of this century of crises.

The anxiety of art is a philosophical quality perceived by artists to be inherent in acts of creation in our time. It manifests itself, first of all, in the questioning of art itself. It places in issue the greatness of the art of the past (How really great was it? How great is it for us?) and the capacity of the contemporary spirit to match that greatness. Anxiety is thus the form in which modern art raises itself to the level of human history. It is an objective reflection of the indefiniteness of the function of art in present-day society and the possibility of the displacement of art by newer forms of expression, emotional stimulation and communication. It relates to the awareness that art today survives in the intersections between the popular media, handicraft and the applied sciences; and that the term "art" has become useless as a means for setting apart a certain category of fabrications. Given the speed and sophistication with which the formal characteristics of new art modes are appropriated by the artisans of the commercial media and semi-media (architecture, highway design, etc.), the art object, including masterpieces of the past, exists under constant threat of deformation and loss of identity. Today, there is no agreed-upon way of identifying works as art except by including them in art history. But art history is constantly being expanded to comprise such new species as photography, TV, cinema, comic books. Moreover, the historical qualification of works as art is today threatened by the transformation of the museum and the art book into media of mass communication.

Confronting this situation, the anxiety of art embodies the freedom of art to remake itself at will. It is present in the recurrent resolve of artists of this century, and especially of the post-World War I vanguard movements—Dada, Surrealism, Action Painting—to liquidate art as a classification of objects and to redefine it in terms of the intellectual acts of artists. Thus "art" has been opened up to include "ready-mades" produced by industry, snapshots of dreams, events on and off the canvas, demonstrations of color relations and tricks of the optical nerve. What is decisive is who does what for what reason.

This can only mean that the art object persists without a sure identity, as what I have called an "anxious object." ("Am I a masterpiece," it must ask itself, "or an assemblage of junk?" Its nature is contingent upon recognition by the current communion of the knowing. Art does not exist. It *declares itself.*

The anxiety of art represents the will that art *shall* exist, despite conditions that might make its existence impossible. Through constant revision of its aims, its techniques, its scope, modern art has made itself into a discipline rooted in the free development of individuals. All the traditional elements of painting have been reconceived in such ways as to make them completely subject to the will of the artist.

In a speech delivered thirty years ago, Fernand Léger summarized the evolution of modernist esthetics as follows:

> The entire effort of artists during the past fifty years has consisted of the struggle to liberate themselves from certain old restraints. . . .

> The effort toward freedom began with the Impressionists and has been continually emphasized to this day.
>
> The Impressionists freed color—we have carried their work forward and have freed form and drawing.

By its conquest of the privilege of freedom within art itself avant-garde art has for the past one hundred years differentiated its activity from other forms of social production, including the craft of the academies. Art alone has been the realm of the free act. It is by this history that the vaguard has reconstituted the concept of art.

With regard to the destiny of the artist's freedom, the current integration of the arts into our society of specialized functions is far from reassuring. The closing of the gap between artist and public has not come about through an expansion of freedom in American occupations generally. On the contrary, it is occurring under conditions in which work and the practice of the intellectual professions are being constantly narrowed and more strictly disciplined. In this environment the present emphasis in art criticism on the end product, rather than on the problematical nature of the art undertaking, opens the way to art produced under direction, as in related professions. Today's socially accepted vanguard already responds to paintings and sculptures executed according to formulas suggested by critics, dealers or collectors without any more surprise or revulsion than is aroused by a TV drama composed to fit the story line of a program producer. Indeed, efforts are continually under way, both here and abroad, to establish "project" art as the ruling principle for the art of tomorrow.

Given what David Jones has called "the actual civilizational situation," the quieting of art's anxiety is bound to suggest the cheerfulness of a sick room. It is a renunciation of that intellectual and emotional ingredient in twentieth-century art that arises from facing the reality of its situation. The anxiety of modern art is the measure of its historical consciousness and of its appreciation of the stature of the past. It is the condition in which art in our time identifies itself with the destiny of man. No wonder Picasso saw it as central in Cézanne.

The essays that follow present contemporary painting and sculpture as a web of problems, and contemporary artists as engaged in a dramatic struggle with those problems. No substantial problem of art is soluble by art alone (technical problems are soluble). For example, Arshile Gorky could not solve the problem of identity, nor can Barnett Newman solve the problem of the absolute.

Instead of solving his problem—"his" because he has chosen it—the artist lives it through the instrumentality of his materials. By fixing his idea in matter he exposes either the crudeness of his thought or the clumsiness of his art; thus he is led to experiment and refinement. In time, he becomes so adept in materializing his hypotheses, and in manipulating his materials as if they were meanings, that the problem itself is transformed. He has translated it into a unique set of terms; besides, he, the investigator, has through his efforts remade himself into a different man.

The adeptness of the artist's mind, achieved through devouring problems of art, is the ultimate art product—its evidences are what confer value on particular paintings and sculptures. This is one reason why I find it appropriate here to devote more reflection to veteran artists than to newcomers whose ideas, whatever they be, are at the beginning of their enactment. The choice is not based on esthetic preference for an earlier style over later ones but on the relative intellectual gravity of the works available for consideration in our period. It matters not in what mode an artist begins, whether with colored squares, a streak of black, the letter "D" or the drawing of a nude. All beginnings are clichés and the formal repertory of modern art was fairly complete by 1914. It is finding the obstacle to going ahead that counts—*that* is the discovery and the starting point of metamorphosis. Uniqueness is an effect of duration in action, of prolonged hacking and gnawing. In the course of engagement a mind is created. Apart from that, every kind of excellence can be copied.

27

The Art Object and the Esthetics of Impermanence*

Harold Rosenberg

In defining a poem in terms of its psychological effect on the reader Poe introduced time into criticism. "All excitements," he argued in "The Poetic Principle," "are, through a psychal necessity, transient" and half an hour "at the very utmost" is the limit of "that degree of excitement which would entitle a poem to be so called at all." There are, of course, poems that take longer to read. But though it is physically present on the page, for Poe "a long poem does not exist."

A comparable time limit on paintings was proposed recently by Marcel Duchamp, except that instead of considering the audience's capacity for "excitement" Duchamp reflected on how long the stimulating power of the work itself can last. Discussing "the short life of a work of art," he declared that a painting possesses an esthetic "smell or emanation" which persists for twenty to thirty years, after which it dissolves and the work dies. As illustration, Duchamp mentioned his own celebrated "Nude Descending a Staircase"; despite all the fuss about it, he said, the "Nude" is dead, "completely dead."

* From *The Anxious Object: Art Today and its Audience.*—The editors.

As against the common-sense notion of the poem or painting as an object to which the beholder reacts, Poe and Duchamp pose the idea of the work as a temporary center of energy which gives rise to psychic events. To attribute independent power to things is a species of fetishism; but the fetishes of these artists are of a modern variety because their potency is measured by the clock. In the introspection of Poe and the history consciousness of Duchamp, an interval of portentous time replaces the transcendental "thing" of the older esthetics and the older magic. The work of art is like an irradiated substance; when its charge dies down it begins to *last*.

The concept of painting as involved in time is of fairly recent origin. The French Catholic philosopher, Etienne Gilson, analyzing the nature of painting in his *Painting and Reality,* refers to "the *received* [i.e., accepted] distinction between arts of time (poetry, music) and arts of space (sculpture, painting and, generally speaking, the 'arts of design')." Gilson endeavors to uphold this distinction by arguing that though the esthetic experience of a painting continues for so many minutes then ceases, the painting itself has a physical existence in space and that it is this spatial existence that determines the nature of painting as an art. The spatial concept has, however, Gilson admits, been meeting resistance among modern estheticians and artists, probably from artists most of all. Gilson's position is in direct conflict with Paul Klee's assertion in his "Creative Credo" that Lessing's famous separation in the *Laokoön,* between arts of space and arts of time is out of date in twentieth-century space-time thinking. It takes time, Klee explained, for a dot to turn into a line, for a line to form a surface, and so forth; in sum, for the picture as a whole to come into being out of its parts. It takes time also for the spectator to appreciate it—"leisure-time," said Klee, plus, he added (quoting the nineteenth-century phenomenologist, Feuerbach), a chair to keep the fatigue of the legs from distracting the mind. All this phenomenology of action and response is applicable, Gilson concedes, but only to "the genesis of the work of art and of its apprehension by a beholder." A painting is of time when it is considered as an encounter between the artist and his audience. It belongs to space when it is conceived as a thing, that is to say, as Gilson puts it, "from the point of view of the work of art itself."

The notion of the art object as worthy of being considered from its own point of view apart from the artist's act of creation and the excitement of the spectator is of capital importance in regard to twentieth-century art. One sets a painting aside as a thing independent of the human circumstances surrounding it not merely for the sake of philosophical completeness but for ideological purposes. This is made amply clear by Gilson in *Painting and Reality*. Art which is, in his words, "in keeping with the physical mode of existence that belongs to painting," that is, with the mode of spatiality, will conform to and uphold values of stability and permanence; which means that it will oppose the evanescent-energy concepts of Poe, Duchamp, Klee and other contemporaries. From the essential "thingness" of painting Gilson derives an esthetics of quiescence, contemplation, pattern, as against the "action" tradition of such paintings as Gericault's "Epsom Derby" or Jacques-Louis David's "Bonaparte Crossing the St. Bernard." Paintings like the David and the Poussin "Rape of the Sabine Women" are to be restudied in such a way as to transform their "motion in time" into a "visual pattern in space." Gilson carries his concept to the literal conclusion that the still-life is the supreme subject of painting since "in a still life nothing acts, nothing gesticulates, nothing does anything else than to be"—a formula of negatives curiously homologous with the anti-Expressionist pronouncements of Ad Reinhardt. In sum, the concept of the art object becomes the basis for imposing on paintings a mental "set" or gridiron of values—in this instance, the values of a religious quietism over and apart from the actual experience of both painters and spectators.

Gilson's metaphysics of the art object provides (in reverse) a clue as to why so many modern paintings and sculptures are deliberately produced out of materials that change or fall apart. The short-lived work of art, as dramatized, for example, by the self-annihilating "sculpture" exhibited by Tinguely a few years ago in the garden of the Museum of Modern Art, displays art as an *event*. To underscore the phenomenon of creation and its effects on the beholder as the exclusive content of a painting, some twentieth-century artists have been willing to condemn the work itself to extinction. Duchamp, though he doubts that esthetic shock is any longer possible, seems himself shocked by the degree to which contemporary artists connive at the self-destruction of their products. "It's the most revolutionary attitude possible," he has asserted, "because they know they're killing themselves. It is a form of suicide, as artists go; they kill themselves by using perishable materials." Apparently, Duchamp can endure the thought that his "Nude" is dead but is awed that a work shall vanish and take its creator with it.

The painting with a "short life" is an antidote to the painting as an object that obstructs the psychic transaction between the artist and the spectator. One who today reacts with excitement to Duchamp's "Nude" is, in the opinion of her creator, stimulated by "the thing he has learned" rather than by the painting itself. From the artist's point of view, better a dead work than one enveloped forever in abstractions. In the end, Duchamp acknowledges that his notion of the fading aroma or "soul" of a painting may be a fantasy. But it has a vital, practical function: "it helps me make a distinction between esthetics and art history."

The esthetics of impermanence stresses the work of art as an interval in the life of both artist and spectator. Compositions into which found objects are glued or affixed or from which they protrude or are suspended make art subject to time on equal terms with nature and commodities for daily use. A German critic's description of a work by Kurt Schwitters shows the direct connection between the embodying of time in a contemporary work and bringing the spectator into contact with the artist: "The MERZbau is a three-dimensional assemblage to which new elements were *merzed on* for sixteen consecutive years until, eventually, it grew upwards through two stories and downward into a cellar in Schwitters' house in the Waldhausenstrasse in Hanover. The important thing is for the spectator to stand *'in'* a piece of sculpture." (His italics.) The yellowing and crumbling newspapers in a collage of Picasso or Schwitters incorporate a rhythm of aging equivalent to the metamorphosis of characters in Proust's *Remembrance of Things Past,* composed in the same period. Art that deteriorates more or less visibly is the reply of the twentieth-century mind to the fixated estheticism of Dorian Gray.

Action painting, which has usually refrained from attacking the physical integrity of the canvas (though there are notable examples of perishable Action Paintings by Pollock, de Kooning, Kline and others), has focussed on the inception of the work in opposition to, as Klee put it, the "end product." Its vocabulary tends to describe its creations in terms of their coming into being: expressions that conceive of a painting as beginning to "happen" or as "working itself out" are typical. Some Action Painters apparently concluded that the picture ought to be begun and finished in Poe's "half an hour" as a guarantee of authentic excitement. In Action Painting the artist is the first spectator, and the audience is invited to repeat with him the experience of seeing the work take shape. Mathieu, for example, actually made painting a picture into a public performance; and analogies have often been drawn between Action Painting and the paintings executed as a spectacle by Zen monks. From Action Paintings to "happenings," which carry painting and sculpture over into theatre, took only a single logical step—a final step, by the way, which in art one should always hesitate to take. In the "happening" the art object, Gilson's "physical existence," is abandoned altogether and composition turns literally into an event.

As an art form the "happening" is superfluous, as are such other coarser manifestations of transience as audience-participation collage and decollage (reassembling torn fragments of posters), art controlled by timers or by photoelectric cells, "making art by eating" (done both in New York and Paris; art-eating has the advantage of combining the art exhibition and the artists' party, the two chief tourist attractions of the art world). Today all works of art have become happenings. A Giotto and a Kaprow are events of differing duration in the psyche of individuals and in the history of art. Ontologically, a painting may be an immobile object to be contemplated; in this respect, however, there is nothing to differentiate it from any other object, and, as we have seen, it can be made to move and act by "ontologists" of a different persuasion. More relevant to the philosophical definition of art than its inherent spatiality is its function in a given human environment. In terms of what it does, the chief attribute of a work of art in our century is not stillness but circulation. Whether through being moved before multitudes in exhibitions and reproductions or through being made available to multitudes in *their* movements, as in the great museums, it is circulation that determines the nature and significance of paintings in the contemporary world.

Circulating as an event in art history, the painting sheds its materiality; it assumes a spectral other self that is omnipresent in art books, illustrated articles, exhibition catalogues, TV and films and the discourses of art critics and historians. Composed in the first instance of the painter's motions in time, the picture also exists temporally in the frequency-rate of its public appearance. To introduce it into and identify it as part of the cultural system, it must carry an art-historical tag that relates it to paintings of other times. Thus the painting becomes inseparable from language (one of Gilson's temporal media); in actual substance it is a centaurlike being—part words, part art supplies.

It is inspiring to imagine with Professor Gilson a painting engaged in "the simplest and most primitive of all acts, namely, to be." To witness an enactment of isolated being, however, one would have to seek out a painting hidden from curators and reviewers. Perhaps a little more than other contemporary museums, the Guggenheim has dedicated itself to hooking up its exhibits historically. Its "Six Painters and the Object" show linked comic strip and billboard art to Seurat and Léger. Its "Cézanne and Structure in Modern Painting" exhibition rounded up such widely separated contemporaries as Jenkins and Marca-Relli, Ferren and Albers, as "heirs of Cézanne" with whom "structure is the guiding principle." Van Gogh has been similarly "explored" in relation to twentieth-century Expressionism, i.e., has been stuffed under a stylistic label with artists far removed from him in motive, intellectual character and conception of the object. It is probably futile to object that these tags interfere with the apprehension of the works shown; and no doubt there are theoretical grounds for connecting Cézanne with "structure" and even the rationale of structure. Yet one would like to see Cézanne associated for a change (and to help free the physical presence of a Cézanne from its ideological casing) with Expressionism and even (via de Kooning and Hans Hofmann) with Action Painting, and to see Van Gogh brought forward among painters of "structure," by way, for example, of his color theories. After all, historical continuity depends on the facets chosen for emphasis, and nothing could be more misleading than the bifurcation of the history of modern art into Formalist and Expressionist limbs. It ought no longer be necessary to point out that every valid artist is both—that Kline is a Formalist, Newman an Expressionist, as well as the vice versa. Mr. Daniel Robbins, who prepared the catalogue for "Cézanne and Structure," strove heroically to enunciate this synthetic character of modern creation: of Albers' "Homage to the Square" series he wrote that the "primary effect is emotional and closely tied to nature," and, noting qualities in Albers' painting that he found "baffling," "moving," "equivocal," he concluded that "in terms of the conventional sense of structural esthetic, it produces a sense of frustration." Then why include Albers in the theme of "Cézanne and Structure," unless a "conventional" and "frustrating" label is better than no label at all?

Once set in motion, a work survives apart from its physical body. Indeed, the art object tends more and more to dissolve into its reproductions and to fixed opinions regarding its meaning. Exhibited for limited periods, frequently to illustrate a concept, the original painting retires leaving the image in the catalogue or historical or biographical monogram by which it is "placed" and comprehended. Duchamp is probably mistaken: perishable materials will not prevent artists from achieving immortality in the future chronicles of art. Today, painters are renowned in places where not a single painting of theirs has ever been displayed; why should they not be equally famous in areas of time never reached by their actual products?

Impermanence of the art object arose as the artist's weapon against art as an intellectual prop for changeless ideas. Today, however, impermanence has become a stylistic device, eagerly appreciated in terms of esthetic precedents. Refuse, old newspapers, rags—ephemera symbolizing the moment of vision when anything that lies at hand is sufficient for esthetic excitement—are embalmed in bronze or plastics to insure the works composed of them against the ravages of time. Art cannot transform the conditons of its own existence. The struggle to preserve the direct encounter between the artist and the spectator will, however, no doubt continue by one means or another. To *épater le bourgeois* may prove far easier than to exorcise the art historian. Perhaps one should look forward to masterpieces on such themes as "The Abuduction from the Studio" and "The Rape of de Kooning's Women."

28

Manifesto

Allan Kaprow

Once, the task of the artist was to make good art; now it is to avoid making art of any kind. Once, the public and critics had to be shown; now the latter are full of authority and the artists are full of doubts.

The history of art and of esthetics is on all bookshelves. To this pluralism of values, add the current blurring of boundaries dividing the arts, and dividing art and life; and it is clear that the old questions of definition and standards of excellence are not only futile but naive. Even yesterday's distinction between art, anti-art and non-art are pseudo-distinctions which simply waste our time: the side of an old building recalls Clifford Still's canvases, the guts of a dishwashing machine doubles as Duchamp's Bottle Rack, voices in a train station are Jackson MacLow's poems, the sounds of eating in a luncheonette are by John Cage, and all may be part of a Happening. Moreover, as the "found-object" implies the found-word, -noise or -action, it also demands the found-environment. Art not only becomes life, but life refuses to be itself.

The decision to be an artist thus assumes both the existence of a unique activity and an endless series of deeds which deny it. The decision immediately establishes the context within which all of one's acts may be judged by others as art, and also conditions one's perception of all experience as probably (not possibly) artistic. Anything I say, do, notice, or think, is art—whether or not desired—because everyone else aware of what is occurring today will probably (not possibly) say, do, notice, and think of it, as art at some time or other.

This makes the identification of oneself as an artist an ironic one, attesting not to talent for a specialized skill, but to a philosophical stance before elusive alternatives of not-quite-art, or not-quite-life. "Artist" refers to a person willfully enmeshed in the dilemma of categories, who performs as if none of them existed. If there is no clear difference between an Assemblage with sound and a "noise" concert with sights, then there is no clear difference between an artist and a junkyard dealer.

Although it is a commonplace to do so, bringing such acts and thoughts to the gallery, museum, concert hall, stage or serious bookshop, blunts the power inherent in an arena of paradoxes. It restores that sense of esthetic certainty which these milieux once proclaimed in a philistine society, just as much as it evokes a history of cultural expectations that run counter to the poignant and absurd nature of art today. Conflict with the past automatically ensues.

But obviously this is not the issue. The contemporary artist is not out to supplant recent modern art with a better kind; *he wonders what art might be*. Art and life are not simply conmingled; *their identities are both uncertain*. To pose these questions in the form of acts that are neither art-like nor life-like, while at the same time locating them within the framed context of the conventional showplace, is to suggest that there are really no uncertainties at all: the name on the gallery or stage door assures us that whatever is contained within is art, and everything else is life.

Speculation. Professional philosophy of the twentieth century has generally removed itself from problems of human conduct and purpose, and plays instead art's late role as professionalistic activity; it could aptly be called philosophy for philosophy's sake. Existentialism for this reason is assigned a place closer to social psychology than to philosophy per se, by a majority of academicians for whom ethics and metaphysics are a definitional and logical inquiry at best. Paul Valéry, acknowledging philosophy's self-analytic tendency, and wishing to salvage from it something of value, suggests that even if Plato and Spinoza can be refuted, their thoughts remain astonishing works of art. Now, as art becomes less art, it takes on philosophy's early role as critique of life. Even if its beauty can be refuted, it remains astonishingly thoughtful.

Precisely because art can be confused with life, it forces attention upon the aim of its ambiguities to "reveal" experience.

Philosophy will become steadily more impotent in its search for verbal knowledge, so long as it fails to recognize its own findings: that only a small fraction of the words we use are precise in meaning; and only a smaller proportion of these contain meanings in which we are vitally interested. When words alone are no true index of thought, and when sense and nonsense today rapidly become allusive and layered with implication rather than description, the use of words as tools to precisely delimit sense and nonsense may be a worthless endeavor. LSD and LBJ invoke different meaning clusters, but both partake of a need for code; and code performs the same condensing function as symbol in poetry. TV "snow" and Muzak in restaurants are accompaniments to conscious activity which, if suddenly withdrawn, produce a feeling of void in the human situation. Contemporary art, which tends to "think" in multimedia, intermedia, overlays, fusions and hybridizations, is a closer parallel to modern mental life than we have realized. Its judgments, therefore, may be acute. "Art" may soon become a meaningless word. In its place, "communications programming" would be a more imaginative label, attesting to our new jargon, our technological and managerial fantasies, and to our pervasive electronic contact with one another.

29

Interview in *Cahiers du Cinéma*

Jean-Luc Godard

Q— *Jean-Luc Godard, you came to the cinema by way of film criticism. What do you owe to this background?*

A— All of us at *Cahiers* considered ourselves as future directors. Frequenting film societies and the Cinémathèque, we were already thinking in strictly cinematic terms. For us, it meant working at cinema, for between writing and shooting there is a quantitative difference—not a qualitative one. The only critic who was one completely was André Bazin. The others—Sadoul, Balazs, or Pasinetti—are historians or sociologists, not critics.

While I was a critic, I considered myself already a cinéaste. Today I still consider myself a critic and, in a sense, I am one more than before. Instead of writing a critique I direct a film. I consider myself an essayist; I do essays in the form of novels and novels in the form of essays; simply, I film them instead of writing them. If the cinema were to disappear, I'd go back to pencil and paper. For me, the continuity of all the different forms of expression is very important. It all makes one block. The thing to know is how to approach this block from the site most appropriate to you.

I think, too, that it's very possible for a person to become a cinéaste without first being a critic. It happened that, for us, it went as I said, but it's not a rule. Rivette and Rohmer made films in 16mm. But if criticism was the first echelon of a vocation, it was not so much a means. It is said: they availed themselves of criticism. No—we were thinking cinema and, at a certain moment, we felt the need to deepen that thought.

Criticism taught us to love Rouch and Eisenstein at the same time. To criticism we owe not excluding one aspect of the cinema in the name of another aspect of the cinema. We owe it also the possibility of making films with more distance and of knowing that if such and such a thing has already been done it is useless to do it again. A young writer writing today knows that Molière and Shakespeare exist. We are the first cinéastes to know that Griffith exists. Even Carne, Delluc, or René Clair, when they made their first films, had no true critical or historical formation. Even Renoir had very little. (It is true that he had genius.)

Q— *This cultural basis exists only in a fraction of the new wave.*

A— Yes, in those from *Cahiers,* but for me that fraction is the whole thing. There is the group from *Cahiers* (and also Astruc, Kast, and Leenhart, who are somewhat apart) to which must be added what we might call the Left Bank Group: Resnais, Colpi, Varda, Marker. Also Demy. These had their own cultural basis, but there are not thirty-six others. *Cahiers* was the nucleus.

They say that now we can no longer write about our colleagues. Obviously, it has become difficult to have coffee with someone if, that afternoon, you have to write that he's made an idiotic film, but what has always differentiated us from others is that we take a stand for a criticism of praise: we speak of a film, if we like it. If we don't like it, we exempt ourselves from breaking its back. All one has to do is hold to this principle.

Q— *Your critical attitude seems to contradict the idea of improvisation which is attached to your name.*

A— I improvise, without doubt, but with material that dates from way back. One gathers, over the years, piles of things and then suddenly puts them in what one is doing. My first shorts had a lot of preparation and were shot very quickly. *Breathless* was started in this way. I had written the first scene (Jean Seberg on the Champs Èlysées) and, for the rest, I had an enormous amount of notes corresponding to each scene. I said to myself, this is very distracting. I stopped everything. Then I reflected: in one day, if one knows what one is doing, one should be able to shoot a dozen sequences. Only, instead of having the material for a long time, I'll get it just before. When one knows where he is going, this must be possible. This is not improvisation, it's decision-making at the last minute. Obviously, you have to have and maintain a view of the ensemble; you can modify a certain part of it, but after the shooting starts keep the changes to a minimum—otherwise it's catastrophic.

I read in *Sight and Sound* that I was improvising in the Actors' Studio style, with actors to whom one says: you are such and such, take it from there. But Belmondo's dialogue was never invented by him. It was written: only, the actors didn't learn it—the film was shot silent and I whispered the cues.

Q— *When you started the film, what did it represent for you?*

A— Our first films were purely films by cinephiles. One may avail one of something already seen in the cinema in order to make deliberate references. This was the case for me. Actually, I was reasoning according to purely cinematographic attitudes. I worked out certain images, schemes with relation to others I knew from Preminger, Cukor, etc. . . . In any case Jean Seberg's character is a follow-up of the one in *Bonjour Tristesse*. I could have taken the last frame of that and linked it with a title: "three years later." . . . This is to reconcile my taste for quotation, which I have always kept. Why reproach us for it? People, in life, quote what pleases them. We have therefore the right to quote what pleases us. I show people "quoting"—only I arrange it so that the quote pleases me. In the notes I keep of what might be useful to me in a film I also put a sentence from Dostoievsky, if I like it. Why be constrained? If you want to say something, there is only one solution: say it.

Moreover, the genre of *Breathless* was such that all was permitted, that was its nature. Whatever people might do—all this could be integrated into the film. This was even my point of departure. I said to myself: there has already been Bresson, we just had *Hiroshima,* a certain kind of cinema has just ended—well, then, let's put the final period to it: let's show that anything goes. What I wanted to do was to depart from the conventional story and remake, but differently, everything that had already been done in the cinema. I also wanted to give the impression of just finding or experiencing the processes of cinema for the first time. The iris-shot showed that it was permissible to return to the sources of cinema and the linking-shot came along, by itself, as if one had just invented it. If there weren't other processes, this was in reaction to a certain cinema, but this doesn't have to be a rule. There are films where they are necessary: from time to time one could do more with them.

What is hardest on me is the ending. Is the hero going to die? At first, I was thinking of doing the opposite of, for example, *The Killing*. The gangster would succeed and leave for Italy with his money. But this would have been a very conventional anti-convention, like having Nana succeed in *My Life to Live*. I finally told myself that since, after all, all my avowed ambitions were to make a normal gangster film I couldn't systematically contradict the genre: the guy had to die. If the descendants of Atreus don't massacre each other any more, they are no longer descendants of Atreus.

But improvisation is fatiguing. I am always telling myself: this is the last time! It's not possible any more! It's too fatiguing to go to sleep every night asking oneself, "What am I going to do tomorrow morning?" It's like writing an article at twenty-to-twelve at a café table when it has to be delivered to the paper at noon. What is curious is that one always arrives at writing it, but working like this month after month is killing. At the same time there is a certain amount of premeditation. You say to yourself that if you are honest and sincere and in a corner and have to do something, the result will necessarily be honest and sincere.

Only, you never do exactly what you believe you're doing. Sometimes you even arrive at the exact opposite. This is true for me, in any case, but at the same time I lay claim to everything I've done. I realized, at a certain point, that *Breathless* was not at all what I believed it to be. I believed I'd made a realistic film and it wasn't that at all. First of all, I didn't possess sufficient technical skill, then I discovered that I wasn't made for this genre of film. There are also a great number of things I'd like to do and don't do. For example, I'd like to be like Fritz Lang and have frames which are extraordinary in themselves, but I don't arrive at that. So I do something else. I like *Breathless* enormously—for a certain period I was ashamed of it, but now I place it where it belongs: with *Alice in Wonderland*. I thought it was *Scarface*.

Breathless is a story, not a subject. A subject is something simple and vast about which one can make a resumé in twenty seconds: revenge, pleasure . . . a story takes twenty minutes to recapitulate. *The Little Soldier* has a subject: a young man is confused, realizes it and tries to find clarity. In *A Woman Is a Woman* a girl wants a baby at any cost and right away. In *Breathless*, I was looking for a subject all during the shooting; finally I became interested in Belmondo. I saw him as a sort of a façade which it was necessary to film in order to know what was behind it. Seberg, on the contrary, was an actress whom I wanted to make do many little things that pleased me—this came from the cinephile side I no longer have.

Q— *How do you think of actors now?*

A— My position with regard to them has always been somewhat like the interviewer and the interviewed—I run behind someone and ask him something. At the same time it is I who have organized the race.

Q— *What led you to* The Little Soldier?

A— I wanted to catch up with the realism I had missed in *Breathless;* the concrete. The film takes off from an old idea: I wanted to speak of brainwashing. One would say to a prisoner, "If it takes twenty minutes or twenty years, we always make someone say something." The happenings in Algeria made me replace brainwashing with torture, which had become the big question. My prisoner is someone who is asked to do something he doesn't want to do; simply doesn't want to do it, and he resists on principle. This is liberty as I see it: from a practical point of view. To be free is to be able to do what pleases you when it pleases you.

The film is witness to an epoch. People speak of politics but it is not *politically* oriented. My style of commitment was to say to myself: they reproach the *new wave* for showing nothing but people in beds—I'm going to show some who are politically involved and have no time to go to bed. Well, politics was Algeria. But I had to show that from the angle I knew and in the way I felt it. If Kyron or the people from *L'Observateur* wanted it to be spoken of otherwise, very well—all they had to do was to go with a camera to the F.L.N. If Dupont wanted another point of view he had only to film Algiers from the point of view of the paratroopers. It's a shame about the things that are never done. Me—I spoke of the things that concerned me insofar as I was a Parisian in 1960, a member of no party. What concerned me was the problem of war and its moral repercussions. Therefore I showed a guy who poses himself a great many problems. He doesn't know how to resolve them, but posing them, even with confusion, is already an attempt. It is more valuable perhaps to pose questions than to refuse to question or to believe oneself capable of resolving everything.

Q— *How did the experience of* Breathless *serve you?*

A— It served me, but I had a great deal of trouble shooting *The Little Soldier.* We could have shot it in two weeks. With stops, it took us two months. I reflected; I hesitated. Quite the opposite of *Breathless,* I couldn't say everything. I could only say certain things, but which ones? Finally, it was already something to know what not to say—by elimination what remained was what had to be said.

Also I came back to improvisation. Well, after *The Little Soldier,* I said to myself: it's finished! Therefore I started from a very preconceived scenario: *A Woman is a Woman.* But there was more improvisation. For *Breathless,* I was staying up nights, writing, all during the shooting; for *The Little Soldier*—in thc morning; and with *A Woman Is a Woman* I was writing in the studio while the actors were making up. But once more, you only hit upon the things you've thought of for a long time. In *My Life to Live* I worked out the scene of *The Oval Portrait* that morning but I knew the story. At the moment I hit upon it I had forgotten it, I said to myself: I'll use that. But I was at a point where in any case I would have found something. If the solution hadn't come then it would have the next day.

With me it's a method: since I make films on small budgets, I can ask the producer for five weeks knowing that there will be about two weeks of actual shooting. The big difficulty is that I have to have people at my disposal all the time. Sometimes they have to wait an entire day before knowing what I can make them do. I have to ask them not to leave the place of shooting, we might start working again any minute. They suffer for it. That's why anyone who works with me is always well paid. The actors suffer, from another point of view: an actor likes to have the impression of being in control of his character, even if it's not true, and with me they rarely get that impression. What is terrible is that it is very difficult to do in the cinema what the painter does naturally: he stops, steps back, is disheartened, starts again, modifies . . . all goes well.

But this method is not valuable for everyone. There are two major classes of cinéastes. In the Eisenstein-Hitchcock group, there are those who write out their film in the most complete fashion possible. They know what they want, they have everything in their heads, they put everything down on paper. The shooting is only a practical application, a construction of some sort resembling as much as possible what was imagined. Resnais is in this category, and Demy. The others, in the Rouch class, don't have a very clear idea of what they're going to do and they are searching. The film is this search. They know that they're going to arrive somewhere, and they have the means for that, but where exactly? The first group makes circle-films, the others—films in a straight line. Renoir is one of the rare people who do both together, this is what makes his charm.

Rossellini is still another thing. He is the only one who has an exact vision and sees things as a totality. He films them, therefore, in the only way possible. No one can film one of Rossellini's scenarios. His vision of the world is so exact that his way of seeing detail, formal or not, is exact also. With him, a frame is beautiful because it is correct; with most other people, a frame becomes right because it is beautiful. They try to construct an extraordinary thing and, in relation to how effective it becomes, we see that there were reasons for doing it. Rossellini, however, does things he had reasons for doing in the first place. It is beautiful because it is.

Beauty and the splendor of truth are two poles. There are cinéastes who seek truth and, if they find it, it will necessarily be beautiful. We find these two poles in the documentary and in fiction. Certain people start with a documentary and arrive at fiction, like Flaherty who ended by making very carefully composed films; others start with fiction and arrive at the documentary: Eisenstein, coming from montage, finished by making *Que Viva Mexico.*

The cinema is the only art which, as Cocteau says (in *Orpheus,* I believe), "films death at work." The person one films is growing older and will die. We film, therefore, a moment when death is working. Painting is immobile; the cinema is interesting because it seizes life and the mortal aspect of life.

Q— *And you—from which pole do you start?*

A— I believe I start more from the documentary, in order to give truth to fiction. That's why I've always worked with excellent, professional actors—without them, my films would not be as good.

I am also interested in the theatrical aspect. In *The Little Soldier,* when I was seeking to arrive at the concrete, I saw that the closer I drew to the concrete the more theatrical my work became. *My Life to Live* is both very concrete and very theatrical. I would like to film a play by Sacha Guitry; I would like to film *Six Characters in Search of an Author* to show, cinematically, what theatre is. By being a realist one discovers the theatre, and by being theatrical. . . . As in *The Golden Coach:* behind the theatre is life and behind life, the theatre.

My point of departure was the imaginary and I discovered the real; but, behind the real there was the imaginary.

According to Truffaut, the cinema consists of the spectacle (Méliès) and research (Lumière). If I analyze myself today I see that I have always wanted, basically, to make a research film in spectacle form. The documentary side is this: a man is in such and such a situation. The spectacle side comes from making the man a gangster or a secret agent. The spectacle side comes, in *A Woman Is a Woman,* out of the fact that the woman is a comedienne; in *My Life to Live,* she is a prostitute.

The producers say: Godard—he talks about Joyce, metaphysics, or painting, but he will always have with him a commercial side. I don't say this at all—I don't see two things, I only see one.

Q— *How do you rank* A Woman Is a Woman *in your work?*
A— As with *Jules and Jim* for Truffaut, it is my first real film.

Q— *Is this the film that resembles you most?*
A— I don't believe so, but it's the film I love the most. It's like *Lady Windermere's Fan* for Preminger: one's sick children are the most loved.

For me, the film also represents the discovery of color and direct sound, since my other films were post-synchronized. The subject, like that of my two previous films, is how a character resolves a certain situation. But I conceived this subject as the interior of a neorealist musical. This is an absolute contradiction, but it is exactly that which interested me in the film. An error, perhaps, but a seductive error. And it fit the subject well, since we are showing a woman who wants a baby in an absurd manner when it's the most natural thing in the world. But the film is not a musical comedy. It's the *idea* of the musical comedy.

Moreover, I hesitated for a long time about doing scenes that were truly musical. Finally, I preferred to suggest the idea that the characters are singing, thanks to the utilization of music while having them speak normally. Nevertheless, the musical comedy is dead. *Adieu Philippine,* in a certain way, is also a musical comedy, but the genre itself is dead. Even for the Americans, there's no longer any sense in doing remakes of *Singin' in the Rain.* Something else is necessary. This is also what my film is saying: it is nostalgia for the musical comedy, as *The Little Soldier* is nostalgia for the Spanish Civil War.

What people must not have liked was the discontinuity, the changes of rhythm or the breaks in tone. Perhaps also the theatrical aspect, *cinéma dell'arte*. The people in the film play and bow at the same time; they know and we know that they are playing, that they are laughing and, at the same time, that they are crying. In sum, it's an exhibition, but that's what I wanted to do. The characters are always playing to the camera: it's a parade: I wanted people to be able to cry for Columbine, even when she's on parade. In *My Life to Live,* on the contrary, we should have the impression that the people are fleeing the camera.

I also discovered 'scope with *A Woman Is a Woman*. I believe that that's a normal format and that (1.33) is an arbitrary ratio. You can shoot everything in 'scope. Not in (1.33)—but it is extraordinary. (1.66) is nothing at all. I don't like intermediate ratios. I hesitated about 'scope for *My Life to Live,* then I didn't use it—it's too sentimental as a ratio. (1.33) is harder, more severe. On the other hand, I regret not having used 'scope for *Breathless*. That's my only regret. *The Little Soldier* is in the right ratio. But these things can be seen more clearly after the fact. These are the surprises and I like being surprised. If you know in advance exactly what you're going to do, it's no longer worth the trouble of doing it. If a spectacle is all written out, what's the point of filming it? What's the use of cinema, if it follows literature? When I write a scenario, I also want to put everything on paper but I don't arrive at it. I am not a writer. To make a film is to superimpose three operations: thinking, shooting, editing. Everything can't be in the scenario; or if it is—if people cry or laugh when they read it, the only thing to be done is to print it and sell it in a bookstore.

What bores me is that when you sign with a producer he wants to know what you're signing for. A producer likes to engage a director about whom he thinks that when he finishes his film it will look like the idea he started out with.

Q— *Is this what has led you to refuse certain projects?*

A— The Hakim brothers proposed that I do *Eva*. To start with, I didn't like the actors they had in mind. I wanted Richard Burton. They thought it was a good idea. They said, "We'll telephone him." I said, "There's the telephone." They said, "Oh, yes—but you know—maybe he's not home!" So I understood that they weren't willing. For the female lead, I saw someone like the Rita Hayworth of five or six years ago. In any case, I wanted only American actors. Film people, if they're not American, I don't know what to do with them. If a Frenchman says, "I am a scenarist," what does that mean? That doesn't exist. Whereas for an American if it doesn't exist it doesn't matter: what is "American" has a mythical side that makes something exist.

Eva caused me pain, also, because it was too much like *La Chienne*. And there was no subject. I did, however, propose this: the story of a guy who is approached by a producer to write a scenario about a woman in order to prove that he is really a writer. This becomes the story of a man who tries to write about a woman but does not succeed. Or maybe he does, I don't know. In any case, what happens is what it is necessary to tell about. I wanted to show the poem he writes and the analysis of the poem. For example, he writes: "I went out; the weather was fine; I met her; she had blue eyes." Then, he asks himself why he wrote that. Finally, I think he doesn't arrive at anything . . . it's a little like the story of the end of Porthos.

The producers didn't want it. The Hakim brothers aren't stupid, but, like all the big postwar producers, they no longer knew what to do. Before, a producer knew what genre of films he ought to do. There were three or four directions and each producer had his own. Braunberger already existed and he knew his direction and it was different from the others. Today, there are ten thousand directions. Braunberger isn't lost, for he always has his own little way, and those who make films like *Ben Hur*—they, too, always have their own way. But 80 percent of the producers are completely lost. At one time they could say, "I'm going to do a film with Duvivier," but today? They can't succeed with either big films or little intellectual films. Everything is mixed up.

So they say to themselves, "There's Antonioni. Two hundred thousand people went to see *La Notte* . . . let's do a film with him." What loses them is that they don't really know why they're doing it. Losey, and Antonioni, when utilized in this fashion and at the wrong moment, no longer bring in anything at all. After following a certain path in cinema for forty years, these people can't adapt. In my contact with the Hakim brothers it was specified that they could, if they so judged, reedit the film in accordance with their ideas. I was disillusioned. They said to me, "Duvivier, Carne, all the others have this kind of contract."

They no longer know. Also, the public baffles them. At one time, they didn't know that they knew nothing. Today they know it. But I shouldn't speak too negatively about producers, because the exploiters and distributors are much worse. The producers, basically, are like us: these are people who don't have money and who need to make films. They're on the same side we are. They want to work without anyone's interference and they are, like us, against censorship. The distributors and exploiters are not in love with what they're doing. I have never seen a producer who didn't have a love for his métier. Compared to an exploiter, the worst producer is a poet. Mad, imbecilic, innocent, or stupid—they are sympathetic. They put their money on things that are uncertain and, often, follow their own pleasure. A producer is often a guy who buys a book and suddenly wants to build a whole production on it. It might or might not go well, but he must push on. The annoying part is that, since most of the time he doesn't have good taste, he buys worthless books. But, whatever he may be, he is sympathetic. And he works. Distributors and exploiters are functionaries and that's what is terrible. The functionary's ideal is this: that every day at the same hour a film should make the same number of spectators come in.

The public is neither stupid nor intelligent. No one knows what it is. It is sometimes surprising and generally deceiving. You can't count on it. And in a sense that's good. In any case, it's changing. The old average-cinema-public has become the television public. When producers speak about the public I say to them, "I know what it is, because I go to the movies and pay for my seat; and you—you never go anywhere—you don't know what's happening."

Q— *Well, let's talk about* My Life to Live. *Was that hard or easy to make?*

A— This film was at the same time very simple and . . . it was as if it was necessary to extract the images from the night, as if they were at the bottom of a pit and had to be attracted to the light. When I extricated the frame, I said to myself, "Everything is there, nothing to retouch, but I mustn't make a mistake about what I'm bringing out, about what should be brought out first." I didn't want to search for effects. I had to risk each stroke. In *A Woman Is a Woman,* it was different; I wanted to obtain certain things, for example—the theatrical aspect. This aspect, I had it in *My Life to Live* but without saying to myself that I must do *this* or *that* to get it. I knew, however, that I would have it. It was a little like *théâtre-vérité.*

This way of getting shots does away with editing. All you have to do is put them end to end. The rushes seen by the crew are pretty close to what the public saw. Not only that. I shot the scenes in order. Neither was there any mixing. The film is a series of blocks. It is sufficient to take the stones and place them one after the other, side by side. The whole thing is to pick up good stones in the first place. The ideal, for me, is to obtain right away what will work—and without retouches. If they are necessary, it falls short of the mark. The immediate is chance. At the same time it is definitive. What I want is the definitive by chance.

I obtain a theatrical realism. The theatre is also a block which cannot be retouched. Realism, in any case, is never exactly the truth and the realism of the cinema is obligatorily faked. I am close to the theatre also by my use of words: in my film you have to listen to the people talking, so much the more because they are often seen from behind and one isn't distracted by the faces. The sound is as realistic as possible. It makes me think of the first talkies. I have always loved the sound of those films, they had a great truth for it was the first time one heard people speaking.

In a general way, we are coming back now to more authentic sound and dialogue. People have made use of this to reproach us for our grossness. In *Monkey in Winter* the word *merde* occurs dozens of times; in *Les Bonnes Femmes,* two or three times—but there people call it grossness since Audiard remains conventional. If a girl says to a boy, "Poor bastard, I detest you" in life, that hurts. Thus, in the cinema, it should hurt as much as in life. That's what people don't accept. That's why they refused *Les Bonnes Femmes,* which told the truth and had an effect on them. There we really had a case of a theatre full of people who saw themselves in a mirror.

Q— *When you made* My Life to Live, *what was your point of departure?*

A— I didn't know exactly what I was going to do. I prefer searching for something I don't know to doing well something I already know. In fact the film was realized right off the bat, as if I was carried away. *My Life to Live* was the equilibrium that makes one suddenly feel good about life, for an hour, a day, or a week. Anna, who is in 60 percent of the film, was a little unhappy never knowing much in advance what she would have to do. But she was so sincere in her will to act for something that it is finally that sincerity which acted. For my part, without knowing exactly what I was going to do, I was so sincere in my desire to make the film that, the two of us together, we succeeded. I like very much to change actors, but, with her, working represents something else. I believe it is the first time that she is absolutely conscious of her means and is utilizing them. Thus, the interrogation scene in *The Little Soldier* is made in the Rouch way: she didn't know in advance the questions I would ask her. Here, in *My Life to Live,* she acted with a text as if she didn't know the questions. Finally one arrives at spontaneity and naturalness.

The film was made in a special state, and Anna is not the only one to have given the best of herself. Coutard achieved his best photography. What astonishes me, on seeing the film again, is that it seems to be the most composed of those I've made when it really wasn't. I took raw material, perfectly round pebbles which I placed one next to the other, and it's organized. And then—this strikes me now—I had a habit of paying attention to the colors of things, even in black and white. In this case—no; what was black was black and what was white was white. And the shooting was done with people wearing their own clothes, except Anna for whom we bought a skirt and a jersey.

Q— *Why the division into twelve tableaux?*

A— Why twelve? I don't know, but as for the tableaux themselves—that accentuates the theatrical aspect, the Brechtian side. I wanted the idea of "the adventures of Miss Nana Untel." The end of the film, that too is very theatrical: the last tableau had to be more theatrical than all the others. Also, this division corresponds to the exterior side of things, to permit me to show the sentiment of the inside to a greater extent, the exact opposite of *Pickpocket* in which the character is seen from inside. How to render the inside? Well, that's it—by wisely staying outside.

In any case, something happens. This is why Antonioni's cinema, with its aspect of non-communication, is not mine. Rossellini said to me that I grazed Antonioni's sin in passing but that I correctly avoided it. I think that with this kind of problem it is sufficient to be of good faith. To say that the more you look at someone the less you understand him—I believe that that's false. But obviously, if you look at people too much you end by asking yourself what's the use; that's inevitable. If you look at a wall for ten hours in a row you end up by posing it questions—when it's a wall. One creates useless problems for oneself. This is another reason for the film's being a series of sketches: it is necessary to let people live their lives, not look at them for too long, or else you'll end by no longer understanding anything about them.

Q— *One of your projects is* The Riflemen. *Will you make the film in color?*

A— Yes, but what color exactly? It's all the same to me. I would be happy to obtain the color of Buñuel's *Robinson Crusoe* or of Rossellini's *Jeanne d'Arc*. And I shall make the film in 16mm. Blown up to 35mm., the image will be somewhat washed out but I see nothing wrong with that. Maybe that'll even make it better. Shooting in 16mm. is in the spirit of this film. The big Mitchell is another spirit. For *My Life to Live* I held absolutely to a big camera. If there had been a bigger one than the Mitchell I'd have taken it. I very much like the shape of the Mitchell: it really looks like a camera. I was very unhappy doing *Sloth* because the producer had everyone using a Debrie. This is a square camera which doesn't have the camera spirit, not at all. Maybe it's foolish but I attach importance to these things.

Also, I am going to do a sketch. A man goes out on the street, everything seems normal, but two or three little details reveal to him that people, his fiancée, are no longer reasoning normally. He discovers for example that a café is no longer called a café. And if his fiancée doesn't come to a rendezvous, it's not that she doesn't love him any more—it's simply that she reasons in a different way. They no longer have the same logic. One day he reads a newspaper and finds out that there has been an atomic explosion somewhere; then he tells himself that he is without doubt the only person on earth who is reasoning normally. Things are the same, but everything is different. It's anti-Rossellini, but that's the way it is.

The Riflemen would be more like the old Rossellini, when he made *La Machine à Tuer les Méchants* and *Où Est la Liberté?* The scenario is so strong that all I have to do is film it without posing problems for myself. The solutions will impose themselves. It's the story of two peasants who see riflemen arrive. They are not there to arrest them but to bring them a letter from the king. In fact it's an order of mobilization. They are annoyed but the riflemen say to them, "War is great; you can do anything, have everything!" They want to know what. Leave a restaurant without paying? Of course! And they continue to ask questions, enumerating things from the most trifling larcenies to the greatest atrocities. May one massacre children? Of course! Steal old men's watches? Why yes! Break people's glasses? That too! Burn women? Obviously! When the enumeration is finished, they leave for the war. The film will be nasty, because each time an idea emerges from their stupidity it is a wicked idea.

They write to their wives: "We have taken the Arc de Triomphe, the Lido, the Pyramids, raped lots of women and burned things; everything is going well!" At the end they come home, happy but mutilated, with a small valise, saying, "We have brought back all the treasures of the world." And they take out heaps of post cards representing the monuments of every land: for them, this is as much as having titles to the property; they believe that as soon as the war ends they will be given all of it. The riflemen say to them, "When you hear shouts and noises in the valley, that will mean the war is over and that the king is coming to reward everyone; go there and you will have everything." Some time later, they hear cries and explosions—they go there, but there is shooting (the scenes are analogous to those of the Liberation). The king has not won the war, but he has signed a peace treaty with the enemy and those who have fought for him are considered as war criminals. Instead of gaining riches, the two peasants are shot. Everything will be very realistic, in a purely theatrical perspective—we will see war scenes, commando style, as in Fuller's films, with some newsreel footage. But now that I've told all about it I'm suddenly less anxious to do it.

Q— *You also want to do* Ubu Roi.

A— Yes, in somewhat the same style. Ubu, for cinema, should be very gangsterish—with raincoat and soft hat—and we should see Ubu and his clique get in their cars and go to cafés.

What annoys me is that the tone of Ubu already exists in *Shoot the Piano Player* and the realistic side was very successful, not to speak of the text which was very fine. The film, from this point of view, was extraordinary.

I should also like to shoot *Pour Lucrèce* by Giraudoux. There I will have theatre in a pure state, for I'd like to specifically reçord a text, record the voices that speak it. I should also like to make an immense film about France. Everything would be in it. It would last two or three days. The film would be in episodes and each episode would be screened for a week or two. If one were to rent a theatre for a year it would be feasible. Anything is possible. To show everything has always been the temptation of novelists in their big books. I'd show people going to the movies and you'd see the film they see. You would see an intellectual with the job of interviewing people and you'd see the interviews. We could interview everyone, from Sartre to the Minister of War including the peasants of Chantal or workers. We'd also see sports, racing, etc. It would have to be organized on principle and then go in all directions. The shooting would last three or four years.

Q— *Do you like television?*

A— Television is the State and the State is functionaries, and functionaries . . . that's the contrary of television. Of what it should be, I mean. But I'd like very much to do something in it. Not make films *for* television, in the sense of making them for cinema, but do *reportage,* for example. I'd like to do some programs in the form of essays, interviews, or travelogs—to speak about a painter or a writer whom I like. Or, quite plainly, some "dramatics." But directly. Television is not a means of expression. The proof is that the more idiotic it is the more it fascinates and the longer people stay hypnotized in their chairs. That's what television is but we may hope that this will change. The annoying thing is that if you start watching TV you can't get away from it. The thing to do is not to watch it.

Television should be considered not as a means of expression but of transmission. It has to be taken as such. If this is the only remaining way to speak about art to people it should be used. For, even with films like *Lola Montes* or *Alexander Nevsky,* something remains in spite of the distortion, the rounded screen, the greyness of the image, or the absence of color. The spirit remains. In *Lola Montes* what you lose of the images you gain by the dialogue since you pay more attention. The film can hold you simply by the dialogue: its spirit comes to you through that. The same is true of all good films: it suffices that one part came through and that part suffices to indicate the whole film. Thus television in spite of everything transmits the spirit of things and that's very important.

And newsreels? That could be extraordinary. And why not make reconstructed newsreels, like Méliès did? Today, we should show Castro and Johnson, played by actors: "This is the sad story of Castro and Johnson. . . ." We would add real footage and people would love all that, I'm sure of it.

And miscellaneous "human interest" stories? They should be shown in the same way that we see them in *France-Soir*. In this genre, the only extraordinary things you can see are the reconstructions of crimes. First of all, it's really "real life" and then the reconstituted part of it is fascinating. In a general fashion, *reportage* is only interesting when it's inserted in fiction, but fiction is interesting only when it is verified by reality.

The *nouvelle vague* is defined, in part, by this new rapport between fiction and reality. It is defined also by regret, by nostalgia for a cinema which no longer exists. As soon as you can make films—you can no longer make films like the ones that made you want to make them. The dream of the *new wave,* which will never be realized, is to shoot—*Spartacus* in Hollywood with ten million dollars. Yet I am not bothered by making small inexpensive films—but people like Demy are very unhappy.

People have always believed that the *nouvelle vague* means cheap films as opposed to expensive ones. It is, simply, good film as opposed to bad film. Only it was found that the only way was to make inexpensive films. It is true that certain films are better for being made on small budgets but you have to think of the films that are better for having cost a great deal.

Q— *And if someone had offered you a hundred million (francs) to make* My Life to Live *with?*

A— I would never have accepted. What would the film have gained? The only thing I could have done would have been to pay more to the people who worked with me, that's all. At the same time I'd refuse to do a film for one hundred million (francs) if I thought it would cost four hundred.

Definitively, it is only in France that the producer recognizes, at least on principle, the notion of the *auteur*. (Hitchcock is one exception: as soon as the directors have their names outside the theatre, he has his photograph!) The best of the Italian producers considers the director as an employee. The difference is that the Italian system isn't worth much while the Americans are very strong. They are doubtless less so since the organization of the big studio has disappeared, but before they were the strongest in the world. Ben Hecht is the strongest scenarist I have ever seen. The Americans, who are much more stupid when it's a question of analysis, instinctively succeed in constructing things. They also have the gift of a simplicity which gives profundity: take the little Western *Ride the High Country*.

In France, if you want to do things like that you seem to be an intellectual.

Q— *We come back to the idea of compartmentalization.*

A— France is made of compartments. Well, in expression everything is linked and all thc means of expression are linked. And life is one. Shooting and not shooting, for me, are not two different lives. Making films should be part of life and should be a natural and normal thing. Shooting hasn't changed my life much, for I was already shooting while doing criticism, and if I were to go back to being a critic it would still be, for me, a way of making films.

The only interesting film of Clouzot's is the one in which he searched, improvised, experimented, and lived something: *The Mystery of Picasso.* Clement or the others don't live their cinema. It is a separate compartment.

In France, as I have already said, you must not mix genres. In America, a murder mystery can also be political and have gags. It is accepted here, of course, because it is American, but do the same thing in France and they shout.

It is true that now people reproach us less because they finally saw that we were arriving at talking about something other than "surprise parties." The only one who hasn't done anything is Vadim and he isn't reproached. Him—he's the worst. He has betrayed everything he could have betrayed, even himself. The public adores that: Vadim is comfortable. He gives people the impression that they are seeing Shakespeare when he presents them with *Confidences* and *À Tout Coeur*. People say to themselves, "This is Shakespeare? Great! Why didn't anyone tell us before?"

I don't believe that a person can feel that he's doing something stupid and nasty and still continue doing it. Vadim must not be aware of what he's doing. Neither did he know what he was doing in the beginning, when he was spontaneous and sincere. Simply, he was on time. The fact of being on time when the rest of the world is behind gives the impression of being ahead. Since then he's stayed in the same place while the rest of the people have come to be on time—which makes him behind.

Having a *métier* is something that has always counted in France. Before the war, a director wasn't compared to a musician or to a writer but to a carpenter, an artisan. It turned out that among these artisans there were artists—like Renoir, Ophuls. Today the director is considered an artist but most of them have remained artisans. The *métier* exists, but not in the way they think. Carne has a *métier:* that's what makes him make bad films. When he was inventing his *métier* he made extraordinary films. Now he no longer invents. Chabrol, today, has more of a *métier* than Carne and it makes him search. It's a good *métier*.

Q— *The* nouvelle vague *cinéastes, in criticism as in cinema—have they in common the will to search?*

A— We have many things in common. As for Rivette, Rohmer, Truffaut—obviously I feel different from them, but we have basically the same ideas about cinema. We have more things in common than we have differences—the details are quite different but on a profound level the differences are tiny.

We don't make the same films, that's true, but the more I see of so-called normal films and the more I see our films the more I am struck by the difference. And it must be a big one, because I have a general tendency to see what things have in common. Before the war, for example, there was a difference between Duvivier's *La Belle Equipe* and Renoir's *La Bête Humaine,* but only one of quality. Whereas now, between our films and a film by Verneuil, Delannoy, Duvivier, or Carne, there is truly a difference in kind.

There were two sorts of values: the true and the false. *Cahiers* said that the true were false and the false were true. But today, there is neither true nor false and everything has become more difficult. The people at *Cahiers* were commandos: today they are an army in time of peace, going off on war games. But I think this is a temporary situation. For the moment, as in any peacetime army, *Cahiers* is divided into clans. It's like when Protestantism divided into an incredible number of sects. If you like one director you have to detest the other.

In other countries *Cahiers* has an enormous influence. People wonder if we're serious. It was bad enough to admit that guys like Ray and Aldrich have genius, but when they see interviews with someone like Ulmer—I am for the *Politique des Auteurs,* but not just anybody—I find that opening the door to absolutely everyone is a very dangerous thing. Inflation is menacing.

The important thing is not to want to discover someone at all cost. The snob aspect of the game of discovery should be left to *L'Express*. What is important is to know how to discern who has genius and who doesn't and to try, if you can, to define the genius or to explain it. There aren't many who try.

It is true that for today's critics everything has become very difficult and that many of *Cahiers'* faults are old ones. In any case, we have in common the fact that we are searching: those who do not cannot for very long give the illusion of doing so; things end by clarifying themselves.

Translated by Rose Kaplin

30

Bodies in Space: Film as "Carnal Knowledge"

Annette Michelson

I

All mastery casts a chill.

Mallarmé

The indefinable, knowing fear which is
the clearest intimation of the metaphysical.

Borgès

In the winter of 1905 the first continuously operated movie theatre opened in Los Angeles. There is an obvious sense in which the history of film is circumscribed by the feature of that theatre's initial program, George Meliès' *Trip to the Moon,* and Stanley Kubrick's *2001: A Space Odyssey*. There is another sense in which its evolution hypostatizes the accelerating dynamics of History. Walking the three blocks between the Museum of Modern Art's screening room and the Loew's Capitol, thinking of that evolution, one finds oneself tracing a vector, exploring, in implication, as one goes, a multi-demensional movement of human consciousness in our century.

In 1961, the year of Meliès' centenary, the Cinémathèque Française and the Union Centrale des Arts Décoratifs presented in the Louvre a commemorative exhibition still present to me as one of the finest I have seen. One wandered through the reconstitution of a life-work prodigious in its inventive abundance as through a forest alive with apparitions and metamorphoses, stopping all at once, however, as before a clearing, arrested as by a shaft of light, the illumination flaring from a photograph upon the wall.

Greatly enlarged, it showed the Meliès Company in action.[1] The Company had been, of course, a family affair, its production something of a "cottage industry," and one saw it here in operation on one of the artfully designed and fastidiously executed sets which were a point of honor and pride for the indefatigable Master Builder. The photograph gave one pause.

It gives us a behind-the-scene view, shows not the action being filmed, but its reverse side, the flats of its set anchored, here and there, in the manner of theatrical décor, to the ground. Men—gentlemen, formally dressed and hatted—stand about, supporting those flats, ready to catch them should the screws fail and they fall. The image is, of course, "moving" because it restores to us the feeling of the primitive, the home-made and artisanal modesty, the fragile and precarious underpinnings of a grandiose venture. It articulates, as well, the matter in which film first made its entrance, through the stage door (*l'entrée des artistes*), and something of the homely mechanics, the dialectic at work in the fabrication of illusion itself, its re-invention for us. It illustrates the manner in which the artisan, the bourgeois family man, the *bricoleur,* prestidigitator and entrepreneur fused in a single figure of genius to engender the art of cinema as we know it.

The 19th century had been dreaming of movies, as all its forms of popular narrative and diversion (photographic album, panoramic view, magic lantern, shadow play, wax museum and the novel itself) conspire to testify, and Meliès' intrepid talent, a synthesis of the imagination and industry which were subsequently to be reified into the opposing terms of the new form's dialectic, fused these dreams into something real. If Lumierè had been the first cinematographer, Meliès was the first of the *réalisateurs,* as distinct from the *metteurs-en-scene;* he *realized* the cinema itself.

Seeing Kubrick's *Space Odyssey,* we sense, we know that its ontogeny recapitulates a philogeny.[2] The very conditions of its making involved the scale of enterprise, the dedicated resolution and intellectual flexibility, the proud marshalling of vast resources brought to bear upon the most sophisticated and ambitious ventures of our culture. Its making required, indeed, a length and complexity of preparation, a breadth of concept and detail of organization analogous only to those invested in the launching of a new regime, a new inter-continental missile system, a fresh episode in the exploration of space. And its appearance has, in fact, generated the same sort of apprehension or "cultural shock" which Arthur C. Clarke describes, in his novelistic rendering of the screenplay, as the reaction to the invention of "the highly advanced HAL 900 Computer, the brain and nervous system" of the narrative's "vehicle," the space-ship *Discovery*.

Like that black monolith whose unheralded materialization propels the evolution of consciousness through the three panels of the movie's narrative triptych, Kubrick's film has assumed the disquieting function of Epiphany. It functions as a disturbing structure, emitting, in its intensity of presence and perfection of surface, sets of signals. That intensity and perfection are contingent upon a conspicuous invisibility of *facture* commanded by the power of a rigorously conceptual imagination, disposing of vast amounts of money. Those signals, received by a bewildered and apprehensive community (tribe? species?) of critics, have propelled them, all unwilling, into a chorus of dismay, a choreography of vacillation, of approach, and recoil, to and from the "object." We know that song and dance; they are the old, familiar projection of a crisis in criticism. And still the "object" lures us on. Another level or "universe" of discourse awaits us.

We are dealing, then, with a work which is revelatory, a "breakthrough," one whose substance and function fuse in the synthetic radicalization of its metaphors. It is precisely because form and surface command the most immediate and complex intensity of physical response that they release a wild energy of speculation, confirming, even as they modify, the character and options of the medium. In that oscillating movement between confirmation and transformation, the film as a whole performs the function of a Primary Structure, forcing the spectator back, in a reflexive gesture, upon the analytic rehearsal of his experience, impelling, as it does so, the conviction that here is a film like any other, like all others, only more so—which is to say, a paradigm, unique. (If one were concerned with an "ontology" of cinema, this film would be a place in which to look for it.) The margin of difference-in-similarity which contains or defines its "edge" over other films is the locus of its poetry.

The play of an inspired primate ("Moonwatcher" is Clarke's name for him) ending the Prologue of this film, issues in the visionary realization which transforms a bone into a weapon, then flings it in a gesture of apperceptive exultation, high into the vacant air. Meliès' extraordinary intuition, realizing (inventing) the possibilities of the medium, created out of forms and materials that lay to hand, a new instrument of the Imagination, an agent of power and delight, launching his cinema in confident optimism out into an unsuspecting world.

Kubrick's transformation of bone into spacecraft through the movement of redescent (through that single cut which concludes the Prologue and initiates the Odyssey) inscribes, within the most spectacular ellipsis in cinematic history, nothing less than the entire trajectory of human history, the birth and evolution of Intelligence. Seizing, appropriating the theme of spatial exploration as narrative metaphor and formal principle, he has projected intellectual adventure as spectacle, converting, through still another leap of the imagination, Meliès' pristine fantasy to the form and uses of a complex and supremely sophisticated structure.

Moving, falling toward us with the steady and purposive elegance of an incomparably powerful "vehicle," Kubrick's masterwork is designed, in turn, as an instrument of exploration and discovery. *A Space Odyssey* is, in fact, in the sustained concreteness and formal refinement which render that design, precisely that which Ortega believed modern poetry to have become: a "higher algebra of metaphors."

II

> The object in motion moves neither in the space
> in which it is nor in that in which it is not.
>
> *Zeno*
>
> The present hath no space.
> Where then is the time which we may call long?
>
> *Saint Augustine*

In a letter, undated but probably of 1894, Pierre Louys called upon Debussy, about to embark upon the career of music critic which produced the brilliant and insolent persona of "Monsieur Croche, Anti-Dilettante," to "do something" to cure the malady of contemporary criticism. Complaining that "one cannot strike a single chord these days without eliciting a flurry of metaphysical speculation," he says that *Lohengrin,* after all is a work "about movement." "It is about a man who arrives and departs," and nothing else. Or, as Valéry was shortly to say,

"The true connoisseur of this art is necessarily the person to whom it suggests nothing."

Like all statements of this kind, these strictures suggest a critical strategy rather than an esthetic, a working hypothesis formulated in terms of a particular historical situation, a re-orientation of critical concern in the interests of immediate usefulness and interest. Like Fénéon's descriptive criticism of painting, like Mallarmé's assertion, to Degas, that "poetry is made with words rather than with ideas," like Robbe-Grillet's attack on Metaphor, Stravinsky's rejection of musical "content" or "subject," and Artaud's indictment of theatrical text, they propose a therapy for an intellectual tradition in which, as in that of our current film criticism, an endemic and debilitating Idealism perpetuates exhausted critical categories. Reductive, double-edged, polemically inflected, they urge a closer, fresher, more innocent and comprehending view of the Object, a respect for form and physicality as the ground of interest and value.

Like *Lohengrin, Space Odyssey,* is, of course, endlessly suggestive, projects a syncretic heritage of myths, fantasies, cosmologies and aspirations. Everything about it is interesting; it proposes, however, nothing of more radical interest than its own physicality, its "formal statement" on the nature of movement in its space; it "suggests" nothing so urgent and absorbing as an evidence of the senses, its discourse on knowledge through perception as action, and ultimately, on the nature of the medium as "action film," as mode and model of cognition.

Reading the critical or journalistic reproaches (and defenses) addressed to this film's supposedly "static quality," its "plotless" structure in which "nothing happens," one recalls the myths which dominated a half-century or so of theatrical criticism's uncomprehending view of Chekhov, as of Wagner. In this *Odyssey,* incident, surprise, discovery, shock and violence abound. Its plot turns, in fact, upon *intrigue,* as the French define plot. And, like a "scenario" (the term adopted by contemporary technocrats such as Herman Kahn for their hypothetical projections of our future), its structure is "open." Like *Lohengrin* and *Uncle Vanya,* above all, however, this work is about "arrival and departure," about movement. Its narrative, a voyage of discovery, a progress towards disembodiment, explores, through a multi-level tactics of displacement, through a constant and intensive re-invention of the possibilities of cinematic immediacy, the structural potentialities of haptic disorientation as agent of cognition.

Navigation—of a vessel or human body—through a space in which gravitational pull is suspended, introduces heightened pleasures and problems, the intensification of erotic liberation and of the difficulty of purposeful activity. In that floating freedom, all directed and purposive movement becomes work, the simplest task an exploit. The new freedom poses for the mind, in and through the body, the problematic implications of all freedom, forcing the body's recognition of its suspended coördinates as its necessity. The dialectic of pleasure and performance principles, projected through camera's radical re-structuring of environment, the creation of ranges of change in light, scale, pace, heighten, to the point of transformation, the very conditions of film experience. Viewing becomes, as always but as never before, the discovery, through the acknowledgement of disorientation, of what it is to see, to learn, to know, and of what it is to be, seeing. Once the theatre seat has been transformed into a vessel, opening out onto and through the curve of a helmet to that of the screen as into the curvature of space, one rediscovers, through the shock of recognition, one's own body living in *its* space. One feels suspended, the mind not quite able to "touch ground." One surveys the familiar ground of experience (as the astronauts have indicated, remarking that a prime reason for space flight lay in the rediscovery and organization of the *earth's* resources), feeling the full meaning of "suspense" as anticipation, *sensing* that though things may possibly be the same again, they will, thanks to Kubrick, never be the same *in quite the same way*.

If, then, *Space Odyssey* proposes, as in Bergson's view all works of art do, "the outline of a movement," it is, as well what Elie Faure claimed all *film* to be: "an architecture of movement." As a film which takes for its very subject, theme and dynamics—both narrative and formal—movement itself, it has a radical, triple interest and urgency, a privileged status in the art that is ours, modern.

III

Form is tinted with meaning.

Quintilian, after Zeno

The secret of the true artist consists in the following:
he effaces nature through form.

Schiller

There is a moment—that present moment which extends a century back into the past—in which the entire system of presuppositions governing the artist's view of subject, content and theme is undermined. That moment initiates in the radical questioning of art as mimesis. It produces a shift or displacement of the artist's aspiration. The movement of displacement is by no means steady or uncontested, as the entirely problematic esthetic implicit in Expressionism (it is, after all, neither school nor style, but the name we give to sixty years of polymorphic contestation) insistently reminds us. In that shift, the culmination of a crisis sustained since the 17th century through philosophy, the authority of the imagination moves to replace that of a transcendence animating the esthetic of transcription or expression. Sustained through the radical art of our century, the shift is pre-figured in Flaubert's celebrated letter of January, 1852, to Louise Colet: "What I consider fine, what I should like to do is a book about nothing, a book without external attachments of any sort, which would hold of itself, through the inner strength of its style, as the earth sustains itself with no support in air, a book with almost no subject. Or at least an almost invisible subject, if possible."

This aspiration toward a work of total autonomy, self-referring, self-sustaining and self-justifying, required the invention of a mediating strategy, a transition. The subject could be eliminated only through a process of dissolution initiated by its re-definition. Therefore, Flaubert's subsequent affirmation, in a letter dated one year later: "Since poetry is purely subjective, there is no such thing as a fine subject. Yvetôt and Constantinople are of equal value. One can write equally well about anything at all. It is the artist who elevates things (through his manner of writing)." (The manner in and degree to which the history of pictorial and sculptural modernism confirms and embodies this position requires no immediate development in this particular journal.)

It is, however, at precisely that moment which instigates the dissolution of the subject, a process crystallized and extended through Mallarmé and Cézanne into the art of our own day, it is when the painter, rendering "seeing rather than things seen," takes painting as his subject, when the novelist commences the relating of "narrativity" itself, that art's aspiration shifts, expands, intensifies, tending, as in a movement of compensation, towards the most radical and all-encompassing of possible functions. Poetry, consenting through Mallarmé to be poetry only, proposes, simultaneously, to become "the orphic explanation of the earth," of a "world meant," moreover, "to end in a book." The dissolution of the subject or figure, the contestation of art as Mimesis, of Realism itself, is grounded in the problematic consciousness of a reality no longer assumed as pre-defined or pre-existent to the work of the imagination. Art now takes the nature of reality, the nature of consciousness in and through perception, as its subject or domain. As exploration of the conditions and terms of perception, art henceforth converges with philosophy and science upon the problem of reality as known and knowable.

Thus, the very ambiguity of Kandinsky's title for his esthetic treatise, *Towards The Spiritual in Art*—translatable, too, from the German as *Toward The Intellectual In Art*—defines with great precision the nature and locus of the shift. Its ambiguity spells out the problems involved in the relocation, through abstraction, of sources of authority, interest and aspiration, which had been dislodged by the crisis in the Western metaphysical tradition. Text and title re-enact, in their ambivalence and contradictions, that crisis; their celebrated "confusion" has the clarity of a syndrome, a syndrome converted into an esthetics bequeathed to us, somewhat in the manner of an hereditary taint or talent, in the sensibility of "Abstract Expressionism."

That movement towards abstraction which animates the style and esthetics of modernism posed, for every art form, the problem of what Ortega calls "the incompatibility of the perception of lived reality with the perception of artistic form," in so far as "they call for different adjustments of our perceptive apparatus." "An art that requires such a double seeing is a squinting art. The 19th century was cross-eyed . . . ." Ortega, speaking with a certain crudeness symptomatic of ambivalence, spoke far truer than he knew.

Surely that statement is nowhere more significant than in its central omission. It stops just short of the recognition that the 19th century ended in producing the cinema, the art form whose temporality created another space in which "lived reality" could once again be figured, restructured. Cinema is the temporal instrument working in a direction counter to that of modernist painting's increasingly shallow space, through which the deep space of illusionism is reinvented. In assuming the burden of illusionism, cinema reintroduces not only "lived reality," but an entirely new and seemingly limitless range of structural relationships allowing for the reconciliation of "lived reality" with "artistic form." In order to do so, of course, film not only rehabilitated the "squint," but elevated it to the status of a dynamics of creation and perception, installed it as the very central principle of an art form, the source of its power and refinement.

Film's relation to modernism is, consequently, delicate and complex in the extreme, and the demands it makes upon its audience have a strenuousness directly proportionate to that complexity and delicacy, contingent upon its illusionistic immediacy. Its fullest experience demands a kind of critical athleticism.

As all who care more than casually for movies know, the point at which one begins to understand the nature of the medium comes when one sees the images before one, not as a sequence of events evolving past or within the limits of a frame, but rather as a structure organized in depth and in relation to the frame by the camera itself. The heightened experience of film henceforth involves the constant oscillation between the two "points of view," the constant "adjustment of the perceptive apparatus" in an activity of experience. The trajectory of both narrative and of camera lens as the extension of the eye and will of the artist begins to describe itself for us when we see, as in the scene of the poisoning of the Czarina in *Ivan The Terrible,* that the slow and devious passage of a goblet through a room is the propulsion, to its destined victim, by design dissembled as chance, through a camera movement, the movement of History. Film's narrative now acquires the dimension of style, as the structural and sensuous incarnation of the artist's will.

One follows, in another celebrated instance, the trolley car ride of Murnau's *Sunrise,* moved to pity by the protagonist's agony of anguish and shame, *borne along,* from a country to a city landscape, *carried away,* as they emerge from an extremity of alienation into reconciliation as into the New Jerusalem, and ultimately *transported* by the movement of the camera, the artist's agent, his mind's eye, defining and sustaining the space and dimensions of narrative as form.

Film proposes, then, and most sharply when it is greatest, a dissociative economy of viewing. That is why, although its "dream-like" quality received an immediate and extensive entry in the Dictionary of Received Ideas, it remains to be stressed that cinema is, more than any other art form, that which Plato claimed art in general to be: *a dream for waking minds.* The paradox testifies to the manner in which film provokes that delicate dissociation, that *contraposto* of the mind, that constantly renewed tension and readjustment whose symptom is, indeed, Ortega's "squint."

If this distance, the alienation of the spectator with respect to his experience, reflecting the elevation of doubt to an esthetic principle, may be said to characterize modernist sensibility as a whole, determining, in fact, the intensity of its very longing for immediacy, then film's conversion of that principle to the uses of a formal dynamics gives it a privileged place as a medium centrally involved with the cognitive aspiration of modern art. The dissociative economy of film viewing heightens our perception of being physical to the level of apperception: one becomes conscious of the modes of consciousness. The athleticism required of the spectator is contingent on the manner in which film reflects or returns that which is brought to it. Like all esthetic situations, it offers—quite beyond the luxury of identification—the occasion to gain awareness of the inner presuppositions that sustain us, so that pleasure is informed with the shock of recognition.

A Space Odyssey, that film of "special effects" in which "nothing happens," is simply one which, in its extremity of stylistic formal coherence and richness, its totally reinvented environment, quite dissolves the very notion of the "special effect." They disappear. Above all, however, it solicits, in its overwhelming immediacy, the *relocation of the terrain upon which things happen.* And they happen, ultimately, not only on the screen but somewhere between screen and spectator. It is the area defined and constantly traversed by our active restructuring and reconstitution, through an experience of "outer" space, of the "inner" space of the body. Kubrick's film, its action generating a kind of cross-current of perception and cognitive restructuring, visibly reaches, as it were, for another arena, redefining the content of cinema, its "shape of content." The subject and theme of *A Space Odyssey* emerge, then, as neither social nor metaphysical; they develop elsewhere, between, in a genetic epistemology.

IV

> My mobility is the way in which I counterbalance the mobility of things,
> thereby understanding and surmounting it.
> All perception is movement.
> And the world's unity, the perceiver's unity,
> are the unity of counterbalanced displacements.
>
> *Merleau-Ponty*

> All things in the heaven of intelligibility are heavenly . . . .
> In this kingdom, all is diaphanous.
> Nothing is opaque or inpenetrable, and light encounters light.
> No traveler wanders there as in a foreign land.
>
> *Plotinus*

This Odyssey traces, then, in its "higher algebra of metaphors," the movement of bodies in space, voyaging, through spheres beyond the pull of terrestrial attraction, in exploration of the Unknown, in and through *Discovery*.

The Voyage as narrative form acts, in its deformation or suspension of the familiar framework of existence (as in the logic of Alice, the geography of Saint Brendan, the reality of Don Quixote, the sociology of Gulliver), to project us, as in space travel, toward the surface of a distant world, its propulsive force contriving, through a Logistics of the Imagination, to redeliver us in rebound from that surface, into the familiar, the known, the Real.

So, too, the voyage of the astronauts ultimately restores us, through the heightened and complex immediacy of this film, to the space in which we dwell. This navigation of a vessel as instrument of exploration, of the human organism as adventurer, dissolves the opposition of body and mind, *bringing home* to us the manner in which "objective spatiality" is but the envelope of that "primordial spatiality," the level on which the body itself effects the synthesis of its commitments in the world, a synthesis which is a fusion of meaning as experienced, tending toward equilibrium.

By constantly questioning that "objective spatiality," Kubrick incarnates the grand theme and subject of learning as self-recognition, of growth as the constant disruption and re-establishment of equilibrium in progress towards knowledge. This succession of re-establishments of equilibrium proposes a master metaphor for the mind at grips with reality, and we re-enact its progress through a series of disconcerting shocks which solicit our accommodation.

As soon as the airline hostess starts her movement through the space-craft's interior, moving up the wall, around and over the ceiling, disappearing upside down into it, we get an intimation—through the shock of surprise instigated by the defiance of our gravity—of the nature of our movement in our space. The delight we take in the absurdity of her progress is the index of our heightened awareness of something fundamental in ourselves. The system of pre-suppositions sustaining our spatial sense, the coördinates of the body itself, are hereby suspended and revised. That revision and its acknowledgment constitute our passport into another space and state of being, from which our own can be observed and known.

The writing pen floating in the space-craft's cabin and retrieved by the hostess prior to her movement over wall and into ceiling had signalled to us, as it were, the passage into the weightless medium. Since, however, we define and comprehend movement—and repose—in terms of our own bodily positions, through the sense of inner coördinates rather than in terms of what is merely seen, that signal could not fully prepare us for, or inform us of, the suspension of those coördinates, inevitable in the weightless environment. (And indeed, judging from the surprised laughter that has followed that second sequence in each of nine viewings of the film, it does not prepare us.) The difference between the two qualities and intensities of response is the difference between things seen and things felt, between situations visually observed and those sensed between a narrative emblem and a radically formal embodiment of, spatial logic.

A weightless world is one in which the basic coördinates of horizontality and verticality are suspended. Through that suspension the framework of our sensed and operational reality is dissolved. The consequent challenge presented to the spectator in the instantaneously perceived suspension and frustration of expectations, forces readjustment. The challenge is met almost instantaneously, and consciousness of our own physical necessity is regenerated. We snap to attention, in a new, immediate sense of our earth-bound state, in repossession of those coördinates, only to be suspended, again, toward other occasions and forms of recognition. These constitute the "subplot" of the Odyssey, plotting its action in us.

The extraordinary repetitive sequence of the woman climbing a staircase in Léger's *Ballet Mecanique* erases the possibility of destination or of completion of action, thereby freezing a woman in a perpetual motion of ascent. So, too, this first sequence of the air-hostess's navigation (and it is only one of an amazing series of variations upon the qualities and modes of movement) suspends us, in its frustration and inversion of our expectations, impelling us to a reflexive or compensatory movement of reversal, clarifying for us something of the essential nature of motion itself.

By distorting or suspending the logic of action as we know it (movement's completion in time, the operation of the coördinates), each sequence questions, thereby stimulating awareness of, the corporeal *a-prioris* which compose our sensory motor apparatus. Sensing, after the fifth ascent or so that Léger's woman will never "arrive," we re-direct our attention, in a movement of recognition, to the fact and quality of movement as such. The recognition of paradox speaks through our laughter, arguing for that double nature of Comedy as Bergson saw it; its delight in the concrete and its unique capacity for play with ideas.

In their reduction of people moving to bodies in motion, both sequences elicit the laughter which Bergson tells us is the response to that transformation or reduction of the human into the mechanical which underlies all comedy. Solicited, then, through a constantly playful succession of surprises to a re-assessment or re-structuring of the real, we see, in our surprised laughter, that here is a work which employs a very serious form of wit to teach us something of the nature of our experience.

A Space Odyssey, then, proposes, in its epistemology, the illustration of a celebrated theory of Comedy. In a film whose terrain or scene of action is, as we have seen, the spectator, the spectator becomes the hero or butt of comedy. The laugh is on us; we trip on circumstance, recognizing, in a reflex of double-take, that circumstances have changed. Tending, in the moment which precedes this recognition, "to see that which is no longer visible," assuming the role of absent-minded comic hero, "taken in," we then adjust in comprehension, "taking it in." Kubrick does make Keatons of us all.

If "any incident is comic that calls our attention to the physical in a person, when it is the moral side that is concerned," *Space Oydssey* indeed provides, through variation and inversion, a fascinating range of comic situations. (On quite another level, of course HAL, the computer as character, reverses the comic "embarrassment of the soul by the body" in being a mere body embarrassed by possession of a soul. A thing which gives the impression of being a person, rather than—as in silent comedy at its paroxysmic best—a person giving the impression of being a thing, "he *acts* as though he has feelings," as one astronaut remarks. Here, God help us, is someone or something who, as R. D. Laing says, "can pretend to be what he—or it—really is.")

As a film whose grand theme is that of learning, whose effect is intimately revelatory, *A Space Odyssey* is, in the strongest and deepest sense of the word, maieutic. Kubrick's imagination, exploring the possibilities of scale, movement, direction as synthesized in a style, works towards our understanding. The intensified and progressively intimate consciousness of one's physicality provides the intimation of that physicality as the ground of consciousness. The film's "action" is felt and we are "where the action is." Its "meaning" or "sense" is sensed, and its content is the body's perceptive awaking to itself.

The briefest, most summary comparison with *Alphaville* shows Godard's film to be, as I have on another occasion suggested, a film of "dis-location," as against this new film of "dis-orientation." Godard installs the future within the landscape of present-day Paris, dislocating the spectator *in situ,* so to speak. Kubrick's suspension and distention of the properties of environment transform it into something radically new and revealing. The difference between the two films is also, of course, the difference between the strategies of *bricolage* or a "do-it-yourself" technique, brilliantly handled, and of technology. Two attitudes toward futurity are inscribed within the conditions of their making.

Alphaville's superimposition of image upon image, of word upon word, of plot upon plot, creates a complex system of visual, verbal and narrative puns within which past and future alternatively and reciprocally mask and reveal each other. Futurity inhabits things as they look now. It is installed, moreover, as a *corruption* of the here-and-now, projecting Godard's essential romanticism in a dislocation that is primarily fictional in its tactics. Figurative, one might say. In this film, Godard, like his Eurydice, looks backward in nostalgia.

In *Space Odyssey,* a total formalization imposes futurity through the eye and ear. The look and sense of things is in their movement, scale, sound, pace and intensity. Unlike most other science fiction films, both unflaggingly sustain a coherent visual style. All others (from *Metropolis* through the *Buck Rogers* series to *Barbarella*) relax, about halfway through, capitulating in a relaxation of the will, a fatigue of the imagination, to the past. (It is generally a Gothic past, a style of medievalism, and these two films are probably the only ones utterly devoid of billowing capes and Gothic arches.) The manner in which both exemplify film's pre-empting of the function, the esthetic mode, of Visionary Architecture, begun by Meliès, presents a striking contrast: Godard adopts a policy of abstinence, of invention in austerity, Kubrick a planned and prodigal expenditure of resources. (The manner in which the different economies at work—European as against American—seem to represent opposing sensibilities making fundamentally esthetic decisions, leads one to remember that Godard's Computer—a Sphinx, speaking with the re-educated voice of a man whose vocal chords have been removed—asks questions, while Hal, that masterpiece of "the third Computer breakthrough," presumably knows all the answers.)

Kubrick's prodigality is, however, totalizing, heightens, through the complete re-invention of environment, the terms, the stylistic potential of cinematic discourse. Therefore, one's thrilled fascination with the majestic movements of the spacecraft through the heavens, with the trajectories of arrival (landing), departure (levitation), seeing (sighting), conjunction (synthesis), action (gauging) through which the parameters of movement, scale, direction, intensity are examined, exploited. Suspended, totally absorbed by their momentous navigation, one remembers only days later, the manner in which the slow, repetitive lifting of the bridge in *Ten Days That Shook The World* shattered action, inventing, in its radically disjunctive force, another kind of cinematic time. The number and kinds of space simultaneously proposed by isometric readings and interior projections—as in the approach toward the space station or in the landing on the Moon—are fused by the spectator who discovers, with a sudden thrill of delight, that *he* is the meeting place of a multiplicity of spaces, depths and scales, his eye their agent of reconciliation, his body the focal point of a multi-dimensional, poly-spatial cosmos.

In the visionary catapulting through the "Star Gate," "beyond infinity," through galactic explosions of forms and sound as landscape, we zoom over a geography photographed in "negative," passing finally, as through a portal, to a scene which reveals itself to be that of the eye itself. Experience as Vision ends in the exploration of seeing. The film's reflexive strategy assumes the eye as ultimate agent of consciousness, reminding us, as every phenomenological esthetic, from that of Ortega to that of Merleau-Ponty, has, that art develops from the concern with "things seen to that of seeing itself."

In a series of expansions and contractions, the film pulsates, leading us, in the final sequence following the "trip," with the astronaut into a suite of rooms, decorated in Regency style. Here, every quality of particularity, every limiting, defining aspect of environment is emphasized. The sudden contraction into these limits, projects us from galactic polymorphism into an extreme formality, insinuating, through the allusion of its décor, the idea of History into Timelessness. It shocks. Everything about the place is defined, clearly "drawn." In the definition of this room lit from beneath the floor, as in the drainage of color (everything is greenish, a bit milky, translucent, reminding one slightly of video images), we perceive the triumph of *disegno* over *colore*. An Idea of a Room, it elaborates the notion of Idea and Ideality as Dwelling. (Poincaré, after all, imagined Utopia as illustrating Riemann's topology.) It is, of course, a temporary dwelling—Man's last Motel stop on the journey towards disembodiment and renascence. Its very sounds are sharper; the clatter of glass falling to the floor informs us that glass is breaking upon glass, evoking through an excruciation of high-fidelity acoustics, something of the nature of Substance. It is this strange, Platonic intensification-through-reduction of the physical which sustains the stepping-up of time, through the astronaut's life and death, to rebirth, ejecting us with him once again, through a final contracting movement of parturition, into the heavens.

V

Structural formation, that reflective process of abstraction
which draws its sustenance not from objects,
but from actions performed upon them.

Piaget

However, the fact that knowledge can be used to designate sexual intercourse . . .
points to the fact that for the Hebrews, "to know" does not simply mean
to be aware of the existence or nature of a particular object.
Knowledge implies also the awareness of the specific relationship
in which the individual stands with that object,
or of the significance the object has for him.

The Interpreter's Dictionary of the Bible

If *A Space Odyssey* illustrates, through its exercise in genetic epistemology, the manner of our acting, it provides the immediate demonstration that the ability to function in space is neither given nor predetermined, but acquired and developed.

Its re-establishment of the notion of equilibrium as open process is central. In a weightless medium, the body confronts the loss of those coordinates through which it normally functions. The manner in which all directed movement is endowed with the momentousness of the task indicates the reinvention of those coördinates for operational efficiency. Total absorption in their reinvention creates a form of motion of extraordinary unity, that of total concentration, the precondition of Style, a style we normally recognize as the quality of dance movement.

It would be interesting, then, to consider a style of movement created by the exact inversion of that negation of weight (its retrieval, in fact), which animates the Dance of our Western historical tradition. More interesting, still, perhaps, is the realization that the style created by the astronauts in movement, in the reinvention of necessity, does indeed have a special affinity with that contemporary dance which proceeds from the radical questioning of balletic movement, the redefining and rehabilitation of the limits of habitual, operational movement as an esthetic or stylistic mode.

In that questioning, initiated by Cunningham, radicalized through the work of Rainer, Whitman, Paxton, and others, dance is re-thought in terms of another economy, through the systematic negation of the rhetoric and hierarchies imposed by classical balletic conventions and language. That rhetoric is, in fact, reversed, destroyed, in what has been called the "dance of ordinary language" and of "task performance." This movement of reversal—revolutionary—traversing the forms of most modernist art, works in Dance as well, toward "the dissolution of the (fine) subject."

The astronauts' movement—as in the very great sequence of the repair of the presumably malfunctioning parts—is invested with an intensity of interest (sustaining itself through every second of its repetition), a "gravity" which is that of total absorption in operational movement (task performance) as a constant reinvention of equilibrium in the interests of functional efficiency. The stress is on the importance, "the fascination of what's difficult," which is to say, the simplest operations. They require the negation of a floating freedom. (It should have been the business of Vadim's recently released *Barbarella* to explore the erotic possibilities of the body floating free in outer space suggested by that film's superb opening credits. Unfortunately *Barbarella's* progress is entirely earthbound; the film is a triumph of iconography over form.)

The astronauts' movements, slowed by weightlessness, reinvent the conditions of their efficiency. This slowness and the majesty with which the space-craft itself moves, are predicated, of course, upon the speed of space travel itself. And the film itself moves ultimately with that momentum, that apparent absence of speed which one experiences only in the fastest of elevators, or jet planes.

The complex maneuvering of tools, craft or the mere navigation of the body involves an adjustment which constitutes an adventure, a stage in the development of the Mind. Seeing films, in general, one gains an intimation of the link between the development of sensory-motor knowledge to that of intelligence itself.

We know, through the systematic investigations which constitute the monumental life-work of Piaget, that the acquisition of the basic coördinates of our spatial sense is a very gradual process, extending roughly over the first twelve years of our lives. There is, presumably, no difference in kind between the development of verbal logic and the logic inherent in coordination of action. Both involve the progress through successive adjustments to perturbation which re-establish, in an open process and through a succession of states of equilibrium, the passage from a "pre-operational" stage, to that of concrete operations, and finally to abstract operations. *"The logic of actions is, however, the deepest and most primitive."*

And here, of course, lies the explanation of the *Space Odyssey's* effect upon its audiences, the manner in which it exposes a "generation gap." This film has "separated the men from the boys"—with implications by no means flattering for the "men."

"Human action consists in the continual mechanism of readjustment and equilibration . . . one can consider the successive mental structures engendered by development as so many forms of equilibrium each representing a progress over the preceding ones. On each successive level the mind fulfills the same function, which is to incorporate the universe, but the structure of assimilation varies. The elaboration of the notion of space is due to the coordination of movements, and this development is closely linked to those of sensory-motor awareness and of intelligence itself." [3]

The structures are to be comprehended in terms of the genetic process linking them. This Piaget calls equilibrium, defined as a process rather than a state, and it is the succession of these stages which defines the evolution of intelligence, each process of equilibration ending in the creation of a new state of disequilibrium. This is the manner of the development of the child's intelligence.

"The development of the coordinates of horizontality and verticality are not innate, but are constructed through physical experience, acquired through the ability to read one's experience and interpret it, and both reading and interpretation always suppose a deductive system capable of assuring the intellectual assimilation of the experience. The construction of the system of coordinates of horizontality and verticality is extremely complex . . . it is, in effect, not the point of departure of spatial knowledge, but the end point of the entire psychological construction of Euclidian space."

And Kubrick has proposed, in the *Space Odyssey,* a re-enactment of the very process of sensory-motor habit formation, soliciting, through the disturbance and re-establishment of equilibrium, the recapitulation of that fundamental educative process which effects "our incorporation of the world." *Space Odyssey* makes the experience of learning both plot and sub-plot of an Action or Adventure film. An invitation to a voyage, it proposes the re-enactment of an initiation, sustained *rite de passage,* "The Passage into Euclidian Space."

The young are, of course, still closer to that slow development of the body's wisdom, to the forming of the sensory-motor apparatus. Above all, however, they are more openly disposed to that kind of formal transcription of the fundamental learning process which negates, in and through its form, the notion of equilibrium as a state of definition, of rest in finality.

To be "mature" in our culture is to be "well-balanced," "centered," not easily "thrown off balance." Acceptance of imbalance is, however, the condition of receptivity to this film. Our "maturity" pre-supposes the "establishment" of experience as acquisition, the primacy of wisdom as knowledge over that of intellectual exploration, of achievement over aspiration. "Adventure," as Simmel observes in an essay of remarkable beauty,[4] "is, in its specific nature and charm, a form of experiencing. Not the content but the experiential tension determines the adventure. In youth the accent falls on the process of life, on its rhythms and antinomies; in old age, it falls on life's substance, compared to which experience . . . appears relatively incidental. This contrast between youth and age, which makes adventure the prerogative of youth may be expressed as the contrast between the romantic and the historical spirit of life. Life in its immediacy counts (for youth). . . . The fascination is not so much in the substance, but rather the adventurous form of experiencing it, the intensity and excitement with which it lets us feel life. What is called the subjectivity of youth is just this; the material of life in its substantive significance is not as important to youth as is the process which carries it, life itself."

The critical performance around this film, object, Structure, revolving as it has about the historical, anecdotal, sociological, concerned as it is with the texture of incident is, of course, the clear projection of aging minds and bodies. Its hostile dismissal constitutes, rather like its timid defense, an expression of fatigue. This film of adventure and of action, of action as adventure is an event, an extraordinary occasion for self-recognition, and it offers, of course, the delights and terrors occasions of that sort generally provide. Positing a space which, overflowing screen and field of vision, converts the theatre into a vessel and its viewers into passengers, it impels us, in the movement from departure to arrival, to rediscover the space and dimensions of the body as theatre of consciousness. Youth in us, discarding the spectator's decorum, responds, in the movement of final descent, as to "the slap of the instant," quickening in a tremor of rebirth, revelling in a knowledge which is *carnal*.

NOTES

1 That photograph, currently unavailable for reproduction, obviously differs from the one reproduced here.

2 For a consideration of this question one does well to compare Meliès admirable text, *Vues Cinématographiques,* reprinted in the catalog of the commemorative exhibition (Paris, 1961), which encompasses, within 15 densely printed pages, a basic course in filmmaking and a discussion of the formal and technical problems involved and resolved in his own work, with the information on the making of 2001: *A Space Odyssey* provided by the *Journal of the American Cinematographer,* June 1968, Vol. 49 no. 6. The parallels on all parameters are striking. In the production of this particular *grande machine,* the use and invention of meta-machines resulted, as one might expect (in a medium, whose history is, more than any, tied to technological development), a number of technical breakthroughs recalling or extending those created by Meliès himself. Here are a very few:

a. Kubrick directed the action in the centrifuge sequences from outside by watching a closed circuit monitor relaying a picture from a small video camera mounted next to the film camera inside the centrifuge itself.

b. In order to attain a slow and "large-scale" movement of doors and other parts, motors were made to drive these mechanisms, then "geared down so far that the actual motion, frame by frame was imperceptible. 'We shot most of these scenes,' says Kubrick, 'using slow exposures of 4 seconds per frame. One couldn't see the movement. A door moving 5 inches during a scene would take 5 hours to shoot. You could never see any unsteady movement. It was like watching the hand of a clock.' "

c. "For the Stargate sequence, a slit-scan machine was designed, using a technique of image scanning as used in scientific and industrial photography. This device could produce two seemingly infinite planes of exposure while holding depth-of-field from a distance of 15 feet to 1½ inches from the lens at an aperture of F ⅛ with exposures of approximately one minute per frame using a standard 65 mm. Mitchell camera."

d. "A huge 10 by 8 foot transparency plate projector for the application of the Alekan-Gerrard method of front-projected transparency" was constructed for the primates sequence. It is expected to open up enormous possibilities for future film production.

3 For detailed consideration of the notion of equilibrium as open learning process, I refer the reader to Piaget's *La Représentation De L'Espace Chez L'Enfant,* Presses Universitaires de France, Paris, 1948, and most particularly to the chapter entitled *Le Passage à L'Espace Euclidien.* Further discussion of this notion and of the development of spatial coordinates is to be found in Volumes 5 and 6 of *Etudes Epistémologiques,* Presses Universitaires, Paris, as well as in *Six Etudes Psychologiques,* Editions Gonthier, Geneva, 1964.

4 *The Adventure,* in George Simmel, *Essays on Sociology, Philosophy and Aesthetics,* Harper and Row, New York, 1965.

31

Le Journal d'un Curé de Campagne and the Stylistics of Robert Bresson

André Bazin

If *The Diary of a Country Priest* impresses us as a masterpiece, and this with an almost physical impact, if it moves the critic and the uncritical alike, it is primarily because of its power to stir the emotions, rather than the intelligence, at their highest level of sensitivity. The temporary eclipse of *Les Dames du Bois de Boulogne* was for precisely the opposite reason. This film could not stir us unless we had, if not exactly analyzed, at least tested its intellectual structure and, so to speak, understood the rules of the game.

While the instantaneous success of *Le Journal* is undeniable, the aesthetic principles on which it is based are nevertheless the most paradoxical, maybe even the most complex, ever manifest in a sound film. Hence the refrain of those critics, ill-equipped to understand it. "Paradoxical," they say, "incredible—an unprecedented success that can never be repeated." Thus they renounce any attempt at explanation and take refuge in the perfect alibi of a stroke of genius. On the other hand, among those whose aesthetic preferences are of a kind with Bresson's and whom one would have unhesitatingly thought to be his allies, there is a deep sense of disappointment in proportion as they expected greater acts of daring from him.

First embarrassed, then irritated by the realization of what the director did not do, yet too long in accord with him to be able to change their views on the spot; too caught up in his style to recapture their intellectual virginity which would have left the way open to emotion, they have neither understood nor liked the film.

Thus we find the critical field divided into two extreme groups. At one end those least equipped to understand *Le Journal* and who, by the same token, have loved it all the more without knowing why; at the other end those "happy few" who, expecting something different, have not liked it and have failed to understand it. It is the strangers to the cinema, the men of letters, amazed that they could so love a film and be capable of freeing their minds of prejudice, who have understood what Bresson had in mind more clearly than anyone else.

Admittedly Bresson has done his best to cover his tracks. His avowal of fidelity to the original from the first moment that he embarked on the adaptation, his declared intention of following the book word-for-word conditioned us to look for just that and the film only serves to prove it. Unlike Aurenche and Bost, who were preoccupied with the optics of the screen and the balance of their drama in its new form, Bresson, instead of building up the minor characters like the parents in *Le Diable au corps,* eliminated them. He prunes even the very essentials, giving an impression as he does so of a fidelity unable to sacrifice one single word without a pucker of concern and a thousand preliminary twinges of remorse. Again this pruning is always in the interest of simplification, never of addition. It is no exaggeration to say that if Bernanos had written the screenplay he would have taken greater liberties with his novel. He had, indeed, explicitly recognized the right of the adaptor to make use of his book according to the requirements of the cinema, the right that is "to dream his story over."

However, if we praise Bresson for his fidelity, it is for the most insidious kind of fidelity, a most pervasive form of creative license. Of course, one clearly cannot adapt without transposing. In that respect, Bernanos was on the side of aesthetic common sense. Literal translations are not the faithful ones. The changes that Aurenche and Bost made to *Le Diable au corps* are almost all entirely justified in principle. A character on the screen and the same character as evoked by the novelist are not identical.

Valéry condemned the novel for being obliged to record that "the

Marquise had tea at five o'clock." On his side, the novelist might in turn pity the film-maker for having to show the marquise actually at the table. It is for this reason that the relatives of the heroes in Radiguet, peripheral in the novel, appear important on the screen. The adaptor, however, must be as concerned with the text as with the characters and with the threat of their physical presence to the balance of the story. Having transformed the narrative into visuals, the film-maker must put the rest into dialogue, including the existing dialogue of the novel although we expect some modification of the latter—since spoken as written, its effectiveness and even its meaning will normally evaporate.

It is here that we see the paradoxical effect of the textual fidelity of *Le Journal*.

While the characters in the book are presented to the reader in high relief and while their inevitably brief evocation by the pen of the curé of Ambricourt never gives us a feeling of frustration or of any limits being put both to their existence and to our knowledge of their existence, Bresson, in the process of showing them to us, is forever hurrying them out of sight. In place of the powerfully concrete evocations of the novelist, the film offers us an increasingly impoverished image which escapes us because it is hidden from us and is never really developed.

The novel of Bernanos is rich in picturesque evocations, solid, concrete, strikingly visual. For example: "The Count went out—his excuse the rain. With every step the water oozed from his long boots. The three or four rabbits he had shot were lumped together in the bottom of his game-bag in a horrible-looking little pile of bloodstained mud and grey hair. He had hung the string bag on the wall and as he talked to me I saw fixed on me, through the intertwining cords, a still limpid and gentle eye."

Do you feel you have seen all this somewhere before? Don't bother to look where. It was probably in a Renoir film. Now compare this scene with the other in which the count brings the two rabbits to the presbytery—admittedly this comes later in the book but the two could have profitably been combined, thus giving them a style in common—and if you still have any doubts, Bresson's own admission will remove them. Forced to throw out a third of his final cut for the exhibitor's copy he ended, as we know, by declaring with a delicate touch of cynicism that he was delighted to have had to do so. Actually, the only "visual" he really cared about was the blank screen at the finale, which we will discuss later.

If he had really been faithful to the book, Bresson would have made quite a different film. Determined though he was to add nothing to the original—already a subtle form of betrayal by omission—he might at least have chosen to sacrifice the more literary parts for the many passages of ready-made film material that cried out for visualization. Yet he systematically took the opposite course. When you compare the two, it is the film that is literary while the novel teems with visual material.

The way he handles the text is even more revealing. He refuses to put into dialogue (I hardly dare to say "film dialogue") those passages from the novel where the curé enters in his diary the report of such-and-such a conversation. Here is a first discrepancy, since Bernanos at no point guarantees that the curé is giving a word for word report of what he heard. The odds are that he is not. In any event, supposing he *is,* and that Bresson has it in mind to preserve, along with the objective image, the subjective character of something remembered, it is still true that the mental and emotional impact of a line that is merely read is very different from that of a spoken line.

Now, not only does he not adapt the dialogue, however circumspectly, to the demands of a performance, he goes out of his way, on the contrary, whenever the text of the novel has the rhythm and balance of true dialogue, to prevent the actor from bringing out these qualities. Thus a good deal of excellent dramatic dialogue is thrown away because of the flat monotone in which the director insists that it be delivered.

Many complimentary things have been said about *Les Dames du Bois de Boulogne,* very little about the adaptation. The critics have, to all intents and purposes, treated the film as if it was made from an original screenplay. The outstanding quality of the dialogue has been attributed to Cocteau, whose reputation has little need of such praise. This is because they have not reread *Jacques le fataliste,* in which they would have found if not the entire script, at least the evidence of a subtle game of hide and go seek, word for word, with the text of Diderot. While it did not make one feel one ought to go back to verify the fact at close quarters, the modern version left one with the impression that Bresson had taken liberties with the story and retained simply the situation and, if you like, a certain eighteenth-century flavor. Since, in addition, he had killed off two or three writers under him, so to speak, it was reasonable to suppose that he was that many steps away from the original. However I recommend fans of *Les Dames du Bois de Boulogne* and aspiring scenarists alike to take a second look at the film with these considerations in mind. Without intending in any way to detract from the decisive part played by the style of the direction in the success of the film, it is important to examine very closely the foundations of this success, namely a marvellously subtle interplay—a sort of counterpoint between faithfulness and unfaithfulness to the original.

It has been suggested in criticism of *Les Dames du Bois de Boulogne,* with equal proportions of good sense and misunderstanding, that the psychological make-up of the characters is out of key with the society in which they are shown as living. True, it is the mores of the time that, in the novel of Diderot, justify the choice of the revenge and give it its effectiveness. It is true again that this same revenge seems to the modern spectator to be something out of the blue, something beyond his experience. It is equally useless on the other hand for those who defend the film to look for any sort of social justification for the characters. Prostitution and pandering as shown in the novel are facts with a very clear and solid contemporary social context. In the film of *Les Dames* they are all the more mystifying since they have no basic justification. The revenge of an injured mistress who forces her unfaithful lover to marry a luscious cabaret dancer seems to us to be a ridiculous gesture. Nor can the fact that the characters appear to be abstractions be explained by deliberate cuts made by the director during the filming. They are that way in the script. The reason Bresson does not tell us more about his characters is not because he has no desire to, but because he would be hard put to do so. Racine does not describe the color of the wall paper in the rooms to which his characters retire. To this one may answer, of course, that classical tragedy has no need of the alibis of realism and that this is one of the basic differences between the theater and the cinema. That is true enough. It is also precisely why Bresson does not derive his cinematographic abstraction simply from the bare episodes but from the counterpoint that the reality of the situation sets up with itself. In *Les Dames du Bois de Boulogne,* Bresson has taken the risk of transferring one realistic story into the context of another. The result is that these two examples of realism cancel one another out, the passions displayed emerge out of the characters as if from a chrysalis, the action from the twists and turns of the plot, and the tragedy from the trappings of the drama. The sound of a windshield-wiper against a page of Diderot is all it took to turn it into Racinian dialogue. Obviously Bresson is not aiming at absolute realism. On the other hand, his stylized treatment of it does not have the pure abstract quality of a symbol. It is rather a structured presentation of the abstract and concrete, that is to say of the reciprocal interplay of seemingly incompatible elements. The rain, the murmur of a waterfall, the sound of earth pouring from a broken pot, the hooves of a horse on the cobblestones, are not there just as a contrast to the simplification of the sets or the convention of the costumes, still less as a contrast to the literary and anachronistic flavor of the dialogue. They are not needed either for dramatic antithesis or for a contrast in decor. They are there deliberately as neutrals, as foreign bodies, like a grain of sand that gets into and seizes up a piece of machinery. If the arbitrariness of their choice resembles an abstraction, it is the abstraction of the concrete integral. They are like lines drawn across an image to affirm its transparency, as the dust affirms the transparency of a diamond; it is impurity at its purest.

This interaction of sound and decor is repeated in the very midst of elements which seem at first to be completely stylized. For example, the two apartments of the women are almost totally unfurnished but this calculated bareness has its explanation. That the frames should be on the walls though the paintings have been sold is undoubtedly a deliberate touch of realism. The abstract whiteness of the new apartment is not intended as part of a pattern of theatrical expressionism. The apartment is white because it has just been repainted and the smell of fresh paint still hangs about. Is there any need to add to this list the elevator or the concierge's telephone, or, on the sound track, the tumult of male voices that follows the face-slapping of Agnes, the text for which reads totally conventionally while the sound quality of it is absolute perfection.

I have referred to *Les Dames* in discussing *Le Journal* because it is important to point out the profound similarity between the mechanics of their respective adaptations.

The style of *Le Journal* indicates a more systematic searching, a rigor that is almost unbearable. It was made under very different technical conditions. Yet we shall see that the procedure was in each case basically the same. In both it was a matter of getting to the heart of a story or of a drama, of achieving the most rigorous form of aesthetic abstraction while avoiding expressionism by way of an interplay of literature and realism, which added to its cinematic potential while seeming to negate it. In any case, Bresson's faithfulness to his model is the alibi of liberty in chains. If he is faithful to the text this is because it serves his purpose better than taking useless liberties. Furthermore, this respect for the letter is, in the last analysis, far more than an exquisite embarrassment, it is a dialectical moment in the creation of a style.

So it is pointless to complain that paradoxically Bresson is at one and the same time the slave and the master of his text because it is precisely from this seeming contradiction that he gets his effects. Henri Agel, for example, describes the film as a page of Victor Hugo rewritten in the style of de Nerval. But surely one could imagine poetic results born of this monstrous coupling, of unexpectedly revealing flashes touched off by a translation made not just from one language into another (like Mallarmé's translation of Poe) but from one style and one content into the style of another artist and from the material of one art transposed into the material of another.

Let us look a little more closely now at *Le Journal* and see what in it has not really come off. While not wishing to praise Bresson for all his weak spots, for there are weaknesses, rare ones, which work to his disadvantage, we can say quite definitely that they are all an integral part of his style; they are simply that kind of awkwardness to which a high degree of sensibility may lead, and if Bresson has any reason here for self-congratulation, it is for having had the sense to see in that awkwardness the price he must pay for something more important.

So, even if the acting in general seems poor, except for Laydu all the time and for Nicole Lamiral some of it, this, provided you like the film, will only appear to be a minor defect. But now we have to explain why Bresson who directed his cast so superbly in *Les Anges du péché* and *Les Dames du Bois de Boulogne* seems to handle them in this film as amateurishly as any tyro with a camera who has roped in his aunt and the family lawyer. Do people really imagine that it was easier to get Maria Casarès to play down her talent than to handle a group of docile amateurs? Certainly some scenes were poorly acted. It is odd however that these were by no means the least moving.

The fact is that this film is not to be measured by ordinary standards of acting. It is important to remember that the cast were all either amateurs or simple beginners. *Le Journal* no more approximates to *Ladri di Biciclette* than to *L'Entrée des artistes*. Actually the only film it can be likened to is Carl Dreyer's *Jeanne d'Arc*. The cast is not being asked to act out a text, not even to live it out, just to speak it. It is because of this that the passages spoken off-screen so perfectly match the passages spoken by the characters on-screen. There is no fundamental difference either in tone or style. This plan of attack not only rules out any dramatic interpretation by the actors but also any psychological touches either. What we are asked to look for on their faces is not for some fleeting reflection of the words but for an uninterrupted condition of soul, the outward revelation of an interior destiny.

Thus this so-called badly acted film leaves us with the feeling of having seen a gallery of portraits whose expressions could not be other than they were. In this respect the most characteristic of all is de Chantal in the confessional. Dressed in black, withdrawn into the shadows,

Nicole Lamiral allows us only a glimpse of a mask, half lit, half in shadow, like a seal stamped on wax, all blurred at the edges.

Naturally Bresson, like Dreyer, is only concerned with the countenance as flesh, which, when not involved in playing a role, is a man's true imprint, the most visible mark of his soul. It is then that the countenance takes on the dignity of a sign. He would have us be concerned here not with the psychology but with the physiology of existence. Hence the hieratic tempo of the acting, the slow ambiguous gestures, the obstinate recurrence of certain behavioral patterns, the unforgettable dream-like slow motion. Nothing purely accidental could happen to these people—confirmed as each is in his own way of life, essentially concerned either against the influence of grace, to continue so, or, responding to grace, to throw off the deadly Nessus-mantle of the old Adam.

There is no development of character. Their inner conflicts, the various phases of their struggle as they wrestle with the Angel of the Lord, are never outwardly revealed. What we see is rather a concentration of suffering, the recurrent spasms of childbirth or of a snake sloughing off its skin. We can truly say that Bresson strips his characters bare.

Eschewing psychological analysis, the film in consequence lies outside the usual dramatic categories. The succession of events is not constructed according to the usual laws of dramaturgy under which the passions work towards a soul-satisfying climax. Events do indeed follow one another according to a necessary order, yet within a framework of accidental happenings. Free acts and coincidences are interwoven. Each moment in the film, each set-up, has its own due measure, alike, of freedom and of necessity. They all move in the same direction, but separately like iron filings drawn to the overall surface of a magnet. If the word tragedy comes to one's pen, it is in an opposite sense since we can only be dealing here with a tragedy freely willed. The transcendence of the Bernanos-Bresson universe is not the transcendence of destiny as the ancients understood it, nor yet the transcendence of Racinian passion, but the transcendence of grace which is something each of us is free to refuse.

If nevertheless, the concatenation of events and the causal efficiency of the characters involved appear to operate just as rigidly as in a traditional dramatic structure, it is because they are responding to an order, of prophecy (or perhaps one should say of Kierkegaardian "repetition") that is as different from fatality as causality is from analogy.

The pattern of the film's unfolding is not that of tragedy in the usual sense, rather in the sense of the medieval Passion Play, or better still, of the Way of the Cross, each sequence being a station along that road. We are given the key to this by the dialogue in the hut between the two curés, when the one from Ambricourt reveals that he is spiritually attracted to the Mount of Olives. "Is it not enough that Our Lord should have granted me the grace of letting me know today, through the words of my old teacher, that nothing, throughout all eternity, can remove me from the place chosen by me from all eternity, that I was the prisoner of His Sacred Passion?"

Death is not the preordained end of our final agony, only its conclusion and a deliverance. Henceforth we shall know to what divine ordinance, to what spiritual rhythm the sufferings and actions of the curé respond. They are the outward representation of his agony. At which point we should indicate the analogies with Christ that abound towards the end of the film, or they may very well go unnoticed. For example, the two fainting fits during the night; the fall in the mud; the vomitings of wine and blood—a remarkable synthesis of powerful comparisons with the falls of Jesus, the Blood of the Passion, the sponge with vinegar on it, and the defiling spittle. These are not all. For the veil of Veronica we have the cloth of Seraphita; then finally the death in the attic—a Golgotha with even a good and a bad thief.

Now let us immediately put aside these comparisons, the very enumeration of which is necessarily deceptive. Their aesthetic weight derives from their theological value, but both defy explanation. Bresson like Bernanos avoids any sort of symbolic allusion and so none of the situations, despite their obvious parallel to the Gospel, is created precisely because of that parallel. Each carries its own biographical and individual meaning. Its Christlike resemblance comes second, through being projected onto the higher plane of analogy. In no sense is it true to say that the life of the curé of Ambricourt is an imitation of its divine model, rather it is a repetition and a picturing forth of that life. Each bears his own cross and each cross is different, but all are the Cross of the Passion. The sweat on the brow of the curé is a bloody sweat.

So, probably for the first time, the cinema gives us a film in which the only genuine incidents, the only perceptible movements are those of the life of the spirit. Not only that, it also offers us a new dramatic form, that is specifically religious—or better still, specifically theological; a phenomenology of salvation and grace.

It is worth noting that through playing down the psychological elements and keeping the dramatics to a minimum, Bresson is left to face two kinds of pure reality. On the one hand, as we saw, we have the countenance of the actor denuded of all symbolic expression, sheer epidermis, set in a surrounding devoid of any artifice. On the other hand there is what we must call the "written reality." Indeed, Bresson's faithfulness to the text of Bernanos, his refusal, that is, not only to adapt it but also his paradoxical concern to emphasize its literary character, is part of the same predetermined approach to the direction of his actors and the selection of his settings. Bresson treats the novel as he does his characters. The novel is a cold, hard fact, a reality to be accepted as it stands. One must not attempt to adapt it to the situation in hand, or manipulate it to fit some passing need for an explanation; on the contrary it is something to be taken absolutely as it stands. Bresson never condenses the text, he cuts it. Thus what is left over is a part of the original. Like marble from a quarry the words of the film continue to be part of the novel. Of course the deliberate emphasis on their literary character can be interpreted as a search after artistic stylization, which is the very opposite of realism. The fact is, however, that in this case the reality is not the descriptive content, moral or intellectual, of the text—it is the very text itself, or more properly, the style. Clearly the reality at one stage removed of the novel and that which the camera captures directly, cannot fit or grow together or become one. On the contrary the effect of their juxtaposition is to reaffirm their differences. Each plays its part, side by side, using the means at its disposal, in its own setting and after its own style. But it is doubtless by this separating off of elements which because of their resemblance would appear to belong together, that Bresson manages to eliminate what is accidental. The ontological conflict between two orders of events, occurring simultaneously, when confronted on the screen reveal their single common measure—the soul.

Each actor says the same things and the very disparity between their expressions, the substance of what they say, their style, the kind of indifference which seems to govern the relation of actor to text, of word and visage, is the surest guarantee of their close complicity. This language which no lips could speak is, of necessity, from the soul.

It is unlikely that there exists anywhere in the whole of French cinema, perhaps even in all French literature, many moments of a more intense beauty than in the medallion scene between the curé and the countess. Its beauty does not derive from the acting nor from the psychological and dramatic values of the dialogue, nor indeed from its intrinsic meaning. The true dialogue that punctuates the struggle between the inspired priest and a soul in despair is, of its very nature, ineffable. The decisive clashes of their spiritual fencing-match escape us. Their words announce, or prepare the way for, the fiery touch of grace. There is nothing here then of the flow of words that usually goes with a conversion, while the overpowering severity of the dialogue, its rising tension and its final calm leave us with the conviction that we have been the privileged witnesses of a supernatural storm. The words themselves are so much dead weight, the echo of a silence that is the true dialogue between these two souls; a hint at their secret; the opposite side of the coin, if one dare to say so, of the Divine Countenance. When later the curé refuses to come to his own defense by producing the countess' letter, it is not out of humility or love of suffering. It is rather because no tangible evidence is worthy to play a part either in his defense or his indictment. Of its nature the evidence of the countess is no more acceptable than that of de Chantal, and none has the right to ask God to bear witness.

The technique of Bresson's direction cannot adequately be judged except at the level of his aesthetic intention. Inadequately as we may have so far described the latter, it may yet be that the highly astonishing paradox of the film is now a little more evident. Actually the distinction of having set text over against image for the first time goes to Melville in his *Silence de la mer*. It is noteworthy that his reason was likewise a desire for fidelity. However, the structure of Vercors' book was of itself unusual. In his *Journal* Bresson has done more than justify Melville's experiment and shown how well warranted it was. He has carried it to its final conclusions.

Is *Le Journal* just a silent film with spoken titles? The spoken word, as we have seen, does not enter into the image as a realistic component. Even when spoken by one of the characters, it rather resembles the recitative of an opera. At first sight the film seems to be somehow made up on the one hand of the abbreviated text of the novel and illustrated, on the other hand, by images that never pretend to replace it. All that is spoken is not seen, yet nothing that is seen but is also spoken. At worst, critical good sense can reproach Bresson with having substituted an illustrated radiophonic montage, no less, for Bernanos' novel.

So it is from this ostensible corruption of the art of cinema that we begin if we are to grasp fully Bresson's originality and boldness.

In the first place, if Bresson "returns" to the silent film it is certainly not, despite the abundance of close-ups, because he wants to tie in again with theatrical expressionism—that fruit of an infirmity—on the contrary, it is in order to rediscover the dignity of the human countenance as understood by Stroheim and Dreyer. Now if there is one and only one quality of the silent film irreconcilable of its very nature with sound, it is the syntactical subtlety of montage and expression in the playing of the film, that is to say that which proceeds in effect from the weakness of the silent film. But not all silent films want to be such. Nostalgia for a silence that would be the benign procreator of a visual symbolism unduly confuses the so-called primacy of the image with the true vocation of the cinema—which is the primacy of the object. The absence of a sound track for *Greed, Nosferatu,* or *La Passion de Jeanne d'Arc* means something quite other than the silence of *Caligari, Die Nibelungen,* or *Eldorado*. It is a frustration, not the foundation of a form of expression. The former films exist in spite of their silence, not because of it. In this sense the invention of the sound track is just a fortuitous scientific phenomenon and not the aesthetic revolution people always say it is. The language of film, like the language of Aesop, is ambiguous and in spite of appearances to the contrary, the history of cinema before and after 1928 is an unbroken continuity. It is the story of the relations between expressionism and realism. Sound was to destroy expressionism for a while before adopting it in its turn. On the other hand, it became an immediate part of the continued development of realism.

Paradoxically enough it is to the most theatrical, that is to say to the most talkative, forms of the sound film that we must look today for a resurgence of the old symbolism while the pre-talkie realism of a Stroheim has in fact no following. Yet, it is evident that Bresson's undertaking is somehow related to the work of Stroheim and Renoir. The separating of sound and of the image to which it relates cannot be understood without a searching examination of the aesthetics of realism in sound. It is just as mistaken to see it as an illustration of a text, as a commentary on an image. Their parallelism maintains that division which is present to our senses. It continues the Bressonian dialectic between abstraction and reality thanks to which we are concerned with a single reality—that of human souls. In no sense does Bresson return to the expressionism of the silent film. On the one hand he excludes one of the components of reality in order to reproduce it, deliberately stylized on a sound track, partially independent of the image. In other words, it is as if the final rerecording was composed of sound directly recorded with scrupulous fidelity and a text postsynchronized on a monotone. But, as we have pointed out, this text is itself a second reality, a "cold aesthetic fact." Its realism is its style, while the style of the image is primarily its reality, and the style of the film is precisely the conflict between the two.

Bresson disposes once and for all of that commonplace of criticism according to which image and sound should never duplicate one another. The most moving moments in the film are those in which text and image are saying the same thing, each however in its own way. The sound never serves simply to fill out what we see. It strengthens it and multiplies it just as the echo chamber of a violin echoes and multiplies the vibrations of the strings. Yet this metaphor is dialectically inadequate since it is not so much a resonance that the mind perceives as something that does not match, as when a color is not properly superimposed on a drawing. It is here at the edge that the event reveals its true significance. It is because the film is entirely structured on this relationship that, towards the end, the images take on such emotional power. It would be in vain to look for its devastating beauty simply in what is explicit. I doubt if the individual frames in any other film, taken separately, are so deceptive. Their frequent lack of plastic composition, the awkwardness and static quality of the actors completely mislead one as to their value in the overall film. Moreover, this accretion of effectiveness is not due to the editing. The value of an image does not depend on what precedes or follows it. They accumulate, rather, a static energy, like the parallel leaves of a condenser. Between this and the sound track differences of aesthetic potential are set up, the tension of which becomes unbearable. Thus the image-text relationship moves towards its climax, the latter having the advantage. Thus it is that, quite naturally, at the command of an imperious logic, there is nothing more that the image has to communicate except by disappearing. The spectator has been led, step by step, towards that night of the senses the only expression of which is a light on a blank screen.

That is where the so-called silent film and its lofty realism are headed, to the disappearance of the image and its replacement simply by the text of the novel. But here we are experimenting with an irrefutable aesthetic, with a sublime achievement of pure cinema. Just as the blank page of Mallarmé and the silence of Rimbaud is language at the highest state, the screen, free of images and handed back to literature, is the triumph of cinematographic realism. The black cross on the white screen, as awkwardly drawn as on the average memorial card, the only trace left by the "assumption" of the image, is a witness to something the reality of which is itself but a sign.

With *Le Journal* cinematographic adaptation reaches a new stage. Up to now, film tended to substitute for the novel in the guise of its aesthetic translation into another language. Fidelity meant respect for the spirit of the novel, but it also meant a search for necessary equivalents, that is to say, it meant taking into account the dramatic requirements of the theater or again the more direct effectiveness of the cinematographic image. Unfortunately, concern for these things will continue to be the general rule. We must remember however that it was through their application that *Le Diable au corps* and *La Symphonie pastorale* turned out so well. According to the best opinions, films like these are as good as the books on which they are modelled.

In the margin of this formula we might also note the existence of the free adaptation of books such as that made by Renoir for *Une Partie de campagne* or *Madame Bovary*. Here the problem is solved in another way. The original is just a source of inspiration. Fidelity is here the temperamental affinity between film-maker and novelist, a deeply sympathetic understanding. Instead of presenting itself as a substitute, the film is intended to take its place alongside the book—to make a pair with it, like twin stars. This assumption, applicable only where there is genius, does not exclude the possibility that the film is a greater achievement than its literary model, as in the case of Renoir's *The River*.

Le Journal however is something else again. Its dialectic between fidelity and creation is reducible, in the last analysis, to a dialectic between the cinema and literature. There is no question here of a translation, no matter how faithful or intelligent. Still less is it a question of free inspiration with the intention of making a duplicate. It is a question of building a secondary work with the novel as foundation. In no sense is the film "comparable" to the novel or "worthy" of it. It is a new aesthetic creation, the novel so to speak multiplied by the cinema.

The only procedure in any way comparable of which we have any examples are films of paintings. Emmer or Alain Resnais are similarly faithful to the original, their raw material is the already highly developed work of the painter; the reality with which they are concerned is not the subject of the painting but the painting itself, in the same way as the text of the novel is Bresson's reality. But the fidelity of Alain Resnais to Van Gogh is but the prior condition of a symbiosis of cinema and painting. That is why, as a rule, painters fail utterly to understand the whole procedure. If you see these films as nothing more than an intelligent, effective, and even a valuable means of popularizing painting—they certainly are that too—you know nothing of their aesthetic biology.

This comparison with films of paintings, however, is only partially valid since these are confined from the outset to the realm of minor aesthetic works. They add something to the paintings, they prolong their existence, they release them from the confines of their frames but they can never pretend to be the paintings themselves.[1] The Van Gogh of Alain Resnais is a minor masterpiece taken from a major work which it makes use of and explains in detail but does not replace. There are two reasons for this congenital limitation. First of all, the photographic reproduction, in projection, cannot pretend to be a substitute for the original or to share its identity. If it could, then it would be the better to destroy its aesthetic autonomy, since films of paintings start off precisely as the negation of that on which this aesthetic autonomy is based, the fact that the paintings are circumscribed in space and exist outside time. It is because cinema as the art of space and time is the contrary of painting that it has something to add to it.

Such a contradiction does not exist between the novel and the film. Not only are they both narrative arts, that is to say temporal arts, but it is not even possible to maintain a priori that the cinematic image is essentially inferior to the image prompted by the written word. In all probability the opposite is the case. But this is not where the problem lies. It is enough if the novelist, like the film-maker, is concerned with the idea of unfolding a real world. Once we accept these essential resemblances, there is nothing absurd in trying to write a novel on film. But *Le Journal* has just proved to us that it is more fruitful to speculate on their differences rather than on their resemblances, that is, for the existence of the novel to be affirmed by the film and not dissolved into it. It is hardly enough to say of this work, once removed, that it is in essence faithful to the original because, to begin with, it *is* the novel. But most of all the resulting work is not, certainly, better (that kind of judgment is meaningless . . .) but "more" than the book. The aesthetic pleasure we derive from Bresson's film, while the acknowledgment for it goes, essentially, to the genius of Bernanos, includes all that the novel has to offer plus, in addition, its refraction in the cinema.

After Bresson, Aurenche and Bost are but the Viollet-le-Duc of cinematographic adaptation.

Translated by Hugh Gray

NOTE

1 At least up to the time of *Le Mystère Picasso* which, as we shall see, may invalidate this criticism.

32

Forerunners of Modern Music

John Cage

The Purpose of Music— Music is edifying, for from time to time it sets the soul in operation. The soul is the gatherer-together of the disparate elements (Meister Eckhart), and its work fills one with peace and love.

Definitions— Structure in music is its divisibility into successive parts from phrases to long sections. Form is content, the continuity. Method is the means of controlling the continuity from note to note. The material of music is sound and silence. Integrating these is composing.

Strategy— Structure is properly mind-controlled. Both delight in precision, clarity, and the observance of rules. Whereas form wants only freedom to be. It belongs to the heart; and the law it observes, if indeed it submits to any, has never been and never will be written.[1] Method may be planned or improvised (it makes no difference: in one case, the emphasis shifts towards thinking, in the other towards feeling; a piece for radios as instruments would give up the matter of method to accident). Likewise, material may be controlled or not, as one chooses. Normally the choice of sounds is determined by what is pleasing and attractive to the ear: delight in the giving or receiving of pain being an indication of sickness.

Refrain— Activity involving in a single process the many, turning them, even though some seem to be opposites, towards oneness, contributes to a good way of life.

The Plot Thickens— When asked why, God being good, there was evil in the world, Sri Ramakrishna said: To thicken the plot.
The aspect of composition that can properly be discussed with the end in view of general agreement is structure, for it is devoid of mystery. Analysis is at home here.

Schools teach the making of structures by means of classical harmony. Outside school, however (*e.g.*, Satie and Webern), a different and correct [2] structural means reappears: one based on lengths of time.[3] [4]

In the Orient, harmonic structure is traditionally unknown, and unknown with us in our pre-Renaissance culture. Harmonic structure is a recent Occidental phenomenon, for the past century in a process of disintegration.[5]

Atonality [6] *Has Happened*— The disintegration of harmonic structure is commonly known as atonality. All that is meant is that two necessary elements in harmonic structure—the cadence, and modulating means—have lost their edge. Increasingly, they have become ambiguous, whereas their very existence as structural elements demands clarity (singleness of reference). Atonality is simply the maintenance of an ambiguous tonal state of affairs. It is the denial of harmony as a structural means. The problem of a composer in a musical world in this state is to supply another structural means,[7] just as in a bombed-out city the opportunity to build again exists.[8] This way one finds courage and a sense of necessity.

Interlude (*Meister Eckhart*)— "But one must achieve this unselfconsciousness by means of transformed knowledge. This ignorance does not come from lack of knowledge but rather it is from knowledge that one may achieve this ignorance. Then we shall be informed by the divine unconsciousness and in that our ignorance will be ennobled and adorned with supernatural knowledge. It is by reason of this fact that we are made perfect by what happens to us rather than by what we do."

At Random— Music means nothing as a thing.

A finished work is exactly that, requires resurrection.

The responsibility of the artist consists in perfecting his work so that it may become attractively disinteresting.

It is better to make a piece of music than to perform one, better to perform one than to listen to one, better to listen to one than to misuse it as a means of distraction, entertainment, or acquisition of "culture."

Use any means to keep from being a genius, all means to become one.

Is counterpoint good? "The soul itself is so simple that it cannot have more than one idea at a time of anything . . . . A person cannot be more than single in attention." (Eckhart)

Freed from structural responsibility, harmony becomes a formal element (serves expression).

Imitating either oneself or others, care should be taken to imitate structure, not form (also structural materials and structural methods, not formal materials and formal methods), disciplines, not dreams; thus one remains "innocent and free to receive anew with each Now-moment a heavenly gift." (Eckhart)

If the mind is disciplined, the heart turns quickly from fear towards love.

Before Making a Structure by Means of Rhythm, It Is Necessary to Decide What Rhythm Is— This could be a difficult decision to make if the concern were formal (expressive) or to do with method (point to point procedure); but since the concern is structural (to do with divisibility of a composition into parts large and small), the decision is easily reached: rhythm in the structural instance is relationships of lengths of time.[9] Such matters, then, as accents on or off the beat, regularly recurring or not, pulsation with or without accent, steady or unsteady, durations motivically conceived (either static or to be varied), are matters for formal (expressive) use, or, if thought about, to be considered as material (in its "textural" aspect) or as serving method. In the case of a year, rhythmic structure is a matter of seasons, months, weeks, and days. Other time lengths such as that taken by a fire or the playing of a piece of music occur accidentally or freely without explicit recognition of an all-embracing order, but nevertheless, necessarily within that order. Coincidences of free events with structural time points have a special luminous character, because the paradoxical nature of truth is at such moments made apparent. Caesurae on the other hand are expressive of the independence (accidental or willed) of freedom from law, law from freedom.

Claim— Any sounds of any qualities and pitches (known or unknown, definite or indefinite), any contexts of these, simple or multiple, are natural and conceivable within a rhythmic structure which equally embraces silence. Such a claim is remarkably like the claims to be found in patent specifications for and articles about technological musical means (see early issues of *Modern Music* and the *Journal of the Acoustical Society of America*). From differing beginning points, towards possibly different goals, technologists and artists (seemingly by accident) meet by intersection, becoming aware of the otherwise unknowable (conjunction of the in and the out), imagining brightly a common goal in the world and in the quietness within each human being.

For Instance— Just as art as sand painting (art for the now-moment [10] rather than for posterity's museum civilization) becomes a held point of view, adventurous workers in the field of synthetic music (e.g. Norman McLaren) finds that for practical and economic reasons work with magnetic wires (any music so made can quickly and easily be erased, rubbed off) is preferable to that with film.[11]

The use of technological means [12] requires the close anonymous collaboration of a number of workers. We are on the point of being in a cultural situation,[13] without having made any special effort to get into one [14] (if one can discount lamentation).

The in-the-heart path of music leads now to self-knowledge through self-denial, and its in-the-world path leads likewise to selflessness.[15] The heights that now are reached by single individuals at special moments may soon be densely populated.

NOTES

1 Any attempt to exclude the "irrational" is irrational. Any composing strategy which is wholly "rational" is irrational in the extreme.

2 Sound has four characteristics: pitch, timbre, loudness, and duration. The opposite and necessary coexistent of sound is silence. Of the four characteristics of sound, only duration involves both sound and silence. Therefore, a structure based on durations (rhythmic: phrase, time lengths) is correct (corresponds with the nature of the material), whereas harmonic structure is incorrect (derived from pitch, which has no being in silence).

3 This never disappeared from jazz and folk music. On the other hand, it never developed in them, for they are not cultivated species, growing best when left wild.

4 Tala is based on pulsation, Western rhythmic structure on phraseology.

5 For an interesting, detailed proof of this, see Casella's book on the cadence.

6 The term "atonality" makes no sense. Schoenberg substitutes "pantonality," Lou Harrison (to my mind and experience the preferable term) "proto-tonality." This last term suggests what is actually the case: present even in a random multiplicity of tones (or, better, sounds [so as to include noises]), is a gravity, original and natural, "proto," to that particular situation. Elementary composition consists in discovering the ground of the sounds employed, and then letting life take place both on land and in the air.

7 Neither Schoenberg nor Stravinsky did this. The twelve-tone row does not offer a structural means; it is a method, a control, not of the parts, large and small, of a composition, but only of the minute, note-to-note procedure. It usurps the place of counterpoint, which, as Carl Ruggles, Lou Harrison, and Merton Brown have shown, is perfectly capable of functioning in a chromatic situation. Neo-classicism, in reverting to the past, avoids, by refusing to recognize, the contemporary need for another structure, gives a new look to structural harmony. This automatically deprives it of the sense of adventure, essential to creative action.

8 The twelve-tone row offers bricks but no plan. The neo-classicists advise building it the way it was before, but surfaced fashionably.

9 Measure is literally measure—nothing more, for example, than the inch of a ruler—thus permitting the existence of any durations, any amplitude relations (meter, accent), any silences.

10 This is the very nature of the dance, of the performance of music, or any other art requiring performance (for this reason, the term "sand painting" is used: there is a tendency in painting (permanent pigments), as in poetry (printing, binding), to be secure in the thingness of a work, and thus to overlook, and place nearly insurmountable obstacles in the path of, instantaneous ecstasy).

11 Twenty-four or *n* frames per second is the "canvas" upon which this music is written; thus, in a very obvious way, the material itself demonstrates the necessity for time (rhythmic) structure. With magnetic means, freedom from the frame of film means exists, but the principle of rhythmic structure should hold over as, in geometry, a more elementary theorem remains as a premise to make possible the obtaining of those more advanced.

12 "I want to be as though new-born, knowing nothing, absolutely nothing about Europe." (Paul Klee)

13 Replete with new concert halls: the movie houses (vacated by home television fans, and too numerous for a Hollywood whose only alternative is "seriousness").

14 "Painting in becoming literally (actually) realistic—(this is the twentieth century) seen from above, the earth, snow-covered, a composition of order superimposed on the "spontaneous" (Cummings) or of the latter letting order be (from above, so together, the opposites, they fuse) (one has only to fly [highways and topography, Milarepa, Henry Ford] to know)—automatically will reach the same point (step by step) the soul leaped to.

15 The machine fathers mothers heroes saints of the mythological order, works only when it meets with acquiescence (cf. *The King and the Corpse,* by Heinrich Zimmer, edited by Joseph Campbell).

33

The Literarization of the Theatre

(Notes to the *Threepenny Opera*)

Bertolt Brecht

THE READING OF PLAYS

There is no reason why John Gay's motto for his *Beggar's Opera*—nos haec novimus esse nihil—should be changed for the *Threepenny Opera.* Its publication represents little more than the prompt-book of a play wholly surrendered to theatres, and thus is directed at the expert rather than at the consumer. This doesn't mean that the conversion of the maximum number of readers or spectators into experts is not thoroughly desirable; indeed it is under way.

The *Threepenny Opera* is concerned with bourgeois conceptions not only as content, by representing them, but also through the manner in which it does so. It is a kind of report on life as any member of the audience would like to see it. Since at the same time, however, he sees a good deal that he has no wish to see; since therefore he sees his wishes not merely fulfilled but also criticized (sees himself not as the subject but as the object), he is theoretically in a position to appoint a new function for the theatre. But the theatre itself resists any alteration of its function, and so it seems desirable that the spectator should read plays whose aim is not merely to be performed in the theatre but to change it: out of mistrust of the theatre. Today we see the theatre being given absolute priority over the actual plays. The theatre apparatus's priority is a priority of means of production. This apparatus resists all conversion to other purposes, by taking any play which it encounters and immediately changing it so that it no longer represents a foreign body within the apparatus—except at those points where it neutralizes itself. The necessity to stage the new drama correctly—which matters more for the theatre's sake than for the drama's—is modified by the fact that the theatre can stage anything: it theatres it all down. Of course this priority has economic reasons.

TITLES AND SCREENS

The screens on which the titles of each scene are projected are a primitive attempt at literarizing the theatre. This literarization of the theatre needs to be developed to the utmost degree, as in general does the literarizing of all public occasions.

Literarizing entails punctuating "representation" with "formulation," gives the theatre the possibility of making contact with other institutions for intellectual activities; but is bound to remain one-sided so long as the audience is taking no part in it and using it as a means of obtaining access to "higher things."

The orthodox playwright's objection to the titles is that the dramatist ought to say everything that has to be said in the action, that the text must express everything within its own confines. The corresponding attitude for the spectator is that he should not think about a subject, but within the confines of the subject. But this way of subordinating everything to a single idea, this passion for propelling the spectator along a single track where he can look neither right nor left, up nor down, is something that the new school of play-writing must reject. Footnotes, and the habit of turning back in order to check a point, need to be introduced into play-writing too.

Some exercise in complex seeing is needed—though it is perhaps more important to be able to think above the stream than to think in the stream. Moreover the use of screens imposes and facilitates a new style of acting. This style is the *epic style*. As he reads the projections on the screen the spectator adopts an attitude of smoking-and-watching. Such an attitude on his part at once compels a better and clearer performance as it is hopeless to try to "carry away" any man who is smoking and accordingly pretty well occupied with himself. By these means one would soon have a theatre full of experts, just as one has sporting arenas full of experts. No chance of the actors having the effrontery to offer such people those few miserable scraps of imitation which they at present cook up in a few rehearsals "any old how" and without the least thought! No question of their material being taken from them in so unfinished and unworked a state. The actor would have to find a quite different way of drawing attention to those incidents which had been previously announced by the titles and so deprived of any intrinsic element of surprise.

Unfortunately it is to be feared that titles and permission to smoke are not of themselves enough to lead the audience to a more fruitful use of the theatre.

ABOUT THE SINGING OF THE SONGS

When an actor sings he undergoes a change of function. Nothing is more revolting than when the actor pretends not to notice that he has left the level of plain speech and started to sing. The three levels—plain speech, heightened speech and singing—must always remain distinct, and in no case should heightened speech represent an intensification of plain speech, or singing of heightened speech. In no case therefore should singing take place where words are prevented by excess of feeling. The actor must not only sing but show a man singing. His aim is not so much to bring out the emotional content of his song (has one the right to offer others a dish that one has already eaten oneself?) but to show gestures that are so to speak the habits and usage of the body. To this end he would be best advised not to use the actual words of the text when rehearsing, but common everyday phrases which express the same thing in the crude language of ordinary life. As for the melody, he must not follow it blindly: there is a kind of speaking-against-the-music which can have strong effects, the results of a stubborn, incorruptible sobriety which is independent of music and rhythm. If he drops into the melody it must be an event; the actor can emphasize it by plainly showing the pleasure which the melody gives him. It helps the actor if the musicians are visible during his performance and also if he is allowed to make visible preparation for it (by straightening a chair perhaps or making himself up, etc.). Particularly in the songs it is important that "he who is showing should himself be shown."

WHY DOES MACHEATH HAVE TO BE ARRESTED TWICE OVER?

From the pseudo-classical German point of view the first prison scene is a diversion, but to us it is an example of rudimentary epic form. It is a diversion if, like this purely dynamic form of drama, one gives priority to the idea and makes the spectator desire an increasingly definite objective—in this case the hero's death; if one as it were creates a growing demand for the supply and, purely to allow the spectator's strong emotional participation (for emotions will only venture on to completely secure ground, and cannot survive disappointment of any sort), needs a single inevitable chain of events. The epic drama, with its materialistic standpoint and its lack of interest in any investment of its spectators' emotions, knows no objective but only a finishing point, and is familiar with a different kind of chain, whose course need not be a straight one but may quite well be in curves or even in leaps. The dynamic, idealistically-orientated kind of drama, with its interest in the individual, was in all decisive respects more radical when it began life (under the Elizabethans) than in the German pseudo-classicism of two hundred years later, which confuses dynamics of representation with the dynamics of what has to be represented, and has already put its individual "in his place." (The present-day successors of these successors are indescribable: dynamics of representation have changed into an ingenious and empirically-based arrangement of a jumble of effects, while the individual, now in a state of complete dissolution, still goes on being developed within his own limits, but only as parts for actors—whereas the late bourgeois novel at least considers that it has a science of psychology which has been worked out to help it analyse the individual—as though the individual had not simply collapsed long ago.) But this great kind of drama was far less radical in its purging of the material. Here the structural form didn't rule out all the individual's deviations from the straight course, as brought about by "just life" (a part is always played here by outside relationships, with other circumstances that "don't take place"; a far wider cross-section is taken), but used such deviations as a motive force of the play's dynamics. This friction penetrates right inside the individual, to be overcome within him.

The whole weight of this kind of drama comes from the piling up of resistances. The material is not yet arranged in accordance with any wish for an easy ideal formula. Something of Baconian materialism still survives here, and the individual himself still has flesh and bones and resists the formula's demands. But whenever one comes across materialism epic forms arise in the drama, and most markedly and frequently in comedy, whose "tone" is always "lower" and more materialistic. Today, when the human being has to be seen as "the sum of all social circumstances" the epic form is the only one that can embrace those processes which serve the drama as matter for a comprehensive picture of the world. Similarly man, flesh and blood man, can only be embraced through those processes by which and in course of which he exists. The new school of play-writing must systematically see to it that its form includes "experiment." It must be free to use connections on every side; it needs equilibrium and has a tension which governs its component parts and "loads" them against one another. (Thus this form is anything but a revue-like sequence of sketches.)

Translated by John Willett

CONTEMPORARY VIOLENCE AND THE NEW SEARCH FOR COHERENCY

PART V

34

From "The Science of the Concrete"

Claude Lévi-Strauss

Examples like these * could be drawn from all parts of the world and one may readily conclude that animals and plants are not known as a result of their usefulness; they are deemed to be useful or interesting because they are first of all known.

It may be objected that science of this kind can scarcely be of much practical effect. The answer to this is that its main purpose is not a practical one. It meets intellectual requirements rather than or instead of satisfying needs.

The real question is not whether the touch of a woodpecker's beak does in fact cure toothache. It is rather whether there is a point of view from which a woodpecker's beak and a man's tooth can be seen as "going together" (the use of this congruity for therapeutic purposes being only one of its possible uses), and whether some initial order can be introduced into the universe by means of these groupings. Classifying, as opposed to not classifying, has a value of its own, whatever form the classification may take. As a recent theorist of taxonomy writes:

* Various primitive classifications of the natural world—Editors.

> Scientists do tolerate uncertainty and frustration, because they must. The one thing that they do not and must not tolerate is disorder. The whole aim of theoretical science is to carry to the highest possible and conscious degree the perceptual reduction of chaos that began in so lowly and (in all probability) unconscious a way with the origin of life. In specific instances it can well be questioned whether the order so achieved is an objective characteristic of the phenomena or is an artifact constructed by the scientist. That question comes up time after time in animal taxonomy . . . . Nevertheless, the most basic postulate of science is that nature itself is orderly . . . . All theoretical science is ordering and if, systematics is equated with ordering, then systematics is synonymous with theoretical science.

The thought we call primitive is founded on this demand for order. This is equally true of all thought but it is through the properties common to all thought that we can most easily begin to understand forms of thought which seem very strange to us.

A native thinker makes the penetrating comment that "All sacred things must have their place." It could even be said that being in their place is what makes them sacred for if they were taken out of their place, even in thought, the entire order of the universe would be destroyed. Sacred objects therefore contribute to the maintenance of order in the universe by occupying the places allocated to them. Examined superficially and from the outside, the refinements of ritual can appear pointless. They are explicable by a concern for what one might call "micro-adjustment"—the concern to assign every single creature, object or feature to a place within a class. The ceremony of the Hako among the Pawnee is particularly illuminating in this respect, although only because it has been so well analysed. The invocation which accompanies the crossing of a stream of water is divided into several parts, which correspond, respectively, to the moment when the travellers put their feet in water, the moment when they move them and the moment when the water completely covers their feet. The invocation to the wind separates the moment when only the wet parts of the body feel cool: "Now, we are ready to move forward in safety." As the informant explains: "We must address with song every object we meet, because Tira'wa (the supreme spirit) is in all things, everything we come to as we travel can give us help. . . ."

This preoccupation with exhaustive observation and the systematic cataloguing of relations and connections can sometimes lead to scientifically valid results. The Blackfoot Indians for instance were able to prognosticate the approach of spring by the state of development of the foetus of bison which they took from the uterus of females killed in hunting. These successes cannot of course be isolated from the numerous other associations of the same kind which science condemns as illusory. It may however be the case that magical thought, that "gigantic variation on the theme of the principle of Causality" as Hubert and Mauss called it, can be distinguished from science not so much by any ignorance or contempt of determinism but by a more imperious and uncompromising demand for it which can at the most be regarded as unreasonable and precipitate from the scientific point of view.

> As a natural philosophy it (witchcraft) reveals a theory of causation. Misfortune is due to witchcraft co-operating with natural forces. If a buffalo gores a man, or the supports of a granary are undermined by termites so that it falls on his head, or he is infected with cerebrospinal meningitis, Azande say that the buffalo, the granary, and the disease, are causes which combine with witchcraft to kill a man. Witchcraft does not create the buffalo and the granary and the disease for these exist in their own right, but it is responsible for the particular situation in which they are brought into lethal relations with a particular man. The granary would have fallen in any case, but since there was witchcraft present it fell at the particular moment when a certain man was resting beneath it. Of these causes the only one which permits intervention is witchcraft, for witchcraft emanates from a person. The buffalo and the granary do not allow of intervention and are, therefore, whilst recognized as causes, not considered the socially relevant ones (Evans-Pritchard *I*, p. 418–19).

Seen in this way, the first difference between magic and science is therefore that magic postulates a complete and all-embracing determinism. Science, on the other hand, is based on a distinction between levels: only some of these admit forms of determinism; on others the same forms of determinism are held not to apply. One can go further and think of the rigorous precision of magical thought and ritual practices as an expression of the unconscious apprehension of the *truth of determinism,* the mode in which scientific phenomena exist. In this view, the operations of determinism are divined and made use of in an all-embracing fashion before being known and properly applied, and magical rites and beliefs appear as so many expressions of an act of faith in a science yet to be born.

The nature of these anticipations is such that they may sometimes succeed. Moreover they may anticipate not only science itself but even methods or results which scientific procedure does not incorporate until an advanced stage of its development. For it seems to be the case that man began by applying himself to the most difficult task, that of systematizing what is immediately presented to the senses, on which science for a long time turned its back and which it is only beginning to bring back into its purview. In the history of scientific thought this "anticipation-effect," has, incidentally, occurred repeatedly. As Simpson has shown with the help of an example drawn from nineteenth-century biology, it is due to the fact that, since scientific explanation is always the discovery of an "arrangement," any attempt of this type, even one inspired by non-scientific principles, can hit on true arrangements. This is even to be foreseen if one grants that the number of structures is by definition finite: the "structuring" has an intrinsic effectiveness of its own whatever the principles and methods which suggested it.

Modern chemistry reduces the variety of tastes and smells to different combinations of five elements: carbon, hydrogen, oxygen, sulphur and nitrogen. By means of tables of the presence and absence of the elements and estimates of proportions and minimum amounts necessary for them to be perceptible, it succeeds in accounting for differences and resemblances which were previously excluded from its field on account of their "secondary" character. These connections and distinctions are however no surprise to our aesthetic sense. On the contrary they increase its scope and understanding by supplying a basis for the associations it already divined; and at the same time one is better able to understand why and in what conditions it should have been possible to discover such associations solely by the systematic use of intuitive methods. Thus to a logic of sensations tobacco smoke might be the intersection of two groups, one also containing broiled meat and brown crusts of bread (which are like it in being composed of nitrogen) and the other one to which cheese, beer and honey belong on account of the presence of diacetyl. Wild cherries, cinnamon, vanilla and sherry are grouped together by the intellect as well as the senses, because they all contain aldehyde, while the closely related smells of wintergreen, lavender and bananas are to be explained by the presence of ester. On intuitive grounds alone we might group onions, garlic, cabbage, turnips, radishes and mustard together even though botany separates liliaceae and crucifers. In confirmation of the evidence of the senses, chemistry shows that these different families are united on another plane: they contain sulphur. A primitive philosopher or a poet could have effected these regroupings on the basis of considerations foreign to chemistry or any other form of science. Ethnographic literature reveals many of equal empirical and aesthetic value. And this is not just the result of some associative madness destined sometimes to succeed simply by the law of chance. Simpson advances this interpretation in the passage quoted above; but he displays more insight when he shows that the demand for organization is a need common to art and science and that in consequence "taxonomy, which is ordering par excellence, has eminent aesthetic value." Given this, it seems less surprising that the aesthetic sense can by itself open the way to taxonomy and even anticipate some of its results. I am not however commending a return to the popular belief (although it has some validity in its own narrow context) according to which magic is a timid and stuttering form of science. One deprives oneself of all means of understanding magical thought if one tries to reduce it to a moment or stage in technical and scientific evolution. Like a shadow moving ahead of its owner it is in a sense complete in itself, and as finished and coherent in its immateriality as the substantial being which it precedes. Magical thought is not to be regarded as a beginning, a rudiment, a sketch, a part of a whole which has not yet materialized. It forms a well-articulated system, and is in this respect independent of that other system which constitutes science, except for the purely formal analogy which brings them together and makes the former a sort of metaphorical expression of the latter. It is therefore better, instead of contrasting magic and science, to compare them as two parallel modes of acquiring knowledge. Their theoretical and practical results differ in value, for it is true that science is more successful than magic from this point of view, although magic foreshadows science in that it is sometimes also successful. Both science and magic however require the same sort of mental operations and they differ not so much in kind as in the different types of phenomena to which they are applied.

These relations are a consequence of the objective conditions in which magic and scientific knowledge appeared. The history of the latter is short enough for us to know a good deal about it. But the fact that modern science dates back only a few centuries raises a problem which ethnologists have not sufficiently pondered. The Neolithic Paradox would be a suitable name for it.

It was in neolithic times that man's mastery of the great arts of civilization—of pottery, weaving, agriculture and the domestication of animals—became firmly established. No one today would any longer think of attributing these enormous advances to the fortuitous accumulation of a series of chance discoveries or believe them to have been revealed by the passive perception of certain natural phenomena.[1]

Each of these techniques assumes centuries of active and methodical observation, of bold hypotheses tested by means of endlessly repeated experiments. A biologist remarks on the rapidity with which plants from the New World have been acclimatized in the Philippines and adopted and named by the natives. In many cases they seem even to have rediscovered their medicinal uses, uses identical with those traditional in Mexico. Fox's interpretation is this:

> . . . plants with bitter leaves or stems are commonly used in the Philippines for stomach disorders. If an introduced plant is found to have this characteristic, it will be quickly utilized. The fact that many Philippine groups, such as the Pinatubo Negritos, constantly experiment with plants hastens the process of the recognition of the potential usefulness, as defined by the culture, of the introduced flora (R. B. Fox, pp. 212–13).

To transform a weed into a cultivated plant, a wild beast into a domestic animal, to produce, in either of these, nutritious or technologically useful properties which were originally completely absent or could only be guessed at; to make stout, water-tight pottery out of clay which is friable and unstable, liable to pulverize or crack (which, however, is possible only if from a large number of organic and inorganic materials, the one most suitable for refining it is selected, and also the appropriate fuel, the temperature and duration of firing and the effective degree of oxidation); to work out techniques, often long and complex, which permit cultivation without soil or alternatively without water; to change toxic roots or seeds into foodstuffs or again to use their poison for hunting, war or ritual—there is no doubt that all these achievements required a genuinely scientific attitude, sustained and watchful interest and a desire for knowledge for its own sake. For only a small proportion of observations and experiments (which must be assumed to have been primarily inspired by a desire for knowledge) could have yielded practical and immediately useful results. There is no need to dwell on the working of bronze and iron and of precious metals or even the simple working of copper ore by hammering which preceded metallurgy by several thousand years, and even at that stage they all demand a very high level of technical proficiency.

Neolithic, or early historical, man was therefore the heir of a long scientific tradition. However, had he, as well as all his predecessors, been inspired by exactly the same spirit as that of our own time, it would be impossible to understand how he could have come to a halt and how several thousand years of stagnation have intervened between the neolithic revolution and modern science like a level plain between ascents. There is only one solution to the paradox, namely, that there are two distinct modes of scientific thought. These are certainly not a function of different stages of development of the human mind but rather of two strategic levels at which nature is accessible to scientific enquiry: one roughly adapted to that of perception and the imagination: the other at a remove from it. It is as if the necessary connections which are the object of all science, neolithic or modern, could be arrived at by two different routes, one very close to, and the other more remote from, sensible intuition.

Any classification is superior to chaos and even a classification at the level of sensible properties is a step towards rational ordering. It is legitimate, in classifying fruits into relatively heavy and relatively light, to begin by separating the apples from the pears even though shape, colour and taste are unconnected with weight and volume. This is because the larger apples are easier to distinguish from the smaller if the apples are not still mixed with fruit of different features. This example already shows that classification has its advantages even at the level of aesthetic perception.

For the rest, and in spite of the fact there is no necessary connection between sensible qualities and properties, there is very often at least an empirical connection between them, and the generalization of this relation may be rewarding from the theoretical and practical point of view for a very long time even if it has no foundation in reason. Not all poisonous juices are burning or bitter nor is everything which is burning and bitter poisonous. Nevertheless, nature is so constituted that it is more advantageous if thought and action proceed as though this aesthetically satisfying equivalence also corresponded to objective reality. It seems probable, for reasons which are not relevant here, that species possessing some remarkable characteristics, say, of shape, colour or smell give the observer what might be called a "right pending disproof" to postulate that these visible characteristics are the sign of equally singular, but concealed, properties. To treat the relation between the two as itself sensible (regarding a seed in the form of a tooth as a safeguard against snake bites, yellow juices as a cure for bilious troubles, etc.) is of more value provisionally than indifference to any connection. For even a heterogeneous and arbitrary classification preserves the richness and diversity of the collection of facts it makes. The decision that everything must be taken account of facilitates the creation of a "memory bank."

It is moreover a fact that particular results, to the achievement of which methods of this kind were able to lead, were essential to enable man to assail nature from a different angle. Myths and rites are far from being, as has often been held, the product of man's "myth-making faculty," turning its back on reality. Their principal value is indeed to preserve until the present time the remains of methods of observation and reflection which were (and no doubt still are) precisely adapted to discoveries of a certain type: those which nature authorised from the starting point of a speculative organization and exploitation of the sensible world in sensible terms. This science of the concrete was necessarily restricted by its essence to results other than those destined to be achieved by the exact natural sciences but it was no less scientific and its results no less genuine. They were secured ten thousand years earlier and still remain at the basis of our own civilization.

NOTE

1 An attempt has been made to discover what would happen if copper ore had accidentally found its way into a furnace: complex and varied experiments have shown that nothing happens at all. The simplest method of obtaining metallic copper which could be discovered consisted in subjecting finely ground malachite to intense heat in a pottery dish crowned with an inverted clay pot. This, the sole result, restricts the play of chance to the confines of the kiln of some potter specializing in glazed ware (Coghlan).

35

Definition of Man

Kenneth Burke

I

First, a few words on definition in general. Let's admit it: I see in a definition the critic's equivalent of a lyric, or of an aria in opera. Also, we might note that, when used in an essay, as with Aristotle's definition of tragedy in his *Poetics,* a definition so sums things up that all the properties attributed to the thing defined can be as though "derived" from the definition. In actual development, the definition may be the last thing a writer hits upon. Or it may be formulated somewhere along the line. But logically it is prior to the observations that it summarizes. Thus, insofar as all the attributes of the thing defined fit the definition, the definition should be viewed as "prior" in this purely non-temporal sense of priority.

Definitions are also the critic's equivalent of the lyric (though a poet might not think so!) in that the writer usually "hits on them." They are "breakthroughs," and thus are somewhat hard to come by. We should always keep trying for them—but they don't always seem to "click."

A definition should have just enough clauses, and no more. However, each clause should be like a chapter head, under which appropriate observations might be assembled, as though derived from it.

I am offering my Definition of Man in the hope of either persuading the reader that it fills the bill, or of prompting him to decide what should be added, or subtracted, or in some way modified.

II

Man Is the Symbol-Using Animal— Granted, it doesn't come as much of a surprise. But our definition is being offered not for any possible paradoxical value. The aim is to get as essential a set of clauses as possible, and to meditate on each of them.

I remember one day at college when, on entering my philosophy class, I found all blinds up and the windows open from the top, while a bird kept flying nervously about the ceiling. The windows were high, they extended almost to the ceiling; yet the bird kept trying to escape by batting against the ceiling rather than dipping down and flying out one of the open windows. While it kept circling thus helplessly over our heads, the instructor explained that this was an example of a "tropism." This particular bird's instinct was to escape by flying *up,* he said; hence it ignored the easy exit through the windows.

But how different things would be if the bird could speak and we could speak his language. What a simple statement would have served to solve his problem. "Fly down just a foot or so, and out one of those windows."

Later, I ran across another example that I cite because it has further implications, with regard to a later clause in our defintion. I witnessed the behavior of a wren that was unquestionably a genius within the terms of its species. The parents had succeeded in getting all of a brood off the nest except one particularly stubborn or backward fellow who still remained for a couple of days after the others had flown. Despite all kinds of threats and cajolery, he still lingered, demanding and getting the rations which all concerned seem to consider his rightful lot. Then came the moment of genius. One of the parent wrens came to the nest with a morsel of food. But instead of simply giving it to the noisy youngster, the parent bird held it at a distance. The fledgling in the nest kept stretching its neck out farther and farther with its beak gaping until, of a sudden, instead of merely putting the morsel of food into the bird's mouth, the parent wren clamped its beak shut on the young one's lower mandible, and with a slight jerk caused the youngster, with his outstretched neck, to lose balance and tumble out of the nest.

Surely this was an "act" of genius. This wren had discovered how to use the principle of leverage as a way of getting a young bird off the nest. Had that exceptionally brilliant wren been able to conceptualize this discovery in such terms as come easy to symbol systems, we can imagine him giving a dissertation on "The Use of the Principle of Leverage as an Improved Method for Unnesting Birds or Debirding a Nest." And within a few years the invention would spread throughout all birddom, with an incalculable saving in bird-hours as compared with the traditional turbulent and inefficient method still in general practice.

There are three things to note about this incident:

1) The ability to describe this method in words would have readily made it possible for all other birds to take over this same "act" of genius, though they themselves might never have hit upon it.

2) The likelihood is that even this one wren never used the method again. For the ability to conceptualize implies a kind of *attention* without which this innovation could probably not advance beyond the condition of a mere accident to the condition of an invention.

3) On the happier side, there is the thought that at least, through lack of such ability, birds are spared our many susceptibilities to the ways of demagogic spellbinders. They cannot be filled with fantastic hatreds for alien populations they know about mainly by mere hearsay, or with all sorts of unsettling new expectations, most of which could not possibly turn out as promised.

The "symbol-using animal," yes, obviously. But can we bring ourselves to realize just what that formula implies, just how overwhelmingly much of what we mean by "reality" has been built up for us through nothing but our symbol systems? Take away our books, and what little do we know about history, biography, even something so "down to earth" as the relative position of seas and continents? What is our "reality" for today (beyond the paper-thin line of our own particular lives) but all this clutter of symbols about the past combined with whatever things we know mainly through maps, magazines, newspapers, and the like about the present? In school, as they go from class to class, students turn from one idiom to another. The various courses in the curriculum are in effect but so many different terminologies. And however important to us is the tiny sliver of reality each of us has experienced firsthand, the whole overall "picture" is but a construct of our symbol systems. To meditate on this fact until one sees its full implications is much like peering over the edge of things into an ultimate abyss. And doubtless that's one reason why, though man is typically the symbol-using animal, he clings to a kind of naïve verbal realism that refuses to realize the full extent of the role played by symbolicity in his notions of reality.

In responding to words, with their overt and covert modes of persuasion ("progress" is a typical one that usually sets expectations to vibrating), we like to forget the kind of relation that really prevails between the verbal and the nonverbal. In being a link between us and the nonverbal, words are by the same token a screen separating us from the nonverbal—though the statement gets tangled in its own traces, since so much of the "we" that is separated from the nonverbal by the verbal would not even exist were it not for the verbal (or for our symbolicity in general, since the same applies to the symbol systems of dance, music, painting, and the like).

A road map that helps us easily find our way from one side of the continent to the other owes its great utility to its exceptional existential poverty. It tells us absurdly little about the trip that is to be experienced in a welter of detail. Indeed, its value for us is in the very fact that it is so essentially inane.

Language referring to the realm of the nonverbal is necessarily talk about things in terms of what they are not—and in this sense we start out beset by a paradox. Such language is but a set of labels, signs for helping us find our way about. Indeed, they can even be so useful that they help us to invent ingenious ways of threatening to destroy ourselves. But even accuracy of this powerful sort does not get around the fact that such terms are sheer emptiness, as compared with the substance of the things they name. Nor is such abstractness confined to the language of scientific prose. Despite the concrete richness of the imagery in Keats's poems, his letters repeatedly refer to his art as "abstract." And the same kind of considerations would apply to the symbol systems of all other arts. Even so bodily a form of expression as the dance is abstract in this sense. (Indeed, in this regard it is so abstract that, when asking students to sum up the gist of a plot, I usually got the best results from dance majors, with music students a close second. Students specializing in literature or the social sciences tended to get bogged down in details. They were less apt at "abstracting.")

When a bit of talking takes place, just what is doing the talking? Just where are the words coming from? Some of the motivation must derive from our animality, and some from our symbolicity. We hear of "brainwashing," of schemes whereby an "ideology" is imposed upon people. But should we stop at that? Should we not also see the situation the other way around? For was not the "brainwasher" also similarly motivated? Do we simply use words, or do they not also use us? An "ideology" is like a god coming down to earth, where it will inhabit a place pervaded by its presence. An "ideology" is like a spirit taking up its abode in a body: it makes that body hop around in certain ways; and that same body would have hopped around in different ways had a different ideology happened to inhabit it.

I am saying in one way what Paul said in another when he told his listeners that "Faith comes from hearing." He had a doctrine which, if his hearers were persuaded to accept it, would direct a body somewhat differently from the way it would have moved and been moved in its daily rounds under the earlier pagan dispensation. Consider the kind of German boys and girls, for instance, who became burghers in the old days, who during the period of inflation and U.S.-financed reparation payments after World War I wanted but to be Wandering Birds, and who with the rise of the Third Reich were got to functioning as Hitlerite fiends.

With regard to this first clause in our definition (man as the "symbol-using" animal) it has often been suggested that "symbol-making" would be a better term. I can go along with that emendation. But I'd want to add one further step. Then, for the whole formula we'd have: the "symbol-using, symbol-making, and symbol-misusing animal."

In referring to the misuse of symbols, I have in mind not only such demagogic tricks as I have already mentioned. I also think of "psychogenic illnesses," violent dislocations of bodily motion due to the improperly criticized action of symbolicity. A certain kind of food may be perfectly wholesome, so far as its sheer material nature is concerned. And people in some areas may particularly prize it. But our habits may be such that it seems to us loathsome; and under those conditions, the very thought of eating it may be nauseating to us. (The most drastic instance is, of course, provided by the ideal diets of cannibals.) When the body rebels at such thoughts, we have a clear instance of the ways whereby the realm of symbolicity may affect the sheerly biologic motions of animality. Instances of "hexing" are of the same sort (as when a tribesman, on entering his tent, finds there the sign that for some reason those in authority have decreed his death by magic, and he promptly begins to waste away and die under the burden of this sheer thought).

A merely funny example concerns an anecdote told by the anthropologist, Franz Boas. He had gone to a feast being given by Esquimaux. As a good anthropologist, he would establish rapport by eating what they ate. But there was a pot full of what he took to be blubber. He dutifully took some, and felt sick. He went outside the igloo to recover. There he met an Esquimau woman, who was scandalized when she heard that they were serving blubber. For they hadn't told her! She rushed in—but came out soon after in great disgust. It wasn't blubber at all, it was simply dumplings. Had the good savant only known, he could have taken dumplings in his stride. But it was a battle indeed for him to hold them down when he thought of them as blubber!

So, in defining man as the symbol-using animal, we thereby set the conditions for asking: Which motives derive from man's animality, which from his symbolicity, and which from the combination of the two? Physicality is, of course, subsumed in animality. And though the *principles* of symbolism are not reducible to sheerly physical terms (quite as the rules of football are not so reducible despite the physicality of the players' hulks and motions as such), the meanings cannot be conceived by empirical organisms except by the aid of a sheerly physical dimension.

One further point, and we shall have finished with our first clause. In his analysis of dream symbolism, Freud laid great stress upon the two processes of "condensation" and "displacement." His observations are well taken. But, since we are here using the term "symbolism" in a much wider sense, we might remind ourselves that the processes of "condensation" and "displacement" are not confined merely to the symbolism of dreams and neuroses, but are also an aspect of normal symbol systems. A fundamental resource "natural" to symbolism is *substitution*. For instance, we can paraphrase a statement; if you don't get it one way, we can try another way. We translate English into French, Fahrenheit into Centigrade, or use the Greek letter *pi* to designate the ratio of the circumference of a circle to its diameter, otherwise stated as 3.14159. . . . In this sense, substitution is a quite rational resource of symbolism. Yet it is but a more general aspect of what Freud meant by "displacement" (which is a confused kind of substitution).

Or, as Horne Tooke pointed out a century and a half ago, a typical resource of language is abbreviation. And obviously, abbreviation is also a kind of substitution, hence a kind of "displacement," while it is also necessarily a kind of "condensation." And language is an abbreviation radically. If I refer to Mr. Jones by name, I have cut countless corners, as regards the particularities of that particular person. Or if I say, "Let's make a fire," think of what all I have left out, as regards the specific doing. Or if I give a book a title, I thereby refer to, while leaving unsaid, all that is subsumed under that title. Thus, condensation also can be viewed as a species of substitution. And a quite "rational" kind of "condensation" has taken place if, instead of referring to "tables," "chairs," and "rugs," I refer to "furniture," or if we put "parents" for "mother and father," and "siblings" for "brothers or sisters."

To say as much is to realize how many muddles such as Freud is concerned with may also be implicit in the symbols of "condensation" in his particular sense of the term. For my remarks are not intended as a "refutation" of Freud's terminology. By all means, my haggling about "condensation" and "displacement" as aspects of *all* symbolizing is not meant to question his line of investigation. All I am saying is that there still are some dividing lines to be drawn between the two realms (of symbolism in his sense and symbolism in general).

In any case, Freud (like Frazer) gives us ample grounds for trying never to forget that, once emotional involvement is added to symbolism's resources of substitution (which included the invitations to both condensation and displacement) the conditions are set for the symbol-using animal, with its ailments both physically and symbolically engendered, to tinker with such varying kinds of substitution as we encounter in men's modes of penance, expiation, compensation, paying of fines in lieu of bodily punishment, and cult of the scapegoat.

Obviously, to illustrate this point, there is an embarrassment of riches everywhere we choose to look, in the history of mankind. But, almost by accident, let us pick one, from a book, *Realm of the Incas,* by Victor W. Von Hagen. I refer to the picture of a

> propitiatory cairn, called *apacheta,* found in all of the high places of Peru on the ancient road. As heavily laden travelers passed along the road, they placed a stone on the *apacheta* as a symbol of the burden, "and so left their tiredness behind."

We are further told that "The Persians, the Chinese, and the Greeks adopted more or less the same custom."

Substitution sets the condition for "transcendence," since there is a technical sense in which the name for a thing can be said to "transcend" the thing named (by making for a kind of "ascent" from the realm of motion and matter to the realm of essence and spirit). The subterfuges of euphemism can carry this process still further, culminating in the resources of idealization that Plato perfected through his dialectic of the Upward Way and Downward Way.

The designation of man as the symbol-using animal parallels the traditional formulas, "rational animal" and *Homo sapiens*—but with one notable difference. These earlier versions are honorific, whereas the idea of symbolicity implies no such temptation to self-flattery, and to this extent is more admonitory. Such definitions as "two-footed land-animal" (referred to in Aristotle's *Topics*) or "featherless biped" (referred to in Spinoza's *Ethics*) would be inadequate because they would confine the horizon to the realm of motion.

So much for our first clause.

III

The second clause is: *Inventor of the negative.* I am not wholly happy with the word, "inventor." For we could not properly say that man "invented" the negative unless we can also say that man is the "inventor" of language itself. So far as sheerly empirical development is concerned, it might be more accurate to say that language and the negative "invented" man. In any case, we are here concerned with the fact that there are no negatives in nature, and that this ingenious addition to the universe is solely a product of human symbol systems. In an age when we are told, even in song, to "accentuate the positive," and when some experts in verbalization make big money writing inspirational works that praise "the power of positive thinking," the second clause of my definition must take on the difficult and thankless task of celebrating that peculiarly human marvel, the negative.

I have discussed elsewhere what an eye-opener the chapter, "The Idea of Nothing," was to me, in Bergson's *Creative Evolution*. It jolted me into realizing that there are no negatives in nature, where everything simply is what it is and as it is. To look for negatives in nature would be as absurd as though you were to go out hunting for the square root of minus-one. The negative is a function peculiar to symbol systems, quite as the square root of minus-one is an implication of a certain mathematical symbol system.

The quickest way to demonstrate the sheer symbolicity of the negative is to look at any object, say, a table, and to remind yourself that, though it is exactly what it is, you could go on for the rest of your life saying all the things that it is not. "It is not a book, it is not a house, it is not Times Square," etc., etc.

One of the negative's prime uses, as Bergson points out, involves its role with regard to unfulfilled expectations. If I am expecting a certain situation, and a different situation occurs, I can say that the expected situation did *not* occur. But so far as the actual state of affairs is concerned, some situation positively prevails, and that's that. If you are here but someone is expecting to meet you elsewhere, he will *not* meet you elsewhere because you positively *are* here. I can ask, "Does the thermometer read 54?" And if it registers anything in the world but 54, your proper answer can be "It is not 54." Yet there's no such thing as it's simply *not* being 54; it *is* 53, or 55, or whatever.

However, I would make one change of emphasis with regard to Bergson's fertile chapter. His stress is a bit too "Scientistic" for specifically "Dramatistic" purposes. Thus, in keeping with the stress upon matters of knowledge, he stresses the propositional negative, "It *is* not." Dramatistically, the stress should be upon the hortatory negative, "Thou *shalt* not." The negative begins not as a resource of definition or information, but as a command, as "Don't." Its more "Scientistic" potentialities develop later. And whereas Bergson is right in observing that we can't have an "idea of nothing" (that we must imagine a black spot, or something being annihilated, or an abyss, or some such), I submit that we *can* have an "idea of No," an "idea of don't." The Existentialists may amuse themselves and bewilder us with paradoxes about *le Néant,* by the sheer linguistic trick of treating no-thing as an abstruse kind of something. It's good showmanship. But there's no paradox about the idea of "don't," and a child can learn its meaning early.

No, I must revise that statement somewhat. In one sense, there is a paradox about "don't." For the negative is but a *principle,* an *idea,* not a name for a *thing*. And thus, whereas an injunction such as "thou shalt not kill" is understandable enough as a negative *idea,* it also has about its edges the positive *image* of killing. But the main point is: Though a child may not always obey the "thou shalt not," and though there may inevitably be, in the offing, an image positively inviting disobedience, the child "gets the idea."

In this sense, though we can't have an "idea of nothing," we can have an "idea of no." When first working on the negative, I thought of looking through the documents on the training of Helen Keller and Laura Bridgeman, whose physical privations made it so difficult to teach them language. And in both cases the records showed that the hortatory negative was taught first, and it was later applied for use as propositional negative, without explicit recognition of the change in application.

There is a superbly relevant passage in Emerson's early long essay, *Nature,* in the chapter "Discipline," a paragraph ending thus: All things "shall hint or thunder to man the laws of right and wrong, and echo the ten commandments." In our scheme, this could be presented thus: "Reverse the statement, start with the principle of negation as in the Mosaic Decalogue, and everything encountered along your way will be negatively infused."

In other words, if our character is built of our responses (positive or negative) to the thou-shalt-not's of morality, and if we necessarily approach life from the standpoint of our personalities, will not all experience reflect the genius of this negativity? Laws are essentially negative; "mine" equals "not thine"; insofar as property is not protected by the thou-shalt-not's of either moral or civil law, it is not protected at all.

The negative principle in morals is often hidden behind a realm of quasi-positives. One can appreciate this situation most readily by thinking of monastic discipline. The day may be filled with a constant succession of positive acts. Yet they are ultimately guided or regulated by proscriptive principles, involving acquiesence to vows consciously and conscientiously taken, while such vows come to fulfillment formally in such admonititions as are embodied in the Decalogue. Next, bearing in mind such clear evidence of the moralistic negativity that underlies the "quasi-positives" of the monastic rituals and routines, look at sheerly secular ambitions, with their countless ways of "justifying" oneself—and all such efforts too will be seen for what they are, not simply positives, but "quasi-positives," countless improvised ways of responding to the negativity so basic to man as moral agent.

Thus, all definitions stressing man as moral agent would tie in with this clause (if I may quote a relevant passage from a recent book of mine, *The Rhetoric of Religion*):

> *Action* involves *character,* which involves *choice*—and the *form* of choice attains its perfection in the distinction between Yes and No (shall and shall-not, will and will-not). Though the concept of sheer *motion* is non-ethical, *action* implies the ethical, the human personality. Hence the obvious close connection between the ethical and negativity, as indicated in the Decalogue.[1]

Is more needed on this point? We might say a few words about the role of antithesis in what are often called "polar" terms, not just Yes-No, but such similarly constructed pairs as: true-false, order-disorder, cosmos-chaos, success-failure, peace-war, pleasure-pain, clean-unclean, life-death, love-hate. These are to be distinguished from sheerly positive terms. The word "table," for instance, involves no thought of counter-table, anti-table, non-table, or un-table (except perhaps in the inventions of our quite positively negative-minded poet, E. E. Cummings).

We need not now decide whether, in such paired opposites, the positive or the negative member of the pair is to be considered as essentially prior. We can settle for the indubitable fact that all *moral* terms are of this polar sort. And we can settle merely for the fact that such positives and negatives imply each other. However, in a hit-and-run sort of way, before hurrying on, I might avow that I personally would treat the negative as in principle prior, for this reason: (1) Yes and No imply each other; (2) in their role as opposites, they *limit* each other; (3) but limitation itself is the "negation of part of a divisible quantum." (I am quoting from the article on Fichte in the *Encyclopaedia Britannica,* eleventh edition.)

There is an implied sense of negativity in the ability to use words at all. For to use them properly, we must know that they are *not* the things they stand for. Next, since language is extended by metaphor which gradually becomes the kind of dead metaphor we call abstraction, we must know that metaphor is *not* literal. Further, we cannot use language maturely until we are spontaneously at home in irony. (That is, if the weather is bad, and someone says, "What a beautiful day!" we spontaneously know that he does *not* mean what the words say on their face. Children, before reaching "the age of reason," usually find this twist quite disturbing, and are likely to object that it is *not* a good day. Dramatic irony, of course, carries such a principle of negativity to its most complicated perfection.)

Our tendency to write works on such topics as "The Spirit of Christianity," or "The Soul of Islam," or "The Meaning of Judaism," or "Buddha and Eternity," or "Hinduism and Metempsychosis," leads us to overlook a strongly negativistic aspect of religions. I refer here not just to the principle of moral negativity already discussed, but also to the fact that religions are so often built *antithetically* to other persuasions. Negative motivation of this sort is attested by such steps as the formation of Christianity in opposition to paganism, the formation of Protestant offshoots in opposition to Catholicism, and the current reinvigoration of churchgoing, if not exactly of religion, in opposition to communism. So goes the dialectic!

Only one more consideration, and we are through with thoughts on this clause in our definition:

In an advertising world that is so strong on the glorification of the positive (as a way of selling either goods or bads), how make the negative enticing? At times the job has been done negatively, yet effectively, by the threat of hell. But what sanctions can we best build on now?

What a notable irony we here confront! For some of man's greatest acts of genius are in danger of transforming millions and millions of human agents into positive particles of sheer motion that go on somehow, but that are negative indeed as regards even the minimum expectations to which we might feel entitled.

And what is this new astounding irony? Precisely the fact that all these new positive powers developed by the new technology have introduced a vast new era of negativity. For they are deadly indeed, unless we make haste to develop the controls (the negatives, the thou-shalt-not's) that become necessary, if these great powers are to be kept from getting out of hand.

Somewhat ironically, even as the possibilities of ultimate man-made suicide beset us, we also face an opposite kind of positive technologic threat to the resources of our moral negativity. I refer to the current "population explosion." In earlier days, the problem was solved automatically by plagues, famines, high rate of infant mortality, and such. But now the positive resources of technology have undone much of those natural "adjustments," so that new burdens are placed upon the Muscles of Negativity as the need arises for greater deliberate limitation of offspring.

However, ironically again, we should not end our discussion of this clause until we have reminded ourselves: There is a kind of aesthetic negativity whereby any moralistic thou-shalt-not provides material for our entertainment, as we pay to follow imaginary accounts of "deviants" who, in all sorts of ingenious ways, are represented as violating these very Don'ts.

IV

Third clause: *Separated from his natural condition by instruments of his own making*. It concerns the fact that even the most primitive of tribes are led by inventions to depart somewhat from the needs of food, shelter, sex as defined by the survival standards of sheer animality. The implements of hunting and husbandry, with corresponding implements of war, make for a set of habits that become a kind of "second nature," as a special set of expectations, shaped by custom, comes to seem "natural." (I recall once when there was a breakdown of the lighting equipment in New York City. As the newspapers the next day told of the event, one got almost a sense of mystical terror from the description of the darkened streets. Yet but fifty miles away, that same evening, we had been walking on an unlit road by our house in the country, in a darkness wholly "natural." In the "second nature" of the city, something so natural as dark roadways at night was weirdly "unnatural.")

This clause is designed to take care of those who would define man as the "tool-using animal" (*homo faber, homo economicus,* and such). In adding this clause, we are immediately reminded of the close tie-up between tools and language. Imagine trying to run a modern factory, for instance, without the vast and often ungainly nomenclatures of the various technological specialties, without instructions, education, specifications, filing systems, accountancy (including mathematics and money or some similar counters). And I already referred to the likelihood that the development of tools requires a kind of attention not possible without symbolic means of conceptualization. The connection between tools and language is also observable in what we might call the "second level" aspect of both. I refer to the fact that, whereas one might think of other animals as using certain rudiments of symbolism and rudimentary tools (for instance, when an ape learns to use a stick as a means of raking in a banana that the experimenter has purposely put beyond arm's length), in both cases the "reflexive" dimension is missing. Animals do not use words about words (as with the definitions of a dictionary)—and though an ape may even learn to put two sticks together as a way of extending his reach in case the sticks are so made that one can be fitted into the other, he would not take a knife and deliberately hollow out the end of one stick to make possible the insertion of the other stick. This is what we mean by the reflexive or second-level aspect of human symbolism. And it would presumably apply also to such complex sign systems as bees apparently have, to spread information about the distance and direction of a newly discovered food supply. Apparently investigators really have "cracked" such a code in certain dancelike motions of bees—but we should hardly expect ever to find that student bees are taught the language by teacher bees, or that there are apiaries where bees formulate the grammar and syntax of such signaling. "Information" in the sense of sheer motion is not thus "reflexive," but rather is like that of an electric circuit where, if a car is on a certain stretch of track, it automatically turns off the current on the adjoining piece of track, so that any car on that other piece of track would stop through lack of power. The car could be said to behave in accordance with this "information."

However, in saying that the human powers of symbolicity are interwoven with the capacity for making tools (and particularly for making tools that make tools), we still haven't answered one objection. If the two powers involve each other, if the same reflexive trait is characteristic of both, why start with symbol-using rather than with toolmaking? I'd propose an answer of this sort:

Formally, is not the choice implicit in the very act of definition itself? If we defined man first of all as the tool-using animal (or, old style, as *homo faber* rather than as *homo sapiens*), our definition would not be taking into account the "priority" of its very own nature as a definition. Inasmuch as definition is a symbolic act, it must begin by explicitly recognizing its formal grounding in the *principle* of definition as an act. In choosing *any definition at all,* one implicitly represents man as the kind of animal that is capable of definition (that is to say, capable of symbolic action). Thus, even if one views the powers of speech and mechanical invention as mutually involving each other, in a technical or formal sense one should make the implications explicit by treating the gifts of symbolicity as the "prior" member of the pair.

Also, we should note that one especially good result follows from this choice. Those who begin with the stress upon *tools* proceed to define language itself as a species of tool. But though instrumentality is an important aspect of language, we could not properly treat it as the *essence* of language. To define language simply as a species of tool would be like defining metals merely as species of tools. Or like defining sticks and stones simply as primitive weapons. Edward Sapir's view of language as "a collective means of expression" points in a more appropriate direction. The instrumental value of language certainly accounts for much of its development, and this instrumental value of language may even have been responsible for the survival of language itself (by helping the language-using animal to survive), quite as the instrumental value of language in developing atomic power now threatens the survival of the language-using animal; but to say as much is not by any means to say that language is in its essence a tool. Language is a species of action, symbolic action—and its nature is such that it can be used as a tool.

In any case, the toolmaking propensities envisioned in our third clause result in the complex network of material operations and properties, public or private, that arise through men's ways of livelihood, with the different *classes* of society that arise through the division of labor and the varying relationships to the property structure. And that brings us to our fourth clause.

V

Fourth clause: *Goaded by the spirit of hierarchy.* But if that sounds too weighted, we could settle for, "Moved by a sense of order." Under this clause, of course, would fall the incentives of organization and status. In my *Rhetoric of Motives,* I tried to trace the relation between social hierarchy and mystery, or guilt. And I carried such speculations further in my *Rhetoric of Religion.* Here we encounter secular analogues of "original sin." For, despite any cult of good manners and humility, to the extent that a social structure becomes differentiated, with privileges to some that are denied to others, there are the conditions for a kind of "built in" pride. King and peasant are "mysteries" to each other. Those "Up" are guilty of not being "Down," those "Down" are certainly guilty of not being "Up."

Here man's skill with symbols combines with his negativity and with the tendencies towards different modes of livelihood implicit in the inventions that make for division of labor, the result being definitions and differentiations and allocations of property protected by the negativities of the law. I particularly like E. M. Forster's novel, *A Passage to India,* for its ingenious ways of showing how social mystery can become interwoven with ideas of cosmic mystery. The grotesque fictions of Franz Kafka are marvelous in this regard. The use of the word "Lord," to designate sometimes the Deity and sometimes an aristocrat, in itself indicates the shift between the two kinds of "worship." In *Book of the Courtier* Castiglione brings out the relationship nicely when he writes of kneeling on one knee to the sovereign, on both knees to God. Or, in ancient Rome, the application of the term *pontifex maximus* to the Emperor specifically recognized his "bridging" relationship as both a god and the head of the social hierarchy. Milton's use of terms such as Cherubim, Seraphim, Thrones, Dominations, Powers, reflects the conceiving of supernatural relations after the analogy of a social ladder. The religious vision of the city on a hill is similarly infused—making in all a ziggurat-like structure without skyscrapers. (Recall a related image, El Greco's painting of Toledo.) And, of course, the principles of such hierarchal order are worked out with imaginative and intellectual fullness in Dante's *Divine Comedy.* The medieval pageant probably represents the perfection of this design. All the various "mysteries" were represented, each distinct from all the others, yet all parts of the same overarching order.

VI

By now we should also have taken care of such definitions as man the "political animal" or the "culture-bearing animal." And for a while, I felt that these clauses sufficiently covered the ground. However, for reasons yet to be explained, I decided that a final codicil was still needed, thus making in all:

Man is
the symbol-using (symbol-making, symbol-misusing) animal
inventor of the negative (or moralized by the negative)
separated from his natural condition by instruments of his own making
goaded by the spirit of hierarchy (or moved by the sense of order)
and rotten with perfection.

I must hurry to explain and justify this wry codicil.

The principle of perfection is central to the nature of language as motive. The mere desire to name something by its "proper" name, or to speak a language in its distinctive ways is intrinsically "perfectionist." What is more "perfectionist" in essence than the impulse, when one is in dire need of something, to so state this need that one in effect "defines" the situation? And even a poet who works out cunning ways of distorting language does so with perfectionist principles in mind, though his ideas of improvement involve recondite stylistic twists that may not disclose their true nature as judged by less perverse tests.

Thoughts on this subject induce us to attempt adapting, for sheerly logological purposes, the Aristotelian concept of the "entelechy," the notion that each being aims at the perfection natural to its kind (or, etymologically, is marked by a "possession of telos within"). The stone would be all that is needed to make it a stone; the tree would be all that is needed to make it a tree; and man would (or should!) be all that is needed to make him the perfectly "rational" being (presumably a harder entelechial job to accomplish than lower kinds of entities confront). Our point is: Whereas Aristotle seems to have thought of all beings in terms of the entelechy (in keeping with the ambiguities of his term, *kinesis,* which includes something of both "action" and "motion"), we are confining our use of the principle to the realm of symbolic action. And in keeping with this view, we would state merely: There is a principle of perfection implicit in the nature of symbol systems; and in keeping with his nature as symbol-using animal, man is moved by this principle.

At this point we must pause to answer an objection. In *Beyond the*

Pleasure Principle (near the end of Chapter V) Freud explicitly calls upon us "to abandon our belief that in man there dwells an impulse towards perfection, which has brought him to his present heights of intellectual prowess and sublimation." Yet a few sentences later in that same closing paragraph, we find him saying, "The repressive instinct never ceases to strive after its complete satisfaction." But are not these two sentences mutually contradictory? For what could more clearly represent an "impulse to perfection" than a "striving" after "complete satisfaction"?

The alternative that Freud proposes to the striving after perfection is what he calls a "repetition compulsion." And near the end of Chapter III he has described it thus:

> One knows people with whom every human relationship ends in the same way: benefactors whose protégés, however different they may otherwise have been, invariably after a time desert them in ill-will, so that they are apparently condemned to drain to the dregs all the bitterness of ingratitude; men with whom every friendship ends in the friend's treachery; others who indefinitely often in their lives invest some other person with authority either in their own eyes or generally, and themselves overthrow such authority after a given time, only to replace it by a new one; lovers whose tender relationships with women each and all run through the same phases and come to the same end, and so on. We are less astonished at this "endless repetition of the same" if there is involved a question of active behaviour on the part of the person concerned, and if we detect in his character an unalterable trait which must always manifest itself in the repetition of identical experiences. Far more striking are those cases where the person seems to be experiencing something passively, without exerting any influence of his own, and yet always meets with the same fate over and over again.

Freud next mentions in Tasso's *Gerusalemme Liberata* the story of the hero Tancred who, having unwittingly slain his beloved Clorinda, later in an enchanted wood hews down a tall tree with his sword, and when blood streams from the gash in the tree, he hears the voice of Clorinda whose soul was imprisoned in the tree, and who reproaches him for having again "wrought" the same "baleful deed."

Freud sees in all such instances the workings of what he calls the neurotic attempt to so shape one's later life that some earlier unresolved problem is lived over and over again. Freud also calls it a "destiny compulsion," to bring out the thought that the sufferer unconsciously strives to form his destiny in accordance with this earlier pattern.

My point is: Why should such a "destiny compulsion" or "repetition compulsion" be viewed as antithetical to the "principle of perfection"? Is not the sufferer exerting almost superhuman efforts in the attempt to give his life a certain *form,* so shaping his relations to people in later years that they will conform perfectly to an emotional or psychological pattern already established in some earlier formative situation? What more thorough illustrations could one want, of a drive to make one's life "perfect," despite the fact that such efforts at perfection might cause the unconscious striver great suffering?

To get the point, we need simply widen the concept of perfection to the point where we can also use the term *ironically,* as when we speak of a "perfect fool" or a "perfect villain." And, of course, I had precisely such possibilities in mind when in my codicil I refer to man as being "rotten" with perfection.

The ironic aspect of the principle is itself revealed most perfectly in our tendency to conceive of a "perfect" enemy. (See on " 'Perfection' as a Motive," in *Permanence and Change,* Hermes edition, pp. 292–294.) The Nazi version of the Jew, as developed in Hitler's *Mein Kampf,* is the most thoroughgoing instance of such ironic "perfection" in recent times, though strongly similar trends keep manifesting themselves in current controversies between "East" and "West." I suppose the most "perfect" definition of man along these lines is the formula derived from Plautus: *homo homini lupus,* or one to suit the sort of imaginary herding animal that would fit Hobbes's notion of the *bellum omnium contra omnes.*

The principle of perfection in this dangerous sense derives sustenance from other primary aspects of symbolicity. Thus, the principle of drama is implicit in the idea of action, and the principle of victimage is implicit in the nature of drama. The negative helps radically to define the elements to be victimized. And inasmuch as substitution is a prime resource of symbol systems, the conditions are set for catharsis by scapegoat (including the "natural" invitation to "project" upon the enemy any troublesome traits of our own that we would negate). And the unresolved problems of "pride" that are intrinsic to privilege also bring the motive of hierarchy to bear here; for many kinds of guilt, resentment, and fear tend to cluster about the hierarchal psychosis, with its corresponding search for a sacrificial principle such as can become embodied in a political scapegoat.

Similar ominous invitations along these lines derive from the terministic fact that, as Aristotle observed in his *Rhetoric,* antithesis is an exceptionally effective rhetorical device. There is its sheerly *formal* lure, in giving dramatic saliency and at least apparent clarity to any issue. One may find himself hard put to define a policy purely in its own terms, but one can advocate it persuasively by an urgent assurance that it is decidedly *against* such-and-such other policy with which people may be disgruntled. For this reason also, the use of antithesis helps deflect embarrassing criticism (as when rulers silence domestic controversy by turning public attention to animosity against some foreign country's policies). And in this way, of course, antithesis helps reinforce unification by scapegoat.

The principle of perfection (the "entelechial" principle) figures in other notable ways as regards the genius of symbolism. A given terminology contains various *implications,* and there is a corresponding "perfectionist" tendency for men to attempt carrying out those implications. Thus, each of our scientific nomenclatures suggests its own special range of possible developments, with specialists vowed to carry out these terministic possibilities to the extent of their personal ability and technical resources. Each such specialty is like the situation of an author who has an idea for a novel, and who will never rest until he has completely embodied it in a book. Insofar as any of these terminologies happen also to contain the risks of destroying the world, that's just too bad; but the fact remains that, so far as the sheer principles of the investigation are concerned, they are no different from those of the writer who strives to complete his novel. There is a kind of "terministic compulsion" to carry out the implications of one's terminology, quite as, if an astronomer discovered by his observations and computations that a certain wandering body was likely to hit the earth and destroy us, he would nonetheless feel compelled to *argue for the correctness of his computations,* despite the ominousness of the outcome. Similarly, of course, men will so draw out the implications of their terminologies that new expectations are aroused (promises that are now largely interwoven with the state of Big Technology, and that may prove to be true or false, but that can have revolutionary effects upon persons who agree with such terministic "extrapolations").

Whereas there seems to be no principle of control intrinsic to the ideal of carrying out any such set of possibilities to its "perfect" conclusion, and whereas all sorts of people are variously goaded to track down their particular sets of terministically directed insights, there is at least the fact that the schemes get in one another's way, thus being to some extent checked by rivalry with one another. And such is especially the case where *allocation of funds* is concerned.

To round out the subject of "perfection," in both honorific and ironic senses, we might end by observing that, without regard for the ontological truth or falsity of the case, there are sheerly technical reasons, intrinsic to the nature of language, for belief in God and the Devil. Insofar as language is intrinsically hortatory (a medium by which men can obtain the cooperation of one another), God perfectly embodies the petition. Similarly, insofar as vituperation is a "natural" resource of speech, the Devil provides a perfect butt for invective. Heaven and Hell together provide the ultimate, or perfect, grounding for sanctions. God is also the perfect audience for praise and lamentation (two primary modes of symbolic action, with lamentation perhaps the "first" of all, as regards tests of biological priority). Such considerations would provide a strictly logological treatment of Martin Buber's "I-Thou Relation."

VII

So much for the clauses of our Definition, a definition which most people would probably want to characterize as "descriptive" rather than "normative," yet which is surely normative in the sense that its implications are strongly admonitory, suggesting the kind of foibles and crotchets which a "comic" theory of education [2] would feature, in asking man to center his attention on the understanding of his "natural temptations" towards kinds of turbulence that, when reinforced with the powers of the new weapons, threaten to undo us.

I'm not too sure that, in the present state of Big Technology's confusions, any educational policy, even if it were itself perfect and were adopted throughout the world, would be able to help much, when the world is so ardently beset by so much distress and malice. The dreary likelihood is that, if we do avoid the holocaust, we shall do so mainly by bits of political patchwork here and there, with alliances falling sufficiently on the bias across one another, and thus getting sufficiently in one another's road, so that there's not enough "symmetrical perfection" among the contestants to set up the "right" alignment and touch it off.

Perhaps because of my special liking for the sympathetically ironic point of view in E. M. Forster's novel, *A Passage to India,* I place a wan hope in the sheer muddle of current international relations. That is, there is the chance that the problem, in its very insolubility, also contains enough elements of self-cancellation to keep things from coming to a perfect fulfillment in a perfect Apocalyptic holocaust. Meanwhile, the most that one can do, when speculating on a definition, is to ask oneself whether it is turned somewhat in the right direction.

But what of an ending for this discussion? After so much talk about "perfection," I feel quite self-conscious. For obviously, my discussion should itself have a perfect ending.

A perfect ending should promise something. In this regard, I guess the most perfect ending is provided by a sermon in which, after a threat of total loss unless we mend our ways, we are promised the hope of total salvation if we do mend our ways. But even though, today, we stand as close as mankind ever has stood, in secular regards, to a choice precisely as radical as that, I can build up no such perfectly urgent pattern (partly because, as we generally recognize now, it is impossible for us truly to imagine that next day, no matter how earnestly some writers try to help us by inventing imaginary accounts of it, accounts which even they can't believe, despite the enterprise of their imaginings).

The best I can do is state my belief that things might be improved somewhat if enough people began thinking along the lines of this definition; my belief that, if such an approach could be perfected by many kinds of critics and educators and self-admonishers in general, things might be a little less ominous than otherwise.

However, at this point I hit upon a kind of *Ersatz* promise for an ending. As you will see, it is concerned with perfection on a grand scale. And it has in its favor the further fact that it involves the modernizing, or perfecting, of a traditional vision, one even so primal as to be expressed in a nursery jingle. I shall give the traditional jingle first, and then my proposed modernized perfecting of it. The older form ran thus:

If all the trees were one tree
What a great tree that would be

If all the axes were one axe
What a great axe that would be.

If all the men were one man
What a great man he would be.

And if all the seas were one sea
What a great sea that would be.

And if the great man
Took the great axe
And chopped down the great tree
And let it fall into the great sea

What a Splish-Splash that would be!

Modernized, perfected, the form runs thus:

If all the thermo-nuclear warheads
Were one thermo-nuclear warhead
What a great thermo-nuclear warhead that would be.

If all the intercontinental ballistic missiles
Were one intercontinental ballistic missile
What a great intercontinental ballistic missile that would be.

If all the military men
Were one military man
What a great military man he would be.

And if all the land masses
Were one land mass
What a great land mass that would be.

And if the great military man
Took the great thermo-nuclear warhead
And put it into the great intercontinental ballistic missile
And dropped it on the great land mass,

What great PROGRESS that would be!

COMMENTS

One might ask the question: "What does it mean, to approach reality through one language rather than another?" Or one might ask: "What does it mean to be the kind of animal that uses *any* language (to view reality through *any* kind of highly developed symbol system)?" Benjamin Lee Whorf's ingenious speculations (many of them collected in his volume, *Language, Thought, and Reality*) suggest answers to the first question. The present "Definition" has been concerned rather with answers to the second.

Men can be studied as individuals, as members of groups (tribes, classes, organizations, and the like), or as generically "human." The present essay has been concerned with the most "universal" of such classifications. But elsewhere we deal with the fact that the analysis of particular idioms can be methodically narrowed even to the study of one particular writer's terminology (with its own unique set of "personal equations").

Given the range of meanings in the ancient Greeks' concept of "politics," the anthropologists' definition of man as the "culture-bearing animal" is not far from Aristotle's view of man as the "political animal." Both imply the ability to develop and transmit conventions and institutions. Just as Aristotle's definition serves most directly for his book on politics, so the anthropologists' definition serves most directly for their studies of tribal cultures. "Social animal" might most directly suit sociologists. Our point is simply that for our purposes a still more general starting point is necessary, analogous to *homo sapiens,* but minus the "built-in" honorific connotations of that formula (though perhaps it did perform a notable rhetorical function in prodding many of the perverse to cherish after the manner of Flaubert the lore of *la bêtise humaine*). For the psychologist, man is a "psychological" animal; for the psychoanalyst a mentally sick animal (a psychopathology being a natural part of even the average or "normal" Everyman's everyday life); for the chemist man should be a congeries of chemicals; and so on. But since man can't be called any of these various things except insofar as, encompassing the lot, he is the kind of animal that can haggle about the definition of himself, in this sense he is what Ernst Cassirer has called the *animal symbolicum;* yet I feel that the post-Kantian way of understanding such a formula tends to get epistemologically ("Scientistically") sidetracked from the more ontological ("Dramatistic") approach grounded in the older scholastic tradition.

The idealizing of man as a species of machine has again gained considerable popularity, owing to the great advances in automation and "sophisticated" computers. But such things are obviously inadequate as models since, not being biological organisms, machines lack the capacity for pleasure or pain (to say nothing of such subtler affective states as malice, envy, amusement, condescension, friendliness, sentimentality, embarrassment, etc., *ad nauseam*). One might so construct a computer that, if its signals got into a traffic jam, it would give forth a cry like a child in agony. And this "information" might make you impulsively, despite yourself, feel compassion for it. Yet, not being an organism, the ingenious artificial construct would all the while be as impassive as a Stoic's ideal of the perfect philosopher. For though the contraption might be so designed that it could *record* its own outcry, it could not "hear" that cry in the sense in which you, as an organism of pleasure and pain, would hear it. Until, like the robots in Capek's *R.U.R.,* men's contrivances can be made actually to ache, they cannot possibly serve as adequate models for the total human condition (that is, for a definition of "man in general").

When two machines get cruelly smashed in an accident, it's all the same to them, so far as pain goes. Hence a definition of man without reference to the animality of pain is, on its face, as inadequate as a definition would be that reduced man to the sheer kinetics of chemistry. Unquestionably, such a reduction could tell us much about the realm of motions that underlies our modes of action, and without which we could not act. But we *intuitively* recognize that such terms alone cannot deal with the qualities of experience as we necessarily suffer and enact it. (Awareness itself, by the way, is ambiguously on the dividing line between "action" and "knowledge"; or, otherwise put, intuitive knowledge is a spontaneous activity much like what we call an "act of faith," as per Santayana's ingenious concept of "animal faith.")

Insofar as the concept of "action" gets reduced to terms of "work," conditions are set for an antithetical stress upon play, as with Huizinga's formula, *homo ludens.* While obviously not general enough to cover all cases, it serves well as an instrument to warn us against an overly instrumentalist view of man's ways with symbols. Here would belong also a related view of man, as the "laughing animal." While laughter, like tears, is grounded in the motions of animality, it also depends upon principles of congruity that are due to conventions or proprieties developed through the resources of symbolicity. It embodies these norms of congruity in reverse, by their violation within limits, a kind of "planned incongruity" (as discussed in my *Permanence and Change*). Thus the incongruously perfect definition of man as a wolf (in keeping with man's traditional attitude towards that much maligned, but highly social-minded animal) comes down to us through comedy.

The reference to proprieties suggests the observation that the definition of man as a "moral being" centers in that mighty symbolic invention, the negative, involving the "thou-shalt-not's" (and corresponding "thou shalt's") of law and conscience, and the saying yes or no to such proscriptions and prescriptions. Here would belong Whitman's celebration of the "Answerer," and Nietzsche's paradoxical, negativity-saturated idea of the "Yea-sayer." I remember having heard that William Blackstone somewhere defines man as a being endowed with the capacity for all kinds of crime. Though I have not been able to verify the reference, such a definition would be the most direct fit for commentaries on the law; yet "crime" is but a reflex of human prowess in the making of laws, that is, man's "symbolicity." And Goethe has offered us an attenuated variant of the same notion when confessing an ability to *imagine* all kinds of crime.

The third essay will illustrate the basic symbolic devices under which one should class man as a being typically endowed with the powers of "transcendence." And many subsequent chapters will provide other instances of such resourcefulness (for instance, the piece on Emersonian transcendentalism) including its relation to the hierarchal motive, as embodied in the social order.

Man's "time-binding" propensities would be a subdivision of his traffic with symbols, though the fourth chapter will also consider a sense in which the past is preserved "unconsciously" in the animal tissues.

All told, we should by now have reviewed a sufficient range of cases to indicate why we feel that any possible definition of man will necessarily fall somewhere within the five clauses in our "Definition." Basically, these involve concepts of motion and action (or otherwise put, physicality, animality, and symbolicity). And above all, we would want to emphasize: Whereas many other animal seem sensitive in a rudimentary way to the motivating force of symbols, they seem to lack the "second-level" aspect of symbolicity that is characteristically human, the "reflexive" capacity to develop highly complex symbol systems about symbol systems, the pattern of which is indicated in Aristotle's definition of God as "thought of thought," or in Hegel's dialectics of "self-consciousness."

As we proceed, there will be other chances to consider these matters.

NOTES

1 It suggests the thought that our second clause might be rephrased: "Moralized by the negative."

2 In his *Parts of Animals,* Chapter X, Aristotle mentions the definition of man as the "laughing animal," but he does not consider it adequate. Though I would hasten to agree, I obviously have a big investment in it, owing to my conviction that mankind's only hope is a cult of comedy. (The cult of tragedy is too eager to help out with the holocaust. And in the last analysis, it is too pretentious to allow for the proper recognition of our animality.) Also, I'd file "risibility" under "symbolicity." Insofar as man's laughter is to be distinguished from that of the Hyena, the difference derives from ideas of *incongruity* that are in turn derived from principles of *congruity* necessarily implicit in any given symbol system.

36

From "Behavior in Extreme Situations: Coercion"

Bruno Bettelheim

THE WILL TO LIVE

The question arises as to why, in the concentration camp, although some prisoners survived and others got killed,[1] such a sizable percentage simply died.

Reports about the mortality rate in the camps vary between 20% and 50%, but any overall figure is misleading.[2] More significant is the fact that the vast majority of the thousands of prisoners who died at Buchenwald each year died soon. They simply died of exhaustion, both physical and psychological, due to a loss of desire to live.

After one had learned how to live in the camps, the chances for survival increased greatly. Except for rare occasions, such as the Hamber episode, large scale executions of old prisoners were rare. While one was never without fear for one's life, the fact that several thousands of the prisoners liberated in 1945 had spent five and even ten years in the camps suggests that the death rate for old prisoners was very different from what overall figures would suggest.

Since the only data we have is for a six month period in 1942, the following estimates are admittedly based on impressions. But I feel safe in assuming that the death rate of old prisoners (always excluding extermination, etc.) was rarely more than 10% a year, reckoned from the number of old prisoners present at any one time. On the other hand, the early death rate of new prisoners, particularly during their first months in the camp, may have been as high as 15% *a month*. This, of course, intensified the terror of new prisoners to an unbearable pitch and explains why many of them soon deteriorated into the deathlike state I will soon speak about.

In addition to their high mortality, this group also lived in the worst barracks, amid the worst overcrowding and least sanitation, all of which was soon considerably worsened by their own deterioration. They received the worst food, the least of it, and often no money or mail for months because it took a long time for money and mail to begin to arrive or be distributed.

THE UNPREDICTABLE ENVIRONMENT

What happened in the concentration camp suggests that under conditions of extreme deprivation, the influence of the environment over the individual can become total. Whether it does or not seems to depend a great deal on impact and timing; on how sudden the impact, and how little (or how much) the individual is prepared for it (because it is also destructive if someone has always expected something terrible to happen to him and it does). It depends even more on how long the condition prevails, how well integrated the person is whom it hits, and finally whether it remains unmitigated. Or to put the last point differently: whether the conviction is given that no matter what one does, no positive response can be drawn from the environment through efforts of one's own.

This was so much so, that whether or not one survived may have depended on one's ability to arrange to preserve some areas of independent action, to keep control of some important aspects of one's life, despite an environment that seemed overwhelming and total. To survive, not as a shadow of the SS but as a man, one had to find some life experience that mattered, over which one was still in command.

This was taught me by a German political prisoner, a communist worker who by then had been at Dachau for four years. I arrived there in a sorry condition because of experiences on the transport. I think that this man, by then an "old" prisoner, decided that, given my condition, the chances of my surviving without help were slim. So when he noticed that I could not swallow food because of physical pain and psychological revulsion, he spoke to me out of his rich experience: "Listen you, make up your mind: do you want to live or do you want to die? If you don't care, don't eat the stuff. But if you want to live, there's only one way: make up your mind to eat whenever and whatever you can, never mind how disgusting. Whenever you have a chance, defecate, so you'll be sure your body works. And whenever you have a minute, don't blabber, read by yourself, or flop down and sleep."

This advice, after a while, I made my own and none too soon for my survival. In my case, trying to find out what went on in the prisoners took the place of the activity he had had in mind when he suggested reading. Soon I became convinced of how sound his advice had been. But it took me years to fully grasp its psychological wisdom.

What was implied was the necessity, for survival, to carve out, against the greatest of odds, some areas of freedom of action and freedom of thought, however insignificant. The two freedoms, of activity and passivity, constitute our two most basic human attitudes, while intake and elimination, mental activity and rest, make up our most basic physiological activities. To have some small token experiences of being active and passive, each on one's own, and in mind as well as body—this, much more than the utility of any one such activity, was what enabled me and others like me to survive.[3]

By contrast, it was the senseless tasks, the lack of almost any time to oneself, the inability to plan ahead because of sudden changes in camp policies, that was so deeply destructive. By destroying man's ability to act on his own or to predict the outcome of his actions, they destroyed the feeling that his actions had any purpose, so many prisoners stopped acting. But when they stopped acting they soon stopped living. What seemed to make the critical difference was whether or not the environment—extreme as it was—permitted (or promised) some minimal choices, some leeway, some positive rewards, insignificant as they seem now, when viewed objectively against the tremendous deprivation.

That may be why the SS vacillated between extreme repression and the easing of tension: the torture of prisoners, but occasional punishment of particularly inhuman guards; sudden respect and reward from the SS for some random prisoner who insisted on his dignity; sudden days of rest, etc. Without these, for example, no identification with the SS could have taken place, to mention only one outcome. Most prisoners who died, as opposed to those who got killed, were those who could no longer believe in, or take advantage of, those sudden remissions that happen in even the most extreme situations; in short those who had given up all will to live.

It was impressive to observe how skillfully the SS used this mechanism of destroying man's faith in his ability to predict the future. For want of evidence we cannot say if this was deliberate or unconscious but it worked with deadly effectiveness. If the SS wanted a group (Norwegians, political prisoners who were not Jewish, etc.) to adjust, survive, and serve in the camps, they would hold out the promise that their behavior had some influence on their fate. To those groups whom they wished to destroy (Eastern Jews, Poles, Ukrainians, etc.) they made it quite clear that no matter how hard they worked or tried to please their masters, it would make no difference whatsoever.

Another means of destroying the prisoners' belief that they had some basis for hope, some influence over their fate, and therefore some reason for wanting to live, was to expose them to sudden radical changes in living conditions. At one camp, for example, a large group of Czech prisoners was utterly destroyed by giving them the promise that they were "honor" prisoners entitled to special privileges, letting them live in relative comfort without any work or hardship for a time, then suddenly throwing them into quarry work where labor conditions were worst and mortality highest, while at the same time reducing their food rations; then back again into good quarters and easy work, and after a few months back into the quarries with little food, etc. Soon they all died.

My own experience of three times being called up to be freed and each time being dressed in civilian clothes to be ready for release, is another example. Possibly it happened because I had provoked an SS official. The first time, nearly all other prisoners called up with me were released while I was sent back into the camp. The second time may have been chance, because quite a few besides myself were sent back, and rumor had it that the SS had run out of money and could not pay the sums due the prisoners for the trip home. In any case, when I was summoned the third time I refused to go and be put into civilian clothes because I was convinced it was just another effort of the SS official to break me. But this time the call was authentic.

The question is: why did I deliberately provoke an SS officer? I believe that in order not to collapse, I had to prove to myself that I had some power to influence my environment. I knew I could not do it positively, so I did it negatively. Nor was this reasoned out. I acted on the unconscious realization of what I needed most to survive.

THE PENALTY FOR SUICIDE

Since the main goal of the SS was to do away with independence of action and the ability to make personal decisions, even negative ways of achieving it were not neglected. The decision to remain alive or to die is probably a supreme example of self-determination. Therefore the SS attitude toward suicide may be mentioned.

The stated principle was: the more prisoners to commit suicide, the better. But even there, the decision must not be the prisoner's. An SS man might provoke a prisoner to commit suicide by running against the electrically charged wire fence, and that was all right. But for those who took the initiative in killing themselves, the SS issued (in Dachau in 1933) a special order: prisoners who attempted suicide but did not succeed were to receive twenty-five lashes and prolonged solitary confinement. Supposedly this was to punish them for their failure to do away with themselves; but I am convinced it was much more to punish them for the act of self-determination.

Also, since protecting life, either one's own or that of others, is a major act of self-assertion, it too had to be inhibited. Therefore the same punishment was threatened to any prisoner who tried to prevent a suicide before it happened, or tried to bring back to life a prisoner who tried it. To my knowledge this punishment for attempted suicide or for helping a suicidal person was only once carried out; but it was not the punishment the SS was interested in, it was the threat of punishment and what that did to destroy self-determination.[4]

MUSELMÄNNER: THE WALKING CORPSES

Prisoners who came to believe the repeated statements of the guards—that there was no hope for them, that they would never leave the camp except as a corpse—who came to feel that their environment was one over which they could exercise no influence whatsoever, these prisoners were, in a literal sense, walking corpses. In the camps they were called "moslems" (*Muselmänner*) because of what was erroneously viewed as a fatalistic surrender to the environment, as Mohammedans are supposed to blandly accept their fate.

But these people had not, like real Mohammedans, made an act of decision and submitted to fate out of free will. On the contrary, they were people who were so deprived of affect, self esteem, and every form of stimulation, so totally exhausted, both physically and emotionally, that they had given the environment total power over them. They did this when they gave up trying to exercise any further influence over their life or environment.

That is, as long as a prisoner fought in any way for survival, for some self-assertion within and against the overpowering environment, he could not become a "moslem." Once his own life and the environment were viewed as totally beyond his ability to influence them, the only logical conclusion was to pay no attention to them whatsoever. Only then, all conscious awareness of stimuli coming from the outside was blocked out, and with it all response to anything but inner stimuli.

But even the moslems, being organisms, could not help reacting somehow to their environment, and this they did by depriving it of the power to influence them as subjects in any way whatsoever. To achieve this, they had to give up responding to it at all, and become objects, but with this they gave up being persons. These walking shadows all died very soon. Or to put it differently, after a certain point of extreme deprivation, the environment can only move around empty shells, as the camp routine did with these moslems; they behaved as if they were not thinking, not feeling, unable to act or respond, moved only by things outside themselves.

One might even speculate as to whether these organisms had bypassed the reflex arc that once extended from external or internal stimulus via frontal lobes to feeling and action. First they had given up all action as being utterly pointless; then feeling, because all feeling was merely painful or dangerous or both. Eventually this somehow extended backwards to blocking out the stimulation itself.

These things could be readily observed in the deterioration of moslems. It began when they stopped acting on their own. And that was the moment when other prisoners recognized what was happening and separated themselves from these now "marked" men, because any further association with them could lead only to one's own destruction. At this point such men still obeyed orders, but only blindly or automatically; no longer selectively or with inner reservation or any hatred at being so abused. They still looked about, or at least moved their eyes around. The looking stopped much later, though even then they still moved their bodies when ordered, but never did anything on their own any more. Typically, this stopping of action began when they no longer lifted their legs as they walked, but only shuffled them. When finally even the looking about on their own stopped, they soon died.

DON'T DARE TO NOTICE

That the process was not accidental may be seen from the ban on daring to notice anything. Compared with the all pervasive order not to be conspicuous (noticeable), the prisoners were less frequently told the commensurate "don't dare to notice." But to look and observe for oneself what went on in the camp—while absolutely necessary for survival—was even more dangerous than being noticed. Often this passive compliance—not to see or not to know—was not enough; in order to survive one had to actively pretend not to observe, not to know what the SS required one not to know.[5]

Among the worst mistakes a prisoner could make was to watch (to notice) another prisoner's mistreatment. There the SS seemed totally irrational, but only seemed so. For example, if an SS man was killing off a prisoner and other prisoners dared to look at what was going on in front of their eyes he would instantly go after them, too. But only seconds later the same SS would call the same prisoners' attention to what lay in store for anyone who dared to disobey, drawing their attention to the killing as a warning example. This was no contradiction, it was simply an impressive lesson that said: you may notice only what we wish you to notice, but you invite death if you notice things on your own volition. The issue was again the same; the prisoner was not to have a will of his own.

Many examples showed that all this happened for a reason and a purpose. An SS man might seem to have gone berserk about what he viewed as some resistance or disobedience, and in this state beat up or even kill a prisoner. But in the midst of it he might call out a friendly "well done" to a passing work column who, having stumbled on the scene, would fall into a gallop, heads averted, so as to pass by as fast as possible without "noticing." Obviously their sudden break into running and their averted heads showed clearly that they had "noticed"; but that did not matter as long as they also showed so clearly that they had accepted the command not to know what they were not supposed to know.

This all important enforced behavior was equally apparent when the SS was provoking a prisoner to commit suicide. If the unfortunate succeeded, anyone watching it was immediately punished. But as soon as the punishment for having observed on one's own was over, the same SS might warn: "See what happened to that man? That's what'll happen to you!"

To know only what those in authority allow one to know is, more or less, all the infant can do. To be able to make one's own observations and to draw pertinent conclusions from them is where independent existence begins. To forbid oneself to make observations, and take only the observations of others in their stead, is relegating to nonuse one's own powers of reasoning, and the even more basic power of perception. Not observing where it counts most, not knowing where one wants so much to know, all this is most destructive to the functioning of one's personality. So is finding oneself in a situation where what once gave security (the power to observe correctly and to draw on one's own the right inferences) not only ceases to offer security, but actually endangers one's life. Deliberate nonuse of one's power of observation, as opposed to temporary inattention, which is different, leads to a withering away of this power.

To make matters worse, while to observe was dangerous, to react emotionally to what one saw was frankly suicidal. That is, a prisoner who noticed mistreatment was punished, but only mildly when compared to what happened if his feelings carried him away to the point of trying to give help. Knowing that such an emotional reaction was tantamount to suicide, and being unable at times not to react emotionally when observing what went on, left only one way out: not to observe, so as not to react. So both powers, those of observation and of reaction, had to be blocked out voluntarily as an act of preservation. But if one gives up observing, reacting, and taking action, one gives up living one's own life. And this is exactly what the SS wanted to happen.

Thus the truly extreme environment first blocks self-stimulated action (resisting or modifying the environment) and later also, response to any stimulus coming from the environment in terms of one's own personality (inner revulsion without overt action based on it). Finally, all this is replaced by no other than environment imposed action without even an inner personal response to it. This last situation leads first to a blotting out of responses, later to a blotting out even of perception; except that death then follows.

Prisoners entered the moslem stage when emotion could no longer be evoked in them. For a time they fought for food, but after a few weeks even that stopped. Despite their hunger, even the food stimulus no longer reached their brain clearly enough to lead to action. Nobody and nothing could now influence these persons or their characters, because nothing from inside or outside was reaching them any more. Other prisoners often tried to be nice to them when they could, to give them food and so forth, but they could no longer respond to the emotional attitude that was behind someone's giving them food. So food they took, up to the point where they had reached the final stage of disintegration, but it no longer replenished them emotionally; it just entered an always empty stomach.

As long as they still asked for food, followed someone to get it, stretched out a hand for it and ate what was given eagerly, they could still, with great effort, have been returned to "normal" prisoner status, deteriorated as they were. In the next stage of disintegration, receiving food unexpectedly still led to a momentary lighting up of the face and a grateful hangdog look, though hardly any verbal response. But when they no longer reached out for it spontaneously, no longer responded with thanks, an effort to smile, or a look at the giver, they were nearly always beyond help. Later they took food, sometimes ate it, sometimes not, but no longer had a feeling response. In the last, just before the terminal stage, they no longer ate it.

THE LAST HUMAN FREEDOM

Even those prisoners who did not become moslems, who somehow managed to remain in control of some small aspect of their lives, eventually had to come to longer range terms with their new environment. The mere fact of survival meant that in the matter of Caesar's dues, it was no longer a question of whether to render them or not, nor even, with rare exceptions, of how much to render. But to survive as a man not a walking corpse, as a debased and degraded but still human being, one had first and foremost to remain informed and aware of what made up one's personal point of no return, the point beyond which one would never, under any circumstances, give in to the oppressor, even if it meant risking and losing one's life. It meant being aware that if one survived at the price of overreaching this point one would be holding on to a life that had lost all its meaning. It would mean surviving—not with a lowered self-respect, but without any.

This point of no return was different from person to person, and changed for each person as time passed. At the beginning of their imprisonment, most inmates would have felt it beyond their point of no return to serve the SS as foreman or block chief, or to like wearing a uniform that made them look like the SS. Later, after years in the camp, such relatively external matters gave way to much more essential convictions which then became the core of their resistance. But those convictions one had to hold on to with utter tenacity. About them, one had to keep oneself informed at all times, because only then could they serve as the mainstay of a radically reduced but still present humanity. Much of the tenacity and relentlessness of political prisoners in their factional warfare is thus explainable; for them, political loyalty to party was their point of no return.

Second in importance was keeping oneself informed of how one felt about complying when the ultimate decision as to where to stand firm was not called into question. While less radical, it was no less essential, because an awareness of one's attitude toward compliance was called for almost constantly. One had to comply with debasing and amoral commands if one wished to survive; but one had to remain cognizant that one's reason for complying was "to remain alive and unchanged as a person." Therefore, one had to decide, for any given action, whether it was truly necessary for one's safety or that of others, and whether committing it was good, neutral or bad. This keeping informed and aware of one's actions—though it could not alter the required act, save in extremities—this minimal distance from one's own behavior, and the freedom to feel differently about it depending on its character, this too was what permitted the prisoner to remain a human being. It was the giving up of all feelings, all inner reservations about one's actions, the letting go of a point at which one would hold fast no matter what, that changed prisoner into moslem.

Those prisoners who blocked out neither heart nor reason, neither feelings nor perception, but kept informed of their inner attitudes even when they could hardly ever afford to act on them, those prisoners survived and came to understand the conditions they lived under. They also came to realize what they had not perceived before; that they still retained the last, if not the greatest, of the human freedoms: to choose their own attitude in any given circumstance. Prisoners who understood this fully, came to know that this, and only this, formed the crucial difference between retaining one's humanity (and often life itself) and accepting death as a human being (or perhaps physical death): whether one retained the freedom to choose autonomously one's attitude to extreme conditions even when they seemed totally beyond one's ability to influence them.[6]

NOTES

1 These include prisoners sent to extermination camps, groups of prisoners ordered to be executed or "finished off," and those who died on the transports before reaching camp.

2 The following data (reported in [Eugen] Kogon [*Der SS-Staat,* Frankfurt, 1946] pp. 118 ff) cover a six month period in 1942, the only period for which such figures were found after the war. These data probably held true for most concentration camps of Type II (i.e., camps neither for forced labor nor extermination).

At the beginning of the period there were an estimated 300,000 prisoners already in these camps. Doubling the figures available for the six months period, to arrive at yearly data, we can estimate that 220,000 new prisoners were sent to the camps in 1942, making an accumulated total of 520,000 for the year. During the same time about 9,500 prisoners were released, 18,500 were executed, and 140,000 died. When the total accumulated number of 520,000 is used, it appears that less than 2% were set free, 3½% were executed and 27% died, yielding a total mortality of a little over 30%. But these yearly statistical figures are, psychologically and factually, grossly misleading. Despite the 220,000 new prisoners added to the 300,000 already in the camps, there were only 52,000 more prisoners in the camps at the end of the year than there were at the beginning. Thus, the population of the camp varied little, comparing one random day of the year with another.
On the gross average this meant a daily population of about 325,000 prisoners. And this, not the 520,000, was the base figure from which deaths and liberations were reckoned by prisoners. Using their base figures, it appears that out of the average daily camp population 3% were set free during the year, nearly 6% were executed, and over 43% died. This may explain the divergent reports about mortality rates in the camps depending, it seems, on whether one used the total additions to the camps as the base figure, or the number imprisoned on any given day.

3 Maybe I should explain why I call it a self chosen act of freedom to force oneself to eat repellent food, etc. Given the initial decision—to stay alive—the forcing oneself to eat was self-imposed, not SS enforced, and unlike turning spy for survival it did not violate inner values or weaken self-respect. The patient who is critically ill likewise indicates an active desire to live when he swallows bitter medicine.

4 So when none of the doomed witnesses in the Hamber affair committed suicide, that too was "quite in order."

5 Even trivial examples illustrate this: during some mistreatment on the transport my eyeglasses were broken. Since I can hardly see without them, I asked for permission, once I was at Dachau, to have new glasses sent to me from home. I had been warned in advance never to admit knowing of any mistreatment, including my own. So when asked why I needed glasses, I simply said that they got broken. When the SS officer heard this he began to deliver a beating and screamed, "*What* did you say happened?" I corrected myself, saying I had broken them accidentally. At this he immediately said, "Okay, just remember that for the future," and matter-of-factly sat down to give me written permission to receive glasses. His reaction, incidentally, was swift but by no means spontaneous; on the contrary, it was deliberate and purposeful. No sadist bent on satisfying his desires will instantly stop mistreatment on getting a correct formula reply. Only a person simply after a specific goal will behave in that way.

6 Kogon (*op. cit.*, p. 62) reports one of many incidents bearing this out: Once a command of Jewish prisoners was working alongside of some

Polish Gentile prisoners. The supervising SS, spying two Jewish prisoners whom he thought to be slacking, ordered them to lie down in the ditch and called on a Polish prisoner, named Strzaska, to bury them alive. Strzaska, frozen in terror and anxiety, refused to obey. At this the SS seized a spade and beat the Pole, who nevertheless still refused to obey. Furiously, the SS now ordered the two Jews to get out of the ditch, Strzaska to get in, and the two Jews to bury *him*. In mortal anxiety, hoping to escape the fate themselves, they shoveled earth into the ditch and onto their fellow prisoner. When only Strzaska's head was barely visible the SS ordered them to stop, and unearth him. Once Strzaska was on his feet, the two Jews were ordered back into the ditch, and this time Strzaska obeyed the renewed command to bury them—possibly because they had not resisted burying him, or perhaps expecting that they too would be spared at the last minute. But this time there was no reprieve, and when the ditch was filled the SS stamped down the earth that still lay loosely over his victims. Five minutes later he called on two other prisoners to unearth them, but though they worked frantically, it was too late. One was already dead and the other dying, so the SS ordered them both taken to the crematorium.

37

Akropolis: Treatment of the Text*

Ludwik Flaszen

Wyspianski's drama has been modified in parts to adjust to the purpose of the director. The few interpolations and changes in the original text do not, however, detract from the style of the poet. The balance of the text has been somewhat altered by the deliberately obsessive repetition of certain phrases such as "our Akropolis" or "the cemetery of the tribes." This liberty is justified because these phrases are the motifs around which the play revolves. The prologue is an excerpt from one of Wyspianski's letters, referring to the "Akropolis" as the symbol of the highest point of any specific civilization.

Of all the plays Grotowski has directed, *Akropolis* is the least faithful to its literary original. The poetic style is the only thing which belongs to the author. The play was transposed for stage conditions totally different from those planned by the poet. In a sort of counterpoint pat-

* *Akropolis* was produced by *Jerzy Grotowski*. His main collaborator in this production was the well known polish stage designer, *Josef Szajna,* who also designed the costumes and props. The scenic architecture was by *Jerzy Gurawski*.

tern, it has been enriched with associations of ideas which bring out, as a secondary result of the enterprise, a specific concept of the technique: the verbal flesh of the work had to be transplanted and grafted on the viscera of foreign stage setting. The transplant had to be done with such skill that the words would seem to grow spontaneously from the circumstances imposed by the theatre.

The action of the play takes place in Cracow cathedral. On the night of the Resurrection, the statues and the characters in the tapestries relive scenes from the Old Testament and antiquity, the very roots of European tradition.

The author conceived his work as a panoramic view of the Mediterranean culture whose main currents are represented in this Polish Akropolis. In this idea of the "cemetery of the tribes," to quote Wyspianski, the concept of the director and that of the poet coincide. They both want to represent the sum total of a civilization and test its values on the touchstone of contemporary experience. To Grotowski, contemporary means the second half of the twentieth century. Hence his experience is infinitely more cruel than Wyspianski's and the century-old values of European culture are put to a severe test. Their merging point is no longer the peaceful resting place of the old cathedral where the poet dreamed and meditated in solitude on the history of the world. They clash in the din of an extreme world in the midst of the polyglot confusion where our century has projected them: in an extermination camp. The characters re-enact the great moments of our cultural history; but they bring to life not the figures immortalized in the monuments of the past, but the fumes and emanations from Auschwitz.

It is indeed a "cemetery of the tribes," but not the same as the one where the old Galician poet wandered and dreamed. It is literally a "cemetery," complete, perfect, paradoxical; one which transforms the most daring poetic figures into realities. "Our Akropolis," blind with hope, will not see the Resurrection of Christ-Apollo: he has been left behind, in the mysterious outer reaches of collective experience. The drama formulates a question: what happens to human nature when it faces total violence? The struggle of Jacob with the Angel and the back-breaking labor of the inmates, Paris' and Helen's love duet and the derisive screams of the prisoners, the Resurrection of Christ and the ovens—a civilization of contrast and corruption. . . .

Trapped at its roots, this image of the human race gives rise to horror and pity. The tragi-comedy of rotten values has been substituted for the luminous apotheosis which concluded the philosophic-historic drama of the old poet. The director has shown that suffering is both horrible and ugly. Humanity has been reduced to elemental animal reflexes. In a maudlin intimacy, murderer and victim appear as twins.

All the luminous points are deliberately snuffed out in the stage presentation. The ultimate vision of hope is squashed with blasphemous irony. The play as it is presented can be interpreted as a call to the ethical memory of the spectator, to his moral unconscious. What would become of him if he were submitted to the supreme test? Would he turn into an empty human shell? Would he become the victim of those collective myths created for mutual consolation?

THE PERFORMANCE: FROM FACT TO METAPHOR

The play is conceived as a poetic paraphrase of an extermination camp. Literal interpretation and metaphor are mixed as in a daydream. The rule of the Theatre Laboratory is to distribute the action all over the theatre and among the spectators. These, however, are not expected to take part in the action. For *Akropolis,* it was decided that there would be no direct contact between actors and spectators: the actors represent those who have been initiated in the ultimate experience, they are the dead; the spectators represent those who are outside of the circle of initiates, they remain in the stream of everyday life, they are the living. This separation, combined with the proximity of the spectators, contributes to the impression that the dead are born from a dream of the living. The inmates belong in a nightmare and seem to move in on the sleeping spectators from all sides. They appear in different places, simultaneously or consecutively, creating a feeling of vertigo and threatening ubiquity.

In the middle of the room stands a huge box. Metallic junk is heaped on top of it: stovepipes of various lengths and widths, a wheelbarrow, a bathtub, nails, hammers. Everything is old, rusty, and looks as if it had been picked up from a junkyard. The reality of the props is rust and metal. From them, as the action progresses, the actors will build an absurd civilization; a civilization of gas chambers, advertised by stovepipes which will decorate the whole room as the actors hang them from strings or nail them to the floor. Thus one passes from fact to metaphor.

COSTUMES

The costumes are bags full of holes covering naked bodies. The holes are lined with material which suggests torn flesh; through the holes one looks directly into a torn body. Heavy wooden shoes for the feet; for the heads, anonymous berets. This is a poetic version of the camp uniform. Through their similarity the costumes rob men of their personality, erase the distinctive signs which indicate sex, age, and social class. The actors become completely identical beings. They are nothing but tortured bodies.

The inmates are the protagonists and, in the name of a higher, unwritten law, they are their own torturers. The merciless conditions of the extermination camp constitute the milieu of their lives. Their work crushes them with its size and its futility; rhythmical signals are given by the guards; the inmates call out in screams. But the struggle for the right to vegetate and to love goes on at its everyday pace. At each command the human wrecks, barely alive, stand up erect like well-disciplined soldiers. The throbbing rhythm of the play underscores the building of the new civilization; the work expresses the inmate's stubborn will to live, which is constantly reaffirmed in every one of their actions.

There is no hero, no character set apart from the others by his own individuality. There is only the community, which is the image of the whole species in an extreme situation. In the fortissimos, the rhythm is broken into a climax of words, chants, screams, and noises. The whole thing seems multishaped and misshapen; it dissolves, then re-forms itself into a shivering unity. It is reminiscent of a drop of water under a microscope.

MYTH AND REALITY

During the pauses in the work, the fantastic community indulges in daydreams. The wretches take the names of biblical and Homeric heroes. They identify with them and act, within their limitations, their own versions of the legends. It is transmutation through the dream, a phenomenon known to communities of prisoners who, when acting, live a reality different from their own. They give a degree of reality to their dreams of dignity, nobility, and happiness. It is a cruel and bitter game which derides the prisoners' own aspirations as they are betrayed by reality.

Jacob tramples his future father-in-law to death while asking for Rachel's hand in marriage. Indeed, his relationship to Laban is not governed by patriarchal law but by the absolute demands of the right to survive. The struggle between Jacob and the Angel is a fight between two prisoners: one is kneeling and supports on his back a wheelbarrow in which the other lies, head down and dropping backward. The kneeling Jacob tries to shake off his burden, the Angel, who bangs his own head on the floor. In his turn the Angel tries to crush Jacob by hitting his head with his feet. But his feet hit, instead, the edge of the wheelbarrow. And Jacob struggles with all his might to control his burden. The protagonists cannot escape from each other. Each is nailed to his tool; their torture is more intense because they cannot give vent to their mounting anger. The famous scene from the Old Testament is interpreted as that of two victims torturing each other under the pressure of necessity, the anonymous power mentioned in their argument.

Paris and Helen express the charm of sensuous love; but Helen is a man. Their love duet is conducted to the accompaniment of the snickering laughter of the assembled prisoners. A degraded eroticism rules the world where privacy is impossible. Their sexual sensitivity has become that of any monosexual community, the army for example. Similarly Jacob directs his expression of tenderness toward compensatory objects: his bride is a stove pipe wrapped into a piece of rag for a veil. Thus equipped, he leads the nuptial procession solemnly followed by all the prisoners singing a folksong. At the high point of this improvised ceremony, the clear sound of an altar bell is heard, suggesting naïvely and somewhat ironically a dream of simple happiness.

The despair of men condemned without hope of reprieve is revealed: four prisoners press their bodies against the walls of the theatre like martyrs. They recite the prayer of hope in the help of God pronounced by the Angel in Jacob's dream. One detects in the recitation the ritual grief and the traditional lament of the Bible. They suggest the Jews in front of the Wall of Lamentation. There is, too, the aggressive despair of the condemned who rebel against their fate: Cassandra. One of the prisoners, a female, walks out of the ranks at roll call. Her body wriggles hysterically; her voice is vulgar, sensuous, and raucous; she expresses the torments of a self-centered soul. Shifting suddenly to a tone of soft complaint, she announces with obvious relish what fate holds in store for the community. Her monologue is interrupted by the harsh and guttural voices of the prisoners in the ranks who count themselves. The clipped sounds of the roll call replace the cawing of crows called for in Wyspianski's text.

As for hope, the group of human wrecks, led by the Singer, finds its Savior. The Savior is a headless, bluish, badly mauled corpse, horribly reminiscent of the miserable skeletons of the concentration camps. The Singer lifts the corpse in a lyrical gesture, like a priest lifting the chalice. The crowd stares religiously and follows the leader in a procession. They begin to sing a Christmas hymn to honor the Savior. The singing becomes louder, turns into an ecstatic lament torn by screams and hysterical laughter. The procession circles around the huge box in the center of the room; hands stretch toward the Savior, eyes gaze adoringly. Some stumble, fall, stagger back to their feet and press forward around the Singer. The procession evokes the religious crowds of the Middle Ages, the flagellants, the haunting beggars. Theirs is the ecstasy of a religious dance. Intermittently, the procession stops and the crowd is quiet. Suddenly the silence is shattered by the devout litanies of the Singer, and the crowd answers. In a supreme ecstasy, the procession reaches the end of its peregrination. The Singer lets out a pious yell, opens a hole in the box, and crawls into it dragging after him the corpse of the Savior. The inmates follow him one by one, singing fanatically. They seem to throw themselves out of the world. When the last of the condemned men has disappeared, the lid of the box slams shut. The silence is very sudden; then after a while a calm, matter-of-fact voice is heard. It says simply, "They are gone, and the smoke rises in spirals." The joyful delirium has found its fulfillment in the crematorium. The end.

PROPS AS DYNAMIC ORCHESTRATION

The strictest independence from props is one of the main principles of the Theatre Laboratory. It is absolutely forbidden to introduce in the play anything which is not already there at the very beginning. A certain number of people and objects are gathered in the theatre. They must be sufficient to handle any of the play's situations.

There are no "sets" in the usual sense of the word. They have been reduced to the objects which are indispensable to the dramatic action. Each object must contribute not to the meaning but to the dynamics of the play; its value resides in its various uses. The stovepipes and the metallic junk are used as settings and as a concrete, three-dimensional metaphor which contributes to the creation of the vision. But the metaphor originates in the function of the stovepipes; it stems from the activity which it later supersedes as the action progresses. When the actors leave the theatre, they leave behind the pipes which have supplied a concrete motivation for the play.

Each object has multiple uses. The bathtub is a very pedestrian bathtub; on the other hand it is a symbolical bathtub: it represents all the bathtubs in which human bodies were processed for the making of soap and leather. Turned upside down, the same bathtub becomes the altar in front of which an inmate chants a prayer. Set up in a high place, it becomes Jacob's nuptial bed. The wheelbarrows are tools for daily work; they become strange hearses for the transportation of the corpses; propped against the wall they are Priam's and Hecuba's thrones. One of the stovepipes, transformed by Jacob's imagination, becomes his grotesque bride.

This world of objects represents the musical instruments of the play: the monotonous cacophony of death and senseless suffering—metal grating against metal, clanging of the hammers, creaking of the stovepipes through which echoes a human voice. A few nails rattled by an inmate evoke the altar bell. There is only one real musical instrument, a violin. Its leitmotiv is used as a lyrical and melancholy background to a brutal scene, or as a rhythmical echo of the guards' whistles and commands. The visual image is almost always accompanied by an acoustic one. The number of props is extremely limited; each one has multiple functions. Worlds are created with very ordinary objects, as in children's play and improvised games. We are dealing with a theatre caught in its embryonic stage, in the middle of the creative process when the awakened instinct chooses spontaneously the tools of its magic transformation. A living man, the actor, is the creative force behind it all.

THE POOR THEATRE

In the poor theatre the actor must himself compose an organic mask by means of his facial muscles and thus each character wears the same grimace throughout the whole play. While the entire body moves in accordance with the circumstances, the mask remains set in an expression of despair, suffering and indifference. The actor multiplies himself into a sort of hybrid being acting out his role polyphonically. The different parts of his body give free rein to different reflexes which are often contradictory, while the tongue denies not only the voice, but also the gestures and the mimicry.

All the actors use gestures, positions, and rhythms borrowed from pantomime. Each has his own silhouette irrevocably fixed. The result is a depersonalization of the characters. When the individual traits are removed, the actors become stereotypes of the species.

The means of verbal expression have been considerably enlarged because all means of vocal expression are used, starting from the confused babbling of the very small child and including the most sophisticated oratorical recitation. Inarticulate groans, animal roars, tender folksongs, liturgical chants, dialects, declamation of poetry: everything is there. The sounds are interwoven in a complex score which brings back fleetingly the memory of all the forms of language. They are mixed in this new Tower of Babel, in the clash of foreign people and foreign languages meeting just before their extermination.

The mixture of incompatible elements, combined with the warping of language, brings out elementary reflexes. Remnants of sophistication are juxtaposed to animal behavior. Means of expression literally "biological" are linked to very conventional compositions. In *Akropolis* humanity is forced through a very fine sieve: its texture comes out much refined.

Translated by Simone Sanzenbach

38

From "Totalitarianism in Power"

Hannah Arendt

The first essential step on the road to total domination is to kill the juridical person in man. This was done, on the one hand, by putting certain categories of people outside the protection of the law and forcing at the same time, through the instrument of denationalization, the non-totalitarian world into recognition of lawlessness; it was done, on the other, by placing the concentration camp outside the normal penal system, and by selecting its inmates outside the normal judicial procedure in which a definite crime entails a predictable penalty. Thus criminals, who for other reasons are an essential element in concentration-camp society, are ordinarily sent to a camp only on completion of their prison sentence. Under all circumstances totalitarian domination sees to it that the categories gathered in the camps—Jews, carriers of diseases, representatives of dying classes—have already lost their capacity for both normal or criminal action. Propagandistically this means that the "protective custody" is handled as a "preventive police measure," [1] that is, a measure that deprives people of the ability to act. Deviations from this rule in Russia must be attributed to the catastrophic shortage of prisons and to a desire, so far unrealized, to transform the whole penal system into a system of concentration camps.[2]

The inclusion of criminals is necessary in order to make plausible the propagandistic claim of the movement that the institution exists for asocial elements.[3] Criminals do not properly belong in the concentration camps, if only because it is harder to kill the juridical person in a man who is guilty of some crime than in a totally innocent person. If they constitute a permanent category among the inmates, it is a concession of the totalitarian state to the prejudices of society, which can in this way most readily be accustomed to the existence of the camps. In order, on the other hand, to keep the camp system itself intact, it is essential as long as there is a penal system in the country that criminals should be sent to the camps only on completion of their sentence, that is when they are actually entitled to their freedom. Under no circumstances must the concentration camp become a calculable punishment for definite offenses.

The amalgamation of criminals with all other categories has moreover the advantage of making it shockingly evident to all other arrivals that they have landed on the lowest level of society. It soon turns out, to be sure, that they have every reason to envy the lowest thief and murderer; but meanwhile the lowest level is a good beginning. Moreover it is an effective means of camouflage: this happens only to criminals and nothing worse is happening than that what deservedly happens to criminals.

The criminals everywhere constitute the aristocracy of the camps. (In Germany, during the war, they were replaced in the leadership by the Communists, because not even a minimum of rational work could be performed under the chaotic conditions created by a criminal administration. This was merely a temporary transformation of concentration camps into forced-labor camps, a thoroughly atypical phenomenon of limited duration.) [4] What places the criminals in the leadership is not so much the affinity between supervisory personnel and criminal elements —in the Soviet Union apparently the supervisors are not, like the SS, a special elite trained to commit crimes [5]—as the fact that only criminals have been sent to the camp in connection with some definite activity. They at least know why they are in a concentration camp and therefore have kept a remnant of their juridical person. For the politicals this is only subjectively true; their actions, insofar as they were actions and not mere opinions or someone else's vague suspicions, or accidental membership in a politically disapproved group, are as a rule not covered by the normal legal system of the country and not juridically defined.[6]

To the amalgam of politicals and criminals with which concentration camps in Russia and Germany started out, was added at an early date a third element which was soon to constitute the majority of all concentration-camp inmates. This largest group has consisted ever since of people who had done nothing whatsoever that, either in their own consciousness or the consciousness of their tormenters, had any rational connection with their arrest. In Germany, after 1938, this element was represented by masses of Jews, in Russia by any groups which, for any reason having nothing to do with their actions, had incurred the disfavor of the authorities. These groups, innocent in every sense, are the most suitable for thorough experimentation in disfranchisement and destruction of the juridical person, and therefore they are both qualitatively and quantitatively the most essential category of the camp population. This principle was most fully realized in the gas chambers which, if only because of their enormous capacity, could not be intended for individual cases but only for people in general. In this connection, the following dialogue sums up the situation of the individual: "For what purpose, may I ask, do the gas chambers exist?"—"For what purpose were you born?" [7] It is this third group of the totally innocent who in every case fare the worst in the camps. Criminals and politicals are assimilated to this category; thus deprived of the protective distinction that comes of their having done something, they are utterly exposed to the arbitrary. The ultimate goal, partly achieved in the Soviet Union and clearly indicated in the last phases of Nazi terror, is to have the whole camp population composed of this category of innocent people.

Contrasting with the complete haphazardness with which the inmates are selected are the categories, meaningless in themselves but useful from the standpoint of organization, into which they are usually divided on their arrival. In the German camps there were criminals, politicals, asocial elements, religious offenders, and Jews, all distinguished by insignia. When the French set up concentration camps after the Spanish Civil War, they immediately introduced the typical totalitarian amalgam of politicals with criminals and the innocent (in this case the stateless), and despite their inexperience proved remarkably inventive in creating meaningless categories of inmates.[8] Originally devised in order to prevent any growth of solidarity among the inmates, this technique proved particularly valuable because no one could know whether his own category was better or worse than someone else's. In Germany this eternally shifting though pedantically organized edifice was given an appearance of solidity by the fact that under any and all circumstances the

Jews were the lowest category. The gruesome and grotesque part of it was that the inmates identified themselves with these categories, as though they represented a last authentic remnant of their juridical person. Even if we disregard all other circumstances, it is no wonder that a Communist of 1933 should have come out of the camps more Communistic than he went in, a Jew more Jewish, and, in France, the wife of a Foreign Legionary more convinced of the value of the Foreign Legion; it would seem as though these categories promised some last shred of predictable treatment, as though they embodied some last and hence most fundamental juridical identity.

While the classification of inmates by categories is only a tactical, organizational measure, the arbitrary selection of victims indicates the essential principle of the institution. If the concentration camps had been dependent on the existence of political adversaries, they would scarcely have survived the first years of the totalitarian regimes. One only has to take a look at the number of inmates at Buchenwald in the years after 1936 in order to understand how absolutely necessary the element of the innocent was for the continued existence of the camps. "The camps would have died out if in making its arrests the Gestapo had considered only the principle of opposition," [9] and toward the end of 1937 Buchenwald, with less than 1,000 inmates, was close to dying out until the November pogroms brought more than 20,000 new arrivals.[10] In Germany, this element of the innocent was furnished in vast numbers by the Jews since 1938; in Russia, it consisted of random groups of the population which for some reason entirely unconnected with their actions had fallen into disgrace.[11] But if in Germany the really totalitarian type of concentration camp with its enormous majority of completely "innocent" inmates was not established until 1938, in Russia it goes back to the early thirties, since up to 1930 the majority of the concentration-camp population still consisted of criminals, counterrevolutionaries and "politicals" (meaning, in this case, members of deviationist factions). Since then there have been so many innocent people in the camps that it is difficult to classify them—persons who had some sort of contact with a foreign country, Russians of Polish origin (particularly in the years 1936 to 1938), peasants whose villages for some economic reason were liquidated, deported nationalities, demobilized soldiers of the Red Army who happened to belong to regiments that stayed too long abroad as occupation forces or had become prisoners of war in Germany, etc. But the existence of a political opposition is for a concentration-camp system only a pretext, and the purpose of the system is not achieved even when, under the most monstrous terror, the population becomes more or less voluntarily co-ordinated, *i.e.,* relinquishes its political rights. The aim of an arbitrary system is to destroy the civil rights of the whole population, who ultimately become just as outlawed in their own country as the stateless and homeless. The destruction of a man's rights, the killing of the juridical person in him, is a prerequisite for dominating him entirely. And this applies not only to special categories such as criminals, political opponents, Jews, homosexuals, on whom the early experiments were made, but to every inhabitant of a totalitarian state. Free consent is as much an obstacle to total domination as free opposition.[12] The arbitrary arrest which chooses among innocent people destroys the validity of free consent, just as torture—as distinguished from death—destroys the possibility of opposition.

Any, even the most tyrannical, restriction of this arbitrary persecution to certain opinions of a religious or political nature, to certain modes of intellectual or erotic social behavior, to certain freshly invented "crimes," would render the camps superfluous, because in the long run no attitude and no opinion can withstand the threat of so much horror; and above all it would make for a new system of justice, which, given any stability at all, could not fail to produce a new juridical person in man, that would elude the totalitarian domination. The so-called "*Volksnutzen*" of the Nazis, constantly fluctuating (because what is useful today can be injurious tomorrow) and the eternally shifting party line of the Soviet Union which, being retroactive, almost daily makes new groups of people available for the concentration camps, are the only guaranty for the continued existence of the concentration camps, and hence for the continued total disfranchisement of man.

The next decisive step in the preparation of living corpses is the murder of the moral person in man. This is done in the main by making martyrdom, for the first time in history, impossible: "How many people here still believe that a protest has even historic importance? This skepticism is the real masterpiece of the SS. Their great accomplishment. They have corrupted all human solidarity. Here the night has fallen on the future. When no witnesses are left, there can be no testimony. To demonstrate when death can no longer be postponed is an attempt to give death a meaning, to act beyond one's own death. In order to be successful, a gesture must have social meaning. There are hundreds of thousands of us here, all living in absolute solitude. That is why we are subdued no matter what happens." [13]

The camps and the murder of political adversaries are only part of organized oblivion that not only embraces carriers of public opinion such as the spoken and the written word, but extends even to the families and friends of the victim. Grief and remembrance are forbidden. In the Soviet Union a woman will sue for divorce immediately after her husband's arrest in order to save the lives of her children; if her husband chances to come back, she will indignantly turn him out of the house.[14] The Western world has hitherto, even in its darkest periods, granted the slain enemy the right to be remembered as a self-evident acknowledgment of the fact that we are all men (and *only* men). It is only because even Achilles set out for Hector's funeral, only because the most despotic governments honored the slain enemy, only because the Romans allowed the Christians to write their martyrologies, only because the Church kept its heretics alive in the memory of men, that all was not lost and never could be lost. The concentration camps, by making death itself anonymous (making it impossible to find out whether a prisoner is dead or alive) robbed death of its meaning as the end of a fulfilled life. In a sense they took away the individual's own death, proving that henceforth nothing belonged to him and he belonged to no one. His death merely set a seal on the fact that he had never really existed.

This attack on the moral person might still have been opposed by man's conscience which tells him that it is better to die a victim than to live as a bureaucrat of murder. Totalitarian terror achieved its most terrible triumph when it succeeded in cutting the moral person off from the individualist escape and in making the decisions of conscience absolutely questionable and equivocal. When a man is faced with the alternative of betraying and thus murdering his friends or of sending his wife and children, for whom he is in every sense responsible, to their death; when even suicide would mean the immediate murder of his own family—how is he to decide? The alternative is no longer between good and evil, but between murder and murder. Who could solve the moral dilemma of the Greek mother, who was allowed by the Nazis to choose which of her three children should be killed? [15]

Through the creation of conditions under which conscience ceases to be adequate and to do good becomes utterly impossible, the consciously organized complicity of all men in the crimes of totalitarian regimes is extended to the victims and thus made really total. The SS implicated concentration-camp inmates—criminals, politicals, Jews—in their crimes by making them responsible for a large part of the administration, thus confronting them with the hopeless dilemma whether to send their friends to their death, or to help murder other men who happened to be strangers, and forcing them, in any event, to behave like murderers.[16] The point is not only that hatred is diverted from those who are guilty (the *capos* were more hated than the SS), but that the distinguishing line between persecutor and persecuted, between the murderer and his victim, is constantly blurred.[17]

Once the moral person has been killed, the one thing that still prevents men from being made into living corpses is the differentiation of the individual, his unique identity. In a sterile form such individuality can be preserved through a persistent stoicism, and it is certain that many men under totalitarian rule have taken and are each day still taking refuge in this absolute isolation of a personality without rights or conscience. There is no doubt that this part of the human person, precisely because it depends so essentially on nature and on forces that cannot be controlled by the will, is the hardest to destroy (and when destroyed is most easily repaired).

NOTES

1 [Theodor] Maunz [*Gestalt und Recht der Polizei,* Hamburg, 1943] p. 50, insists that criminals should never be sent to the camps for the time of their regular sentences.

2 The shortage of prison space in Russia has been such that in the year 1925–26, only 36 per cent of all court sentences could be carried out. [David J. Dallim & Boris I. Nicolaevsky, *Forced Labor in Russia,* 1947] p. 158 ff.

3 "Gestapo and SS have always attached great importance to mixing the categories of inmates in the camps. In no camp have the inmates belonged exclusively to one category" [Eugen Kogon, *Der SS-Staat,* Munich, 1946] p. 19.

In Russia, it has also been customary from the beginning to mix political prisoners and criminals. During the first ten years of Soviet power, the Left political groups enjoyed certain privileges; only with the full development of the totalitarian character of the regime "after the end of the twenties, the politicals were even officially treated as inferior to the common criminals." (Dallim, *op. cit.,* p. 177 ff.)

4 [David] Rousset's book [*The Other Kingdom,* New York, 1947] suffers from his overestimation of the influence of the German Communists, who dominated the internal administration of Buchenwald during the war.

5 See for instance the testimony of Mrs. Buber-Neumann (former wife of the German Communist Heinz Neumann), who survived Soviet and German concentration camps: "The Russians never . . . evinced the sadistic streak of the Nazis. . . . Our Russian guards were decent men and not sadists, but they faithfully fulfilled the requirements of the inhuman system" (*Under Two Dictators*).

6 Bruno Bettelheim, "Behavior in Extreme Situations," in *Journal of Abnormal and Social Psychology,* Vol. XXXVIII, No. 4, 1943, describes the self-esteem of the criminals and the political prisoners as compared with those who have not done anything. The latter "were least able to withstand the initial shock," the first to disintegrate. Bettelheim blames this on their middle-class origin.

7 Rousset, p. 71.

8 For conditions in French concentration camps, see Arthur Koestler, *Scum of the Earth,* 1941.

9 Kogon, p. 6.

10 See *Nazi Conspiracy,* IV, 800 ff.

11 [F.] Beck & [W.] Galin [*Russian Purge & the Extraction of Confession,* 1951] state explicitly that "opponents constituted only a relatively small proportion of the [Russian] prison population" (p. 87), and that there was no connection whatever between "a man's imprisonment and any offense" (p. 95).

12 Bruno Bettelheim. "On Dachau and Buchenwald," when discussing the fact that most prisoners "made their peace with the values of the Gestapo," emphasizes that "this was not the result of propaganda . . . the Gestapo insisted that it would prevent them from expressing their feelings anyway" (pp. 834–35).

Himmler explicitly prohibited propaganda of any kind in the camps. "Education consists of discipline, never of any kind of instruction on an ideological basis." "On Organization and Obligation of the SS and the Police," in *National-politischer Lehrgang der Wehrmacht,* 1937. Quoted from *Nazi Conspiracy,* IV, 616 ff.

13 Rousset, p. 464.

14 See the report of Sergei Malakhov in Dallin, pp. 20 ff.

15 See Albert Camus in *Twice A Year,* 1947.

16 Rousset's book consists largely of discussions of this dilemma by prisoners.

17 Bettelheim describes the process by which the guards as well as the prisoners became "conditioned" to the life in the camp and were afraid of returning to the outer world.

Rousset, therefore, is right when he insists that the truth is that "victim and executioner are alike ignoble; the lesson of the camps is the brotherhood of abjection" (p. 588).

39

From "The Survivor"*

Robert Jay Lifton

FORMULATION

We have seen that the dropping of the atomic bomb in Hiroshima annihilated a general sense of life's coherence as much as it did human bodies. We have also seen that mastery of the experience depended upon re-establishing form within which not only the death immersion but the survivor's altered identity could be grasped and rendered significant. This quest for formulation turns both *hibakusha* and concentration camp survivors into what has been called "collectors of justice." Beyond medical and economic benefits as such, they seek a sense of world-order in which their suffering has been recognized, in which reparative actions by those responsible for it can be identified.

As part of the "work of mourning" Freud described the survivor's need to come to gradual recognition of the new reality, of the world which no longer contains that which has been lost. He must, as a later psychoanalytic writer on depression put it, "rebuild with anguish the inner world, which is felt to be in danger of deteriorating and collapsing." And an investigator of acute grief reactions speaks specifically of the effort to "find an acceptable formulation of his future relationship to

* From *Death in Life: Survivors of Hiroshima.*—The editors.

the deceased," which includes "emancipation from bondage to the deceased" and "formation of new relationships." What has not been generally recognized is that this "anguish of formulation" is the basic reparative process following any significant psychic disruption.

The process begins early, even before the actual death encounter. For the "explanations" of Hiroshima people, just prior to the disaster, as to why their city had not been bombed could be viewed as anticipatory formulations. And the psychic closing-off which occurred when the bomb fell represented another formulation ("If I feel nothing, death is not taking place"), which, however magical and laden with denial, was a functional way of relating self to world under those extreme conditions. To be completely deprived of formulation at any time, even at the moment of the death encounter, is psychically intolerable. As Chaim Kaplan said in a journal he left recording experiences in the Warsaw ghetto: "The worst part of this ugly kind of death is that you don't know the reason for it. . . . The lack of reason for these murders especially troubles the inhabitants of the ghetto." The diary goes on to record that "We feel compelled to find some sort of system to explain these nightmare murders," especially a system which would permit each to imagine his survival:

> If there is a system, every murder must have a cause; if there is a cause, nothing will happen to me since I myself am absolutely guiltless.

Kaplan knows the truth: "The system is a lack of system. . . . The guiding principle is the annihilation of a specific number of Jews every night. . . . Indiscriminately." But this truth is greatly resented because *"People do not want to die without cause."* And years later, in the evaluation of the kinds of stress experienced under Nazi persecution which led to later emotional disturbances, a psychiatric examiner emphasized "the abrogation of causality." What the survivor feels deprived of is not causality in its literal eighteenth-century scientific sense (precisely this cause produces precisely that effect) so much as the existence of an ordered symbolic universe. For any experience of survival—whether of large disaster, intimate personal loss, or (more indirectly) severe mental illness—involves a psychic journey to the edge of the world of the living. The formulative effort is the survivor's means of "return."

Impaired formulation, therefore, becomes a central problem for survivors. In tracing the many impediments faced by *hibakusha,* we noted that a capacity for indignation and anger could, to some degree, enhance the formulative process. We recall the young keloid-bearing hospital worker who channeled her diffuse rage ("a confused mixture of anger, indignation, hatred, and resentment") into active participation in protest movements in a way that gave significance to her experience, purpose to her life, and generally enhanced her self-esteem. But where indignation and rage become fixed and repetitive, there frequently develops what can be termed the *survivor's embittered world-view*. Within this bitterness—or biting anger—is contained the mixture of need and mistrust we have associated with the theme of counterfeit nurturance. It resembles the "embittered vehemence" one psychiatrist has observed in people prone to depression; and I would stress its tendency to dominate the survivor's entire cognitive and emotional life. The embittered world-view becomes his total vision of the way things were and the way things are. Not having been able to "vomit" his "bitter water," such a survivor finds his entire psychic life poisoned by it. The *hibakusha's* "underground" wish for ultimate retaliation or total nuclear conflagration can be understood as the most extreme expression of the survivor's embittered world-view, and finds its analogy in various emotions of former concentration camp inmates—such as Wiesel's temporary wish "To burn the whole world!" For if he is unable to reconstitute his own psychic world, the survivor finds this sharing of annihilation to be the only kind of relationship with others that he can imagine.

Rawicz suggests the importance of impaired formulation in his protagonist's retrospective realization, concerning the time just prior to his death immersion, "that the moment that lay ahead was to provide me, not only with a lifetime's bitterness, but with an eternal alibi." The "eternal alibi" is the survivor's need to justify his being alive. His "lifetime's bitterness" has to do with the permanent "bad taste" he retains, with his inability to "savor" that which is offered him, and his "biting anger" toward a world he cannot re-enter.

The indelible image we spoke of earlier is also an expression of impaired formulation. The image can include, in addition to the death encounter itself, memories of pre-bomb existence—as in a revealing statement written by a university professor nineteen years after his exposure to the bomb:

> The brightness of the Inland Sea on summer days and the unpleasantly loud noises of a military city. . . . The images of this life of my youth . . . have been fixed in the back of my mind as though held there by the flash of the atomic bomb. The form of that period does not alter. It is the picture of me in my young days, and at the same time is like seeing the picture of a child who died before I did. . . . What would a psychologist call the fixation of memories of individual

> experience which have resisted every interpretation or solution, and have instead become like a still picture. . . . It is very much like asking the meaning of a picture of one's younger days which is dusted off and hung up, in the midst of a service being held on the twentieth anniversary of one's death. . . .

In one sense these early recollections could be looked upon as "screen memories," which substitute for and shield against the more disturbing memories of the bomb itself. But they are also much more. The writer's equation of an image of himself in his youth with "the picture of a child who died before I did" suggests his inability to overcome either his loss of pre-bomb innocence, or his guilt over survival priority (he makes the latter clear in additional comments as well). The "still picture" of himself conveys a sense of cessation of psychic motion; and the phrase about participation in a service commemorating the twentieth anniversary of one's own death suggests the close relationship between this kind of indelible image and the identity of the dead. He goes on to speak of the bomb as having "fixed everything in one moment," of there being "no words of comfort I could utter to friends who . . . were dying . . ." since (as we quoted him before as saying) "there exist no words in any human language which can comfort guinea pigs who do not know the cause of their death." There can, in other words, be no formulation—the experience must remain an indelible and ineffable image—because no words can convey either its vastness and totality or its suffusion with death and guilt. One remains fixed upon the world that has been annihilated, held motionless because unable to give form to that annihilation and its consequences.

Rawicz tells us of the survivor "living out his memories and the memory of his memories," so that

> The present is present like a lump of dead meat dried up by the malevolent sun. . . . It shortens our lives, and yet remains dead and dumb itself.

Now we can recognize the indelible image as part of still another vicious circle confounding the survivor's psychic life: death anxiety and death guilt confer unique value upon his memories, while at the same time devitalizing all subsequent experience and undermining attempts at formulation; he is thrown back upon these memories (of the event itself and his life preceding it) as his only form of authentic connection; they become all the more indelible, and he is further fixed in unformulatable death imagery, etc. Should he try to forget the memories, he is brought back to them by the call of the survivor mission, by the demand that he (in Rawicz' words) "remember everything" because "The only thing that matters, that *will* matter, is the integrity of witnesses." Hence the sacredness of the literal details of his death encounter we have so often noted, and the worshipful stasis surrounding its image. Indeed we begin to understand why religious and political movements take shape as forms of survival: the significance of the witnessing of the death of Jesus for the emergence of Christianity, and that of the surviving of the Long March for Chinese Communism. The survivor may become a "disciple" not only of a dead leader, or of the collective "dead," but of the death immersion itself. The guilt with which he embraces that event is by no means devoid of love, but should he move toward psychic forms which could free him from its bondage, he risks the disturbing self-accusation of betrayal.

The concept of the survivor's impaired formulation is relevant for much recent psychiatric and medical research which has attributed a variety of disorders to problems of grief and mourning. Among widows, for instance, complaints of bodily and mental difficulties have been noted to increase during the period following their husbands' deaths; and the tendency toward delinquency and antisocial behavior has been described as "a manifestation of the mourning process—a substitutive pathologic grief reaction" (reminding us of the case referred to before in which grief stimulated rage to the point of attempted murder). There have also been correlations between childhood bereavement (from the early death of a parent) and adult psychiatric disorder. A distinguished German psychoanalyst has recently gone further and suggested that "repressed mourning" for Hitler and the Nazi movement has interfered with social and political progress in postwar Germany.[1] We can well understand the insistence that grief itself be considered a disease. I shall explore some of these issues more fully in my later volume, but there are two important principles I would stress concerning these general findings and theories. First, we can better grasp the phenomena involved by a concept of impaired formulation on the part of various kinds of survivors than by focusing upon traditional interpretations of the mourning process per se. And second, the "disease" to be contended with is not grief as such, but a symbolic disruption which can accompany grief or any other form of individual or collective emotional upheaval.

SCAPEGOATING

The survivor's conflicts can readily lead him to a scapegoating formulation. By focusing total blame upon a particular person, symbol, or group of people, he seeks to relieve his own death guilt. When *hibakusha* single out such objects of focused resentment as President Truman, the pilot of the A-bomb plane, Japanese leaders, American scientists, American capitalists, or "Americans," we can observe the process by which the search for responsibility spills over into scapegoating. More specific scapegoating (because its objects are more removed from actual responsibility) can be found in *hibakusha* resentments toward Koreans, Chinese, *burakumin,* foreign residents of Hiroshima at the time of the bomb, outsiders who came in later, the financially successful, and non-*hibakusha* in general; as well as toward city officials, welfare administrators, physicians, and research scientists, through the overall constellation of guinea pig imagery and suspicion of counterfeit nurturance. On the whole, however, my impression was that scapegoating in Hiroshima has been fragmentary, and without strong conviction, less part of clear-cut formulations than of a generally embittered world-view. The urge toward scapegoating has hardly been absent, but the weapon's impersonality and cosmic destructiveness interfered with scapegoating just as they did with general assigning of responsibility.

In contrast, there is evidence that scapegoating formulations have been much stronger among concentration camp survivors and groups identified with them. These again often enter a borderline area which includes reasonable labeling of responsibility. But we may observe the scapegoating phenomenon where resentments, *instead* of being expressed toward the Nazis, are directed almost exclusively toward groups concerned with restitution payments, outsiders, or other camp survivors; toward the Catholic Church or the Allied powers for their failure to do more for Nazi victims; or toward Jewish leaders thought to have, in their associations with their persecutors, aided the work of extermination. Without arguing the legitimacy of these accusations, I would suggest that the intensity with which they have been expressed has to do with the general issue of death guilt, since all parties involved are survivors (and some are initiators) of the events debated.

The Nazis themselves, coming to power as survivors of Germany's national humiliation during and following World War I, made use of a scapegoating formulation in the extreme: the vision of Jewish responsibility for Germany's various forms of literal and symbolic death immersion, and for all of the world's ills, and the prescription of a "final solution" to the "Jewish problem." That kind of formulation, moreover, had a long history. During the plague of the fourteenth century "many blamed the Jews, accusing them of poisoning the wells or otherwise acting as agents of Satan." But at that time a form of "internal scapegoating" was also prominent, a self-accusatory interpretation of the plague as "a punishment by God for human sins." This interpretation not only gave rise to intensified prayer, but to "half-naked flagellants, members of the century-old cult of flagellantism, march[ing] . . . in procession whipping each other and warning the people to purge themselves of their sins before the coming day of atonement." Very different, but by no means psychologically unrelated, was the behavior of groups of survivors of the Tokyo-Yokohama earthquake of 1923, who simply massacred every Korean in sight in a wild outbreak of murderous scapegoating.

Scapegoating formulations, then, emerge from struggles between internal and external blaming, and create for the survivor an opportunity to cease being a victim and make one of another. But these formulations may not only be dangerous to the newly chosen (or, more frequently, reinstated) victim; they meet with limited success in accomplishing their object, the purging of death guilt. In fact, they add a new psychic burden of guilty anger. They are, moreover, difficult to sustain as coherent entities, and readily disintegrate into amorphous bitterness. The intervention of contemporary technology, as we saw in the case of the A-bomb, further blurs the entire process by creating an adversary whose "magic" is so difficult to grasp, blame, or hate.

Yet a process at least bordering on scapegoating seems necessary to the formulation of any death immersion. It enters into the survivor's theory of causation, and his need to pass judgment on people and forces outside of himself to avoid drowning in his own death guilt and symbolic disorder. The more closely these scapegoating tendencies attach themselves to the actuality of events, the greater their adaptive usefulness, and the better the survivor's chance to transcend them, or at least combine them with more inclusive formulative approaches. What the survivor seeks from his scapegoating formulation is the reassuring unconscious message that "You, and not I, are responsible for the others' deaths and my suffering, so that I have a right to be alive after all." It is a message that he can neither fully believe nor entirely cease to reassert.

In Hiroshima we observed the preponderance of the alternative message: "Having survived at the expense of the dead, I can justify my existence only by emphasizing their virtue and my guilt, and by embracing them to the point of becoming one of them." But this tendency for the survivor to saturate his formulation with self-blame and identification with the dead has its own pitfalls, notably that of lifelong psychic numbing.

One can observe the operation of these formulative paradoxes in other situations related to survival—perhaps most strikingly in a group of severely ill people described by two psychiatric investigators as "predilection patients," because prior to undergoing major surgery, they correctly predicted their own deaths. One of them, described as "The Widow Who Could Not Die," had experienced a series of survivals which she found herself increasingly unable to justify. Having undergone an extensive operation for carcinoma of the rectum at the age of forty-one, she lived as an invalid for the next twenty-eight years, burdened by a colostomy (an opening from the colon through the abdominal wall) and by frequent rectal abscesses. Prior to the operation, she had been pregnant three times, but on each occasion miscarried. Then, over the years, her "favorite brother" died, having also developed carcinoma of the rectum; three sisters died in rapid succession; and finally, her devoted husband died of coronary thrombosis. The psychiatric examiner observed that she "thought of herself as a plump and sickening slug wallowing and feeding on death," and that she had the feeling "that her survival had been at the expense of other lives, even those of her unborn children." He noted the "solemn immobility" of her face, which "resembled a death mask," and a "sickening atmosphere of death in her room." She expressed to him both her desire to die, and the calm conviction that her death would result from a lung hemorrhage following surgery (she had experienced one after a previous operation, but had been saved by prompt treatment), which it did. Her emotional status "was not that of depression but of flattened affect"—or what we would call psychic numbing—and the investigators' further comments raise a key question about the formulative problem we have been discussing:

> It would be difficult to conceive of a patient who welcomed death as did this woman. She had survived at the cost of every person to whom she was devoted, and managed to live on with a disease of unusually rapid mortality. It was as though something indeed was wrong with her. The persistent sense of being soiled and repulsive clung to her. Her loneliness in the later years and preoccupation with the fate of those she had lost held her encased in the little room, but still she

> did not die. The important question is not, however, that she wished to die. She had understood for many years that only death could resolve her difficulties. Why had she survived so long?

There is no certain answer to the question. What we can say is that she was an "eternal survivor," but unlike the paranoid despots who seek external solutions for guilt in the form of an unending series of antagonists whom they can survive, she internalized her guilt to create a life of grief. Indeed, I believe that her guilt-ridden formulation of her responsibility for others' deaths was her means of granting herself unconscious permission to go on living—much in the fashion we have described for *hibakusha*. If we accept the likelihood that her psychic state contributed to her death, we may further suspect that her increasing loneliness, together with her mounting guilt, finally negated the adaptational usefulness of her formulation—possibly to the point where it became mobilized to the cause of biological death.

What I am suggesting is that at a certain point the balance can be tipped, so that the survivor's self-accusatory formulation linking him with the dead no longer contributes to his sense of connection and his "right" to life. At that point he becomes overwhelmed by death guilt, experiences a marked diminution of vitality, and embraces a "death-welcoming" formulation, which although not fundamentally different from the one he held before, now accelerates the process of dying. Even this kind of formulation, at least in the "predilection patients" we have been describing, may be said to reflect a kind of mastery. For these "survivors" are neither psychiatrically disturbed nor possessed by the suicidal patient's fantasy of magically conquering death, but achieve a certain degree of integration in which elements of numbing and despair presage the death that is anticipated and inwardly embraced. It is quite possible that such death-welcoming formulations accelerated the process of dying in many Hiroshima and Nazi concentration camp survivors, both during their initial ordeal and later on; and where particularly severe, contributed to the onset of leukemia and other malignancies within the former group.[2]

A key issue in the survivor's capacity to make his self-accusatory formulation adaptive is the retrospective conferring upon the dead of a quality of glory or of symbolic immortality. Only in this way can the survivor reassert his own sense of immortality. Hence the profound fear of "betraying" the dead which pervades both Hiroshima and concentration camp survivors. For, as Camus tell us in words written in the midst of repeated survivals of comrades in the French anti-Nazi underground in 1943:

> In the period of revolution, it is the best who die. The law of sacrifice brings it about that finally it is always the cowardly and prudent who have the chance to speak since the others have lost it by giving the best of themselves. Speaking always implies a treason.

The "treason" is being alive to have a voice at all. But by recognizing it in one's formulation, as Camus did, one can share in the enduring power of the dead.

"Golden Age" and Significant "Messages"— Both Hiroshima and concentration camp survivors, in discussing their early lives, frequently presented images of a "golden age," of "idyllic childhoods, spent in the bosom of close, harmonious families." While expiatory needs to idealize the dead are important here, this kind of image serves another important function: it is the survivor's effort to reactivate within himself old and profound feelings of love, nurturance, and harmony, in order to be able to apply these feelings to his new formulation of life beyond the death immersion. Inevitably these relate to early childhood, a universal "golden age" in which, whatever its pain, one is capable of uncomplicated happiness. Even if drawn from later periods of life, the image is likely to include a childlike sense of the joy of spontaneous play in an ordered world—precisely what the survivor now feels himself most in need of. He must combine these old emotions with a new sense of significant purpose. The Hiroshima survivors' stress upon their "peace city" finds its parallel in concentration camp survivors' actions on behalf of preventing the re-emergence of Nazi or Nazilike movements, and in the participation of many of them in the formation of a "Jewish State" in Israel. This stress upon significant purpose is most vivid where the formulation takes the shape of a specific survivor mission, but it is also quietly present in tendencies toward psychological non-resistance.

In either case, the purpose must in some way derive from a symbolic message from the dead, whether that message emphasizes an enlarged vision or simple revenge. We can look upon the *hibakusha* stress upon the general theme of peace, so prominent in their struggles with their overall experience, as an effort to achieve wisdom and transcend revenge. But the theme of "avenging the dead" is universal. It has been overtly prominent in Japanese tradition, and covertly at issue in postwar controversies over shrines for the war dead and national holidays memorializing them.[3] Moreover, it is present in diffuse form in *hibakusha* imagery of ultimate retaliation ("Let A-bombs fall all over the world!"). Among concentration camp survivors themes of revenge have been more publicly prominent. But usually associated with them have been efforts to impose responsibility, to punish the guilty, to reassert moral order—all part of the "collection of justice" we spoke of earlier. This dual quest for revenge and moral order has been present in the reaction of concentration camp survivors to later trials of Nazi war criminals, and has contributed to the sense of renewed vitality observed in many following the Eichmann trial and execution.

There is little doubt that a perceived message of wisdom from the dead is, for the survivor, the superior pattern both ethically and psychologically. But emotions surrounding the idea of revenge must be contended with, and in some way expressed, in relationship to any form of death immersion, especially where the sense of being victimized is strong. With atomic bomb survivors the nature of the weapon makes specific revenge—that is revenge "in kind"—virtually "unthinkable," as compared with the accessibility to concentration camp survivors of specific objects for such feelings. This does not mean that retaliatory emotions do not exist among *hibakusha,* but rather that they tend to become more indirect and ambiguous. Yet however vague, they create extremely strong inner pressure upon the survivor to renounce and overcome them.

These general formulative principles can be observed in parents of children dying of leukemia. It has been observed that among such parents the conclusion that the child's fatal condition was caused by something they did, or failed to do, often seemed preferable to "the intolerable conclusion that no one is responsible." Formulated guilt is preferable to meaningless innocence. Beyond this, they often take on a survivor mission of combating the general scourge of leukemia, through first familiarizing themselves with the medical aspects of the problem and then participating in various programs and campaigns aimed at fighting the disease. Some take comfort in the idea that their own child's case contributed to this goal by what it revealed about the condition. Here we may speak of a guinea pig image that is not devoid of honor, the image of an unpreventable death (whatever the parents' feelings of responsibility) and maximum use of for the benefit of mankind—in contrast to the Hiroshima survivor's sense of having been made into a historical victim by a willful human experiment, and then asked to contribute to medical knowledge.

We observed in Hiroshima the tendency for this negative form of guinea pig imagery to be associated with fantasies of retaliation. In a general sense, any survivor's fixed focus upon revenge as the predominant message from the dead may be understood as a profound formulative impairment, in which he is unable to imagine the existence of relevant wisdom emanating from them or any other source.

Images of Survival and Mastery— We are now in a better position to understand why formulation is so intimately bound up with mastery. For it relates not only to the death immersion itself but to the entire constellation of life-and-death imagery within each individual psyche. This constellation includes three polarities which we have already hinted at: connection-separation, integrity-disintegration, and movement-stasis. To avoid the misleading instinctual language of classical psychoanalysis, and at the same time recognize the presence of the precursors of these polarities at birth, they are best referred to as *innate images*. That is, they form the earliest basis for the individual's world-picture, and for his way of acting upon that world-picture. They are also, inevitably, the prototypes for his later death imagery. And however primitive and unconscious they are during early stages of life, they are from the beginning involved in the creation and re-creation of significant patterns which concern the entire organism.

The first, the connection-separation polarity, has been given considerable stress by psychoanalytic writers, most recently in John Bowlby's elaboration of "attachment behavior" in the very young child. But although much has been written about infantile fears of being devoured or annihilated, and about the young child's terror at being deprived of its mobility, the last two polarities, *as lifelong constellations,* have received relatively little attention. Bowlby and his associates rightly emphasize the significance of very early separation anxiety in the child, and have described a pattern of infantile mourning consisting of three stages—protest, disorganization, and reorganization—which is renacted in adult reactions to death and loss. But when they observe that the eighteen- to twenty-four-month-old child, if separated from his mother, behaves "as if his world has been shattered," we may suspect that the anxiety involved includes primitive images of disintegration and stasis which are inseparable from the sense of separation itself. We of course recognize in this kind of separation the prototype for later survival experiences. But what must also be kept in mind is that the early image formed around it can be reactivated by any subsequent suggestions of disintegration or stasis, as well as separation. The task of formulation is to reassert their polar opposites—connection, symbolic integrity, and movement. Just as one has "known" the experience of survival in every threat to these life-affirming themes, so has one called upon formulation to reconstitute one's inner and outer worlds after each of these "survivals."

This is not to say that childhood experiences "cause" the patterns we have been discussing in this chapter, or that the massive death immersion is "nothing new" and "merely a repetition" of prior psychological tendencies. Rather, we may say that the death immersion reactivates, and at the same time adds new dimensions to, the earlier imagery. Indeed, the emotional power of the death immersion lies precisely in this combination of shock of newness and "shock of recognition."

Of great importance is the age at which the death immersion takes place. In Hiroshima my impression was that the younger a person was, the more fundamental the effect upon his evolving psychic life, but also the greater latitude and flexibility in formulation. The young survivor, therefore, could often achieve considerable mastery over even a severe and indelibly imprinted death immersion. In contrast, older surviors did not "imbibe" the experience in as fundamental a way but retained more incapacitating patterns of despair and psychic numbing. A particularly powerful imprint occurred with those exposed to the bomb during or just prior to adolescence, a period of life when one is extremely sensitive to death imagery, and at the same time old enough for that imagery to take its adult form rather than occur in less specific emotional prototypes. In this group of survivors there tended to occur a formulative struggle of lasting intensity, leading neither to numbed despair nor to mastery. But at whatever age he is exposed, the survivor must call forth life-affirming elements from his own past even as he molds these into a new formulation.

We have noted how formulation enables the survivor to recapture a sense of "active tension"—or of "actuality"—with his environment. All three of the polarities I spoke of are involved in this quest, but particularly those concerned with symbolic integrity and psychic mobility. Yet the seemingly inactive formulative approach of psychological non-resistance, can be, as we have also seen, the most effective one. In a very general sense, psychological non-resistance can be related to an Eastern philosophical emphasis, and the more active idea of "survivor mission" to a Western one. But we have observed the importance of the survivor mission among Japanese in Hiroshima. And Western concentration camp survivors have shown considerable inclination toward psychological non-resistance—as expressed recently in Elie Wiesel's public request for an "accumulation of silence." [4] Not only has there been so much cultural interchange that philosophical origins have become obscure, but we are in fact dealing with two related aspects of universal psychic forms. Both "non-resistance" and "survivor mission" are means of avoiding a sense of being inactivated or overwhelmed with death to the point of marked psychic numbing. And both provide symbolic integrity, including an active reassertion of the sense of immortality.

To reassert this connection to continuous life, the survivor reverts not only to his personal past but to his historical past as well. We recall the *hibakusha's fear of psychohistorical extinction,* as expressed by some individually and also in Agawa's novel. Wiesel describes similar feelings when he discovers, upon his return to his native town, that all was the same as before except that "the Jews had disappeared." He is angry with the Gentile townspeople, not for their misbehavior at the time of the persecutions but "for having forgotten them," and "So quickly, so completely." The survivor cannot formulate from a void. He requires the psychological existence of a past as well as a present, of the dead as well as the living. Without these, neither mastery of his death encounter nor a place in human society is possible.

A WORLD OF SURVIVORS

The atomic survivor, then, is both part of a historical legacy of survivorhood, and a representative of a new dimension of death immersion. He experiences the same general psychological themes we have enumerated for all survivors of massive death immersion, but the unique features of nuclear weapons and of the world's relationship to them give a special quality to his survivorhood.

His death imprint is complicated by a sense of continuous encounter with death—extending through the initial exposure, the immediate post-bomb impact of "invisible contamination," later involvement with "A-bomb disease," and the imagery surrounding the *hibakusha* identity. Death guilt, stimulated at each of these stages, is reinforced by group patterns within a "guilty community," and further reawakened by every flexing of nuclear muscles—whether in the form of threatening words or weapons testing—anywhere in the world. Psychic closing-off is extraordinarily immediate and massive; and later psychic numbing, inseparable from radiation fears, gives rise to a particularly widespread form of psychosomatic entrapment. Suspicion of counterfeit nurturance is markedly strong, and lends itself readily to guinea pig imagery. Contagion anxiety is similarly great because of the radiation-intensified death taint. Formulation is made profoundly difficult, both by the dimensions of the original experience, and by the complexity and threat surrounding the general nuclear problem. And here we arrive at another quality of atomic survival not unique to it but of unique importance: we all share it.

I say this not only because if Japan or Germany had developed the bomb first, I might have been either among the A-bomb dead or else the American equivalent of a *hibakusha;* just as if my grandparents had not elected to emigrate from Eastern Europe, I might have been a concentration camp victim or survivor. Such accidents of history must be kept in mind. But what I refer to is the universal psychological sharing of any great historical experience and particularly of this one in this epoch. In a large sense history itself is a series of survivals, but in our century the theme of survival is more immediate and more ominous.

We have observed the effects of a relatively localized impact of a "small" nuclear bomb, with the existence of an "outside world" to help. There is no need to dwell on the magnification and dissemination of destructive power since Hiroshima, or on the uncertainty of there being an "outside world" to help in a future holocaust. We may simply say that Hiroshima gave new meaning to the idea of a "world war," of man making war upon his own species.

Only man, we are often reminded, "knows death," or at least knows that he will die. To which we must add: only man could invent grotesquely absurd death. Only man, through his technology, could render the meaningful totally meaningless. And more, elevate that "invention" to something in the nature of a potential destiny that stalks us all. For, after Hiroshima, we can envisage no war-linked chivalry, certainly no glory. Indeed, we can see no relationship—not even a distinction—between victimizer and victim, only the sharing in species annihilation.

Yet we know that great discoveries have in the past been made by survivors—of dying historical epochs as well as of actual catastrophes. By confronting their predicament, they have been able to break out of the numbing and stasis of unmastered survivorhood and contribute to the enlargement of human consciousness. Our present difficulty is that we can no longer be sure of this opportunity. We can no longer count upon survivor wisdom deriving from weapons which are without limit in what they destroy.

I have tried throughout this book to write with restraint about matters that make their own emotional statements. But behind that restraint has been a conviction that goes quite beyond judgments of individuals or nations, beyond even the experience of Hiroshima itself. I believe that Hiroshima, together with Nagasaki, signifies a "last chance." It is a nuclear catastrophe from which one can still learn, from which one can derive knowledge that could contribute to holding back the even more massive extermination it seems to foreshadow.

Hiroshima was an "end of the world" in all of the ways I have described. And yet the world still exists. Precisely in this end-of-the-world quality lies both its threat and its potential wisdom. In every age man faces a pervasive theme which defies his engagement and yet must be engaged. In Freud's day it was sexuality and moralism. Now it is unlimited technological violence and absurd death. We do well to name the threat and to analyze its components. But our need is to go further, to create new psychic and social forms to enable us to reclaim not only our technologies, but our very imaginations, in the service of the continuity of life.

NOTES

1 In a talk delivered at Yale University in 1964, Dr. Alexander Mitscherlich offered the thesis that Germans have been unable to confront the combination of ambivalent love and residual guilt felt toward their former leader, and have consequently had to rely heavily upon denial.

2 William A. Greene, whose work on psychogenic factors in malignancies I have quoted before, relates leukemic symptoms and other forms of physical illness to "disruption . . . of a sense of sequence," of "a feeling of continuity in reference to . . . experiences to date and . . . aspirations for the future"; and "con-sequence in association with another or other persons," which involve "some type of . . . attachment," whether pleasant or unpleasant." Greene's concepts are consistent with what I have called "impaired" and "death-welcoming" formulation. The phenomenon of death-welcoming when in the midst of severe stress is well known, and was observed, for instance, in large numbers of American prisoners of war in North Korea who at a certain point would begin to cease trying to stay alive and would resist whatever help was offered by others. The phenomenon was sometimes called "give-upitis."

3 The related themes of revenge and military glory became so closely associated with all memorial ceremonies in prewar and wartime Japan that any postwar ceremonial becomes suspect unless clearly associated with an anti-war formulation. Thus, in an exchange published in English translation in the *Japan Times* of June 8, 1963, Tomoji Abe, a university professor and Director of the Association in Memory of Japanese Student War Dead, recalls the "grand ceremonies during and before the last war" held in the name of commemorating the dead but "designed to instill the general public with a militaristic spirit" and opposes a government-sponsored plan for a large national ceremony on August 15, the day of surrender. He contrasts the implicit ethos of his

own group's program of "lecture meetings, symposiums and . . . homage to tombs of students who were killed in service during the war." His antagonist, Asataro Yamamoto, Director of the Repatriation Bureau of the Health and Welfare Ministry, defends the government plan as responsive to a growing need for "spiritual solace" on the part of bereaved families devoid of "ulterior motives" and dissociated from "revival of militarism in Japan."

4 Wiesel was speaking before a dinner marking the twentieth anniversary of the liberation of the Bergen-Belsen camp. Significantly, however, he referred to the silence of Job's comforters, who sat with him for seven days and seven nights without speaking a word, so that the form of psychological non-resistance advocated is mixed with a Biblical sequence notable for its questioning of God's actions, as well as with Wiesel's own continuing survivor mission of bearing witness.

40

The Art of Suicide

A. Alvarez

> After Stephane Mallarmé, after Paul Verlaine,
> after Gustave Moreau, after Puvis de Chavannes,
> after our own verse, after all our subtle colour
> and nervous rhythm, after the faint mixed tints of Conder,
> what more is possible? After us the Savage God.
>
> W. B. Yeats, *The Trembling of the Veil.*

To put it most simply: one of the most remarkable features of the arts in this century has been the sudden, sharp rise in the casualty rate among the artists. Of the great premodernists, Rimbaud abandoned poetry at the age of twenty, Van Gogh killed himself, Strindberg went mad. Since then the toll has mounted steadily: in the first great flowering of modernism, Kafka wanted to turn his premature natural death from tuberculosis into artistic suicide by having all his writings destroyed. Virginia Woolf drowned herself, a victim of her own excessive sensitivity. Hart Crane devoted prodigious energy to aestheticizing his chaotic life—a desperate compound of homosexuality and alcoholism—and finally, thinking himself a failure, jumped overboard from a steamer in the Caribbean. Dylan Thomas and Brendan Behan drank themselves to death. Artaud spent years in lunatic asylums. Delmore Schwartz was found dead in a run-down Manhattan hotel. Camus died absurdly in a car crash. Cesare Pavese and Paul Celan, Randall Jarrell and Sylvia Plath, Mayakovsky, Yesenin and Tsvetayeva killed themselves. Among the painters, the suicides include Modigliani, Arshile Gorki, Mark Gertler, Jackson Pollack and Mark Rothko. Spanning the generations was Hemingway, whose prose was modeled on a kind of physical ethic of courage and the control necessary at the limits of endurance. He stripped his style to the bone in order to achieve the aesthetic corollary of physical grace—a matter of great economy, great precision, great tension under the appearance of ease. In such a perspective, the natural erosions of age—weakness, uncertainty, clumsiness, imprecision, an overall slackening of what had once been a highly tuned machine—would have seemed as unbearable as losing the ability to write. In the end, he followed the example of his father and shot himself.

Each of these deaths has its own inner logic and unrepeatable despair, and to do them justice would require a degree of detail beyond my purposes here. But a simple point emerges: before the twentieth century it is possible to discuss cases individually, since the artists who killed themselves or were even seriously suicidal were rare exceptions. In the twentieth century the balance suddenly shifts: the better the artist the more vulnerable he seems to be. Obviously, this is in no way a firm rule. The Grand Old Men of literature have been both numerous and very grand: Eliot, Joyce, Pound, Mann, Forster, Frost, Stevens, Marianne Moore. Even so, the casualty rate among the gifted seems out of all proportion, as though the nature of the artistic undertaking itself and the demands it makes had altered radically.

There are, I think, a number of reasons. The first is the continuous, restless urge to experiment, the constant need to change, to innovate, to destroy the accepted styles. "If it works," says Marshall McLuhan, "it's obsolete." But experiment has a logic of its own which leads it unceasingly away from questions of formal technique into a realm where the role of the artist himself alters. Since art changes when the forms available are no longer adequate to what has to be expressed, it follows that every genuine technical revolution is parallel to a profound internal shift. (The superficial changes need not concern us since they are a matter merely of fashion, and, as such, are dictated not by any inner necessities but by the economics of the art industry and the demands of art consumers.) Thus for the Romantic poets, a major gesture of their new emotional freedom was to abandon the straitjacket of the classical rhymed couplet. Similarly, the first modernists jettisoned traditional rhymes and meters in favor of a free verse which would allow them to follow precisely and without deflection the movement of their sensibilities. Technical exploration, in short, implies a degree of psychic exploration; the more radical the experiments, the deeper the responses tapped. That, "presumably," is why the urge to experiment faded in the nineteen-thirties when it seemed that left-wing politics should provide all the answers, and again in England in the nineteen-fifties when the Movement poets were busy immortalizing the securities and complacencies of the commuter suburbs. Not that an experimental, avant-garde appearance guarantees anything; it can be as easily assumed as any other fancy dress and, more easily than most, becomes an embarrassment to the timid and conventional, since its see-through design effortlessly reveals the user's lack of originality: witness the drab followers of Ezra Pound and William Carlos Williams, on both sides of the Atlantic.

But for the more serious artists experiment has not been a matter of merely tinkering with the machinery. Instead, it has provided a context in which he explores the perennial question, "What am I?" without benefit of moral, cultural or even technical securities. Since part of his gift is also a weird knack of sensing and expressing the strains of his time in advance of other people, the movement of the modern arts has been, with continual minor diversions, toward a progressively more inward response to a progressively more intolerable sense of disaster. It is as though, by taking to its limits Conrad's dictum "In the destructive element immerse," his whole role in society had changed; instead of being a Romantic hero and liberator, he has become a victim, a scapegoat.

One of the most beautiful, and certainly the saddest statement of this new fate is by Wilfred Owen, who was dead before the great Modernist change had properly begun. On New Year's Eve, 1917/18, he wrote to his mother:

> I am not dissatisfied with my years. Everything has been done in bouts:
>
> Bouts of awful labour at Shrewsbury and Bordeaux; bouts of amazing pleasure in the Pyrenees, and play at Craiglockhart; bouts of religion at Dunsden; bouts of horrible danger on the Somme; bouts of poetry always; of your affection always; of sympathy for the oppressed always.
>
> I go out of this year a Poet, my dear Mother, as which I did not enter it. I am held peer by the Georgians; I am a poet's poet.
>
> I am started. The tugs have left me; I feel the great swelling of the open sea taking my galleon.

> Last year, at this time (it is just midnight, and now is the intolerable instant of the Change), last year I lay awake in a windy tent in the middle of a vast, dreadful encampment. It seemed neither France nor England, but a kind of paddock where the beasts are kept a few days before the shambles. I heard the revelling of the Scotch troops, who are now dead, and who knew they would be dead. I thought of this present night, and whether I should indeed—whether we should indeed—whether you would indeed—but I thought neither long nor deeply, for I am a master of elision.
>
> But chiefly I thought of the very strange look on all the faces in that camp; an incomprehensible look, which a man will never see in England, though wars should be in England; nor can it be seen in any battle. But only in Etaples.
>
> It was not despair, or terror, it was more terrible than terror, for it was a blindfold look, and without expression, like a dead rabbit's.
>
> It will never be painted, and no actor will ever seize it. And to describe it, I think I must go back and be with them.

Nine months later Owen was back in France. Two months after that he was killed in action, exactly one week before the war ended.

There are two forces at work in this letter, each pulling in the opposite direction: nurture and nature, training and instinct or, in Eliot's phrase, "tradition and the individual talent." Both are personal yet both also correspond to vital elements in his poetry. The first is traditional, which is inevitable since Owen was, in many ways, still at one with the comfortable Georgians who had no truck with the poetic changes already beginning around them. As such, he was responding in the heroic tradition of Sir Philip Sidney and, say, Captain Oates, as "a brave man and an English gentleman." He was going back to France because he had to do his duty as a soldier; since duty invariably means sacrifice, even the chance of the ultimate sacrifice must be accepted without fuss.

But even more strongly, there is an antiheroic force at work which corresponds to all those elements in his writing which went to make him one of the British forerunners of modernism; it corresponds, that is, to his poems' harsh, disabused vision of the war and, technically, to their subtle, decisive use of half-rhymes which helped effectively to dispose of the chiming sweetness of much Georgian verse. It was this second force which impelled him to return to France not as "an officer and a gentleman" but as a writer. The letter is, after all, about his coming-of-age as a poet, and it was in the context of this newly matured power that he made his decision to return to the front. It seems, literally, to have been a decision: he had already seen a great deal of active service and, as a result, had been hospitalized with shellshock. Moreover, his poetry had brought him powerful friends, one of whom, Proust's translator Scott Moncrieff, worked in the War Office and had been using his influence to get Owen a safe posting in England. It may, then, have taken as much effort and organization to return to the fighting as to stay away. What drew him back, I think, had nothing to do with heroism and everything to do with poetry. The new powers he felt in himself seem to have been inextricably linked with the strange, unprecedented vision he had had in France:

> But chiefly I thought of the very strange look on all the faces in that camp; an incomprehensible look, which a man will never see in England, though wars should be in England; nor can it be seen in any battle. But only in Etaples.
>
> It was not despair, or terror, it was more terrible than terror, for it was a blindfold look, and without expression, like a dead rabbit's.
>
> It will never be painted, and no actor will ever seize it. And to describe it, I think I must go back and be with them.

That numbness—beyond hope, despair, terror and, certainly, beyond heroics—is, I think, the final quantum to which all the "modish" forms of twentieth-century alienation are reduced. Under the energy, appetite and constant diversity of the modern arts is this obdurate core of blankness and insentience which no amount of creative optimism and effort can wholly break down or remove. It is like, for a believer, the final, unbudgeable illumination that God is not good. A psychiatrist has defined it, in more contemporary terms, as that "psychic numbing" which occurs in an overwhelming encounter with death.[1] That is, when death is everywhere and on such a vast scale that it becomes indifferent, impersonal, inevitable and, finally, without meaning, the only way to survive, however briefly, is by shutting oneself off utterly from every feeling, so that one becomes invulnerable, not like an armored animal but like a stone.

> . . . [P]sychic closing-off can serve a highly adaptive function. It does so partly through a process of denial ("If I feel nothing, then death is not taking place") . . . . Further, it protects the survivor from a sense of complete helplessness, from feeling himself totally inactivated by the force invading his environment. By closing himself off, he resists being "acted upon" or altered . . . . We may thus say that the survivor initially undergoes a radical but temporary diminution of his sense of actuality in order to avoid losing this sense completely and permanently; he undergoes a reversible form of symbolic death in order to avoid a permanent physical or psychic death.

Dr. Lifton is, as it happens, describing the defense mechanisms brought into play by the survivors of the Hiroshima atom bomb and the Nazi concentration camps. But that awareness of a ubiquitous, arbitrary death—which descends like a medieval plague on the just and unjust alike, without warning or reason—is, I think, central to our experience of the twentieth century. It began with the pointless slaughters of the First World War, continued through Nazi and Stalinist extermination camps, through a Second World War which culminated in two atomic explosions, and has survived with genocide in Tibet and Biafra, a senseless war in Vietnam, atomic testing which poisons the atmosphere and the development of biological weapons which kill haphazardly and more or less without control; it ends with the possibility of the globe itself shadowed by nuclear weapons orbiting in outer space.

It is important not to exaggerate; after all, this sense of disaster is, for the moment, mercifully peripheral to the lives most of us lead. To harp on it like Cassandra is as foolish, and ultimately as boring, as to ignore it completely. Yet the fact remains that the context in which our arts, morals and securities are created has changed radically:

> After Hiroshima we can envisage no war-linked chivalry, certainly no glory. Indeed, we can see no relationship—not even a distinction—between victimizer and victim—only the sharing in species annihilation. . . . In every age man faces a pervasive theme which defies his engagement and yet must be engaged. In Freud's day it was sexuality and moralism. Now it is unlimited technological violence and absurd death. [—*Dr. Lifton*]

In other words, that sense of chaos which, I suggested, is the driving force behind the restless experimentalism of the twentieth-century arts has two sources—one developing directly from the period before 1914, the other emerging for the first time during the First World War and growing increasingly stronger and more unavoidable as the century has gone on. Both, perhaps, are consequences of industrialism: the first is connected with the destruction of the old social relationships and the related structures of belief during the Industrial Revolution; the second is produced by the technology itself which, in the process of creating the wherewithal to make life easier than ever before, has perfected, as a kind of lunatic spin-off, instruments to destroy life completely. More simply, just as the decay of religious authority in the nineteenth century made life seem absurd by depriving it of any ultimate coherence, so the growth of modern technology has made death itself absurd by reducing it to a random happening totally unconnected with the inner rhythms and logic of the lives destroyed.

This, then, is the Savage God whom Yeats foresaw and whose intolerable, demanding presence Wilfred Owen sensed at the front. To be true to his vocation as a poet Owen felt he must describe that "blindfold look, and without expression, like a dead rabbit's"; which meant he had to return to France and risk his life. This double duty—to forge a language which will somehow absolve or validate absurd death, and to accept the existential risks involved in doing so—is, I think, the model for everything that was to follow. "There exist no words, in any human language," wrote a Hiroshima survivor, "which can comfort guinea pigs who do not know the cause of their death." It is precisely the pressure to discover a language adequate to this apparently impossible task which is behind the curious sense of strain characteristic of nearly all the best and most ambitious work of this century.

There are, of course, other, more obvious pressures, some of which I have already touched on: the collapse of traditional values, impatience with worn-out conventions, the minor pleasures of iconoclasm and experiment for their own sakes. There is also the impact of what Marshall McLuhan calls the "electronic culture," which has so effortlessly usurped both the audience and many of the functions of the "formal" highbrow arts. But beyond all these, and becoming continually more insistent as the atrocities have grown in size and frequency, has been the absolute need to find an artistic language with which to grasp in the imagination the historical facts of this century; a language, that is, for "the destructive element," the dimension of unnatural, premature death.

Inevitably, it is the language of mourning. Or rather, the arts take on the function of mourning, breaking down that "psychic numbness" which follows any massive immersion in death: "The books we need," wrote Kafka in a letter to his friend Oscar Pollack, "are the kind that act upon us like a misfortune, that make us suffer like the death of someone we love more than ourselves, that make us feel as though we were on the verge of suicide, or lost in a forest remote from all human habitation—a book should serve as the axe for the frozen sea within us." Clearly, books of this order will not be written simply by invoking the atrocities—a gesture which usually guarantees nothing but rhetoric and the cheapening of all those millions of deaths. What is required is something a good deal more difficult and individual: the creative act itself, which gives shape, coherence and some kind of gratuitous beauty to all those vague depressions and paranoias art is heir to. Freud responded to the First World War by positing a death instinct beyond the pleasure principle; for the artist, the problem is to create a language which is both beyond the pleasure principle and, at the same time, pleasurable.

This ultimately is the pressure forcing the artist into the role of scapegoat. In order to evolve a language of mourning which will release all those backed-up guilts and obscure hostilities he shares with his audience, he puts himself at risk and explores his own vulnerability; it is as though he were testing out his own death in his imagination—symbolically, tentatively and with every escape hatch open. "Suicide," said Camus, "is prepared within the silence of the heart, as is a great work of art." Increasingly, the corollary also seems to be true: under certain conditions of stress, a great work of art *is* a kind of suicide.

There are two opposite ways into this dimension of death. The first is through what might be called Totalitarian Art (which is, incidentally, different in kind from traditional art in a totalitarian society). It tackles the historical situation frontally, more or less brutally, in order to create a human perspective for a dehumanizing process. The second is what I have called elsewhere Extremist Art: the destruction is all turned inwards and the artist deliberately explores in himself that narrow, violent area between the viable and the impossible, the tolerable and the intolerable. Both approaches involve certain radical changes in the relationship of the artist to his material.

For Totalitarian Art the changes are both inevitable and unwilling. The simple reason is that a police state and its politics of terror produce conditions in which the intense individualism on which art is traditionally based—its absolute trust in the validity of the unique personal insight—is no longer possible. When the artist is valued like an engineer or factory worker or bureaucrat, only to the extent to which he serves the policies of the state, then his art is reduced to propaganda—sometimes sophisticated, more often not. The artist who refuses that role refuses everything; he becomes superfluous. In these circumstances the price of art in the traditional sense and with its traditional values is suicide—or silence, which amounts to the same thing.

Perhaps this explains the phenomenal casualty rate among the generation of Russian poets who had begun to work before the convulsions of 1917 and refused the Joycean alternative of "silence, exile and cunning." In 1926, after Sergei Yesenin hanged himself, first cutting his wrists and then, as a last great aesthetic gesture, writing a farewell poem in his own blood, Mayakovsky wrote, condemning him:

In this life it is not difficult to die
it is more difficult to live.

Yet less than five years later Mayakovsky himself, poetic hero of the Revolution and inveterate gambler who had twice already played Russian roulette with a loaded revolver, came to the conclusion that his political principles were poisoning his poetry at its source. He played Russian roulette for the last time and lost. In his suicide note he wrote laconically, "I don't recommend it for others." Yet several others did, in fact, follow him, apart from all those who, like Mandelshtam and Babel, disappeared in the purges. Boris Pasternak wrote an epitaph on them all:

> To start with what is most important: we have no conception of the inner torture which precedes suicide. People who are physically tortured on the rack keep losing consciousness, their suffering is so great that its unendurable intensity shortens the end. But a man who is thus at the mercy of the executioner is not annihilated when he faints from pain, for he is present at his own end, his past belongs to him, his memories are his and, if he chooses, he can make use of them, they can help him before his death.
>
> But a man who decides to commit suicide puts a full stop to his being, he turns his back on his past, he declares himself a bankrupt and his memories to be unreal. They can no longer help or save him, he has put himself beyond their reach. The continuity of his inner life is broken, his personality is at an end. And perhaps what finally makes him kill himself is not the firmness of his resolve but the unbearable quality of this anguish which belongs to no one, of this suffering in the absence of the sufferer, of this waiting which is empty because life has stopped and can no longer fill it.
>
> It seems to me that Mayakovsky shot himself out of pride, because he condemned something in himself, or close to him, to which his self-respect could not submit. That Yesenin hanged himself without having properly thought out the consequences of his act, still saying in his inmost heart: "Who knows? Perhaps this isn't yet the end. Nothing is yet decided." That Maria Tsvetayeva had always held her work between herself and the reality of daily life; and when she found this luxury beyond her means, when she felt that for her son's sake she must, for a time, give up her passionate absorption in poetry and look round her soberly, she saw chaos, no longer screened by art, fixed, unfamiliar, motionless, and, not knowing where to run for terror, she hid in death, putting her head into the noose as she might have hidden her head under her pillow. It seems to me that Paolo Yashvili was utterly confused, spellbound by the Shigalyovshchina of 1937 as by witchcraft; and that he watched his daughter as she slept at night and, imagining himself unworthy to look at her, went out in the morning to his friends' house and blasted his head with grapeshot from his

> double-barrelled gun. And it seems to me that Fadeyev, still with the apologetic smile which had somehow stayed with him through all the crafty ins and outs of politics, told himself just before he pulled the trigger: "Well, now it's over. Goodbye, Sasha."
>
> What is certain is that they all suffered beyond description, to the point where suffering has become a mental sickness. And, as we bow in homage to their gifts and to their bright memory, we should bow compassionately before their suffering.

Pasternak writes, I think, with the poignancy of a man who has been there himself. This is not, in any way, to imply that he had considered taking his own life—a question which is none of our business—but simply that he had endured those conditions in which suicide becomes an unavoidable fact of society. As he describes them, they are precisely the same as those which obtain, according to Hannah Arendt, when a totalitarian system achieves full power: like the victim of the totalitarian state, the suicide assists passively at the cancellation of his own history, his work, his memories, his whole inner life—in short, of everything that defines him as an individual:

> The concentration camps, by making death itself anonymous (making it impossible to find out whether a prisoner is dead or alive) robbed death of its meaning as the end of a fulfilled life. In a sense they took away the individual's own death, proving that henceforth nothing belonged to him and he belonged to no one. His death merely set a seal on the fact that he had never existed.

For both the exterminated millions Miss Arendt writes about and for Pasternak's suicides the conditions of terror were the same: "chaos, no longer screened by art, fixed, unfamiliar, motionless." But the suicides retained at least one last shred of freedom: they took their own lives. In part this is a political act, both a gesture of defiance and a condemnation of the set-up—like the self-immolation of the student, Jan Palach, in Prague in 1968. It is also an act of affirmation; the artist values life and his own truths too much to be able to tolerate their utter perversion. Thus the totalitarian state presents its artists with suicide as though with a gift, a final work of art validating all his others.

It was part of Pasternak's own genius and uniqueness that he refused to be canceled in this way and continued, by some political miracle, to write his poems and his novel as though all those improbable personal values still survived. No doubt he paid for his understanding with isolation and depression, but few others got out so cleanly. Yet neither those who survived contaminated nor those who went under even managed to hold up the mirror to that complete corruption of nature which is the totalitarian system in action. Not necessarily for lack of trying. But despite the hundreds of attempts, police terror and the concentration camps have proved to be more or less impossible subjects for the artist; since what happened in them was beyond the imagination, it was therefore also beyond art and all those human values on which art is traditionally based.

The most powerful exception is the Pole, Tadeusz Borowski. Where the Russian poets to whom Pasternak paid his homage continued to write up to the point where they felt their whole life and work had been canceled by history, Borowski was unique in beginning with that cancellation. In one of his Auschwitz stories, "Nazis," he remarks sardonically:

> True, I could also lie, employing the age-old methods which literature has accustomed itself to using in pretending to express the truth—but I lack the imagination.

Lacking the imagination, he avoided all the tricks of melodrama, self-pity and propaganda which elsewhere are the conventional literary means of avoiding the intolerable facts of life in the camps. Instead, he perfected a curt, icy style, as stripped of feeling as of ornament, in which the monstrous lunacies of life in Auschwitz were allowed to speak for themselves, without comment and therefore without disguise:

> Between two throw-ins in a soccer game, right behind my back, three thousand people had been put to death.

Following an almost idyllic, almost pastoral description of a lazy game of football in a setting for the moment as peaceful as an English village cricket green, the sentence explodes like a bomb. Borowski's art was one of reduction; his prose and his stories are as bare and deprived as the lives described in them. A Polish critic has pointed out that his notion of tragedy "has nothing to do with the classical conception based on the necessity of choice between two systems of value. The hero of Borowski's stories is a hero *deprived of all choice*. He finds himself in a situation without choice because every choice is base." Because death in the ovens came to all, regardless of their innocence or their "crimes," "the de-individualization of the hero was accompanied by a *de-individualization of the situation*." Borowski himself called his stories "a journey to the utmost limit of a certain kind of morality." It is a morality created out of the absence of all morality, a skillful, minimal yet eloquent language for the most extreme form of what Lifton called "psychic numbing." By reducing his prose to the facts and images of camp life and refusing to intrude his own comments, Borowski also contrived to define, as though by his omissions and silences, precisely that state of mind in which the prisoners lived: brutal, depersonalized, rapacious, deadly. Morally speaking, it is a posthumous existence, like that of the suicide, as Pasternak described him, who "puts a full stop to his being . . . turns his back on his past, . . . declares himself a bankrupt and his memories to be unreal."

This, then, is Totalitarian Art; it is as much an art of successful suicide, as Extremist Art is that of the attempt. And in order to achieve it, Borowski himself underwent a progressive, triple suicide. Although he had behaved with great courage in Auschwitz, voluntarily giving up the relatively easy post of an orderly in order to share the lot of the common prisoners, his first person singular narrator is callous, corrupt, well-placed in the camp hierarchy, a survival artist who hates his fellow victims more than the guards because their weakness illuminates his, and each new death means a further effort of denial and a sharper guilt. Thus his first self-destruction was moral: he assuaged his guilt for surviving when so many others had gone under by identifying with the evil he described. The second suicide came after his concentration camps stories were written: he abandoned literature altogether and sank himself into Stalinist politics. Finally, having escaped the Zyklon B of Auschwitz for so long, he gassed himself at home in 1951, when he was twenty-seven years old.

The politicians and economists of disaster may talk glibly of "thinking about the unthinkable," but for the writers the problem is sharper, closer and considerably more difficult. Like the Hiroshima survivor I mentioned earlier, Borowski seems to have despaired of ever communicating adequately what he knew: "I wished to describe what I have experienced, but who in the world will believe a writer using an unknown language? It's like trying to persuade trees or stones." The key to the language turned out to be deprivation, a totalitarian art of facts and images, without frills or comments, as depersonalized and deprived as the lives of the victims themselves. In the same way, when Peter Weiss created his documentary tragedy, *The Investigation,* he invented nothing and added nothing; he simply used a blank stage, unnamed, anonymously dressed actors and skillfully edited fragments of the Auschwitz trials in Frankfurt. The result was a great deal more shocking than any "imaginative" re-creation of the camps could ever have been.

Similarly, Samuel Beckett began at the other end of the spectrum with an Irish genius for words, words, words and finished by creating a world of what Coleridge called "Life-in-Death." His people lead posthumous, immobile lives, stripped of all personal qualities, appetites, possessions and hope. All that remains to them is language; they palliate their present sterility by dim, ritual invocations of a time when things still happened and their motions still stirred. The fact that Beckett's detachment and impeccable timing produces comedy out of this universal impotence only serves, in the end, to make the desolation more complete. By refusing even the temptation to tragedy and by stylizing his language to the point of minimal survival, he makes his world impregnable. As a—presumably—lapsed Catholic he is creating a world which God has abandoned, as life might abandon some burnt-out star. To express this terminal morality he uses a minimal art, stripped of all artifact. It is the complement of Borowski's concentration camp stories, and equally deprived; the totalitarianism of the inner world.

It is here that Totalitarian and Extremist Art meet. When Norman Mailer calls the modern, statistical democracies of the West "totalitarian," he is not implying that the artist is bound and muzzled and circumscribed as he would be in a dictatorship—a vision not even the most strenuous paranoia could justify. But he is implying that mass democracy, mass morality and the mass media thrive independently of the individual, who joins them only at the cost of at least a partial perversion of his instincts and insights. He pays for his social ease with what used to be called his soul—his discriminations, his uniqueness, his psychic energy, his self. Add to that the ubiquitous sense of violence erupting continually at the edges of perception: local wars, riots, demonstrations and political assassinations, each seen, as it were, out of the corner of the eye as just another news feature on the television screen. Add, finally, the submerged but never quite avoidable knowledge of the possibility of ultimate violence, known hopefully as the balance of terror. The result is totalitarianism not as a political phenomenon but as a state of mind.

"To extreme sicknesses, extreme remedies," said Montaigne. In this instance the remedy has been an artistic revolution as radical and profound as that which took place after Wordsworth and Coleridge published the *Lyrical Ballads* or Eliot brought out *The Waste Land*. In a sense it completes the revolution which began with the first Romantics' insistence on the primacy of their subjective vision. The implied ideal of spontaneity was acceptable in principle but not wholly in practice since it seemed to deny what was self-evidently undeniable: the intelligence of the artist—his realistic understanding of the value and practical uses of his inspiration—and the whole drab, boring labor of creativity. Hence the excesses of Romanticism were continually counterbalanced by the criterion which Matthew Arnold, Flaubert, James, Eliot and Joyce made so much of: that of the artist as disembodied, utterly detached creator whose work is objective, autonymous, "containing in itself," in Coleridge's words, "the reason why it is so and not otherwise." These Arnoldian concepts acted as a substitute classicism which defended the best nineteenth- and twentieth-century artists against the weaknesses, conceit and often downright silliness inherent in their beliefs, from that split between feeling and intelligence which has bedeviled decadent Romanticism from Shelley to Ginsberg.

The opposite of all this is the post-Arnold, post-Eliot art we have now, where the work is not set off on its own, a law unto itself, but is, instead, in a continual, cross-fertilizing relationship with the artist's life. The existence of the work of art, that is, is contingent, provisional; it fixes the energy, appetites, moods and confusions of experience in the most lucid possible terms so as to create a temporary clearing of calm, and then moves on, or back, into autobiography. Camus first hinted at this in *The Myth of Sisyphus* when he suggested that a man's works "derive their definitive significance" only from his death: "They receive their most obvious light from the very life of their author. At the moment of death, the succession of his works is but a collection of failures. But if those failures all have the same resonance, the creator has managed to repeat the image of his own condition, to make the air echo with the sterile secret he possesses." This idea was taken up by the American poet Hayden Carruth and applied eloquently to the situation of the arts now:

> In its authenticity life is our own interpretation and re-organization of experience, structured metaphorically. It is the result of successive imaginative acts—it is a work of art! By conversion, a work of art is life, *provided it be true to the experiential core.* Thus in a century artists had moved from an Arnoldian criticism of life to an Existential creation of life, and both the gains and the losses were immense.
>
> The biggest loss perhaps was a large part of what we thought we had known about art. For now we saw in exactly what way art is limitless. It is limitless because it is free and responsible: it is a life. Its only end is the adventitious cutting off that comes when a heart bursts, or a sun. Still, the individual "piece" of art must be objective in some sense; it lies on the page, on the canvas. Practically speaking, what is a limitless object? It is a fragment; a random fragment; a fragment without intrinsic form, shading off in all directions into whatever lies beyond. And this is what our art has become in the past two decades: random, fragmentary, and open-ended.

> Hence in literature any particular "work" is linear rather than circular in structure, extensible rather than terminal in intent, and at any given point inclusive rather than associative in substance; at least these are its tendencies. And it is autobiographical, that goes without saying. It is an act of self-creation by an artist within the tumult of experience.

The break with classicism has produced, then, not a new form of Romanticism—which remains too cozy, self-indulgent and uncritical to be adequate to the realities of the period—but an Existential art, as tense and stringent as its classic forebears but far less restricted, since its subject is precisely those violent confusions from which both the Augustans and the Neoclassicists of the last hundred years withdrew nervously and with distaste.

For example, a poem by T. S. Eliot is opaque; it gathers the light into itself and gives back only the image of its own perfection. In contrast, a poem by Robert Lowell, though no less carefully constructed, is like a transparent filter; you look through it to see the man as he is. Similarly, in *The Armies of the Night,* Norman Mailer takes a fragment of contemporary history in which he played a part (the March on the Pentagon in October, 1967), presents it, like a good journalist, in all its attendant farce, muddle and political jostling, and yet at the same time transforms it into an internal scenario in which all the conflicting, deadening facts take on a sharpened coherence as reflections in the somewhat bloodshot eye of his own developing consciousness as an artist. The politics of power are replaced by the politics of experience.

None of this absolves the artist from the labor of art—which is one reason, among many, why the confessional poets who follow Ginsberg seem so sad. On the contrary, the more directly an artist confronts the confusions of experience, the greater the demands on his intelligence, control and a certain watchfulness; the greater, too, the imaginative reserves he must tap so as not to weaken or falsify what he knows. But the intelligence required is essentially different from that of classical art. It is provisional, dissatisfied, restless. As D. H. Lawrence said of his own free verse: "It has no finish. It has no satisfying stability, satisfying for those who like the immutable. None of this. It is the instant; the quick." What is involved, then, is an artistic intelligence working at full pitch to produce not settled classical harmonies but the tentative, flowing, continually improvised balance of life itself. But because such a balance is always precarious, work of this kind entails a good deal of risk. And because the artist is committed to truths of his inner life often to the point of acute discomfort, it becomes riskier still.

It is here that post-Arnoldian art joins with what I have called the dimension of absurd death: the artistic revolution of the last decade and a half has occurred, I think, as a response to totalitarianism in Mailer's sense of the word: not as so many isolated facts out there in another country and another political system for which somebody else is responsible, but as part of the insidious atmosphere we breathe. The nihilism and destructiveness of the self—of which psychoanalysis has made us sharply and progressively more aware—turns out to be an accurate reflection of the nihilism of our own violent societies. Since we can't, apparently, control it on the outside, politically, we can at least try to control it in ourselves, artistically.

The operative word is "control." The Extremist poets are committed to psychic exploration out along that friable edge that divides the tolerable and the intolerable; but they are equally committed to lucidity, precision and a certain vigilant directness of expression. In this, they have more in common with the taxingly high standards set by Eliot and the other grandmasters of the nineteen-twenties than with the Surrealists, who were concerned with the wit, or whimsicality, of the unconscious. Out of the haphazard, baroque connections of the mind running without restraints the Surrealists created what is, essentially, a landscape art. In comparison, the Extremist artists are committed to the stage below this, a stage before what Freud called "the dream-work" begins. That is, they are committed to the raw materials of dreams; all the griefs and guilts and hostility which dreams express only elliptically, by displacement and disguise, they seek to express directly, poignantly, skillfully and in full consciousness. Extremism, in short, has more in common with psychoanalysis than with Surrealism.

In poetry the four leading English-language exponents of the style are Robert Lowell, John Berryman, Ted Hughes and Sylvia Plath, all of whom are highly disciplined and highly aware of formal demands and possibilities. All begin with a thickly textured, wary, tensely intelligent style they inherited ultimately from Eliot, and progress in their different ways, towards a poetry in which the means, though no less demanding, are subordinate to a certain inner urgency which makes them push continually at the limits of what poetry can be made to bear. Inevitably so, since each of them is knowingly salvaging his verse from the edge of some kind of personal abyss. The crucial work was Lowell's *Life Studies* in which he turned away from the highly wrought Roman Catholic symbolism of his earlier poetry in order to face—without benefit of clergy, and in a translucent, seemingly more casual style—his own private chaos as a man subject to periodic breakdowns. By some odd creative logic, compounded partly of his great natural gifts and partly of some hitherto unrecognized need in his audience—an impatience, perhaps, with strictly aesthetic criteria which took no count of the confusions and depressions of a life unredeemed by poetry—the more simply and personally he wrote, the more authentic and authoritative his work became. He transformed the seemingly private into a poetry central to all our anxieties.

In much the same way, John Berryman turned from the public, literary world of *Homage to Mistress Bradstreet* to the still stylized but far more intimate cycle of *Dream Songs*. These began as a quirky poetic journal of misdemeanors, gripes, hangovers and morning-after despair, then gradually clarified and deepened into an extended act of poetic mourning for the suicide of a father, the premature deaths of friends and his own suicidal despair. Berryman had always been a poet of bristling nervous energy; now his sense of grief and loss added an extra, urgent dimension to his work, impelling it through the whole process of mourning—guilt, hostility, expiation—which ends with the beautifully lucid acceptance of his own mortality. He ends, that is, writing his own epitaph.

Ted Hughes and Sylvia Plath, belonging to a younger generation, began further along the road and explored further into the hinterland of nihilism. Thus Hughes starts with a series of extraordinary animal poems, full of sharp details and unexpected shifts of focus, in which he elegantly projects onto a whole zooful of creatures whatever unpredictable violence he senses in himself. Then gradually, as in a case of demonic possession, the animals begin to take over; the portraits turn into soliloquies in which murder is no longer disguised or excused, the poet himself becomes both predator and prey of his own inner violence. Like the Yugoslav poet Vasco Popa, Hughes exercises strict control over his private monsters by making them subject to arbitrary rules, as in some psychotic child's game, but he also carries the hunt on into the darkness with exceptional single-mindedness.

It is with Sylvia Plath that the Extremist impulse becomes total and, literally, final. In the briefest terms, her dissatisfaction with the elegant, rather arty style of her early poems more or less coincided with the appearance of *Life Studies*. Lowell proved that it was possible to write about these things without sinking into the witless morals of "confessional" verse. And this was the excuse she had been waiting for, the key to unlock the reserves of pain which had built up steadily since her father's premature death when she was a child and her own suicide attempt at the age of twenty. In the mass of brilliant poems which poured out in the last few months of her life she took Lowell's example to its logical conclusion, systematically exploring the nexus of anger, guilt, rejection, love and destructiveness which made her finally take her own life. It is as though she had decided that, for her poetry to be valid, it must tackle head-on nothing less serious than her own death, bringing to it a greater wealth of invention and sardonic energy than most poets manage in a lifetime of so-called affirmation.

If the road had seemed impassable, she proved that it wasn't. It was, however, one-way, and she went too far along it to be able, in the end, to turn back. Yet her actual suicide, like Lowell's breakdowns or the private horrors of Berryman and Hughes, is by the way; it adds nothing to her work and proves nothing about it. It was simply a risk she took in handling such volatile material. Indeed, what the Extremists have in common is not a style but a belief in the value, even the necessity, of risk. They do not deny it like our latter-day aesthetes, nor drown it in the benign, warm but profoundly muddied ocean of hippy love and inarticulateness. This determination to confront the intimations not of immortality but of mortality itself, using every imaginative resource and technical skill to bring it close, understand it, accept it, control it, is finally what distinguishes genuinely advanced art from the fashionable crowd of pseudo-avant-gardes. On these terms, an artist could live to be as old as Robert Frost or Ezra Pound and yet still, in his work, be a suicide of the imagination.

I am suggesting, in short, that the best modern artists have in fact done what that Hiroshima survivor thought impossible: out of their private tribulations they have invented a public "language which can comfort guinea pigs who do not know the cause of their death." That, I think, is the ultimate justification of the highbrow arts in an era in which they themselves seem less and less convinced of their claims to attention and even existence. They survive morally by becoming, in one way or another, an imitation of death in which their audience can share; to achieve this the artist, in his role of scapegoat, finds himself testing out his own death and vulnerability for and on himself.

It may be objected that the arts are also about many other things, often belligerently so; for example, that they are preoccupied as never before with sex. But I wonder if sexual explicitness isn't a diversion, almost a form of conservatism. After all, that particular battle was fought and won by Freud and Lawrence in the first quarter of this century. The old guard may grumble and occasionally sue, but in a society where *Portnoy's Complaint* is a record-breaking best seller sexual permissiveness is no longer an issue. The real resistance now is to an art which forces its audience to recognize and accept imaginatively, in their nerve ends, the facts not of life but of death and violence, absurd, random, gratuitous, unjustified and inescapably part of the society we have created. "There is only one liberty," wrote Camus in his *Notebooks,* "to come to terms with death. After which, everything is possible."

NOTE

1 Robert Jay Lifton. *Death in Life: The Survivors of Hiroshima.*

Acknowledgments

The editors wish to express their gratitude for the help and advice of Sybil Wuletich.

"The Art of Suicide," by A. Alvarez. Copyright © 1970 by A. Alvarez. From a forthcoming book on suicide to be published by Random House, Inc. Reprinted by permission of the publisher. (First appeared in *Partisan Review,* Volume XXXVII, Number 3, 1970.)

From *The Origins of Totalitarianism* (Cleveland and New York, 1958), New Edition, copyright, 1951, 1958, 1966, by Hannah Arendt. Reprinted by permission of Harcourt Brace Jovanovich, Inc. (Grateful acknowledgment is also made of permission by the English publishers, George Allen & Unwin, Ltd., London.)

"Excerpts from *The Theater and Its Double*" (New York, 1958) by Antonin Artaud. Translated from the French by Mary Caroline Richards. Reprinted by permission of Grove Press, Inc. Copyright © 1958 by Grove Press, Inc. (Grateful acknowledgment is also made of permission by the English publishers, Calder & Boyars, Ltd., London.)

From *Writing Degree Zero* (New York, 1968) by Roland Barthes. Translated from the French *Le Degre Zéro de L'Ecriture,* © 1953 by Editions du Seuil. Translation © 1967 by Johathan Cape Ltd. Preface copyright © 1968 by Susan Sontag. Reprinted by permission of Hill & Wang, Inc.

"The Death of the Author," by Roland Barthes, translated by Richard Howard. Reprinted by permission of the author from *Aspen Magazine,* Section 3, No. 5–6, 1968.

What Is Cinema? (Berkeley and Los Angeles, 1967), by André Bazin. Translated from the French by Hugh Gray as edited by Andre Bazin. Copyright © 1967 by The Regents of the University of California. Reprinted by permission of the University of California Press.

"Three Dialogues," by Samuel Beckett and Georges Duthuit. Copyright 1949 by Samuel Beckett and Georges Duthuit. Reprinted by permission of Georges Duthuit and Grove Press, Inc., from *Transition Forty-Nine,* No. 5 (1949).

The Informed Heart: Autonomy in a Mass Age (New York, 1960), by Bruno Bettelheim. Copyright © 1960 by The Free Press, A Corporation. Reprinted by permission of The Free Press. (Grateful acknowledgment is also made of permission by the English publishers, Thames & Hudson, Ltd., London.)

"The Existential Analysis School of Thought," by Ludwig Binswanger. Translated from the German by Ernest Angel. Copyright © 1958 by Basic Books, Inc. Selection reprinted by permission of the publishers, from *Existence: A New Dimension in Psychiatry and Psychology* (New York, 1958), ed. by Rollo May, Ernest Angel, and Henri F. Ellenberger.

Jorge Luis Borges, *Labyrinths: Selected Stories and Other Writings* (New York, 1962), ed. by Donald A. Yates and James E. Irby. Copyright © 1962 by New Directions Publishing Corporation. Reprinted by permission of New Directions Publishing Corporation. (Grateful acknowledgment is also made of permission by the English publishers, Penguin Books Limited and the Proprietors, Laurence Pellinger Limited, London.)

Copyright © 1957, 1963, and 1964 by Suhrkamp Verlag, Frankfurt am Main. From *Brecht On Theatre* (New York, 1966), translated by John Willett. This translation and notes © 1964 by John Willett. Reprinted by permission of Hill & Wang, Inc. (Grateful acknowledgment is also made of permission by the English publishers, Methuen & Co. Ltd., London.)

"Chance-Imagery," by George Brecht. Copyright © 1966 by Something Else Press, Inc., 276 Park Avenue South, New York, N.Y. 10010. All rights reserved. Reprinted by permission.

Reprinted by permission of the publishers from P. W. Bridgman, *The Way Things Are* (New York, 1961), Cambridge, Mass.: Harvard

University Press, Copyright © 1959, by the President and Fellows of Harvard College.

Copyright © 1959 by Wesleyan University. Reprinted from *Life Against Death* (New York, 1959), Norman O. Brown, by permission of Wesleyan University Press. (Grateful acknowledgment is also made of permission by the English publishers, Routledge & Kegan Paul Ltd., London.)

Language as Symbolic Action (Berkeley and Los Angeles, 1968), by Kenneth Burke. Copyright © 1966 by The Regents of the University of California. Second printing, 1968. Reprinted by permission of The Regents of the University of California.

"Experimental Music," Copyright © 1958 by John Cage. Reprinted from *Silence* (Cambridge, Massachusetts and London, 1966) by John Cage, by permission of Wesleyan University Press. (Grateful acknowledgment is also made of permission by the English Publishers, Calder and Boyars, Ltd., London.)

"Forerunners of Modern Music," Copyright © 1949 by John Cage. Reprinted from *Silence* (Cambridge, Massachusetts and London, 1966) by John Cage, by permission of Wesleyan University Press. (Grateful acknowledgment is also made of permission by the English publishers, Calder and Boyars, Ltd., London.)

"An Interview with Jean Luc Godard," by *Cahiers du Cinéma,* December, 1962. Copyright by Joseph Weill, Cahiers Publishing Company, Inc.

"*Akropolis:* Treatment of the Text," by Ludwik Flaszen. Copyright © 1968 by Jerzy Grotowski and Odin Teatrets Ferlag. Reprinted by permission of H. M. Bergs Ferlag, Copenhagen, from *Towards a Poor Theatre* (New York, 1969) by Jerzy Grotowski.

"The Representation of Nature in Contemporary Physics," by Werner Heisenberg. Reprinted by permission from *Daedalus,* Journal of the American Academy of Arts and Sciences, Boston, Massachusetts, Volume 87, Number 3, Summer, 1958.

"Excerpts from *Notes And Counter Notes: Writings on the Theater* (New York, 1964) by Eugene Ionesco. Translated from the French by Donald Watson. Reprinted by permission of Grove Press, Inc. Copyright © 1964 by Grove Press, Inc. (Grateful acknowledgment is also made of permission by the English publishers, Calder and Boyars, Ltd., London.)

"Manifesto," by Allan Kaprow. Copyright © 1966 by Something Else Press, New York. Reprinted by permission of the publishers.

"The Icon and the Absurd," by Jan Kott. Copyright © 1969 by *The Drama Review*. Reprinted by permission from *The Drama Review,* Volume 14, Number 1, Fall, 1969.

From *The Divided Self* (Middlesex, England, 1965), Copyright © 1960 by Tavistock Publications Ltd. © 1969 by R. D. Laing. Reprinted by permission of Pantheon Books, Inc., a division of Random House, Inc. (Grateful acknowledgment is also made of permission by the English publishers, Methuen & Co. Ltd., London.)

The Savage Mind (Chicago, 1966) by Claude Lévi-Strauss. Translated from the French, *La Pensée Sauvage* © 1962 by Librarie Plon, 8 rue Garanciere, Paris 6e. English translation permission of the author and the University of Chicago Press. (Grateful acknowledgment is also made of permission by the English publishers, George Weidenfeld & Nicholson Ltd., London.)

From *Death in Life: Survivors of Hiroshima* (New York, 1969) by Robert Jay Lifton. Copyright © 1967 by Robert Jay Lifton. Reprinted by permission of the author and the University of Chicago Press. (Grateful acknowledgment is also made of permission by the English publishers, George Weidenfeld & Nicholson Ltd., London.)

Reprinted by permission of The World Publishing Company from *The Armies of the Night* by Norman Mailer. An NAL book. Copyright © 1968 by Norman Mailer. Also reprinted by permission of the author and the author's agent, Scott Meredith Literary Agency, Inc., 580 Fifth Avenue, New York, N.Y. 10036.

"Bodies in Space: Film as 'Carnal Knowledge,' " by Annette Michelson. Copyright © 1969 by Annette Michelson and *Artforum*. Reprinted by permission of the author, from *Artforum,* February, 1969.

From *Understanding Media* (New York, 1965) by Marshall McLuhan. Used with permission of McGraw-Hill Book Company.

"Findings in a Case of Schizophrenic Depression," by Eugene Minkowski. Translated from the French by Barbara Bliss. Copyright © 1958 by Basic Books, Inc. Selection reprinted by permission of the publishers, from *Existence: A New Dimension in Psychiatry and Psychology* (New York, 1958), ed. by Rollo May, Ernest Angel, and Henri F. Ellenberger.

"The Omnipresence of the Grotesque," by Benjamin Nelson. Reprinted by permission of the author, of the Society for the Arts, Religion and Contemporary Culture, and of The Psychoanalytic Review, from *The Psychoanalytic Review,* Volume 57, Number 3, 1970.

"Excerpts from *For a New Novel* (New York, 1965), by Alain Robbe-Grillet. Translated by Richard Howard. Reprinted by permission of Grove Press, Inc. Copyright © 1965 by Grove Press, Inc. (Grateful acknowledgment is also made of permission by the English publisher, Calder and Boyars, Ltd., London.)

Reprint by permission of the publisher, Horizon Press, from *The Anxious Object: Art Today and Its Audience* (New York & Toronto, 1969) by Harold Rosenberg. Copyright 1964, 1966 by Harold Rosenberg.

Reprinted with the permission of Farrar, Straus & Giroux, Inc. from *Styles of Radical Will* (New York) by Susan Sontag, copyright © 1967, 1969 by Susan Sontag.

From *Opus Posthumus* (New York, 1957) by Wallace Stevens, ed. Samuel French Morse. Copyright © 1957 by Elsie Stevens and Holly Stevens. Reprinted by permission of Alfred A. Knopf, Inc. Reprinted by permission of Faber and Faber Ltd.

Index